W9-AMT-090

PRAIRIE POPULISM

RURAL AMERICA

Hal S. Barron
David L. Brown
Kathleen Neils Conzen
Cornelia Butler Flora
Donald Worster

Series Editors

PRAIRIE POPULISM

The Fate of Agrarian Radicalism
in Kansas, Nebraska, and Iowa,
1880–1892

Jeffrey Ostler

 University Press of Kansas

© 1993 by the University Press of Kansas
All rights reserved

Published by the University Press of Kansas (Lawrence, Kansas 66049), which was organized by the Kansas Board of Regents and is operated and funded by Emporia State University, Fort Hays State University, Kansas State University, Pittsburg State University, the University of Kansas, and Wichita State University

Library of Congress Cataloging-in-Publication Data

Ostler, Jeffrey.
    Prairie populism : the fate of agrarian radicalism in Kansas,
Nebraska, and Iowa, 1880-1892 / Jeffrey Ostler.
        p.   cm. — (Rural America)
    Includes bibliographical references and index.
    ISBN 0-7006-0606-8
    1. Populism—Kansas—History—19th century. 2. Populism—
Nebraska—History—19th century. 3. Populism—Iowa—History—19th
century. 4. Kansas—Politics and government —1865-1950.
5. Nebraska—Politics and government. 6. Iowa—Politics and
government. I. Title. II. Series: Rural America (Lawrence, Kan.)
F621.O88   1993
320.978—dc20   93-14828

British Library Cataloguing in Publication Data is available.

Printed in the United States of America.
10 9 8 7 6 5 4 3 2 1

The paper used in this publication meets the minimum requirements of the American National Standard for Permanence of Paper for Printed Library Materials Z39.48-1984.

For my parents
Don Ostler and Barbara Ostler

Contents

Maps and Tables

Acknowledgments

As I began this project I benefited greatly from the advice of several scholars who kindly responded to my queries: Allan Bogue, Robert Cherny, Stanley Parsons, Roy Scott, and Robert Swierenga. In the course of my research I relied heavily on interlibrary loan materials; the staffs of the Inter-Library Loan Department of the University of Iowa and the Cooperative Services Division of the New York Public Library were always cheerful and efficient in responding to my deluge of requests, and the reference librarians of the state historical societies of Kansas, Nebraska, and Iowa provided me with invaluable help in locating materials. The Graduate College and the Department of History of the University of Iowa provided financial assistance at crucial points in my research, and I simply could not have done the statistical analysis without the technical expertise and assistance of John Kolp, Russ Johnson, Cathy Riley, and Steven Rappaport. I also wish to thank the Western Historical Association for allowing me to draw upon an article that I published in the *Western Historical Quarterly* in November 1992, which was a forerunner to this book.

Many individuals offered valuable comments on papers and drafts that eventually led to this book; I would especially like to thank Peter Argersinger, Richard Bensel, Dick Brown, Jeff Cox, Kim Geiger, Roger Hart, Robert Johnston, Linda Kerber, Dan Kryder, Don McCloskey, Robert McMath, Mac Rohrbough, Elizabeth Sanders, Tom Smith, Wayne TeBrake, Charles Tilly, and an anonymous reader for the University Press of Kansas. I owe special debts of gratitude to Daniel Pope, whose keen eye and good sense saved me from making more errors than I actually have, and to Cynthia Miller of the University Press of Kansas for her understanding of populism and for her helpful editorial advice.

It was my good fortune to have worked with a truly remarkable dissertation adviser; this book would not have been possible without Shel Strom-quist's generosity, enthusiasm, and incisive mind. I am deeply grateful to Rosemarie for sharing this project as part of our lives and, finally, to my parents for their encouragement.

1

Insurgency and Its Limits

The influence of factious leaders may kindle a flame within their particular states but will be unable to spread a general conflagration through the other states. . . . A rage for paper money, for an abolition of debts, for an equal division of property, or for any other improper and wicked project, will be less apt to pervade the whole body of the Union than a particular member of it, in the same proportion as such a malady is more likely to taint a particular county or district than an entire state.

In the extent and proper structure of the Union, therefore, we behold a republican remedy for the diseases most incident to republican government.

—James Madison, *The Federalist*, No. 10

Between the close of the Civil War and 1900, the United States emerged as one of the world's foremost economic powers. Industrialists forged revolutionary methods of production, created vast new markets, and invented new forms of corporate organization; a rapidly expanding railroad system and innovations in farm machinery led to a phenomenal growth of agricultural productivity. But the spectacular economic growth of the late nineteenth century was accompanied by social dislocation, acute economic instability, and an alarming increase in the inequality of wealth.

In the opinion of millions of men and women the new industrial order threatened to destroy the republic. The concentration of immense wealth and power in a few hands was inimical to liberty; not only did monopolies undermine the economic independence of farmers, laborers, and small proprietors, but huge aggregations of capital also corrupted democracy. When federal troops shot down strikers, when railroad lawyers manipulated state legislatures, when corporations purchased U.S. senators, it was clear that the people no longer ruled. For those people who saw themselves as the producers of wealth, it seemed that a new aristocracy had arisen and that, bloated on tribute exacted from their toil, that plutocracy was determined to

1

crush those freedoms they still possessed. Under these conditions, it was only a matter of time before the people rebelled. Some Americans talked of revolution, but most looked to the ballot box. There they could reclaim the republic.

Of the many "producer movements" that arose in the late nineteenth century—the Grange, the Greenback Labor Party, the Knights of Labor— the strongest was the People's Party. Organized in 1891 with the support of farmer and labor organizations, the Populists entered the 1892 presidential campaign with a platform that called for the nationalization of railroads, sweeping revisions of the banking and currency systems, and safeguards to ensure democratic control of politics. Not since the Republican Party in the election of 1856 had a new party seemed so capable of achieving success. James B. Weaver, the party's presidential candidate, proclaimed in late August that the "whole group of States west of the Missouri is with us and the tide is sweeping eastward," and another prominent Populist forecast that the new party would carry more states than Cleveland or Harrison.[1]

The results of the November balloting showed that those hopes had been far too sanguine. The Populist Party had done well in the Rocky Mountain and Plains states (Kansas, Nebraska, and South Dakota), where it won twenty-one of its twenty-two electoral votes, but it had gained no more than a foothold in the South and had failed entirely to achieve meaningful levels of support east of the Missouri River (see Map 1.1). In crucial farm states such as Missouri, Wisconsin, Illinois, and Indiana, the Populists had fared poorly, receiving 2–8 percent of the total vote. Even in Weaver's home state of Iowa, voters had spurned their native son, giving him just 5 of every 100 ballots.[2] It was as if a prairie fire originating in the Plains had somehow burned out, or had been extinguished, at the border between the Plains states and those to the east.

What accounts for the success of the People's Party in the Plains states, and why did the party fail to achieve support in other states of the Midwest? There are two ways to answer these questions. One response is that the economic conditions necessary for a widespread revolt did not exist. Like Werner Sombart's famous answer to the question of why is there no socialism in America, it may have been that farmers and workers farther east were amply supplied with roast beef and apple pie and saw little need for the economic reforms proposed by the Populists.[3] The other response is that although the economic conditions were present for a third party to succeed throughout the Midwest, populism failed because of internal weaknesses or because it was co-opted by the existing economic and political order. Although the first response assumes a direct correspondence between eco-

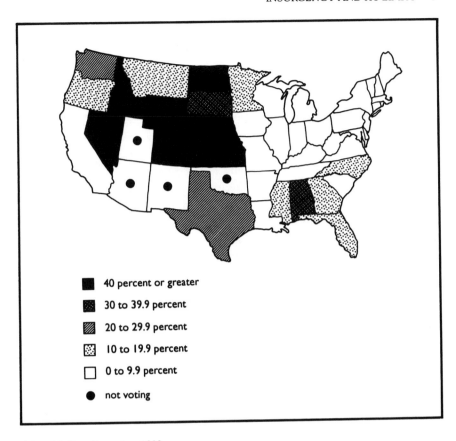

Map 1.1. Populist voting, 1892

nomic conditions and political outcomes, the second allows for noneconomic mediating factors.

Historians of populism have been influenced much more by Frederick
Jackson Turner than by Werner Sombart, but their explanations for the failure of populism to generate support across the nation have generally had
much in common with Sombart's reasons for the weakness of socialism in
the United States. The first comprehensive account of the Farmers' Alliance
and the People's Party, written by John D. Hicks, offered what amounted to
a roast-beef-and-apple-pie explanation. Building upon Turner's frontier thesis, Hicks explained populism as the product of severe economic hardship
following the collapse of a speculative boom on the Great Plains frontier. In
states where the frontier had already passed—Iowa, Missouri, and states
east—farmers "suffered less from debts and drought" and, because of prox-

imity to markets, received prices that "would have broken the back of frontier Populism in a season."[4]

In the 1950s historians challenged the sympathetic view of populism held
by Hicks and other progressive historians. Although critical of almost everything the earlier generation of historians had written, the revisionists continued to accept, evidently without question, the view that populism had
little potential to attract farmers outside those few areas with severe and
unique conditions of economic hardship. Richard Hofstadter, the most celebrated antagonist to Hicks, ironically restated the latter's explanation for
the regional patterns of Populist support. The appeal of populism, Hofstadter concluded, "was confined to the areas of the most acute agricultural discontent where one-crop cash staple farming, heavily dependent upon the
export market, was found in combination with exceptional transportation
problems or a high rate of mortgage indebtedness." In states such as Iowa, Illinois, and Wisconsin, Hofstadter asserted, agriculture was "prosperous"
and farmers had no reason to embrace a third party.[5]

Other historians in the 1950s and 1960s informed by modernization theory made similar observations. One writer portrayed Populists as backward-
looking upholders of the outmoded values of "island communities" and associated populism exclusively with frontier wheat-producing areas; another
contended that Populists in the "wheat belt" of the Dakotas, Kansas, and
Nebraska were "bewildered" by the new industrial economy. In states such
as Illinois, Wisconsin, and Iowa, however, where farmers had made the adjustment to a more advanced dairy and corn/hog economy, they accepted
the new industrial order and "responded coolly to Populism."[6] Whether critical or sympathetic, most other general interpretations of populism written
in the 1960s reiterated this economic explanation.[7]

The first historian to question the standard explanation was Lawrence
Goodwyn, whose *Democratic Promise*, published in 1976, marked a major
breakthrough in Populist studies. Beginning with the premise that many
more farmers were "potential Populists" than actually became Populists,
Goodwyn argued that populism did not form simply in response to economic distress but was a dynamic movement with the potential to become
national in scope. Although he did not provide evidence that farmers outside areas of Populist strength faced substantial economic hardship and despite his flawed contentions that radical agrarianism was based on economic
cooperatives and that a "shadow" free-silver movement absorbed populism,
Goodwyn nonetheless showed the vital importance of noneconomic factors
such as movement organization, party loyalties, and ideology in shaping the
course of populism. Goodwyn's answer to the question of why the People's

Party failed to attract substantial support across the nation may not have been precisely on target, but he was clearly pointing in the right direction.[8]

Most studies of populism in the 1970s and 1980s focused on single states that had relatively strong Populist movements. This research has revealed a great deal about the characteristics separating Populists from non-Populists within the movement's areas of strength, but the concentration on states where populism succeeded has meant that questions unanswerable within such a framework have received little attention. Not much progress has been made in explaining why the kinds of farmers who became Populists in Populist states did not do so in other states. One of the most important findings of several of the state studies is that economic hardship alone cannot explain why populism emerged in particular states. Kansas populism arose from political alienation as well as from economic distress, and in Colorado, "third parties [were] a function of the existing political structure: the responsiveness of established parties; the accessibility of political institutions and decision makers; the extent of democratic processes; and the general sense of political efficacy."[9] These insights based upon examination of states of Populist strength are important, but they have not been applied to regional or national patterns of Populist support. It remains unclear whether noneconomic factors explain these patterns, and if so, how.[10]

Why did populism succeed in the Plains states; why did it fail in other states of the Midwest? The work of the French historian Marc Bloch demonstrates that comparison can be a powerful tool for explaining differences. Bloch focused on divergences among European societies, but his "logic of comparative history" is broadly applicable.[11] To explain why strong People's Parties developed in some states but not in others, I adopt Bloch's approach and focus on two Populist states (Kansas and Nebraska) and on one non-Populist state (Iowa). This method allows us to investigate the extent to which economic conditions actually varied from an area of Populist strength to an area of Populist weakness; to date, historians have only made assumptions about this question. A comparative approach also allows us to see the relevance of noneconomic factors: in particular, how differences in political conditions among the three states were critical in explaining why populism emerged in Kansas and Nebraska but not in Iowa.

Despite the unquestionable congruence of severe economic hardship and of Populist regional strength, there are strong reasons to think that the potential of the Populist movement was much greater than its actual achievements would indicate and that variations in support for the movement depended on several factors besides simple economic distress. In the first place, the sharp distinction in much of the literature between "hardship" in areas of Populist strength and "prosperity" in other areas is overdrawn. All farmers, regardless of where they lived, operated within the deflationary economy of the late nineteenth century. The impact of falling prices was particularly severe for those farmers, weighed down with debt, who saw prices plummet while their obligations remained the same. No matter where they lived, indebted farmers in the 1880s and 1890s found themselves squeezed in a vise, trapped between the money market and the market for crops.

As a result of falling prices and crushing debt but also because of a more general objection to the growing monopolization of economic and political power, angry midwestern farmers banded together in the late 1880s in thousands of local Farmers' Alliances. State Farmers' Alliances began demanding legislation to curb the abuses of railroads and other monopolies and to increase the supply of currency. It is vital to recognize that radical agrarian movements appeared in Iowa, Missouri, Illinois, and Indiana, states that eventually gave populism little support.[12] The crucial distinction between the Alliance in these states and in Populist states is that in the former the Alliances remained nonpartisan, pursuing their agenda within the two-party system, but in Populist states they eventually opted for a third-party strategy. The question is not why agrarian radicalism was strong in the Plains and absent elsewhere, a question based on a false premise; the problem is to explain the divergent strategies of state Farmers' Alliances, and to do so of course involves consideration of the larger political context in which these protest movements contended for power.

Recent students of social movements have argued persuasively against simplistic theories explaining protest solely in terms of temporary hardship associated with structural strain. These theorists contend that the conditions for protest in a society are more or less constantly present. Movements form because of "long-term changes in group resources, organization, and opportunities for collective action," and their subsequent course of development is "critically shaped by the larger political environment."[13] I do not wish to deny the existence or relevance of variations in economic hardship over time or geographically. Yet as resource-mobilization theorists make clear, economic hardship is not directly translated into protest; rather, numerous cultural, societal, and political variables can mediate economic hardship, favoring the emergence of certain types of movements and shaping their course of development.

The federal structure of the United States created a set of barriers and opportunities that encouraged differentiation within the midwestern agrarian protest movement. The federal Constitution gave the states significant powers to tax their citizens, regulate business and commerce, and provide basic social services such as education or police protection. Although the Civil War extinguished extreme claims of states' rights, the national government remained relatively weak, and states continued to be the basic units of government in the late nineteenth century. The state's responsibilities, Lord James Bryce observed in 1893, "practically cover nearly all of the ordinary relations of citizens to one another and to their Government."[14]

Federalism favored decentralized political parties composed of relatively autonomous state organizations. The state party was almost continually mobilized to win a constant succession of elections; the national party was merely "a loose confederation of state and local bosses" that came into existence only once every four years.[15] Patronage was usually controlled by state bosses rather than by any national organization. State party organizations sustained the basic work of organization, recruitment, and fund-raising. Many electoral issues, from purchasing schoolbooks to regulating the railroads to licensing saloons, were state specific; and although national issues such as the tariff often figured in state campaigns, state party organizations mediated these issues, tailoring them to fit local concerns. Even in presidential elections, national issues were colored by a state's political environment.[16]

A decentralized federal system afforded an agrarian protest movement significant opportunities for state-level political action.[17] State governments had the power to alter the economic environment in important ways: railroad regulation, tax reform, and legislation against usury. Because of these significant targets for reform at the state level, farmers' organizations in the Midwest invariably turned first to the states to secure remedial legislation. The profusion of political activity at the state and the local level further invited a state approach by making available numerous points of entry into the state political system. Iowa, for example, elected a governor and the legislature in every odd-numbered year and a full slate of congressmen (representing separate districts) in even-numbered years; a presidential election occurred only once every four years. At almost any given moment an agrarian organization could contend for political power at the state or the congressional-district level; it could do the same at the national level only once every four years. Moreover, the chances of obtaining reform were much better at the state rather than at the national level. An agrarian movement in any given state could hope to pressure a sufficient number of legislators or to elect a governor in sympathy with its principles. It would be much more difficult, however, to alter the composition of the U.S. Congress or to influence the election of the president. Thus, although farmers ultimately sought reforms requiring national legislation, they focused their initial efforts at the state level.

Alliances in all midwestern states initially opposed third-party political action. Most Alliance leaders envisioned that the organization would have social and educational functions in addition to its political activity. With good reason Alliance leaders feared that if the organization became a third party, it would lose its identity as a community of farmers. Many leaders believed that the entry of the Grange into independent politics in the 1870s had caused its demise. Alliance leaders recognized that third-party formation was inherently controversial and risked dividing the organization and diverting its energies from its important nonpolitical purposes. To guard against destructive partisanship, state Alliances included in their constitutions strong statements of the organization's nonpartisan character. To carry out their nonpartisan strategy, Alliance leaders urged members to attend regular party conventions to nominate candidates sympathetic to the hardships facing farmers and then to vote for candidates, regardless of party affiliation, who had an acceptable record on the issues or who made adequate pledges to support the Alliance platform.

The response of state party systems to agrarian demands was pivotal in determining the political course of the Alliance. By the late 1880s important political differences had arisen among midwestern states. At the close of the Civil War, the Republican Party had been dominant in most states of the Midwest. The GOP's successful prosecution of the war gave it substantial resources for reinforcing party loyalty through prolonging the emotional aftermath of the conflict. For three decades the party ritually reminded voters of Democratic treason by waving the "bloody shirt" and cemented wavering loyalties with generous outlays for war pensions. The GOP's promotion of policies for the egalitarian economic development of the West allowed it to stand as the party of growth and prosperity for the common man. The embodiment of the Republicans' original slogan "free soil, free labor, free men" in the Homestead Act of 1862 and in aid for railroad expansion clearly identified the party with western sectional interests.[18]

After the war midwestern state Republican Party organizations increasingly became identified with business. During Reconstruction the ideological republicanism of the radicals was replaced by a new organizational politics controlled by men such as Roscoe Conkling of New York, Philetus Sawyer of Wisconsin, and William B. Allison of Iowa, managers primarily concerned with building strong state party organizations. These conservative GOP leaders sought to use their power to direct the resources of the federal government—jobs, contracts, and money—to their states and to preserve a climate conducive to investment and economic development. They had strong connections to powerful railroad and business interests.[19]

Precisely because the GOP was the dominant party, it had difficulty maintaining the allegiance of voters during periods of pronounced economic discontent, and Republican majorities in the Midwest hemorrhaged in the depression of 1873–1878.[20] Although the party recuperated in the early eighties, economic discontent and ethnocultural conflict in the mid- and late eighties further eroded its base. By the mid-1880s significant challenges to the dominance of the conservative Republicans had appeared, the first from within the GOP. Although Republican Party leaders with their substantial resources of patronage exercised considerable control over party organizations, their power was far from complete. State Republican organizations in the late nineteenth century suffered from chronic factionalism over ethnocultural issues, such as compulsory education or prohibition, and from economic issues such as rate regulation for railroads or restrictions on subsidies. Antimonopoly Republicans, usually lower-level politicians, contended that the GOP had strayed from its initial origins as an egalitarian party committed to progressive reform and had become subservient to the interests of corporations. Although antimonopolists were often able to write reform proposals into party platforms and to introduce reform bills in the state legislature, probusiness Republicans could usually defeat these initiatives. Antimonopolists nonetheless posed a significant threat not only to conservative party leaders but to the party's unity and strength.

The hegemony of the Republicans in many states was also threatened by a resurgent Democratic Party. Bourbon leaders of state Democratic parties, in their opposition to business subsidies and protective tariffs, were even more committed to laissez-faire than their Republican counterparts; but they were frequently willing to make opportunistic appeals to voters on economic issues and to participate in "fusion" arrangements with radical third parties (particularly the Greenback Party in the 1870s and early 1880s) in order to win elections.[21] These fusion campaigns appealed to farmers and to labor because of their discontent with Republican economic policy. A Democratic/Greenback antimonopoly coalition proved especially fruitful in Michigan and Iowa, where it created a viable opposition to the GOP in the mid-eighties. (In Missouri, Republican/Greenback fusion helped accomplish the same purpose.)[22]

By the mid-1880s Republican dominance had disappeared in most of the Midwest. The Democrats were competitive in Ohio, Indiana, Illinois, Michigan, Wisconsin, Iowa, and, to a lesser extent, in Minnesota. (In Missouri the Republicans were challenging the dominant Democrats.) The only states in the region that remained safely Republican were Kansas and Nebraska. Ironically, in the states where the GOP seemed truly secure the farmers' movement would most damage Republican fortunes in the 1890s.[23]

The crucial difference between Iowa and Kansas/Nebraska was party competition. In Iowa, where the Democratic Party had become a genuine threat to the Republicans in the mid-1880s, a competitive party system produced reform in response to Alliance demands, therefore discouraging third-party formation. In Kansas and Nebraska, where the Republicans seemed secure, a one-party dominant political system failed to respond to agrarian demands, leading the Farmers' Alliance to organize the People's Party. Party competition in Iowa facilitated the integration of the protest movement into the existing political structure and discouraged the manifestation of the movement's more radical tendencies, particularly as the Alliance leadership became dependent on the existing sources of political power. In Kansas and Nebraska, however, the Alliance was outside the political system and became increasingly alienated politically; the movement advanced a more radical program, formed a national strategy, and developed an alternative political culture.[24]

The extent to which the presence or absence of party competition was decisive in other states that faced agrarian insurgency requires further study, as does the possibility that different political dynamics within those states had a more important effect than party competition. The comparison of Kansas and Nebraska with Iowa warrants this general observation, however: state political environments were crucial in determining whether agrarian radicalism took a third-party turn.

Political scientists have clarified many of the difficulties facing third parties in the U.S. electoral system. To have succeeded in implementing the Omaha platform, populism would have had to develop a strong organization in a sufficient number of states to control the Congress and to win the presidency. This was an exceedingly difficult task; there was no room for partial success in the U.S. electoral system. Under the winner-take-all system of congressional elections, a minority party could not obtain representation in proportion to its electoral strength. Likewise, the ultimate goal of controlling the presidency could be obtained only by winning a majority in the electoral college. Anything short of this unrealistic level of success brought no rewards at all. In short, the rules of the game made it virtually impossible for a new party to build strength gradually over an extended period of time.[25] Another kind of third party might have been able to survive through gradual growth, perhaps by exercising a balance of power in a closely divided Congress. But populism's millennial spirit encouraged expectations of rapid national triumph and required immediate success to sustain momentum.

Once the People's Party took root in its initial strongholds, enormous obstacles hindered its spread. Not the least was the difficulty of establishing a strong alliance with labor, a subject that has received a great deal of attention from scholars.[26] An even more fundamental problem for populism, however, was the difficulty of recruiting farmers across the nation; for example, by the time populism had taken root in Kansas and Nebraska, conditions were unfavorable for mobilization in Iowa.

Ideological or organizational shortcomings do not explain the failure of the People's Party to expand its agrarian base throughout the Midwest; nor did it fail because of roast beef and apple pie. Both of these explanations—internal weaknesses and insufficient hardship—obscure the fact that populism, in the final analysis, was defeated. The opponents of populism won for many reasons: their superior financial resources, their monopoly on ideas about political economy, and their manipulation of sectional and racial divisions. Yet the framework allowing them to wield these weapons so effectively was the deeper structure of federalism. That populism did not become, in Madisonian terms, a "general conflagration" does not indicate a lack of fuel for such a fire; rather, its containment illustrates how a vast, decentralized republic controlled the initial flames.

2
Deflation and the Geography
of Economic Hardship

From the Civil War to the end of the nineteenth century prices of agricultural products fell dramatically. The erosion in the value of wheat summarizes the general trend: The five-year average price for winter wheat in New York City from 1864 through 1868 was $1.96 per bushel; from 1885 through 1889, the years immediately preceding the Populist revolt, the average price in New York was only 90 cents.[1] The impact of falling prices was particularly severe for those farmers, weighed down with debts, who saw prices plummet while their obligations remained the same.

Contemporaries disagreed about the impact of falling prices. Radical agrarians, who believed deflation resulted from government policies to restrict the supply of money, saw a bleak economic landscape of increasing debt, unemployment, and inequality of wealth. The Populists' 1892 Omaha platform blamed the "inadequate" supply of currency for "falling prices, the formation of combines and rings, [and] the impoverishment of the producing class."[2] William A. Peffer, the Populist senator from Kansas, contended that falling prices worked particular hardship on farmers with mortgage obligations: "We borrowed money when times were good and prices high, but our contracts were changed without our consent, the value of our property was lessened by law, our debts were increased at the instance of the lender, so that we are compelled to pay two dollars of money, two bushels of wheat or two days' labor where we agreed to pay only one."[3]

Most contemporary economists and conservative political leaders, who maintained that falling prices resulted from overproduction rather than from currency contraction, minimized the harmful consequences of declining agricultural prices. Although the price of wheat had fallen, they pointed out that the cost of shipping wheat to market had also dropped. And if the amount of money the farmer received for wheat was less than it once had been, the farmer's dollar would now go further in purchasing teakettles, farm implements, or other goods. Yet it was impossible for contemporaries, even if they regarded the economic transformations of the late nineteenth century as beneficial, to overlook the adverse impact of deflation altogether. The economist David A. Wells contended that deflation, having resulted from technological progress, was not a calamity but a "great improvement" to mankind; still, he acknowledged that "great material interests have been for a time . . . injuriously affected" because of declining prices.[4]

Subsequent interpretations of the late nineteenth-century agricultural economy and the agrarian revolt have continued to reflect the contemporary debate over whether deflation was harmful. Historians sympathetic to populism, from John D. Hicks to Lawrence Goodwyn, have generally accepted the validity of agrarian grievances.[5] Other scholars have been decidedly more skeptical about the seriousness of an agricultural depression in the late nineteenth century. Like conservatives of the time, revisionists have argued that farmers did not really suffer from deflation since prices for nonagricultural products, transportation costs, and interest rates also fell.[6]

The revisionists are right about the first two points: Prices of nonagricultural commodities and transportation costs did decline by about as much as prices of farm products.[7] Had all farmers in the late nineteenth century owned farms free of debt and had they needed no short-term credit, the effects of deflation would have been fairly benign. But most midwestern farmers were not in this situation since the majority either lived on mortgaged farms or were tenants. In 1890 in midwestern states 30.7 percent of families owned mortgaged farms; 27.0 percent of families were tenants.[8]

For farm families with mortgages, several sources of capital were available for real estate mortgage loans. In eastern parts of the corn belt, credit was often furnished by local sources: individual farmers, retired farmers, townspeople, and bankers. Outside insurance companies and mortgage companies were also an important source of credit, although to a lesser extent than local individuals and institutions. Farther west farmers relied more heavily on outside institutions for mortgage loans. In Iowa insurance companies played an important role. Mortgage companies were also active in Iowa and were especially prevalent in Kansas, Nebraska, and the Dakotas. These mortgage companies, which proliferated in the 1880s, served as the agents for eastern individuals and institutions to invest in western farm mortgages either through purchasing assigned mortgages or through investing in debenture bonds secured by a pool of mortgages.[9] Banks played a relatively small role in financing real estate mortgage loans since national banks were not permitted to loan on real estate security. State banks in Iowa occasionally provided farm mortgage loans, but in general, state and private banks took advantage of their knowledge of local conditions to engage in the more lucrative short-term loan business.[10]

Farm mortgages were not in themselves a sign of economic distress. Most farmers took out mortgages for productive purposes: to buy land or to make improvements on their farms.[11] But regardless of the original purpose of a loan, a substantial erosion in the price of farm commodities over the course of the loan could place a sizable burden on the indebted farm household. Assuming that the price of wheat remained constant at $1.00 per bushel, the farmer who contracted for a $1,000 mortgage loan at 8 percent interest per annum maturing in five years would be obligated to pay the equivalent of 80 bushels of wheat ($80) in interest each year and then pay the equivalent of 1,000 bushels of wheat ($1,000) as repayment of principal at the end of five years.[12] If, however, the price of a bushel of wheat were to fall over the course of the loan, the farmer's real obligation would be greatly increased. For example, if the price of wheat were to fall by 5 percent each year of the loan, the interest obligation the first year, with the price of wheat now at 95 cents would be 84 bushels instead of 80. By the fifth year, with the price of wheat at 75 cents, the farmer would be required to produce 107 bushels of wheat to pay the interest. Repayment of the principal would require the equivalent of 1,333 bushels. Economic historians have contended that the impact of deflation was insignificant because "mortgages were so short that no substantial changes occurred in the price level over those brief periods of time." But the preceding illustration is based on historical realities: Prices did fall by as much as 25 percent over some five-year periods in the late nineteenth century.[13]

The logic behind the revisionists' contention that declining interest rates offset the impact of deflation for debtors is decidedly circular. We know that interest rates fell at the same rate as prices, the revisionists insist, because they must have done so. Beginning from certain assumptions about market behavior, they reason that farmers would have adjusted their price expectations and demanded lower rates. Yet the revisionists offer no evidence to support this contention, leaving those individuals who may have reservations about the efficiency of markets to wonder if interest rates actually complied with economists' expectations.[14]

Several local studies of farm mortgages in various midwestern locales provide a general sense of the movement of nominal interest rates, revealing a pattern: Nominal interest rates were fairly constant in the 1860s. They rose slightly in the early 1870s and remained stable through the late seventies, then declined quite significantly (by as much as 2 percentage points) in the early 1880s and continued to decline at a slower rate from the mid-eighties through the late nineties. Although at any one time interest rates were one-half a point to one point higher in Nebraska and Kansas than in Iowa and higher by a similar proportion in Iowa than in Illinois, the timing of interest-rate movement followed the same general pattern throughout the Midwest.[15]

Given that interest-rate movements throughout the Midwest were synchronized, it is possible to use the data from any one of these studies along with a suitable index of agricultural prices in order to determine the course of real interest rates. The best of the local farm-mortgage studies for this purpose examines Champaign County, Illinois, and can be employed in conjunction with the index of Indiana farm prices.[16]

A five-year loan negotiated in 1861 with a maturity date in 1866 carried a nominal interest rate of 8.7 percent (see Table 2.1). Because of Civil War inflation, the real interest on this loan actually would have been negative at −3.3 percent. With the onset of deflation following the war, however, real interest rates began to exceed nominal interest rates. Real interest rates on loans maturing in the early 1870s were between 11 and 14 percent; real rates were also high on loans maturing from 1878 through 1882. Although apparently some adjustment in nominal rates occurred in the early 1880s, it was incomplete. For loans maturing in the last half of the decade the real interest rate exceeded the nominal rate. For loans maturing in the five-year period prior to the Populist revolt (1886–1890), the real interest rate averaged 8.7 percent, which was identical to the nominal rate during the Civil War. These data clearly indicate that the market simply did not function as the revisionists would have wished. The rate at which interest rates fell lagged behind prices, and real interest rates remained higher than nominal rates. Indebted farmers who complained of being squeezed in the late nineteenth century were not under an illusion; the vise was real.[17]

Two further points will refine this analysis. First, the analysis assumes five years as the length of a loan, which reflects accurately conditions in the 1880s and 1890s when the standard contract required semiannual payment of interest with principal due after five years. The specified term of real estate mortgages, however, averaged about three years in the 1860s and about four years in the 1870s.[18] Lengthening the term for loans further increased the burden on indebtedness in a deflationary economy because fixed obligations extended over a longer period of time, thus increasing the interest burden and preventing farmers from renegotiating the terms of their loans with the same or other lenders. Second, the analysis assumes that the volume of borrowing was relatively constant from year to year; in fact, farmers tended to borrow more frequently in those years when deflationary pressures briefly relaxed and prices rose. Mortgage borrowing increased significantly in the

TABLE 2.1. Nominal and Real Interest Rates, Champaign County, Illinois, 1861/66 to 1885/90

Year of Maturity of Loan	Nominal Interest Rate	Real Interest Rate
1866	8.7	−3.3
1867	8.9	−5.8
1868	8.7	1.1
1869	8.8	8.9
1870	8.5	10.1
1871	8.8	10.2
1872	9.1	12.3
1873	9.3	13.5
1874	9.5	13.0
1875	9.7	12.5
1876	9.8	9.4
1877	9.8	8.4
1878	9.6	9.6
1879	9.6	12.8
1880	9.6	13.9
1881	9.4	11.7
1882	9.0	10.2
1883	8.6	2.8
1884	8.0	5.3
1885	7.2	4.9
1886	6.4	8.4
1887	6.5	9.1
1888	6.5	9.9
1889	6.8	8.7
1890	6.8	7.5

Sources: Robert F. Severson, Jr., Frank F. Niss, and Richard D. Winkelman, "Mortgage Borrowing as a Frontier Developed: A Study of Farm Mortgages in Champaign County, Illinois, 1836–1895," Journal of Economic History 26 (June 1966): 152, and Howard J. Houk, A Century of Indiana Farm Prices, 1841 to 1941, Purdue University Agricultural Experiment Station Bulletin 476 (Lafayette, Ind., 1943), 8–9.

early eighties, indicating that farmers hoped the deflationary trend of the previous decade or more would be reversed.[19] But by the time their loans became due, prices had fallen and real interest rates had increased. On the other hand, farmers borrowed less during years of particularly severe price depression, such as the late seventies, and fewer therefore actually had loans maturing in the early eighties when real interest rates were fairly low.

Apart from deflation's effect on real interest rates, the system of mortgage financing in western states increased the cost of credit in a more general sense. In addition to the face value of the loan, borrowers were obligated to pay from 4 to 15 percent of the principal as commission to obtain funds from the farm mortgage companies. This commission was usually paid by deducting the sum from the principal or sometimes by executing a second mortgage, with the commission payable over a series of installments. Local agents who operated as the middlemen between borrowers and mortgage companies also received a commission. These charges increased the effective annual interest rate of a loan by as much as 2 percent. Insurance companies also charged commissions and required that the borrower purchase property insurance. It was reasonable to require insurance to protect the value of the lenders' mortgage, but to require borrowers to purchase their own life insurance, as these companies frequently did, was unfair in that such insurance was often more costly than the premiums offered by cooperative insurance associations.[20]

The mortgage note itself, as a Kansas attorney observed, contained "all conceivable provisions for the protection of the lender." Upon default of one of the semiannual interest payments, the loan's principal was immediately due. The borrower, of course, lacking funds to pay the interest, let alone the principal, would wish to have the loan reinstated. This could be arranged but not without compounding interest on the defaulted payment and charging a further commission for renewal. The borrower might choose to seek funds from another lender to pay the defaulted loan, but this once again entailed payment of various commissions. The mortgage note also required the borrower to stay current on tax payments. If taxes were not paid, the lender, as before, could declare the principal due immediately. Usually the mortgagee would either pay the taxes or purchase the tax certificate at the tax sale to maintain a clear title. In either case the borrower would be required to pay interest on the taxes due. In Kansas tax certificates bore a rate of 24 percent per annum; in Iowa, a delinquent taxpayer was liable for interest of 12 percent a year and penalties, making the rate 16 percent.[21]

In addition to their needs for long-term financing, farmers also required short-term loans to purchase seed, livestock, and machinery and to pay wages, taxes, and interest. Farmers also assumed short-term debts because of unforeseen circumstances. John and Rosie Ise, Kansas farmers, required $300 for medical care for a sick child, and the best rate they could obtain was 15 percent. Although Rosie worried that "interest is a terrible thing . . . the way it eats and eats, due twice as often as it ought to be, and always at the hardest time," the Ises had no choice but to borrow the money. There are few important subjects in midwestern agricultural history of the nineteenth century about which less is known than short-term credit. We know a great deal about the exploitation associated with the crop-lien system in southern agriculture but almost nothing about corresponding types of credit in the midwestern agricultural economy.[22]

Short-term loans constituted a significant part of total borrowing in the Midwest. In 1880 in Illinois, 38,175 chattel mortgages were recorded for a total of $10.4 million; in 1887, 62,263 were executed for $17.4 million. By comparison, fewer farm mortgages were filed (24,248 in 1880; 25,334 in 1887) but for larger total amounts ($30.5 million in 1880; $37.0 million in 1887). In Nebraska for fiscal year 1894–1895, 85,025 chattel mortgages were filed for a total value of $16.1 million. This amount approached that of the 23,622 farm mortgages recorded during the same period valued at $21.7 million. The chattel mortgage was simply a fact of life for many farm families. In four Kansas counties in 1892, one of every two head of cattle and one of every seven hogs were under mortgage.[23] Chattel mortgages represented but a portion of total nonmortgage loans; unsecured loans were presumably as common. Probably most short-term loans financed normal agricultural operations although many were for medical care or to cover expenses after a year of poor crops.

It was a rural axiom that bankers and moneylenders exploited farmers, especially those in serious straits, through usurious interest rates on short-term loans. One Iowa farmer voiced the common wisdom in reminding his fellows that "the pirate looks for the rich laden ship, the loan shark for the struggling farmer." The oppressive weight of short-term obligations was captured in a piece of verse widely circulated in Kansas:

> A chattel mortgage in the West
> Is like a cancer on your breast;
> It slowly takes your life away,
> And eats your vitals day by day.
>
> A cloud by day, a fire by night,
> It keeps him in a dreadful plight;
> And haunts him in his dreams and sleep,
> While salt tears trickle down his cheek.
>
> The sorghum lapper, tired and poor,
> Sees "Bank" in gold above the door. .
> And when the threshold once is crossed,
> The trap is sprung—the lapper's lost.
>
> His team, his grain, his cow, his hog,
> His bed and breeches, wife and dog,

Upon the altar of three-per-cent are tossed,
Time rolls on and all is lost.[24]

As the reference to "three-per-cent" suggests, Populists frequently charged that bankers charged exorbitant rates of interest, citing instances of 2, 3, 5, and even 10 percent per month on short-term loans. Such claims were made not only for the frontier in Kansas and Nebraska but also for the well-established farming districts of Iowa.[25] Historians have not taken these charges of high interest rates seriously; they have pointed out that interest rates on mortgage loans did not exceed 10 percent per annum in the late 1880s, suggesting on this basis that Populists overstated interest rates for political reasons. When charging usury, however, the Populists generally did not have in mind long-term mortgages but were referring to short-term loans. On this score, Populist claims were not exaggerated.[26]

Although the development of banking was more advanced in the Midwest than in the South, significant structural constraints limited the supply of funds available for loans, thus keeping short-term interest rates high in the Midwest. In the Populist era, local sources, primarily private and state banks and local merchants, provided most of the funds for short-term loans. National banks rarely were chartered outside of cities because federal law required high levels of capitalization; consequently, these banks played a limited role in providing short-term funds for agriculture.[27] This lack of participation by national banks in short-term agricultural financing was important because it restricted potential competition. When capital requirements for national banks were eased in 1900, the number of banks in the Midwest increased dramatically; in Indiana the number almost doubled, and in the Dakotas it grew from 52 to 256.[28] Such a rapid increase in the number of chartered national banks clearly indicates that a substantial gap existed between the demand for credit and the institutions available to service these requirements before 1900.

The national banking system further constrained the development of inexpensive short-term rural credit because it was unable to stimulate the growth of currency and banking capital in rural areas and because it failed to provide a currency with sufficient elasticity to respond to seasonal fluctuations in the demand for money.[29] These two problems exerted upward pressure on interest rates in rural areas in the Populist era and well into the 1910s.

The first problem stemmed from disincentives to the formation of banking capital in peripheral areas of the country. Because note issue was predicated upon the relative profits of holding government securities, in midwestern states, where high interest rates made investments in other fields more lucrative than government bonds, national banks held low quantities of government bonds and consequently issued fewer notes than in eastern states, where lower interest rates made government bonds an acceptable investment, resulting in higher levels of note issue. In 1898 the per capita national bank note circulation was only 1.20 in Iowa, 1.65 in Kansas, and 1.55 in Nebraska, but it was 11.07 in Vermont, 13.10 in Massachusetts, and 20.46 in Rhode Island. There was also a corresponding disparity in total bank capital per capita.[30]

The second problem grew from the centralization of reserves in New York. During autumn, country banks required currency to finance the movement of crops and called upon their reserves held in New York banks. As the demand for currency increased, interest rates on call loans backed by stock collateral increased, often dramatically, thus aggravating stock market volatility and sometimes leading to financial panic. An examination of average weekly interest rates from 1890 through 1908 for New York call loans shows substantial fluctuations related to the demand for currency in agricultural regions. From mid-September through early January the average interest rate was usually above 4 percent and sometimes as high as 7 percent on call loans in comparison to the summer months, when rates averaged close to 2.5 percent. After falling off in the late winter months, interest rates increased again to between 3.5 percent and 4 percent in March and April as the need for short-term loans in agricultural regions placed renewed demand on the supply of currency.[31] Analysts of this situation were more concerned with the instability in financial markets than with the system's impact on interest-rate levels in rural areas. Yet the rigidities in the system undoubtedly placed upward pressure on interest rates in rural areas during periods of high seasonal demand. The Country Life Commission in 1909 cited the lack of "an adequate system of agricultural credit, whereby the farmer may readily secure loans on fair terms" as one of the "most prominent deficiencies" in American agriculture. The problem was chronic; if anything, it had been worse in the 1880s and 1890s.[32]

Although there are no comprehensive data for short-term interest rates in the Populist era, we can use data from 1913 to arrive at estimates for short-term rates in 1890. Since we know the rate of interest on short-term loans for 1913 and the rates on long-term mortgage loans in 1913 and in 1890, under the assumption that the rate of decline of short-term loans from 1890 to 1913 was the same as the rate of decline on mortgage loans over the same period, it is possible to make an estimate of short-term rates in 1890.[33] This method yields a conservative estimate, because short-term interest rates probably declined by a larger percentage from 1890 to 1913 than did rates on mortgage loans since the minimal structural changes that did occur between 1890 and the passage of the Federal Reserve Act in 1913 would have increased the supply of credit for short-term loans more than for mortgage loans.[34]

Under the conservative assumption of a constant relationship between interest rates on mortgage and nonmortgage loans between 1890 and 1913, annual interest rates on short-term loans in 1890 would have ranged from 10 to 11 percent in Indiana, Michigan, Illinois, Missouri, and Iowa; in Minnesota, Nebraska, and Kansas rates would have been about 12 percent. These figures take on significance when compared with estimates for the South, where there is little question about the onerousness of short-term credit. In Georgia, Texas, and Alabama, the estimated rate was 13 percent, which was, as expected, higher than in the Midwest. But it is significant that rates in the South were only slightly higher, thus indicating that the situation for midwestern farmers requiring short-term credit was not much better.

An abundance of evidence suggests that these estimates may understate average short-term interest rates in the 1890s and that in any case instances of much higher rates of interest were certainly common. For example, one report indicates that interest rates on loans to finance cattle-feeding operations in Omaha ranged from 10 to 18 percent per annum in the 1880s and 1890s.[35] The Kansas Bureau of Labor and Industrial Statistics, given the task to investigate "exorbitant rates of interest," found that the prevailing rate on chattel mortgages in rural Osage County in 1885 and 1886 was 2 percent per month. A few years later, the state's Republican governor, John A. Martin, pleaded with the Kansas legislature to enact meaningful penalties against usury since laws allowing high interest rates and facilitating easy collection of security on chattel mortgages "invite outrages on property rights that are as flagrant as grand larceny." Had Martin been a Populist, his recognition that rates exceeded the 12 percent legal maximum might be discounted as inflated political rhetoric, but the statement of "flagrant" and widespread abuses, coming from a Republican, cannot be so easily dismissed.[36]

Interest rates on short-term loans were often exorbitant in Iowa as well. Several correspondents to the *Iowa Tribune* in 1884 reported rates ranging from 1 to 3 percent a month. Three years later a Farmers' Alliance official in Hamilton County reported that "money is drawing a big interest, from fifteen to twenty-four per cent, which is entirely too much, considering the times and crops."[37] To this direct testimony can be added the observation that the high cost of borrowing made it impossible for most Iowa farmers to purchase purebred stock to improve their herds.[38]

Arguments over a bill before the 1890 Iowa General Assembly to reduce the legal rate of interest from 10 to 8 percent further indicate that the rate on short-term loans often exceeded 10 percent. State senator C. H. Gatch, a conservative Republican opposing the bill, contended that honest borrowers, paying the legal maximum would be unable to contract loans at the new maximum and would be forced into "fifteen and twenty percent 'shaving shop' transactions." The casual reference to "shaving shops" suggests that such establishments were not unknown in Iowa. The observations of another legislator reinforced the existence of a shady underworld of usurious transactions. Representative Albert Head favored reducing the legal rate of interest but feared it would do little good without strong penalties; under Iowa's usury law, which he described as a "dead letter," many borrowers preferred to pay rates above the maximum 10 percent in order to retain the lender's good will.[39] Such testimony clearly indicates that even in non-Populist Iowa, short-term rates frequently exceeded 10 percent.

Across the Midwest, farmers faced significant burdens in contracting for short-term loans. Although interest rates were not as high in the Midwest as in the South, farmers needing to borrow money for planting, for harvesting, or to meet emergencies faced substantial burdens in attempting to repay these loans. Falling prices only added to the weight of these obligations.

Deflation also had an adverse impact on tenant farmers. Tenancy generally increased during the late nineteenth century: In all midwestern states except Missouri the percentage of total farmers who were tenants grew larger between 1880 and 1900. The extent of tenancy varied from Wisconsin, where only 13.3 percent of farmers were tenants in 1900, to Illinois, with 38.8 percent. Studies of nineteenth-century tenancy in Iowa and Illinois demonstrate that rising land prices made it more and more difficult for people who aspired to farm ownership to make a down payment. This problem was especially severe for young farm families, who by 1880 found it virtually impossible to purchase farms. Thus they chose tenancy as a step on the "agricultural ladder" toward eventual ownership, or they moved west to purchase less expensive farmland.[40]

As it became harder to buy land, demand for rental farms increased and landlords gained the advantage in bargaining over the terms of leases. In a deflationary economy, it was to the landlord's advantage to stipulate cash rents, which would guarantee rent at a fixed cash level. In some years when prices increased the landlord would gain less from cash rent than from receiving a share of the crop, but more often than not prices would decline, making share rents less attractive. Not surprisingly, then, landlords demanded cash rents in the late nineteenth century. In 1880 only 19 percent of leases in Iowa required payment in cash; by 1900 this figure had increased to 56 percent. Yet in years of low prices the fixed obligation of cash rent assumed a higher real value and was undoubtedly burdensome. Tenants might wish to bargain for lower cash rent or to return to renting for shares, but in a tight rental market, they did not bargain on equal terms.[41]

Cash rent was associated with the worst abuses of tenancy in the Midwest. The notorious William Scully, a name synonymous with extortionate rents and merciless evictions from Ireland to the Grand Prairie of Illinois and the Great Plains of Kansas, insisted upon contracts that specified payment in cash. During times of low prices Scully refused to decrease rents and threatened to enforce payment by preventing tenants from selling their crops. Anti-Scully feeling became especially pronounced in the late eighties when Scully and other landlords purchased large tracts in Illinois and Kansas, a development that led to the passage of laws prohibiting land ownership by noncitizens. Perhaps Scully's rental policy was not as abusive as Irish landlordism, but there was much truth in the charges of rack-renting levied against Scully and other Illinois landlords.[42]

A northwest Iowa landlord, M. A. Wiley of Castana, was less well known than Scully but equally despised. In late December 1895 Wiley sent a deputy sheriff to seize the property of one H. Smith in satisfaction of past-due rent. Fifty persons, one with a rope, greeted the deputy and ordered him to depart. After the deputy's prompt compliance, the crowd then hanged Wiley in effigy, declaring that they would no longer allow renters to be "stripped to destitution." Two weeks later a local newspaper linked these troubles to cash rents: "The low prices of all farm products this year demonstrates the wrongfullness [sic] of the cash rent system. . . . There is scarcely a tenant in this county who agreed to pay a cash rent for 1895, who can fulfill his contract and have enough left to buy the wife he loves a calico dress."[43] Many landlords were probably more lenient with their tenants during hard times than Scully or Wiley. Individual acts of kindness may have ameliorated the hardship of low prices for some tenants, but the larger reality remains that the incidence of cash rental increased. As a result, tenants bore the brunt of deflation.

Certainly not all farmers in the Midwest were in a state of acute distress; by the eighties and nineties many of them had become quite prosperous. Perhaps they had started out with a larger-than-average supply of capital or had had the good fortune to choose land of exceptional quality. Many farmers avoided incurring debts at inopportune times, or, because of an exceptional number of hard-working sons and daughters, saved on labor costs. Through these or other factors, many farm families realized a good measure of the promise in the fertile soils of the American prairies. But for the majority the fruits of a land of promise remained elusive as they struggled through seasons of poor crops or low prices. The burden of deflation in the late nineteenth century fell on farmers throughout the Midwest, particularly on those carrying long-term mortgages and on tenant farmers whose landlords shifted from share to cash rents. Short-term interest rates were quite high, frequently at the usurious levels Populists claimed.[44] But how much did economic hardship vary across the Midwest? Can such variations explain divergences in patterns of support for the Populist Party?

Before comparing economic conditions in Kansas and Nebraska (Populist states) and Iowa (a non-Populist state), it is important to realize that the pattern of Populist voting shows a decisive break at the political boundary between the two Populist and the non-Populist states (see Map 2.1). Missouri is included on the map, although it is not central to the analysis.[45] Although numerous counties in eastern Nebraska showed strong Populist support, significant levels of Populist voting utterly disappeared across the Missouri River in Iowa. The break in Populist voting at the Kansas-Missouri border is also striking. It is doubtful that farmers in counties of western Iowa or Missouri were prosperous if their neighbors in eastern Nebraska or Kansas were in desperate straits. The definition of the geography of populism by a political boundary is a strong indication of the importance of state-specific political factors in shaping the voting behavior of farmers.

Strictly in terms of material conditions, the logical location for a break between Populist and non-Populist areas would not be at the Missouri River at all but at the ninety-eighth meridian, about 100 miles west of Omaha and 175 miles west of Kansas City. Geographers have used the ninety-eighth meridian to demarcate two major continental regions: the arid Great Plains to the west and the humid Prairie Plains to the east.[46] Roughly speaking, the Great Plains region includes the western and central thirds of Kansas and Nebraska; the eastern third of those states is part of the humid Prairie region. There is little question that economic conditions in the Great Plains region of Kansas and Nebraska were more severe than elsewhere in the Midwest. Central and western Kansas and Nebraska were true frontier regions, having been settled only in the 1880s. Although abnormally high rainfall in the early phase of settlement encouraged the belief that "rain follows the plow," this article of faith evaporated when drought gripped the region beginning in 1887, ushering in a period of acute depression. In central and

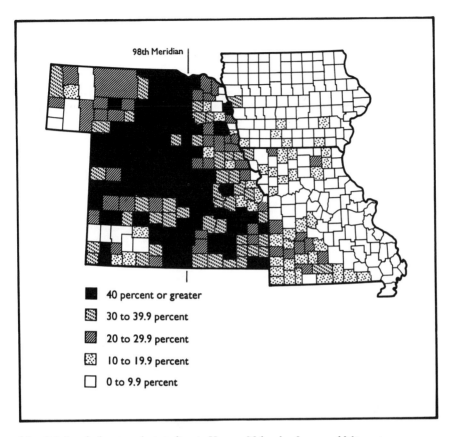

Map 2.1. Level of support for populism in Kansas, Nebraska, Iowa, and Missouri.

western Kansas and Nebraska the usual story associating populism with severe hardship following the collapse of a frontier boom is most fitting.[47]

If that were the only story, there would be little reason to question the traditional economic explanation of support for the People's Party. Yet the Populist movement was remarkably strong in eastern Kansas and Nebraska under conditions much more like those in Iowa or Missouri than on the Great
Plains.[48] Although there were a few pockets where populism did not take
root in eastern Kansas and Nebraska, the overall level of support for the
third party was quite strong. The average Populist support in the thirty-
three eastern Kansas counties was 33.1 percent, which in a three-way election was at virtual parity with the other parties. In the twenty-six eastern
Nebraska counties the Populist average was a substantial 23.3 percent.[49]

Indeed because of the greater degree of urbanization in eastern Kansas and Nebraska, these figures obscure the strength of populism among farmers in the eastern counties. These aggregate county percentages present a misleading impression of weakness for the third party. Returns from Shawnee County, Kansas, for example, show that 11 percent of all voters supported the Independent ticket in 1890, suggesting that populism was fairly weak. But outside of Topeka, which accounted for well over half the county's total vote and recorded only a handful of Populist ballots, the People's Party was stronger, receiving 23 percent of the total vote. A second example is found in Lancaster County, Nebraska, where the aggregate returns show only 13 percent of the voters casting ballots for the People's Party. In the rural areas outside of Lincoln, however, the Independent ticket won a comfortable plurality, gaining 45 percent of the total vote.[50]

The relatively strong support for the People's Party in eastern Kansas and Nebraska challenges the usual association of populism with uniquely severe conditions of economic hardship, since by several measures conditions in eastern Kansas and Nebraska do not differ greatly from those in Iowa. Consider precipitation: A 1948 study indicated that the normal rainfall in the wet months from April through September was twenty-five inches in eastern Kansas, twenty-one inches in eastern Nebraska, and twenty-three inches in Iowa.[51] Examine population density: Farmers had settled in eastern Kansas and Nebraska as early as the 1850s, and after the Civil War agriculture had developed rapidly in the eastern counties. By 1880, with population densities above twenty persons per square mile, eastern Kansas and Nebraska had long since passed the frontier stage.[52] Agricultural practices were also much the same on both sides of the Missouri River. "Corn is king" was the common saying in all three states. Very little wheat was grown either in Iowa or in eastern Kansas and Nebraska during the eighties, and the dairy industry, limited to northeastern Iowa, remained undeveloped.[53] Despite the fact that the identification of agrarian radicalism with areas of wheat production has often assumed the status of a sociological axiom, wheat was not the major crop anywhere in Kansas and Nebraska, even in the arid regions of the central and western sections. Wheat eventually became the most important crop in central and western Kansas and Nebraska, but this did not happen until after the Populist revolt.[54] It is misleading, then, to posit a distinction in the type of agricultural economy as an explanation for divergent patterns of Populist voting. Populism emerged in the corn/livestock economy common to most of the Midwest.

Another tendency has been to associate populism with particularly severe drought.[55] Although drought was more severe in Kansas and Nebraska than in Iowa in the 1880s, Iowa farmers did face moderate drought during these years. In 1888, following several seasons of poor crops, the *Iowa State Register* observed that "climatic changes or planetary influences have given us summers lately that have roasted our fields, decreased our crops, and killed our meadows." Although the *Register* beseeched the Lord to reduce the temperature "about 10 degrees from its . . . burning point in July and August," crops continued to wither. A few years later the director of the Iowa Crop and Weather Service reported a deficiency in rainfall of fifty inches from 1887 through 1890. Because of the "scorching, desolating" southwest winds the 1890 corn crop had been a disappointment, "and now the croakers are saying the State is going dry, that the arid belt is gradually extending eastward." The prospect of Iowa's desertification prompted the state legislature to order an investigation into the causes of this alarming trend.[56]

A look at corn yields from 1886 through 1890 for the three states affords a more precise sense of the relative levels of drought. Years in which the corn yield was above thirty bushels per acre can be considered drought-free. Years when the yield was between twenty and thirty bushels per acre are classified as periods of moderate drought and when the yield fell below twenty bushels per acre as severe. By this measure conditions over the five years were the worst in Kansas, which suffered two years of severe and two years of moderate drought. Nebraska farmers endured two years of moderate and one of severe drought. Iowa farmers were somewhat better off, but they did face moderate drought in three of the five years.[57]

Drought was common in other midwestern states during this period. Inadequate rainfall in 1887 resulted in low corn yields in Michigan (22.5 bushels per acre), Indiana (20), and Illinois (19). Three years later insufficient precipitation and hot winds were recorded from Missouri to Michigan. Yields averaged only around twenty-five bushels per acre. The USDA's annual summary reported that because of "unfavorable conditions . . . there is hardly a prominent grain state in which the yield per acre of corn, oats, or winter wheat is as large as the average of the past ten years."[58]

The pattern of drought within Kansas and Nebraska is also relevant. County-level data on corn yields are available for Kansas for the severe drought of 1890 and convey a general sense of intrastate divergences. Many counties in the western and central parts of the state reported yields below five bushels per acre, and the average for these counties was only eight bushels per acre, clear evidence of disaster. But the drought was less severe in the eastern parts of the state, where the average yield was about twenty-one bushels per acre. The situation in eastern Kansas was similar to that in Iowa, where the average yield was twenty-seven bushels per acre.[59] The severity of drought in central and western Kansas may have added fuel to the fire of populism there, but farmers in eastern Kansas, less hard hit by drought, also turned to the People's Party.

Another important factor scholars have identified in explaining patterns of support for populism is transportation costs.[60] In considering the significance of railroad rates, it is helpful to understand how tariffs were set in the Midwest. There were two basic types of tariffs in the late nineteenth century: local tariffs between points within the same state and through tariffs on interstate shipments over a single line or prorated over two or more lines. Significantly most important for the farmer was the through rate for interstate shipments, by which the bulk of grain and livestock traveled to market. Only a small proportion of farm shipments remained within the same state.[61]

Several factors influenced the pattern of rates on bulk agricultural commodities from western points to eastern markets. In theory through rates were not made on a straight mileage basis because fixed terminal costs made a short haul more expensive per mile than a long haul. Tariff schedules generally showed larger increases per mile in the first few hundred miles from a terminal point than after several hundred miles. Thus rates could be lower per mile farther from market, which often appeared discriminatory to shippers located closer to markets. Although the relative cheapness of long hauls worked to decrease the per-mile shipping cost for western farmers, a countervailing factor operated against them. Because of high traffic density along eastern lines, eastern railroads could afford to charge relatively low rates, but western lines required higher tariffs to compensate for their lower volume of traffic. Rates were further affected by complex competitive relationships among railroad lines and by commercial rivalries between cities.[62]

Of particular importance in affecting the pattern of rates across the Midwest was the structure of the American railroad system from the East Coast to the Plains. The system consisted of two integrated, although distinct, networks. The region east of the Mississippi River was dominated by the major trunk lines that provided through traffic from Chicago and St. Louis to New York and other points on the eastern seaboard. Because of demands for parity by wholesalers at Mississippi River crossings and the conflicting interests of railroads with commitments to different cities (particularly Chicago and St. Louis), a compromise was achieved in the 1870s whereby rates between New York and St. Louis, Burlington, Davenport, and other Mississippi River crossings were set at 125 percent of the trunk-line Chicago–New York rate, regardless of variances in distance to Chicago or the eastern seaboard.

The region west of the Mississippi was dominated by the western trunk lines and the transcontinentals. Rates on shipments to New York from points west of the Mississippi River were generally set at the rate to Chicago or to St. Louis plus the trunk-line rate to New York. Thus, the tariff on a shipment from Des Moines to New York was the sum of the Des Moines–Chicago rate and the Chicago–New York rate. A shipment from Topeka routed through St. Louis to New York would be billed at the Topeka–St. Louis rate plus the St. Louis–New York rate.[63] The result was a dual-tariff structure in the Midwest. In trunk-line territory east of the Mississippi all rates were set in relationship to the distance to New York along the shortest route. West of the Mississippi rates were set according to distance to Chicago or to Mississippi River points plus the rate from Chicago or the Mississippi to New York.

This dual-tariff structure meant that the point at which rates increased significantly was not between Iowa and Kansas-Nebraska but between Iowa and Illinois, as is illustrated by the published tariff on corn in effect in January 1889. From Chicago to New York the rate per 100 pounds on corn was 25 cents; from Mississippi River points the rate was 29 cents. West of the Mississippi rates jumped significantly. From Des Moines the rate to New York was 41 cents (16 cents to Chicago plus 25 cents to New York), an increase of 41 percent in only 175 miles. Rates increased only slightly from Des Moines to the Missouri River, where the rate to New York was 45 cents via Chicago (20 cents to Chicago plus the Chicago–New York charge) or 44 cents via St. Louis (15 cents to St. Louis plus the St. Louis–New York charge). From points in Nebraska and Kansas 150 miles west of the Missouri the tariff was 50 cents (25 cents to Chicago and the additional Chicago–New York rate).[64]

The dual-tariff structure can also be seen by examining the average rate on corn to New York from seven midwestern states as reported by the Interstate Commerce Commission (ICC) in early 1890. In trunk-line territory, the average tariff on corn ranged from 15.5 cents in Ohio to 22 cents in Illinois. At the Mississippi River rates increased markedly to 33.5 cents in Missouri and to 35 cents in Iowa. The ICC reported a further increase west of the Missouri River to 40.5 cents in Kansas and Nebraska, but the increase at the Missouri was much less than the abrupt rise at the Mississippi.[65]

In a certain sense, Iowa farmers suffered a greater disadvantage than farmers in other midwestern states. Iowans were at the eastern end of the trans-Mississippi railroad network, which meant they paid high fixed costs on a short haul to Chicago over low-density lines. The per-mile rate from Des Moines to Chicago based on the tariff in effect in January 1889 was .044 cents per 100 lbs., an extremely high figure. This expensive short-haul rate combined with the long-haul rate to New York meant that Iowa had the highest cost per mile of any midwestern state, at .028 cents per 100 lbs., compared with .024 cents in Ohio, .022 in Indiana and Illinois, and .026 in Kansas and Nebraska.[66]

Farmers felt the effects of railroad rates through their impact on prices at the farm. Generally, farmers sold their produce at local markets to shippers, who assumed the cost of transportation from local to central markets. The price actually received by farmers, then, was the terminal market price less the costs of transportation, commission, and storage (and the profit realized on the transaction by the shipper). For example, if the price of wheat in New York was $1.00 per bushel and the cost of transporting a bushel of wheat from a local market in Iowa to New York was 35 cents, the local market price would have been 65 cents. With this in mind it is revealing to observe that corn prices in the winter of 1889–1890 were nearly equal in the three states: 19 cents in Iowa, 18 cents in Kansas, and 17 cents in Nebraska. Iowa prices were at such ruinous levels that the *Iowa State Register* urged farmers to burn corn in place of coal instead of selling it at a loss. Clearly, Iowa farmers gained little real benefit from their closer proximity to markets.[67]

Differences in the economic geography between Iowa and Kansas-Nebraska were much less pronounced than described by the literature on populism. Several economic indicators in the 1890 census provide a more refined understanding of the differences in economic conditions across the three states. At the most basic level, it is important to note that the proportion of indebted farmers or tenants was about the same in all three states. At the 1890 census, 37.5 percent of all Iowa farms were mortgaged compared with 38.3 percent in Kansas and 37.9 in Nebraska. The percentage of tenant farmers in Iowa was 29.6, similar to 31 percent in Kansas and 27 percent in Nebraska.[68]

Two indicators bearing upon the relative profitability (or unprofitability) of agriculture are the value of livestock and of farm products. These two measures were higher in Iowa (by about half a point) than in eastern Kansas and Nebraska. A third indicator, however, property values, is a superior measure of the relative degree of hardship since they indicate conditions over a longer period of time and reflect an aggregate of conditions (see Table 2.2). Because the price of land embodies judgments about the past levels of profitability, it reflects influences such as drought, transportation rates, and the productivity of the land.[69] The average farm value was greater in Iowa than in central and western Kansas or Nebraska. But the average farm value in eastern Kansas and Nebraska was virtually identical to the value in Iowa,

TABLE 2.2. Selected Indicators of Economic Conditions, 1890 Census

	Kansas	Nebr.	Iowa	Eastern Kansas/Nebr.	Central Kansas/Nebr.	Western Kansas/Nebr.
Value of livestock per farm	$769	$818	$1,025	$889	$796	$536
Value of farm products per farm	$571	$588	$789	$659	$626	$265
Value of average farm	$3,359	$3,542	$4,247	$4,207	$3,426	$1,678
Value of mortgage to value of mortgaged property	36.0%	32.4%	33.3%	31.9%	36.2%	41.1%
Interest rate	8.15%	8.22%	7.36%	7.89%	8.46%	9.33%
Annual debt to value of mortgaged property	10.13%	9.14%	9.11%	8.88%	10.22%	12.03%

Sources: U.S. Census Office, *Report on the Statistics of Agriculture in the United States at the Eleventh Census: 1890* (Washington, D.C., 1895), table 6; U.S. Census Office, *Report on Farms and Homes: Proprietorship and Indebtedness in the United States at the Eleventh Census: 1890* (Washington, D.C., 1896), tables 103, 108.

a strong indication that no substantial difference in economic conditions existed between non-Populist Iowa and Populist eastern Kansas-Nebraska.[70] This conclusion is reinforced by considering three further variables related to the level of indebtedness. The first is the ratio of the value of mortgages to the value of mortgaged property, which, although much higher in central and western Kansas and Nebraska, was actually somewhat lower in eastern Kansas-Nebraska than in Iowa, indicating that Iowa farmers were generally in the same economic condition as farmers in eastern Kansas-Nebraska. The second variable, however, the interest rate on mortgage loans, was lower in Iowa than in any section of Kansas and Nebraska, suggesting that the burden of indebtedness may have been less for Iowa farmers.

Did the half-point disparity in interest rates at the Missouri River indicate a point at which the burden of indebtedness became particularly oppressive? Stepwise multiple-regression analysis would appear to lend some support for an affirmative answer. The highest coefficient of any independent variable in the 1890 census and the Populist percentage, the dependent variable, is the interest rate ($r = +.56$). Adding other variables to the regression equation increases the correlation coefficient only slightly (multiple $r = .60$), indicating that no combination of independent variables can explain much more of the variance in the Populist vote than the variance in interest rates by itself. Because the coefficient between Populist voting and the rate of interest is above .50, a level most analysts would agree is meaningful, it is conceivable that higher interest rates defined a critical threshold of hardship.

But before erroneously concluding that high interest rates "caused" populism, it is important to recognize that the statistical association between interest rates and areas of Populist voting does not necessarily demonstrate a causal relationship between the two variables. These variables show strong correlation because, to a much greater extent than is the case for most other variables from the 1890 census, interest rates reveal a regular increase from the Mississippi River to the Great Plains (partly resulting from lenders using longitudinal location as a proxy for risk in setting interest rates). Since Populist voting begins west of a definite longitude there is obviously an association between the two variables, but the point at which the increase in interest rates intersects with Populist voting does not necessarily represent a threshold of hardship. It is plausible that some other factor explains the sudden emergence of populism west of the Missouri River and that higher interest rates had no independent effect. The fact that the point at which populism emerged happened to be a state political boundary suggests the involvement of noneconomic factors.

But more important, interest rates were only one factor determining the burden of indebtedness. A mortgage loan for a relatively low percentage of the property value, even with a higher interest rate, may not have been as burdensome as a loan for a relatively high percentage of the property value with a lower rate of interest. Thus, to measure the level of indebtedness accurately it is necessary to turn to the third variable, the ratio of the annual debt obligation to the value of mortgaged farms.[71] This ratio, the debt-to-property-value ratio, should be a fairly good indicator of relative levels of hardship across the three states as it encompasses a number of factors, including transportation costs, drought, productivity, costs of borrowing, interest rates, and the level of indebtedness. The fact that this ratio was lower in eastern Kansas and Nebraska (8.88) than in Iowa (9.11) is a strong indication that the level of hardship in Populist eastern Kansas and Nebraska was no greater than in Iowa.

This conclusion is reinforced by examining the pattern of the debt-to-property-value ratio across Kansas, Nebraska, and Iowa; Missouri is in-

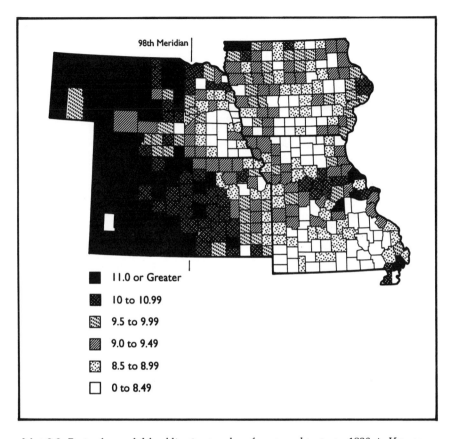

Map 2.2. Ratio of annual debt obligation to value of mortgaged property, 1890, in Kansas, Nebraska, Iowa, and Missouri

cluded as a contiguous state (see Map 2.2). As would be expected, those counties with the highest ratio were concentrated in the western and central regions of Kansas and Nebraska. There were, however, some counties in Iowa and Missouri with a debt-to-property-value ratio above 10 percent, which was comparable to the ratio in some Great Plains counties. Most significant, the overall pattern of the debt-to-property-value ratio was not defined by a state boundary, unlike the voting patterns. Counties with both relatively low and moderate ratios were scattered throughout eastern Kansas-Nebraska, Iowa, and Missouri, demonstrating that conditions in much of non-Populist Iowa and Missouri were similar to conditions in many parts of Populist Kansas and Nebraska. The evidence from the debt-to-property-value ratios justifies a division of the tri-state region into two areas: an area of severe economic hardship in central and western Kansas-Nebraska and one of moderate economic hardship in eastern Kansas-Nebraska and Iowa.[72]

That farmers in Iowa faced significant economic hardship in the late 1880s and early 1890s is confirmed by the results of an assessment of the economic condition of Iowa's farmers undertaken by the state Bureau of Labor Statistics. By far the majority of the 1,015 respondents to the bureau's questionnaire reported that the yield of Iowa's primary agricultural products, with one exception, had not been profitable from 1885 through 1890. Over 90 percent of farmers judged that raising cattle, wheat, oats, and barley had been conducted at a loss, and a full 85 percent reported the same results about growing corn. A clear consensus of unprofitability was absent only for hogs; a majority of farmers (57 percent) responded that raising hogs had made money over the period.[73] Since few farmers depended entirely on hogs and most relied on selling some surplus corn and other grains or specialized in cattle raising, the findings taken together point to the conclusion that farming in Iowa had been a marginal proposition at best.[74]

To determine the rate of foreclosure in Iowa the Bureau of Labor Statistics asked leading farmers throughout the state to estimate "the per cent of farmers losing their farms through foreclosure since 1880" in their county of residence. These estimates were averaged by county, and then a state average was determined. The methodology was somewhat crude, but the results convey a rough sense of the incidence of foreclosure. Only twelve of Iowa's ninety-nine counties had a mean above 10 percent, and the average for the state was 6 percent. If this figure was at all accurate, it would have entailed an annual foreclosure rate of less than 1 percent. These figures are corroborated by two twentieth-century studies of foreclosure rates, confirming the accuracy of the bureau's research and indicating the general reliability of its work.[75]

Although the rate of foreclosure was low in Iowa, the response of several hundred farmers who complied with the bureau's investigation shows clearly that the burdens of indebtedness weighed heavily on farm households in Iowa. Farmers took pains to point out that although few of their neighbors had suffered foreclosure, many of them had been forced to sell their farms or to deed their property to the mortgagee in lieu of actual foreclosure. In a typical response, one farmer reported that although only 5 percent of farms in his county had been lost through foreclosure since 1880, 40 percent of farms had undergone "forced sales to avoid foreclosure." Another observed that even those farmers who had not yet been forced to sell were "hanging on with a death grip, trusting that better times will come."[76]

Other farmers stressed the difficulty of making interest payments. Because most moneylenders wanted to collect interest rather than obtain land through foreclosure, even when farmers were delinquent with interest payments or could not repay the principal, lenders preferred to grant extensions when it seemed at all possible. Had it not been for extensions, claimed one farmer, 80 percent of the farmers in his area would have lost their farms after 1880. Perhaps this was an exaggerated figure, but it illustrates much better than simple data on foreclosures the pervasiveness of the chains of debt. Iowa farmers were not in a state of utter destitution, but they were seriously burdened by debt because of low prices and felt that if conditions did not improve, thousands, perhaps tens of thousands, would fail. "Two years' [crop] failures," one farmer somberly judged, "would close out ninety per cent and less than ten years of present prices will bring the same result."[77]

On the eve of the Populist revolt, farmers faced total disaster in the arid regions west of the ninety-eighth meridian, but the situation was also serious in eastern Kansas and Nebraska and in Iowa. This geographical division clearly shows the inadequacy of a strictly economic interpretation of Populist voting. Had the appeal of populism been limited to exceptional areas of extreme hardship, its level of support would have declined sharply at the eastern boundary of the Great Plains. Populism would have been as weak in eastern Kansas and Nebraska as it was in Iowa. But the strong manifestation of support for populism in eastern Kansas-Nebraska, under conditions similar to those in Iowa, demonstrates that populism could also develop in conditions of moderate economic hardship common to much of the Midwest. I am not suggesting that economic conditions were irrelevant to the process of third-party formation or that variations in hardship had no impact on political behavior. But I do stress that although farmers in eastern Kansas and Nebraska and in Iowa (and in much of the rest of the Midwest) escaped the severe economic crisis that occurred on the Great Plains, they nevertheless endured significant economic hardship because of falling prices in the late 1880s and were not necessarily immune to the message of a third party. Farmers confronted different levels of hardship according to geographical location, but all of them, no matter where they lived, shared the same position in an economy of ruthless deflation. No place afforded security from the brutal facts of a world market.

A series of agrarian revolts surged across the Midwest beginning with the Grange and the Greenback movements in the 1870s and continuing with the Farmers' Alliance in the late 1880s. Each wave of unrest affected the entire region. The fact that the Alliance movement gave birth to strong People's Parties only in states west of the Missouri River does not obviate the hardship and discontent prevalent throughout the Midwest; it only suggests that in many states unrest was channeled in a different direction. An investigation of politics in Iowa during the 1880s and early 1890s reveals the constant presence of underlying economic discontent, the resurgence of agrarian radicalism, and mounting demands for reform. The response of the political system in Iowa to these developments had much to do with the chances of a third party in the Hawkeye state.

3
Antimonopoly and the Emergence of Party Competition in Iowa

At the close of the Civil War, the Republican Party was in a commanding position in Iowa. Gen. Ulysses S. Grant carried the Hawkeye state with an overwhelming 62 percent of the vote in 1868, and all six Republican congressional candidates won election with ease.[1] It seemed that Republican politicians only had to remind voters of the Union victory and characterize the Democrats as traitors unfit to govern; Iowa might remain a one-party state forever.

Yet despite the GOP's electoral dominance, the party was racked with factionalism. For the most part, divisions among Republican leaders were not ideological; factionalism centered on competition for the spoils of office. Serious cleavage in the Iowa GOP first appeared in 1866 during a bitter contest for the Senate seat that had been vacated by James Harlan upon his appointment as secretary of the interior by President Lincoln the previous year. Having become disillusioned with the conservative administration of Andrew Johnson, the radical Harlan resigned his position in Washington, returned to Iowa, and reclaimed "his seat" by defeating Samuel J. Kirkwood, the candidate of a faction led by Gen. Grenville M. Dodge, chief engineer of the Union Pacific Railroad.[2] Vowing to avenge their defeat, "Dodge & Co." spent the next six years organizing a powerful political machine with Dodge's protégé William Boyd Allison as standard-bearer. Although a Harlan man defeated Allison for the Senate in 1870, the anti-Harlanites gained an especially sweet revenge two years later when Allison defeated Harlan. Allison's victory inaugurated the reign of the "Des Moines Regency," a powerful clique of politicians and railroad men that would control the Iowa Republican Party for the next thirty years.[3]

To understand Iowa politics in the Gilded Age, it is important to realize that there were constant challenges to the Regency's dominance. Even as Allison left for Washington, he could hear expressions of unrest and demands for economic reform among his rural constituents. As farm prices fell in the late sixties and early seventies, thousands of Iowa farmers joined the Patrons of Husbandry, popularly known as the Grange. The state Grange was organized in January 1871; by May 1873 there were about 1,500 local Granges in the state, more than in any other.[4] At first the Iowa Grange emphasized cooperative purchasing but quickly turned to the issue of railroad reform. In early 1873 the Grange lobbied the General Assembly for a bill to fix maximum passenger and freight rates. When the lawmakers defeated this legislation, a faction within the Grange launched the Anti-Monopoly Party. Starving for victory, the opportunistic Democrats convinced the Anti-Monopolists to cooperate in the upcoming campaign.[5]

Mobilizing during a period of economic recession, the antimonopoly movement represented a major threat to Republican hegemony. It did not help matters any that Dodge, Allison, and their associate James F. Wilson had recently been implicated in the Crédit Mobilier scandal or that the Republican state treasurer had been caught stealing $38,000 from the Agricultural College. Gov. Cyrus Clay Carpenter, independent of the Regency, had sensed the seriousness of the situation early in 1873; he endorsed railroad reform during the legislative session, joined the Grange, and spoke at numerous Grange gatherings throughout the fall. Carpenter's popularity in rural areas gave him a 12 percent margin of victory, but the GOP almost lost control of the state's house, which was evenly split with fifty Republicans and fifty Anti-Monopolist/Democrats.[6]

The Regency responded to the near catastrophe of 1873 by endorsing reform. James S. "Ret" Clarkson, editor of the *Iowa State Register* and a key member of the Regency, called upon the legislature to enact a stringent rate bill; otherwise, the "Republican Party in Iowa may be written of[f] as dead, and its last platform will prove its epitaph." With little opposition, in 1874 the General Assembly passed a measure fixing maximum freight rates known as the "Iowa Granger Law."[7]

The response of the Republican leaders to the agrarian insurgency of the early 1870s suggested not only political flexibility but also a degree of genuine sympathy for antimonopoly sentiment. As the economic depression of the 1870s deepened, however, Republican leaders became increasingly resolved to secure economic prosperity by giving free reign to business enterprise. In 1877 the railroads began a vigorous campaign for repeal of the Granger Law, claiming that state regulation had brought railroad construction to a halt. This argument ignored the impact of the economic depression on capital investment, but it was effective nonetheless. Under the tutelage of railroad propagandists who obtained open access to the columns of

Clarkson's *Register*, many Iowa voters, particularly in the less developed sections, regarded repeal as the solution to hard times. In a close vote the 1878 General Assembly repealed the 1874 law, replacing it with a toothless new law establishing a board of commissioners to be appointed by the governor.[8] Although the depression of the 1870s induced most Republicans to embrace conservative nostrums, a sizable minority of Republicans led by Gen. James B. Weaver moved in the opposite direction. In the early 1870s Weaver had earned a reputation as one of the strongest Republican orators and debaters in the state and as a powerful voice for the "suppression of the saloons and the public control of the railways and other semi-public corporations."[9] The front-runner for the Republican nomination for governor in 1875, Weaver was defeated by antiprohibitionists and business interests. He was undoubtedly offended by his rejection, but it was the deepening economic depression and his belief that the national Republican Party, with its firm commitment to currency contraction, was no longer responsive to the common people that led him to turn to the recently formed Greenback Party in 1877.[10]

Conservative Republicans responded more aggressively to the Greenback movement than they had to the Grange. The Grange had appeared at a time when Republican leaders still remembered the moral commitments of radicalism and were slightly embarrassed about the discovery of their corporate ties. But a few years later, deep into the depression, the Regency was an entrenched machine fiercely devoted to corporate development. Accordingly, it greeted the more ideologically advanced, combative Greenbackers with wrath and ridicule, savaging them as "communists" and "dishonest agitators."[11] The Greenback ticket won 14 percent of the vote in the gubernatorial election of 1877; though this level of support showed that the Greenback Party posed little direct threat to the GOP, the Greenbackers pulled a sufficient number of voters away from the GOP to deny the Iowa Republicans an outright majority for the first time in post–Civil War politics. The Republican plurality was a comfortable 17 percent, but the combined opposition of the Greenback and Democratic Parties was almost equal to the Republican vote.[12]

Weaver combined a belief in the basic principles of a moral economy with an earnest desire to obtain office. His critics sneered that he was "merely" an office-seeker, but the general contended that in order to achieve one's principles, it was essential to obtain political power. Ever alert to political opportunities, Weaver and his associate, Edward H. Gillette, were elected to Congress in 1878 on a Greenback/Democratic fusion ticket. Only once since Appomattox had anyone except a Republican won a congressional race in

Iowa (in 1874 when the Anti-Monopolists had won one seat); now Iowa had sent two proponents of financial heresy to the national halls of legislation.[13] Believing that the Greenback vote would increase substantially, Weaver opposed fusion with the Democrats in 1879. When the Greenbackers won just 16 percent of the vote—only a slight increase over 1877—Greenback momentum clearly had stalled. As the depression of the 1870s eased and agricultural prices began to rise, the Greenback Party declined. Weaver was the party's presidential candidate in 1880, but he won only 10 percent of the vote in Iowa; the Republican candidate, James A. Garfield, won the state by an overwhelming plurality of 24 percent. Iowa Republicanism, so it seemed, had emerged from the trials of the 1870s triumphant.[14]

In fall 1885 the Republican orator John P. Dolliver assured his audiences that "Iowa will go Democratic when Hell goes Methodist."[15] Such a claim would have been unassailable just a few years earlier, but by 1885 it was rather an incantation against an impending danger. Four years would elapse before the Democrats would elect a governor, but even by 1885, hell, to use Dolliver's metaphor, was undergoing something of a religious revival.

In 1881 not even the most sanguine Democrat would have expressed much hope for the future. The party's Bourbon leadership seemed content with permanent minority status and was unwilling or unable to develop issues that could mobilize voters. The Democrats' passivity was largely due to its defensiveness about the Civil War. With Republican charges of treachery ringing in their ears, Democrats at their 1881 state convention countered that at the outbreak of the war, Iowa Democrats had "responded nobly" and "fought side by side with the Republican party." This feeble pronouncement did little more than salute the bloody shirt. The Democrats proclaimed free trade as their "grand principle" and declared their firm abhorrence of "sumptuary regulation," but these general statements did little to justify the party's existence.[16]

The Republican Party in the early 1880s remained in the capable hands of the Regency. By then Allison had earned a national reputation through his service on the Senate Finance Committee and as chairman of the Committee on Appropriations; he would become a serious contender for the presidential nomination in 1888. Clarkson was also on his way to national prominence. By the end of the eighties, he would become a member of the Republican National Committee and serve as first assistant post master general in the Harrison administration.[17] The control Allison and Clarkson exercised over the GOP continued to rest upon their strong alliances with railroad managers and on their ability to direct patronage. Allison was a close friend of Charles E. Perkins, president of the Chicago, Burlington, and Quincy Railroad. Other associates, Joseph W. Blythe, chief counsel for the CB&Q, and Nathaniel M. Hubbard of the Chicago and North Western, directed much of the day-to-day work maintaining the Iowa Republican Party as an organization friendly to capital and loyal to Allison, seeing to the distribution of passes for free railroad transportation, shaping public opinion through contacts with local journalists, and lobbying the state legislature. Clarkson and Allison used their influence in Washington to ensure that patronage in Iowa rewarded those people loyal to the organization and punished those individuals who threatened to act independently.[18]

Having weathered the challenges spawned by the economic depression of the 1870s, the most immediate threat to the Iowa GOP came from another quarter altogether, the prohibition movement. Although the saloon had been an issue in Iowa politics since the 1850s, it was not until the late 1870s that a well-organized movement spearheaded by the State Temperance Alliance succeeded in capturing the Republican Party. By 1879 the drys had enough delegates at the Republican state convention to pass a resolution favoring a referendum on a prohibition amendment to the state constitution, and the 1880 Republican legislature fulfilled the platform pledge and passed legislation mandating a referendum.[19] Whatever their personal views on the matter, Republican Party managers, whose primary concern was to maintain party stability, regarded the prospect of prohibition warily since it threatened disruption within the Republican ranks and the defection of thousands of voters.

At a special election in June 1882 Iowa voters favored the prohibition amendment by a margin of fifty-five to forty-five.[20] With the Republican Party now fully committed to prohibition, many previously Republican antiprohibition voters, particularly Germans, began to leave the GOP. Disaffection over prohibition contributed to large Democratic gains in the eastern river counties in 1882 and 1883, where there was the greatest concentration of antiprohibition voters, and was the most obvious explanation for the increase in the Democratic vote from 31.2 percent in 1881 to 42.8 percent in 1883. Historians of the ethnocultural school of political history would see the Democratic gains from 1881 to 1883 as due primarily to the movement of antiprohibition voters, but to do so would be seriously misleading. The striking fact about the election of 1883 is that the Democrats gained heavily everywhere in the state. In only one county in the state the Democratic percentage for governor did not increase from 1881 to 1883, and the Democratic percentage increased by 10 percent or more in sixty-three of the state's ninety-nine counties.[21]

A close look at the 1883 election campaign suggests that Democrats made some of their gains by contending that the GOP was controlled by corporations. At stake in the election of 1883 was not only the governorship and other state offices but the seats of all members of the state house and half of the members of the state senate. The election of members to the General Assembly had particular significance because when it convened in early 1884 this body would decide the fate of William B. Allison's bid for a third term in the U.S. Senate. Although the question of Allison's past record was not strictly relevant to a gubernatorial candidacy, James B. Weaver, the Greenback nominee for the state's chief executive, campaigned as if Allison were his opponent. In a "bitter fight" Weaver alleged that Allison consistently had acted in league with corporations and had showed little regard for the common people. Weaver accused Allison of making a fortune by using his influence to change the route of the Sioux City & Pacific Railroad; he further charged that Allison was connected with the Cedar Rapids & Missouri Railroad Company and had supported their suit to evict settlers in southwestern Iowa.[22]

Economic conditions in the early 1880s were not as severe as they had been during the depression of the 1870s, yet significant political and economic discontent still existed. Weaver himself polled only 7 percent of the total vote, but his campaign against the GOP may have resulted in some previously Republican voters casting Democratic ballots in protest. More important, Weaver's attacks on Allison had concrete ramifications in the state legislature. In at least twenty house and eight senate districts Democrats and Greenbackers joined in fielding a fusion ticket in opposition to Allison. As a result of the anti-Allison campaign, the number of Republicans in the House fell from seventy-two in 1882 to fifty-two in 1884. Because of the large number of holdover Republicans in the senate, Allison had a comfortable margin of victory, but the Republican losses in the General Assembly indicated the presence of a strong sentiment against the Allison-dominated Republican Party.[23]

That Democratic gains came not just from the shift of antiprohibition voters is confirmed by looking at estimates of how particular groups voted in the 1881 and 1883 elections.[24] Let us first consider estimates for that portion of the electorate of national origins likely to oppose prohibition (Germany, Ireland, Bohemia, Austria, Belgium, France, Ireland, Italy, and Poland). In 1881 an estimated 38 percent of antiprohibition voters voted Democratic, and 10 percent voted Republican (the remaining 52 percent did not vote). Two years later, the Democratic vote among antiprohibition voters increased to 51 percent, the Republican vote fell to 5 percent, and 44 percent did not vote.[25] The movement of antiprohibition voters from 1881 to 1883 is as expected, but the significant shift in native-born voters from 1881 to 1883 is surprising. Only 14 percent of native-born males of voting age voted Democratic in 1881, but in 1883 the percentage of native-born voters casting ballots for the Democrats increased to 29 percent. The Republicans also gained among native-born voters (32 to 41 percent), but the Democratic increases were larger. Another surprising shift from 1881 to 1883 occurred among farmers. In 1881 only 12 percent of the farmers had voted Democratic; two years later this figure increased to 27 percent.[26]

The success of fusion at the local level in 1883 made it clear to many Democrats and Greenbackers that their alliance was the road to the promised land. Within each party, however, factions opposed cooperation. At a Democratic convention held in early 1884, delegates from the river counties, who regarded the repeal of prohibition as the primary goal of the party, supported a strongly worded resolution to use "every legal means to blot the foul stigma from the face of Iowa." The adoption of this resolution would have seriously hampered efforts to cooperate with the Greenback Party in the fall since many Greenbackers favored prohibition. Recognizing this, delegates from the interior and western counties secured the passage of a more moderate resolution favoring "liberty of individual conduct," thus enhancing the prospects for fusion.[27] Most Greenbackers were former Republicans, and many of them saw cooperation with the Democrats as a pact with Lucifer; but Greenbackers also realized that they would never get anywhere without fusion. The election of 1882, in particular, afforded a clear lesson in the comparative advantages of political realism: Weaver had been crushed in a three-way race for Congress, but another Greenbacker, Luman H. "Calamity" Weller, had won a glorious victory with Democratic support.[28]

The Democratic and Greenback central committees completed fusion arrangements at a joint meeting held in August 1884. The Democrats agreed to support General Weaver and "Calamity" Weller for Congress in the sixth and fourth congressional districts, and the Greenbackers consented to back Judge W. H. McHenry in the seventh. Seven of the state's thirteen presidential electors would be Democrats, and six would be Greenbackers; the parties divided evenly the nominations for secretary of state, state treasurer, auditor, and attorney general. These arrangements encountered minimal opposition at the state conventions. The Democratic convention, chaired by Judge L. G. Kinne of the profusion faction, unanimously backed the decisions of the central committee. At the Greenback convention a majority of delegates ignored warnings that fusion would "crush out the hope of the

Greenback party" and ratified cooperation in order to defeat the hated GOP.[29]

In the fall Democratic campaigners attacked the Republicans for fostering corruption and for building monopolies through a high protective tariff. State party chairman John F. Duncombe declared that a vote for the GOP was a "vote for a trade in official influence, and for a perpetuation of a monopolistic power already grown too great for the safety of the rights and liberty of the people." Democrats contended that the protective tariff was a tax on the necessities of life and, as such, that it imposed particular hardship on farmers. One congressional challenger demanded the Republican incumbent "to show the farmers of [this] district why a tariff of two dollars per thousand [on lumber] is a good thing for their interest." Greenback orators gladly joined their Democratic allies in attacking the GOP's tariff policy. Capt. George W. Bell characterized the protective tariff as "class legislation" that had given "herculean powers" to a few. Not only did the high tariff exacerbate labor strife, but it was also the primary reason why agriculture "wears the shackles of slavery." Why was the price of grain low, Bell demanded: "Don't be deceived; we have driven away our customers and enjoyed the triumph with unsold crops."[30]

Greenbackers also attributed the woes of farmers to insufficient currency and exorbitant railroad charges. Weaver blamed low prices on the national banking system—supported by the Republican Party—that failed to allow the supply of currency to expand commensurate with the growth of population. "Following the policy now in force" was like "trying to crowd a yearling Shanghai rooster into the eggshell that once held it." By the time bankers and railroads finished with the farmer, there was little left: "The banker has hold of one end of the grain sack, the railway magnate the other, and the farmer has what he can scoop up with his hands." The only way for farmers to free themselves from "servitude to monopolies," Weaver declared, was to "take the reins of government out of republican hands."[31]

The campaign focused mainly on national issues, but as election day drew near some Democrats sought to counter the Republicans' natural advantage in a presidential election by emphasizing state economic issues. In late October S. L. Bestow, a former Republican turned antimonopoly Democrat, reminded "Republican and Independent Voters of Iowa" of pledges in the 1883 Republican platform to pass legislation to promote safe conditions for underground coal miners, to regulate railroads, and to abolish free passes, pledges that had been unfulfilled by the Republican-dominated 1884 General Assembly. This attempt to appeal to voters on the basis of state issues, although it played a minor role in the 1884 campaign, signaled the beginning of a fruitful strategy for the Democratic/Greenback antimonopoly coalition in the future.[32]

The results of the November balloting were persuasive evidence to both parties of the advantages of fusion. Greenbackers elected Weaver to Congress although Weller suffered defeat by the narrow margin of 200 votes. Democrats elected three congressmen of their own and won 47 percent of the presidential vote (their previous high in a presidential election had been 38 percent in 1880).[33] The election revealed a deep vein of political unrest in the state and clearly established the Democratic/Greenback coalition as a serious contender in Iowa politics.

The challenge for the new coalition as it approached the next election was to avoid splitting over prohibition. For antimonopoly Democrats the key was to secure a high-license platform. As their leading organ, the *Des Moines Leader*, put it, a high license of $500 to $1,000 was the "mean between the two extremes of prohibition and low license." A policy of low license, as demanded by the river counties, would be "obnoxious to our allies," the Greenbackers, and, furthermore, would be counterproductive to the repeal of strict prohibition as it would ruin the opportunity to elect a majority in the legislature. The *Leader* counseled that the Democratic candidate for governor should be "right on the prohibition question," but he must "stand for something else as well. He should have a record as an honest man, a friend of labor and a foe of monopoly." The candidate should not be a national banker or a railroad attorney; a farmer, thought the *Leader*, would "be worth five to ten thousand votes to the ticket."[34]

The high-license/profusion faction narrowly controlled the Democratic convention in August. For governor the Democrats nominated Charles E. Whiting, a wealthy farmer, but a farmer nonetheless, and for lieutenant governor they chose the Greenback candidate, Edward Gillette. The convention endorsed a platform calling for a $500 license.[35] A jubilant *Keokuk Constitution* proclaimed the birth of a new Democratic Party "cut loose from the old Bourbon traditions," a party that "lives and breathes a new life."[36]

Republicans approached the 1885 election with apprehension. In April William Larrabee, a potential gubernatorial candidate, informed John Dolliver that "many Republicans in various parts of the state are entertaining doubts of our capability to hold the state this year."[37] The GOP desperately needed a strong campaign; Larrabee, one of the wealthiest men in Iowa, was just the man to head the ticket. Congressman David B. Henderson informed Clarkson that even though Larrabee was "not much of a speaker," he would support him because Larrabee would be "most liberal in meeting the legitimate expenses of the campaign" and could "put more strong men upon the 'stump' than any man we can nominate."[38] Larrabee was experienced, having served eighteen years in the state senate, and he appeared safe on controversial questions. He took the moderate position that prohibition should be given a "fair trial"; he was not too close to the members of the Regency to be vulnerable on this score, nor did it seem likely that he would alienate the powerful corporate influences within the party.[39]

Even with a strong candidate heading the ticket, Republicans felt fear in their hearts, and they waved the bloody shirt ever more furiously. In an editorial, "Mr. Whiting of Alabama," the *Register* attacked the Democratic nominee as a Copperhead who had never relinquished his "hatred of the Union and the Union soldier." Later, a *Register* correspondent collected several statements from individuals living in Whiting's home territory of northwestern Iowa alleging him to have been, in the words of one, a "bitter and vindictive Copperhead . . . scolding and abusing Lincoln and the Government, and giving all his sympathy to the South." Under the headline "Here is the Proof," the paper devoted an entire front page to this testimony and other unsubstantiated rumors that upon hearing of Lincoln's assassination Whiting "threw up his hat . . . and gave a prolonged hurrah."[40] Republicans also sought to drive a wedge into the Democratic/Greenback alliance by exploiting possible divisions in the coalition. Senator Allison reminded Greenbackers of President Cleveland's opposition to further coinage of silver (Greenbackers favored free coinage of silver), and the *Register* gleefully informed Democrats that Gillette, the fusion candidate for lieutenant governor, "still retains his membership in the Prohibition and Enforcement Club and in the Polk County Women Suffrage Society."[41]

When they were not too busy scouring western Iowa for men willing to attest to Whiting's wartime loyalty to the Union, the fusionists sought to portray their candidate as a friend of the people, opposed to monopoly and privilege. Antimonopoly newspapers drew a sharp contrast between "Farmer Whiting," who was "pitching hay when the telegram was brought him announcing his nomination," and Larrabee, "a professional politician, a skinflint banker in a dozen banks of the two-percent a month kind."[42] In a counterthrust to the *Register*'s exposé of Whiting's disloyalty, the *Leader* published under the headline "Shylock Larrabee" a full page of documents culled from public records purporting to show Larrabee as "the most inveterate mortgagee in Iowa," a tax cheat, and a usurer.[43]

In addition to these personal attacks, the fusionists sharply challenged the Republican Party's record on economic issues. Weaver reminded voters that in 1878 a Republican-controlled legislature had repealed the 1874 Granger Law and pledged that the Democratic/Greenback slate would reenact legislation to control the railroads.[44] Whiting, too, castigated the GOP for repealing the Granger Law and for rejecting a measure to make the railroad commission responsive to the people through direct election of its commissioners.[45] By the close of the campaign, the fusionists had defined several issues at the state level. The *Leader* focused less on Larrabee's sins as a banker and more on his record in the state senate, indicting him for his opposition to an array of antimonopoly measures: maximum rates on railways in Iowa, an elective railroad commission, reduction of the legal rate of interest, reduction of the tax burden on mortgaged farms, and requirements that coal be weighed prior to screening in order to increase compensation to miners.[46]

The identification of these specific issues marked an important transition among antimonopoly Democrats. Prior to the election of 1884 the Democrats had limited their message to the tariff, and their attacks on the GOP had been haphazard and ill focused. But by the close of the 1885 campaign they had developed a much more comprehensive, radical critique of the GOP and had made a number of concrete demands. It had become difficult to tell a Democrat from a Greenbacker. At the campaign's closing rally, D. O. Finch and Fred Lehman, lifelong Democrats, shared the platform with Greenbackers such as Gillette and Marion Todd of Michigan; they excoriated the "regency" and the "monopolistic character of the legislation of the republican party."[47]

On election day only 7,000 ballots out of 345,000 cast stood between the Republicans and defeat. Like Republicans everywhere, John Dolliver breathed a deep sigh of relief in a letter to Clarkson:

On the whole, we have escaped the most threatening political reverse of recent Iowa politics—Considering the whole field, it was no vain expectation,—this hope of the Fusion arrangers to beat Larrabee. That night Bro Jones showed me those fatal figures, at your office, I woke up with the ratio of our comparative off year losses staring me in the face like a shopsign on Main Avenue. From that minute I had no peace until I showed up under the clock tower on Tuesday night.[48]

Historians of the ethnocultural school of political history have attributed the resurgence of Democratic strength in Iowa and other midwestern states exclusively to the shift of voters (especially Germans) alienated by Republican policy on the cultural issues of liquor legislation and control of public education. Although in the long run Democrats would benefit from the fallout over prohibition, the movement of ethnocultural blocs of voters opposed to sumptuary legislation was not the primary factor in the emergence of the Democratic Party as a competitive force in Iowa politics in the early and mid-eighties. The electorate showed cleavages along ethnocultural lines, but the Democrats became competitive in 1885 because of shifts that were the result of the Democratic/Greenback coalition's capacity to attract voters on economic issues. These issues mattered to most voters, and they were capable of initiating significant shifts in partisan allegiance that had a critical impact on the state party system.

Thus the Democratic increases from the preprohibition election of 1881 to the postprohibition election of 1883 were only partly attributable to disaffection over Republican policy on prohibition. Even more significant, the further gains enabling the Democrats to become fully competitive in 1885 were negatively associated with concentrations of antiprohibition voters. Estimates for the elections of 1883 and 1885 indicate that the proportion of antiprohibition foreign-born voters casting Democratic ballots actually declined from 1883 (51 percent) to 1885 (47 percent). On the other hand, the percentage of native-born voters supporting the Democrats rose substantially from 29 percent in 1883 to 39 percent in 1885, and the percentage of farmers voting Democratic increased from 27 to 36 percent. Most farmers continued to vote Republican (an estimated 51 percent, with 13 percent not voting), but the fusionists' ability to draw as many farmers as they did, given the strong bonds of loyalty that held farmers to the GOP, proved the antimonopoly movement's vitality.[49]

By 1886 Iowa politicians, whether with hope or with apprehension, recognized the potential of the antimonopoly coalition to sweep the state. One development helping the antimonopolists was the surge in membership of the Knights of Labor (KOL) in 1885 and 1886 among railroad and manufacturing workers and coal miners. KOL candidates scored victories in spring 1886 in mayoral elections in Clinton, Marshalltown, Lyons, and Boone.[50] Further political activity by the Knights would certainly favor the Democratic/Greenback antimonopolists. Another factor working to the advantage of the coalition was the deepening of economic discontent among farmers. To some extent agrarian unrest had subsided in the early eighties with the temporary interruption of the secular decline in prices. Since 1882, however, prices had fallen rapidly. By 1886 Iowa cattle had lost one-fourth of their 1882 value, and hogs had lost almost one-half; the price of corn was less than one-half its 1882 level.[51]

With the resumption of deflation, farmers began to seek out their neighbors to understand why they continued to endure hard times, despite years of toil and the solemn promises of politicians. Soon, farmers were forming local Alliances where they could discuss the source of their grievances and formulate plans of action. The Iowa Farmers' Alliance (IFA), formally organized in 1881 as an affiliate of the National Farmers' Alliance (NFA), had been dormant since 1883.[52] In August 1886 the *Iowa Homestead* announced a meeting to reorganize the state Alliance since numerous Alliances "have been springing up spontaneously in many counties of the State, and they feel the need of a central organization."[53]

Chief among the farmers' concerns was railroad transportation. In 1885 the president of the Iowa State Agricultural Society testified before a congressional committee that most Iowa farmers believed that a corporate lobby had been behind the repeal of the Granger Law in 1878 and that the railroad commission had since neglected the legitimate interests of producers.[54] By advocating an elective railroad commission in the 1885 campaign, fusionists had seized the agrarian side of this issue and were in a strong position to capitalize on further unrest among farmers.

The Republican-dominated General Assembly that met in early 1886 did little to reverse the perception that the GOP was promonopoly. The house passed a version of the Cassatt mining bill, which required weighing coal prior to screening to increase compensation to miners, an idea the fusionists had endorsed in 1885, and it also passed a bill for the election of railroad commissioners. But the senate proved to be the graveyard of reform—these two measures died in the upper house along with a measure sponsored by the KOL to regulate factory conditions.[55] The failure of reform in the legislature was a matter of serious concern to Charles Beardsley, chairman of the Republican state central committee. At the close of the session, he informed Allison of the likelihood of "some complaint because the R. R. Commissioners were not made elective; and on the part of some miners because of the coal (Casselt) [sic] bill did not pass." Seeking to avoid the consequences of these liabilities at the state level, Beardsley advised a "campaign on national issues."[56] Such a strategy, he evidently thought, would avoid sticky state questions and afford ample room for waving the bloody shirt and promising prosperity for all through protective tariffs.

Even on national issues, however, the GOP was vulnerable. In addition to the tariff, which the Democrats had shown in 1884 could work to their advantage, was the highly volatile question of regulating interstate commerce. Since 1874 Congress had debated this issue, but no bill had ever passed both houses. In May 1886, with the pressure for legislation mounting, the House and the Senate passed two different bills. The Reagan bill, passed by the House, was the more stringent measure; it outlawed pools, prohibited long- and short-haul discrimination, and required grievances to be settled in the courts. The Senate-approved Cullom bill failed to prohibit pooling, and its provisions regulating long and short hauls allowed numerous exceptions. Rather than judicial review, it proposed a commission to review complaints.[57] Managers of railroads in Iowa detested regulation of any sort, but if they were forced to swallow government interference, they far preferred Cullom to Reagan. In a letter to Senator Allison, the president of the Illinois Central Railroad termed the Reagan bill a "monstrosity" and regarded the long- and short-haul clause as its "most obnoxious feature." Allison's good friend of the Burlington, Charles Perkins, wrote that the Cullom bill "does not seem likely to do very much good, and I think that if it had any effect at all it would be harmful, but they tell me Old Reagan says he won't accept it. I suppose it is too mild to suit his complaint."[58]

In late summer and fall 1886 the debate on the merits of the respective bills moved from the halls of Congress to the crossroads of Iowa. The regulation of interstate commerce first emerged as a campaign issue in the eighth congressional district, a thin strip of counties on the Missouri border, where farmers felt particularly oppressed by high freight rates. According to the *Homestead*, the rate on hogs to Chicago was $50 to $70 from some points in the district, but the rate was only $25 from Council Bluffs, farther west on the Missouri River.[59] Farmers in the recently organized suballiances in the eighth district felt betrayed by William P. Hepburn, their Republican congressman, who had voted against the Reagan bill.[60]

The campaign in the eighth district opened dramatically in July when a convention of "independent Republicans" nominated Albert R. Anderson on a platform demanding the "prohibition of pooling and special rates by which . . . fictitious values of stocks [are] maintained and markets annihilated, common bribery exalted into common courtesy, public morals corrupted, [and] certain persons and localities enriched at the expense of the toiling masses." The platform further characterized Hepburn, the Republican incumbent, as a "friend of the corporations."[61] Although the convention was designed to appear as the initiative of antimonopoly Republicans, Anderson's "independent Republican" candidacy was in reality a clever move by the Democratic/Greenback coalition. Rather than nominate someone from their own ranks, who would probably be vulnerable to charges of Copperheadism or political opportunism, fusionists evidently decided to create the illusion of a spontaneous uprising of antimonopoly Republicans. Anderson was the perfect front for this ploy: He was a Civil War major, and he possessed a credible record of service to Iowa as a regular Republican and as a state railroad commissioner from 1881 to 1884.[62] He could represent himself as a genuine Republican opposing the unprincipled Regency that was betraying the noble ideals of the Grand Old Party. Democratic papers feigned surprise at Anderson's nomination, but their prominent and favorable coverage of the independent convention belied this pretense. After a decent interval of ten days the Democratic and Greenback conventions of the eighth district, meeting simultaneously, saw fit to nominate the insurgent Republican.[63]

At the beginning of the campaign, Anderson and Hepburn agreed to three joint debates. In our own age of sound bites, it is difficult to imagine voters attending closely to a political debate consisting of a fifty-minute speech by one candidate, a seventy-five-minute reply, and a twenty-five-minute rebuttal. But crowds numbering 3,000 listened raptly as Hepburn and Anderson used this format to argue about the respective bills for the regulation of interstate commerce. At the conclusion of the three contests, public interest was so great that the candidates arranged six more dates.[64]

From the moment he took the platform, Anderson was on the offensive. He continually arraigned Hepburn for supporting the Cullom bill, castigating him as "the tool of corporations who [has] not served the people of this district one single hour since he was first elected to Congress."[65] Anderson further attacked railroads in general, detailing the abuses of watered stock, pools, and discriminatory rates. Stunned by Anderson's frontal assault, Hepburn attempted to characterize the Reagan bill as a "pro-railroad measure" by asserting that it had the support of Perkins of the CB&Q even though Perkins favored the Cullom bill.[66] Unable to sustain a defense of the Cullom bill before gatherings of outraged farmers, Hepburn resorted to attacking Anderson's motives, characterizing him as a disgruntled office seeker who "never knew . . . that the Republican party was ruled by the regency and the corporations until he had a grievance."[67]

The debate on the Reagan and Cullom bills defined important questions about basic conditions of life in Iowa. Were the railroads serving the people of the state? Was Iowa's agricultural economy in a prosperous condition? Were Iowa farmers getting their fair share? Was the Republican Party on the side of the people, or was it an instrument of corporations? Affirmative answers to these questions implied a vote for Hepburn, negative replies, a vote for Anderson. For Hepburn and conservative Republicans, railroads had played a vital role in helping Iowa to flourish as an agricultural state. Infrequent cases of discrimination or excessive charges could be resolved through an impartial national commission. Prorailroad Republicans acknowledged that some individuals were discontented but attributed such cases to bad luck, thriftlessness, or improvidence. From these premises, Anderson's campaign against the railroads was, as the *Register* put it, "the rankest kind of demagoguery." His efforts to "excite the farmers and workingmen" were of "the orthodox socialist style; & but a step removed from the doctrine of the anarchists."[68] For Anderson and other antimonopolists there was no demagoguery about it: The relations between producers and railroads were fundamentally unjust. Abuses were not sporadic; they were systemic. Strong measures were necessary, they argued, because of deteriorating economic conditions for producers. Discontented farmers were not so unusual, nor was their condition the result of personal failure.

The Anderson-Hepburn debates stimulated fervent discussion among ordinary citizens in the eighth district. A reporter for the *Register* in Corning was astonished to find that the "interest overshadows that of [a] Presidential campaign." From Osceola another Republican correspondent reported that "Reagan and Cullom have become household words, and one can't go five rods on the street without hearing some excited individual instructing his fellow citizens on the relative merits of the two Inter-State Commerce bills."[69] The clash in the eighth district reverberated throughout Iowa; the *Register* (located in the seventh district) broadcast blow-by-blow accounts of the debates to the far corners of the state, and the Reagan and Cullom bills were the subject of innumerable editorials in Democratic and Republican papers. The railroad issue was a factor in other congressional campaigns. In the ninth district, for example, the Greenback organization endorsed Democrat John H. Keatley after he declared his support for the Greenback platform.[70] In case any farmers had missed the partisan press, the state's foremost agricultural journal and unofficial organ for the Farmers' Alliance, the *Homestead*, informed them of the controversy through editorials praising the Reagan bill (and Anderson) and condemning the Cullom bill (and Hepburn). The *Homestead*'s editor, "Uncle Henry" Wallace (father of Henry C. and grandfather of Henry A. Wallace), regarded the battle in the eighth district as crucial in the struggle for economic justice: "On the issue of this contest there hangs more than on any election held in Iowa for twenty years."[71]

Although Anderson primarily focused on interstate commerce, his campaign also directed the state's attention to related questions such as the election of state railroad commissioners. Throughout the fall the antimonopolist *Leader* reminded Iowans that the previous Republican legislature had brushed aside an elective railroad commission. On the eve of the election the *Leader* contended that a Democratic vote was a vote for a state railroad commission "elected by the people, on the only fair plan."[72] Many Republicans felt defensive about these issues. Governor Larrabee acknowledged that his party had not provided for the election of railroad commissioners, but he promised that "if after mature consideration a change is thought to be for the best interests of the people, it will be made, and the Republicans will make it."[73]

The verdict on election day sent Republicans reeling: Anderson soundly defeated the three-time choice of eighth-district voters by a margin of over 6 percent. Fusionists also elected Weaver and Judge Walter I. Hayes in the second district and narrowly lost in four other districts. Had it not been for a notorious gerrymander, the GOP's losses would have been deeper. Statewide, the combined opposition to the Republican Party, which included a separate Knights of Labor ticket in the second district, actually exceeded the Republican total by a few hundred votes.[74] Hepburn attributed his demise to a "revival of the granger craze of 1873 and 1878. My vote in all of the towns . . . has been up to the state ticket—except in Fremont Co. It is the countryside that did the business for me."[75] Another shaken Republican, James W. McDill, confided to Allison, "I am just getting my breath from our terrible defeat in the Eighth District" and attributed the disaster to the new Farmers' Alliances, which he described as "secret political societies hav[ing] for their sworn purpose regulation of inter-state commerce." McDill warned that unless Congress passed some kind of interstate commerce legislation, "Iowa will not go republican next year."[76]

By 1886 the terms of Iowa politics had been completely redefined. In 1881 the Republican Party could still lay claim to the loyalty of the vast majority of voters as the defender of the Union and the guardian of state and national prosperity; the feeble Democrats were making almost no effort to expand their base of support. The five years before the 1886 elections had seen the emergence of a viable opposition to Republican dominance in Iowa. Key to the success of the Democratic/Greenback coalition was its ability to mobilize voters on the basis of economic discontent while retaining most foreign-born antiprohibition voters. The rise of the antimonopoly coalition coupled with the emergence of the Iowa Farmers' Alliance threatened nothing less than a realignment of Iowa politics. With the "revival of the granger craze," Republican politicians faced the unaccustomed and unwelcome prospect of losing their monopoly on public office.

4

The Iowa Farmers' Alliance and the Politics of Railroad Reform

In the early 1870s Iowa's Republican leaders responded to the Grange by making concessions; but after repealing the Granger Law, the Regency was determined to resist any attempt to limit the prerogatives of capital. By the 1880s, Allison, Clarkson, and their railroad allies believed that the future of Iowa—and the GOP in Iowa—depended upon making the state a fertile field for investment, thus ensuring boundless economic growth. In the face of a new wave of agrarian unrest represented by the Democratic/Greenback anti-monopoly coalition, Iowa's Stalwart Republicans elected to defend the rights of property, bait antimonopolists as demagogues and anarchists, and hope the madness would go away.

Yet some Republicans questioned the economic and political wisdom of unbridled corporate hegemony and ever since the repeal of the Granger Law many had sought to reestablish control over the railroads. Most of these antimonopolists were middle-level politicians or newspaper editors who had influence in a particular locale or region of the state but were outside the councils of the Regency. Antimonopolists were in the majority at the Republican state conventions of 1883 and 1885, which adopted platforms in favor of railroad reform.[1] In the 1886 General Assembly two antimonopoly Republicans, George L. Finn of Taylor County and James G. Berryhill of Polk County, led an abortive fight for an elective railroad commission and a schedule of maximum freight rates.[2] Newspaper editors were becoming more vocal opponents of the Regency's domination of the GOP. Fred Faulkes, editor of the Republican *Cedar Rapids Gazette*, expressed sympathy to "Farmer" Whiting's Democratic candidacy in 1885 and had since made it his personal mission to agitate for a law to reduce passenger fares.[3] The voice with the greatest influence among farmers, Henry Wallace of the *Homestead*, remained loyal to the party of Lincoln, but this did not prevent him from endorsing the Anderson insurgency.

By late 1886 factional lines between conservative and antimonopoly Republicans were hardening, leaving many party members caught in the middle. Republicans who might have opposed reform in the past began to ask themselves if the grievances against the railroads were really just the trumped-up charges of cunning demagogues; perhaps they were legitimate. Perhaps the GOP had strayed from its original mission as the vehicle for the aspirations of free labor and had become the tool of powerful monopolies. And, most important, perhaps the GOP would lose its mandate for reform if it ignored the demands for it.

Among the Republican politicians asking themselves such questions, the man who eventually played the most crucial role in shaping the GOP's position on railroad reform was Gov. William Larrabee. As Larrabee assumed office in 1886 he faced a complicated set of political calculations. The most pressing issue was the saloon. Although Larrabee was not closely identified with the prohibitionist movement, upon assuming office he vowed to give the will of the majority a fair trial and to uphold his oath of office to enforce the law. After the murder of an activist clergyman fighting to close saloons in Sioux City in August 1886, Larrabee resolved to rid the state of lawlessness and disorder. During his first term he forced the saloons out of thirty-seven of the fifty-nine counties where they had openly conducted business in 1885. Larrabee was aware that strict enforcement of prohibition carried political risks, but he contended that "our foreign-born citizens" were becoming "more and more inclined to tolerate and even advocate its enforcement."[4]

Larrabee firmly believed his party was on the right side of the prohibition question, but he was less certain about the party's record on antimonopoly. During the 1886 campaign Larrabee had pledged support for an elective railroad commission, provided it was deemed desirable after "mature consideration."[5] With the debacle of 1886 fresh in his mind, Larrabee began an inquiry that would grow into an exhaustive investigation of the railroad question when he stumbled upon some apparently discriminatory shipping charges to state institutions.[6] On 6 December 1886 the governor directed the state Board of Railroad Commissioners to investigate the reasonableness of the CB&Q's charge of $1.80 per ton on coal shipped from Cleveland, Iowa, to the State Institute for the Feeble-Minded at Glenwood since the charge from the same point to the Deaf and Dumb Institute at Council Bluffs, twenty miles farther, was only $1.25. Larrabee instructed the commissioners to "have the discrimination corrected" if they found it unjustified.[7] In reply to the commission's inquiry, Charles E. Perkins (CB&Q's president) defended the disparity on the standard ground that Council Bluffs, unlike

Glenwood, was a competitive point.[8] Unimpressed, Larrabee vented his annoyance to the board: "I think it is high time the coal rates in the State were revised. Much of the argument offered by Mr. Perkins has served its purpose too long and is now outlawed. . . . The managers of great corporations cannot afford to continue the prosecution of such unjust discrimination. The sense of justice of intelligent minds rebels against it, and nothing can be gained to the corporations or the public by delay in such cases."[9]

The governor's irritation gave way to indignation when in March, following the board's request that the CB&Q revise its coal tariff to remove the discrimination against Glenwood, the road raised the rate to Council Bluffs instead of lowering it to Glenwood.[10] Larrabee demanded a rehearing before the railroad commission and chastised not only the railroads but the commission as well. The railroad managers he likened to 300 convicts he had recently interviewed: "They all tell the same story."[11] As for the board, the governor was convinced that "if the commissioner law was enacted and lived up to, the people of the State would have no reason to complain." But, Larrabee dryly observed, "The idea is general that the railway companies make no great sacrifice by complying with the rulings of the Commission." Many citizens, convinced the commissioners would not give their complaints proper attention, simply refused to bring them before the board. In an unmistakable allusion to the recent political turmoil in the state, Larrabee further lectured the commission that its failure to correct unjust discriminations had allowed "demagogues" to exploit popular dissatisfaction. Unless the commissioners upheld the law better than they had in the past few years, Larrabee concluded, "I am sorry to say this commission will have to go."[12]

Yielding to the governor's tirade, the board in May established a "reasonable rate" for hauling coal and ordered the railroads to comply, although not without two of the three commissioners protesting the "anomalous" situation whereby the board had been "arraigned by the Executive of the State, put on trial before the bar of public opinion," and threatened with extinction unless it conformed to the governor's will.[13] The governor's bold stand against the railroads, culminating in the Glenwood decision, was greeted with almost universal approval. The *Homestead* praised Larrabee for having "fearlessly done his duty to the State and the people," sentiments that were shared by dozens of previously quiescent newspapers such as the Marshalltown *Times-Republican*, which applauded, "Go it, Governor Larrabee! The people of the state are back of you." In the face of such an outpouring of public support, even the *Register* conceded the justice of the Glenwood decision, although it hoped that the commission's positive action would put to rest any more talk of an elective commission.[14]

The *Register* was forced to trim its sails for the time being, but its editor was privately concerned with the disruptive potential of the governor's crusade. In the midst of the Glenwood investigation Clarkson wrote at length to Senator Allison, recounting his recent meeting with Larrabee to discuss the future of the Republican Party in Iowa. Clarkson was alarmed to find that Larrabee "is taking the counsel of such men as Wallace and Finn, who are masking behind pretended anti-railroad feeling, but are prompted in fact by hostility to the party and in a desire to break it up." Apparently Larrabee believed that the previous year's election returns required a change in the party's approach to railroad reform because Clarkson had advised Larrabee that "the plan of party wisdom" was to remain on "the same path we took last year." Recalling that "last year when it was a dead pull on State issues almost entirely, the majority of the State was pulled up over ten thousand [sic]," Clarkson contended that the party's conservative policy was "increasing its strength with the people." He also tried to convince Larrabee that to "force in any new issues in the party to appease certain unappeasable elements" (i.e., antimonopolists such as Wallace and Finn) would "still not appease them" and would serve only "to make lukewarm or alienate other elements in the State [i.e., the railroads] just as necessary to Republican success."[15]

Larrabee's initial clash with the railroads, however, strengthened his sense that removing railroad abuses was desirable ethically, legally, and politically. Threats by a "prominent railway attorney" that if Larrabee continued in his present course the railroads "would have no further use for me in the Governor's office and they would set me out" merely fueled the governor's growing conviction that the railroads had corrupted Iowa politics for too long. Although railroad men became "exceedingly scarce about the Executive Office," Larrabee apparently judged that the cost from losing railroad support would be offset by regaining the confidence of ordinary voters. The GOP was certain to benefit by embracing reforms both popular and just.[16]

The activities of the Iowa Farmers' Alliance (IFA) in 1887 validated Larrabee's concern that the GOP's opposition to railroad reform was a political liability. Since its reorganization in fall 1886, the Alliance had experienced moderate growth. At the annual meeting in September 1887 the state secretary reported that 240 charters had been issued over the past year (making a total of perhaps 340 local alliances); there were probably between 6,000 and 8,000 members in the state. Delegates were present from forty counties located mainly in southwestern and central Iowa.[17] Although the Alliance was still in its early stages of development and had yet to make inroads in the northwest and eastern sections of the state, as it would during its major surge in membership in 1889 and 1890, the organization nonetheless had the potential to cause significant disruption in the Iowa political system should it bolt traditional party lines. This possibility was quite real in summer 1887 when Farmers' Alliances in several counties called independent conventions and in at least one case nominated a "People's Ticket."[18]

The leadership of the IFA and its national affiliate, the National Farmers' Alliance (NFA), opposed such forays into third-party politics. Milton George, founder of the NFA, believed (with good reason) that one of the reasons for the decline of the Grange was its involvement in third-party politics. Although George urged farmers to exert political power to obtain legislation to curtail railroad abuses, he instructed them to work within the existing two parties to nominate and to elect men sympathetic to their views.[19] Henry Wallace of the *Homestead* also took pains to discourage independent political action, arguing that partisan politics would destroy local suballiances by opening the door to political manipulators who would sow discord among members. Reform, Wallace cautioned, could be accomplished "only by non-partisan effort." If members stayed clear of partisan politics and with "each man working in his own party," the Alliance would be able to "control public sentiment in all parties." The Democratic and Republican Alliance member, he advised, "should use his influence to have candidates chosen who are in accord with the principles of the Alliance."[20]

Wallace also regarded a nonpartisan approach as necessary in order to establish a coalition of interests with jobbers and manufacturers. To compete with Chicago, Iowa jobbers and manufacturers had to be able to receive raw materials or wholesale merchandise from outside the state and to ship finished goods or merchandise to consumers or retailers within the state at a combined rate that was the same or not much greater than the rate at which Chicago jobbers and manufacturers shipped directly to consumers and retailers in Iowa.[21] Iowa jobbers and manufacturers were particularly interested in securing redress from some of the adverse consequences stemming from the passage of the Interstate Commerce Act in 1887. The act's provision against long- and short-haul discrimination had caused a reduction in through rates from Chicago to many previously noncompetitive Iowa points, thus lowering costs for Chicago jobbers on shipments direct to Iowa retailers. At the same time, the act did not lower through rates on interstate shipments of goods to Iowa jobbers, located at points that were already competitive, nor did it lower their costs for shipping to Iowa retailers since these shipments were made on local rates unaffected by the new federal legislation.

Whether these changes placed Iowa jobbers at a severe competitive disadvantage with respect to Chicago or whether they simply reduced their competitive advantages, Iowa jobbers sought redress.[22]

Given the jobbers' interest in reducing rates within Iowa, Wallace saw the possibility for forming a coalition of farmers and jobbers. Observing that the interstate commerce law had given jobbers and manufacturers a "dose of the farmers' medicine," the *Homestead* challenged this heretofore "selfish and short-sighted gang" to "consider the farmer's interest and demand justice for the farmer as well as themselves." Such a "combination of influences," the *Homestead* predicted, would prove "invincible."[23] Obviously, the prospects for achieving this alliance were brightest if farmers avoided third-party action.

To steer the Alliance clear of the hazardous shoals of third-party politics at this crucial moment, Wallace launched an initiative designed to encourage farmers to work within the two-party system. The plan was simple: The *Homestead* printed a document listing several railroad reforms; readers were asked to clip this document and to obtain signatures from those people promising to "vote for no man as a delegate to a State [Democratic or Republican] convention who will not pledge himself to an effort to make his party commit itself to the above measures."[24] Evidently this pledge drive was successful because most farmers worked to influence one of the two parties during the campaign of 1887. Although the precise role of farmers in the county conventions held in July and August is unclear, nonpartisan agrarian activism pressured both parties to take strong antimonopoly positions during the summer. In some cases farmers may have taken control of or played a leading role in the conventions. Elsewhere, opportunistic Democratic and Republican politicians exploited grass-roots antimonopoly sentiment to defeat a rival "ring."[25] The most potent dynamic, however, was the threat of independent Alliance or antimonopoly Democratic candidacies, which spurred Republican politicians to make solid pledges for reform.

From the perspective of the Regency, the GOP county conventions were out of control. One Republican newspaper was alarmed at the "uncommonly aggressive" character of the conventions and noted that almost all of them were adopting antimonopoly platforms.[26] In the eighth district, where Anderson had defeated Hepburn in the all-too-memorable campaign of 1886, the Page County regular Republican organization wasted little time donning overalls and raising pitchforks. For the legislature they nominated "Farmer" S. E. Field on a platform denouncing corporations for "amassing colossal fortunes at the expense of a debt-ridden people" and demanding substantial reductions in both local and through rates.[27] Madison County

Republicans responded to the bid of an antimonopoly Democrat for a seat in the state senate by adopting a platform demanding that railroads pay an equal share of taxes, that the principles of the interstate commerce law be applied to Iowa rates, and that the mortgagee pay property taxes on mortgages.[28] In Sac County the Republican convention bypassed Phil Schaller for another term in the state house—he was suspect as a "legislative jobber"— and chose instead an "antimonopoly republican," I. O. Hunter, on a platform that looked as though it had been written in the offices of the *Homestead*.[29] In Calhoun County the Farmers' Alliance convened a "Farmers' Mass Meeting" and demanded that the Republican Party nominate Edgar Hobbs, a man who had tilled Iowa's soil for twenty years and was judged well suited to represent the farmers' interests in the Iowa house.[30]

Conservative Republicans feared that the upcoming state convention would adopt a platform "cater[ing] to every ism and hobby which has been made known up to date."[31] The *Register* exhorted Republicans to ignore "the cry of the demagogue" and to reject the demand for "specific things." A radical platform would disrupt the party by committing it to measures that upon further consideration by "honest men" in the legislature would prove unwise; the party would then be "charged up with perfidy" for contravening its platform.[32] Accordingly, as the *Sioux City Journal* advised, the platform should be "direct, forcible, and short; . . . theories, details, methods should be left for the stump and the newspaper, and the legislature."[33]

Antimonopoly Republicans, however, deemed it imperative that the convention endorse specific demands to remedy genuine grievances and to counter the threat from the Democratic/Greenback coalition. The *Cedar Rapids Evening Gazette* foresaw that a "storm is coming and with great force, and the people of the state will expect relief from the unjust discriminations and unfair treatment received at the hands of the corporations." The Republican Party had a "glorious opportunity," but the *Gazette* warned that if it "fails to do its duty courageously, it may perhaps be sent to the rear."[34]

At the state convention, the two factions battled to a draw. Antimonopolists administered the Regency a "terrible black eye" by denying the nomination for supreme court justice to the prorailroad incumbent, Judge Austin Adams.[35] But conservatives achieved a victory on the transportation plank of the platform. Written by Clarkson, this plank favored the application of the principles of the interstate commerce law to Iowa but avoided mention of an elective commission or a schedule of maximum rates.[36]

Just as a strong reform faction was emerging in the Republican Party, strains were beginning to appear within the Democratic/Greenback antimonopoly coalition. Although antimonopoly Democrats continued to advocate fusion and delivered another platform favoring high license (despite the usual opposition of river-county delegates) and containing endorsements of an elective commission and other economic reforms, they were unable to prevent the nomination for governor of Maj. Thomas Jefferson Anderson, a former attorney for the Rock Island Railroad.[37] But the main problems arose from the Greenbackers themselves, among whom bitter disagreements over fusion had surfaced. Although "Calamity" Weller had been elected to Congress on a fusion ticket in 1882, he had since become an uncompromising opponent of cooperation with the Democrats. At the Greenback state convention Weller outmaneuvered Weaver and forced through resolutions prohibiting any nominee from withdrawing prior to the election (thus precluding any basis for bargaining with the Democrats) and harshly denouncing the national Democratic administration. For governor, the convention nominated an antifusionist, M. J. Cain.[38]

Determined to resist being pulled into a "no-fusion, no-succeed, no-sense" party,[39] Weaver convened a meeting of the state central committees of the Greenback Party and the recently formed Union Labor Party, which called for a new convention of both parties either to ratify the first Greenback convention or "to take such other action as they may deem best." This second convention resolved in favor of yet another convention to nominate a new ticket, but the third convention was never held. Lacking a mandate from a party convention, Weaver was unable to effect fusion with the Democrats and his newspaper reluctantly endorsed Cain.[40]

Antimonopoly Democrats were unable to campaign effectively. The Republican incumbent William Larrabee had just won a stirring victory over the railroads at the same time that the Democratic challenger had been pocketing legal fees from the Rock Island. The *Leader* tried to make an issue out of the governor's alleged underassessment of railroad property and Major Anderson delivered a few feeble jabs at "money loaner Larrabee," but these blows fell far short of the mark.[41] The campaign did rejuvenate "wet" Democrats who ardently desired to remove Larrabee from office because of his strict enforcement of the prohibition law. Indeed, Democrats made substantial gains among antiprohibition voters although Larrabee's strength among foreign-born supporters of prohibition (primarily Scandinavians) and native-born voters was sufficient to give him a fairly narrow victory.[42] The Democratic share of the farm vote declined significantly, but Larrabee was able to retain about the same level of support among farmers as he had enjoyed in 1885, despite a Union Labor ticket in the field and a decrease in turnout.[43]

Although antimonopoly issues were not central to the gubernatorial contest, they were paramount in several races for seats in the General Assembly. Antimonopoly Republicans had been unable to force the state GOP to adopt a radical platform. Still, they and nonpartisan Alliance leaders sought to put their stamp on the next legislature by working to elect candidates, regardless of party affiliation, who were sound on railroad reform. By fall many legislative candidates had pledged themselves to support reform; others, however, remained noncommittal. The *Cedar Rapids Evening Gazette*, identifying transportation as the "great question before the people today," advised voters to reject anyone for the legislature "who is not straight on this matter." Although the *Gazette* preferred that antimonopoly legislators be Republican, it was not averse to supporting Democrats, Union Laborites, or fusion candidates if necessary.[44] The leading proponent of selective endorsement was Henry Wallace, who targeted thirteen incumbents (seven Republicans and six Democrats) as having unacceptable records in the previous legislature. With funds from railroad advertising (as Wallace claimed) or from the "boodle fund" of the rum-soaked Democratic Party (as the *Register* alleged), Wallace flooded the districts of the designated candidates with thousands of copies of special editions of the *Homestead* assailing their voting records.[45] In other districts local Alliances, threatening to cross party lines if they did not obtain adequate answers, requested legislative candidates to state their position on equalization of taxation, reduction of freight and passenger rates, abolition of free passes, election of railway commissioners, and reduction of the legal rate of interest.[46]

Conservative party managers regarded the tactics of Wallace and other "guerrillas" as a mortal threat to their own control over the party and to their laissez-faire policy objectives. Apart from the unlikely possibility that voters might elect enough Democratic legislators to send a Democrat to the U.S. Senate, conservatives feared that the potential of Republican voters in any district to bolt the ticket on economic issues would cause Republican candidates to make radical commitments. And with the election of a few antimonopoly Democrats, the result might be an extremist assembly that would adopt unacceptable legislation. Not only would this damage the railroads, but an outbreak of hostility toward corporate capitalism in Iowa might also be fatal to Allison's ambition of winning the presidential nomination in 1888.

The *Register*'s near-hysterical attacks on Wallace showed how seriously the Regency took the threat posed by nonpartisan agrarian radicalism. In a typical editorial the *Register* condemned Wallace as the "Arnold and Davis of the Republican party," whose sole object was to create "dissension and discord in the party to which he claims he belongs, but which he disgraces." Although the *Homestead* featured engravings of cows, windmills, and corn shellers, these images were illusions; the paper, sneered the *Register*, was nothing more than a "Democratic paper under agricultural colors."[47] With this charge, the *Register* could now unfurl the bloody shirt and fan the smoldering embers of sectional animosity. Reminding its readers that the "ex-rebels of the South are holding Confederate jubilees and boldly declaring that . . . Jeff Davis and not Lincoln was then the real President of the Country," the *Register* framed the battle in Iowa as part of the national struggle with the unrepentant rebels. "In voting for the Legislature in Iowa this year," the *Register* advised, "the voter is choosing men who are to help elect two United States Senators, enough to turn the scale in the Senate in favor of the South." To further deflect attention from economic issues, the *Register* stressed prohibition as the sole state question and urged Republicans to sustain "the party of order, loyalty, temperance, and honest government."[48]

Ultimately, the *Register* was spared the nightmare of a Democratic legislature. Twelve of the thirteen incumbents on Wallace's list lost their seats, but neither party gained the advantage as six Democrats were among the defeated. Republicans gained one seat in the senate and four in the house, but the Republicans in the new legislature would not be to the Regency's liking. One indication that the new assembly represented a departure was simply that the number of farmers in the house increased from thirty-one to fifty-one.[49] Most nonfarmers in the house and senate had also made pledges to support reform, either at the time of their nomination or during the campaign when faced with the political risks of equivocation. Although the *Register* feigned relief that the majority of the new legislators was not in sympathy with the demands of "a few wrecking and communistic newspapers," Clarkson was more candid in confiding to Larrabee his fear that the next legislature "elected on a campaign of distrust . . . will enact the most radical and sweeping legislation."[50]

Any hopes the Regency may have held that the reliable man of business affairs whom they had endorsed for governor in 1885 would regain his senses and steer the legislature clear of a course hostile to business were dashed when Larrabee delivered his second inaugural address on 12 January 1888. In a Gilded Age statement of progressive Republicanism, Larrabee offered a compelling justification for state regulation of private enterprise. He began by reviewing the "progressive spirit of the people of Iowa" as evidenced by their support for abolitionism, their unswerving loyalty to the Union, and, later, their enactment of prohibition. But, Larrabee admonished, "The work of a progressive commonwealth is never done." Iowa faced a new challenge: "Gigantic interests, the creation of our inventive age, are constantly striving to usurp illegitimate, as well as to assert legitimate rights."[51]

Having identified corporations as an object of concern for progressive Republicans, Larrabee then reviewed the history of railroad regulation in the state. The Granger Law of 1874 had been a "great achievement, illustrating the power of the people under our system of government to correct evils when defended by organized capital." Under great pressure from the railroads, the people had agreed to repeal the Granger Law but only because they were willing to give an appointive commission "an honest trial." Since then, however, the railroads had used pools and other devices to destroy competition so that the charges for transportation "are by far too high, and bear little or no relation to the cost of service."[52] The governor then refuted the railroads' rationale for their rates: Was the wealth generated by high rates justified as the railroads' reward for making possible the remarkable material progress of the country? "It appears to me that this argument, if carried to its logical result, would transfer the title to a large share of their income to the heirs of Mr. Watt, the inventor of the steam engine." Would reducing rates result in lower wages for railway workers? Again, the governor was unimpressed: "Such reasoning might apply if those men were now paid a proper share of the receipts of the roads; this is not the case."[53]

Larrabee then affirmed the authority of the state to establish a schedule of reasonable rates. "Corporations," he instructed, "have no rights save such as have been granted to them by the commonwealth." Accordingly, when railroads had "usurped powers dangerous to the public welfare, and have practiced extortions perhaps less cruel, but in the aggregate, more gigantic, than those of the British landlord," it was imperative that the state assert its sovereignty. Indeed, Iowa's economic future was at stake. Iowa farmers, miners, millers, jobbers, and manufacturers were the victims of discriminatory practices akin to those of Grecian pirates who "ravaged villages and plundered unfortified places."[54] Yet Larrabee warned that it would not be easy to pass legislation to end railway extortion. "By retaining the ablest attorneys, by influencing the press, and by flattering and favoring politicians," the railroads had managed until recently to "prevent an open outburst of popular indignation," and they would undoubtedly continue to employ their vast resources to thwart hostile legislation. The governor concluded with a solemn exhortation that each legislator "subordinate all personal ambition and private interests to the welfare of the State and the needs of his constituency."[55]

Stalwart Republicans were appalled at what Clarkson termed the governor's "savage assaults and dangerous recommendations"; Larrabee's inaugural address, he informed Allison, was "absolutely unaccountable. Weaver and his demagoguism [sic] has never equalled this." Charles Perkins implored Allison to "come out here and make the Jackasses see the harm they will do if they carry out Larrabee's insane notions."[56] Although Allison chose to remain safely behind the scenes in Washington, Clarkson devised a plan to defeat measures for an elective commission and a schedule of maximum rates. Calling for a "full hearing of all interests . . . so that the Legislature may be able to proceed intelligently and justly," the *Register* suggested an alternative proposal to retain the appointive commission and to give it the capacity to set rates on particular commodities in the event of a complaint. This conservative approach was embodied in a bill introduced by the future star of the early twentieth-century progressive movement in Iowa, first-term representative Albert B. Cummins.[57]

Clarkson's strategy was designed to exploit divisions between jobbers and manufacturers, who favored such a plan, and farmers, who were committed to more stringent measures. On 25 January a "shippers' convention" composed of 100 members of the Des Moines Commercial Club and over 100 other wholesalers and manufacturers from both Mississippi River and interior cities adopted resolutions in favor of the Cummins bill and the supplementary Gatch bill for the appointment of railway commissioners by the governor with the consent of the senate.[58] Henry Wallace and Jesse Kennedy, president of the Iowa Farmers' Alliance, tried to persuade the convention to endorse an elective commission and the Berryhill bill, which set a schedule of maximum rates, but to no avail.[59]

The agrarian rationale for these measures was as political as it was economic. The *Homestead* objected to the Cummins bill because it made no provision for holding the commission "responsible to the people," a fatal omission given that the commission "has habitually seen all subjects through railway spectacles."[60] A maximum-rate law, on the other hand, would restore popular sovereignty:

A maximum rate is to a railroad what a three-board and three-wire fence is to an unruly beast, a definite fixed, permanent and immovable definition of the limit beyond which the railroad cannot go, the expression of the inflexible will of the people in the exercise of a power as clearly defined and firmly settled as the power of self-government. This maximum rate is not only the assertion of the power of control, but the control itself in such a palpable way that it acts as a perpetual reminder both to the people and the railroads of the sovereignty of the State in visible, potential exercise. No power can remove it but the people.[61]

With the governor sympathetic and most legislators pledged to reform, the moment seemed auspicious for the people to reestablish sovereignty. But as the *Homestead* warned, farmers had to pressure their elected representatives. As in the previous fall campaign, the *Homestead* printed petitions to be circulated for signatures and forwarded to the legislature and local and county Alliances flooded the assembly with their responses. A typical suballiance, "in view of the many pledges of the various platforms and candidates in the last campaign," petitioned the legislature to slash freight rates by 33 percent, reduce passenger rates, and abolish free passes.[62] The Alliance also made its power felt through the continual presence at the capitol of its state president, Jesse Kennedy. Although vastly outnumbered by a "legion of hirelings" lobbying for the railroads, Kennedy daily reminded legislators and key committee chairmen that although his organization was poor in the resources available to corporations, it was rich in ballots, representing 50,000 to 60,000 voters.[63]

To one beleaguered railroad lobbyist it was only too clear that the farmers would have their way. "I am here trying to stay the storm of madness against the railroads," James McDill reported to Allison in late February, "but it is a hopeless task. One might as well try to stop a cyclone." From the eye of the storm J. H. Sweeney, chairman of the senate committee on railroads, wrote to apprise Allison of the situation. "Our political parties have been improvident in promises, and members of the Legislature are held responsible for their fulfillment," he explained. "They are elected upon the platform of their parties and are placed between two very hot fires." Although Sweeney professed his belief in "conservatism," the heat from his constituents evidently exceeded the heat from a U.S. senator; with reluctance, he informed Allison, he would support reform.[64]

With the Alliance implacably opposed to the Cummins-Gatch bills and the jobbers and manufacturers having endorsed this approach, the prospects for reform were uncertain. In late February, however, the wholesalers abruptly changed their position and declared for a maximum-tariff law reducing rates across the board by 40 percent. The *Register* attributed this "sudden flop" to the "chagrin of one member of the Legislature [evidently Berryhill] who had sought assiduously to induce the Jobbers' State Convention to endorse his ideas and bill." A "few" Des Moines jobbers, the *Register* complained, had not known what sort of legislation they wanted and were "willing to subordinate everything else to their personal and factional desire to please this one man."[65] Despite the *Register*'s attempt to attribute their shift in position to personalities, the jobbers had good reason to support the Berryhill bill. Faced with the farmers' unyielding opposition to the Cummins bill, jobbers recognized that their only hope for any reform legislation lay in supporting the Berryhill bill, which, by legislating lower rates across the board, would also meet their objectives. The jobbers could get what they wanted either way; when faced with the choice between Berryhill or nothing, they chose Berryhill. Once they had agreed to support the bill, the jobbers worked closely with the house committee on railroads to prepare a schedule of rates.[66]

The house passed the Berryhill bill (House File 374) on 8 March by a vote of eighty-seven to twelve and forwarded it to the senate.[67] To give themselves maximum leverage with the traditionally more conservative senate, on 28 February house antimonopolists had also passed a similar bill (HF 373) outlawing free passes, pooling, long- and short-haul discrimination, and secret rebates. HF 373 did not fix maximum rates by law but instead required the railroad commissioners to set a schedule of maximum rates based on specific guidelines; still, it was much closer to the Berryhill bill than the Cummins bill, which required the commission to set rates for particular commodities only upon complaint.[68] With the majority of senators pledged to support reform and having before them two options for fulfilling this obligation, they would have a hard time explaining the death of both bills. Accordingly, the senate passed HF 373, the less radical measure, with minor amendments on 23 March. The bill was then sent to a joint conference committee to adjust minor differences in the senate and house bills. The final version passed both houses unanimously on 2 April; one day later the passage of the bill for the election of railroad commissioners completed the antimonopoly triumph.[69]

The *Homestead* hailed the new railroad legislation as a "moral law like the ten commandments," although it expressed concern that the railroad commissioners would fail to arrive at an acceptable schedule of rates.[70] These fears were alleviated in May, however, when the commission published a schedule of maximum rates that reduced charges on agricultural and other commodities, except for carload lots over 200 miles, to a level below rates in Illinois, a move clearly in line with the antimonopoly sentiment of the legislature.[71] Immediately the railroads appealed to the circuit court and obtained a temporary injunction against the new schedule on the grounds that it did not guarantee an adequate return on invested capital. Following a lengthy series of hearings and legal motions, the court refused to grant a permanent injunction; two days later the CB&Q decided to comply with the schedule.[72]

The 1888 railroad legislation resulted from the nonpartisan tactics of the Iowa Farmers' Alliance in a competitive political environment. Both party competition and the pressure from the Alliance were necessary to bring about reform. The first step in the process leading to this reform was the Democratic/Greenback coalition's successful exploitation of antimonopoly sentiment. By helping to define railroad reform as a critical issue and by showing Republican vulnerability, the fusionists impelled many GOP politicians to fight against their image as the servants of corporations and to side with the party's antimonopoly wing. Whether the many Republican politicians who eventually supported reform did so from principle, political expedience, or some mixture of the two, the threat from the Democratic/Greenback coalition was crucial in shifting the balance of power within the Republican Party toward the antimonopolists. This threat, especially as it was manifested in the uprising that defeated Hepburn in 1886, was clearly a major factor in Larrabee's conversion to the cause of reform. It was not just Hepburn's loss that concerned the governor; he saw that conservative party leaders were perhaps on the wrong side of the railroad question. Larrabee's dealings with the recalcitrant railroads in the Glenwood case had affirmed his view that reform was necessary for both moral and political reasons. For Larrabee the ethical and the political were inextricably bound together: The Republican Party had been dominant in Iowa precisely because it had always adopted principled positions. Larrabee's belief in the political necessity for Republicans to embrace railroad reform is revealed in Clarkson's desperate plea to the governor following his inaugural message:

What are we to gain by the new order? Nearly all the powerful elements in the State are antagonized, and forced to be our enemies. In return we will never gain the Weavers. They and the Democrats will take your indictment of your own party and use it to build up their own party. . . . No doubt it was your hope and ambition to unify and strengthen the party, as well as serve the people faithfully, but in endeavoring to placate implacable elements I fear you have succeeded only in alienating those who are necessary to the party's success.[73]

The dynamics of party competition and nonpartisan political pressure in Iowa help illuminate at a more general level the relationships that one historian describes as "the links between the process of popular voting and legislative activity," connections that political historians, given their primary focus on electoral behavior and realignment, have left chiefly unexplored.[74] One political scientist's classic work on the structure of state politics in the South remains the most ambitious attempt to relate policy outcomes to political competition. V. O. Key, Jr., presumed that a competitive party system would more or less automatically respond to social needs, but as the findings of later scholars indicate, party competition does not necessarily translate into policy output.[75] The situation in Iowa suggests that pressures from outside the formal party system are, if not absolutely necessary, at least conducive to stimulating a competitive party system to produce policy reform.

Simple competitive politics probably would not have been sufficient to translate antimonopoly sentiment into actual legislation in Iowa. To ensure that the legislature actually passed laws, an organized movement of farmers had to pressure the party system. At every step of the way—in the county conventions summer 1887, during the fall campaign, and during the legislative session itself—farmers, acting primarily through the Alliance, pressured politicians to support reform. Although the formal membership of the Iowa Alliance was still fairly small, the organization articulated the demands of tens of thousands of voters and was perceived as a serious threat by politicians throughout the state. On the other hand, the farmers' resolve to reject candidates if their positions were unacceptable probably would not have succeeded without the competitiveness of Iowa's political system. For Republican politicians to take these threats seriously, the genuine possibility that opposition candidates could be elected was essential.

An alternative explanation for the 1888 legislation would cite the agitation of mercantile interests. Yet jobbers and manufacturers clearly attempted to realize their goals through non-political means, by appeals to the railroads either directly or through the Iowa commission, and only after railroad reform became an issue in Iowa politics did they consider legislative solutions. Even then it was the agrarians who initiated a coalition of interests and who pushed forward more radical measures. Ironically, the jobbers and manufacturers, who endorsed a maximum tariff and an elective commission as a matter of political expedience only in February 1888, received a much greater economic benefit from the legislation than the farmers who had been agitating for these reforms for at least three years. The legislation helped jobbers and manufacturers by reducing the cost of shipping to Iowa retailers; although the commissioner's schedule reduced the local tariff on agricultural commodities, the benefits to Iowa farmers were probably marginal, considering the small percentage of agricultural freight shipped within the state.[76] Certainly the legislation did nothing directly to redress deflation, a more basic problem.

If state-level railroad reform was inherently unable to redress farmers' economic grievances, why did Iowa farmers concentrate almost exclusively on this particular avenue rather than on an approach such as currency reform, which would have more accurately addressed the problem of deflation? Farmers were aware of proposals such as free silver or reform of the national banking system: Under grass-roots pressure the Iowa Alliance eventually endorsed these measures. Quite probably most farmers and Alliance leaders believed that lower local rates would have a direct impact on interstate rates, an idea based on the commonly held assumption that interstate rates were the sum of the relevant local rates although in fact this was not the case. Given the common wisdom among farmers that it cost a bushel of wheat to ship another bushel to market, it was rational for them to seek reduced local rates because they thought it would reduce overall transportation costs, thereby raising prices.[77]

Ultimately, however, the focus on railroad reform had more to do with the question of political sovereignty than with judgments of economic efficacy. Farmers targeted railroads because they embodied the corruption of republican values and the manipulation of politics for selfish ends. Regulation of these "soulless corporations" meant wresting politics from powerful private interests and restoring sovereignty to the people. Wallace's primary justification for a schedule of maximum rates was not framed in the language of economic utility: He regarded a maximum rate written into law as a reminder of the sovereignty of the people expressed through the state.

Since the battle for reform was essentially political, victory vindicated the farmers' faith in the American form of government. The legislation proved that an organization of farmer-citizens, acting through their representatives in a legislative assembly, could prevail over powerful corporations and secure laws for the benefit of everyone. The secretary of the state Alliance regarded the legislature's accomplishments as "a matter of profound satisfaction," which proved that "when the farmers stand together in demanding right and just things, these demands will become laws."[78] Ordinary farmers were proud to find that political leaders had listened to their voices. One farmer reported that the members of his suballiance had been "watching the Iowa Legislature" and had found a renewed faith in representative government: "The Alliance organization can 'speak out in meeting' on these questions and issues which concern them and make themselves heard."[79] More remained to be done—in fall 1888 the Iowa Alliance demanded reduction of passenger fares, equalization of taxation, and reduction of the legal rate of interest from 10 to 8 percent—but members were certain they could obtain these and any other necessary reforms.[80]

The success of the Iowa Alliance in the political arena during its formative stage was critical in solidifying its commitment to pursue political activity within the two-party system. Iowa's competitive political environment would further reinforce the Alliance's nonpartisanship and integrate the organization's leadership firmly into the two-party system over the next few years. Third-party advocates would attempt to use the Alliance as a vehicle to form a viable Populist Party in Iowa, but the Iowa Alliance's success at obtaining reform from within the existing party system would argue powerfully against a third-party approach.

5

Bastions of Republicanism: Kansas and Nebraska in the 1880s

Although the GOP was under siege in Iowa during the mid- and late 1880s, it remained secure in Kansas and Nebraska. The political identity of Kansas had been forged during the bloody battle against the "Slave Power" in the late 1850s; during the Civil War no state provided a greater proportion of its fighting-age men for the Union cause than Kansas.[1] After the war thousands of veterans came to Kansas and Nebraska to establish homes under the generous terms of the Republican-initiated Homestead Act. Nebraska's statehood in 1867 represented the culmination of the Republican crusade for "free soil, free labor, free men" that had begun a decade earlier. Over the next twenty-five years Republican dominance in the two states was reinforced as settlers from Republican strongholds in the Midwest and New England streamed west to take up land. Nowhere were Democrats scorned as traitors and villains more vehemently or for a longer duration than in Kansas and Nebraska. Republican politicians had only to deliver pensions, promise further economic growth, and remind the rank and file to vote as they had shot. The remarkable increase in population and the rapid economic expansion from 1880 to 1887 seemed to most Kansans and Nebraskans irrefutable evidence of the blessings of Republican governance.

Nonetheless, Republican Party leaders in Kansas and Nebraska did face several challenges both from outside the party and from within their own ranks. The first of these came from the Grange, which grew rapidly in both states during 1873. By March 1874 Nebraska had more local Granges per farmer than any other state; Kansas was second.[2] Yet the Kansas and Nebraska Granges lacked the assertiveness of the Iowa Grange. They denounced railroad abuses at a national level, but because the railroad network in these states remained undeveloped, Kansas and Nebraska farmers were more reluctant to antagonize the railroads through restrictive state legislation. The Grange elected several Independents to the Kansas legislature

72

in 1873 but did not try to pass regulatory legislation. In Nebraska Grangers helped secure a new state constitution in 1875 empowering the legislature to set maximum rates and to outlaw other railroad abuses, but no attempt was made to use these provisions until the 1880s.[3] The Grange's impact on electoral patterns was minor. In Kansas the Democrats may have benefited slightly by economic discontent in 1874, as the GOP's margin of victory declined from 32 to 16 percent, but Republicans still commanded a landslide. In Nebraska the Grange ran its own ticket in 1874, but it gained a mere 12 percent of the vote, with Democrats receiving only 25 percent; the GOP won easily with almost 60 percent.[4]

The Greenback Party also threatened Republican dominance in Kansas and Nebraska, gaining almost 20 percent of the vote in both states in 1878. Although the Greenback vote declined in 1880, the party rebounded in both states in the early 1880s.[5] The Kansas and Nebraska Greenback Parties might have formed part of a viable Democratic/Greenback antimonopoly coalition like the one in Iowa, but it never solidified. Kansas and Nebraska Democrats utterly scorned the idea of cooperation with Greenbackers. Nebraska's leading Democrats, J. Sterling Morton and Dr. George L. Miller, were doctrinaire Bourbons who held laissez-faire as a religious principle and opposed cooperation with any group that advocated restricting enterprise. In 1882 the Anti-Monopoly Party, a union of Greenbackers and the Nebraska Farmers' Alliance (organized as an affiliate of Milton George's National Farmers' Alliance one year earlier) made overtures to the Democrats. But Morton, the Democratic candidate for governor, rejected fusion, leading the Anti-Monopolists to nominate their own candidate, E. P. Ingersoll. Anti-Monopolists and Democrats did agree, however, to nominate Phelps D. Sturdevant for state treasurer. Republicans won the governorship, but the combined vote for Morton and Ingersoll exceeded the Republican total, and Sturdevant became the first non-Republican state official in Nebraska's history. These results argued powerfully for fusion at all levels; two years later Anti-Monopolists and Democrats agreed on a full fusion slate with Morton at the head of the ticket.[6]

The 1884 Democratic/Anti-Monopoly coalition in Nebraska found common ground opposing the GOP-supported protective tariff, but it was fatally divided from the outset over railroad regulation. Anti-Monopolists were highly suspicious of Morton for his activities as publicist for the Burlington and Missouri Railroad and for his inflexible position on railroad regulation. Edward Rosewater, editor of the *Omaha Weekly Bee* and a leading Anti-Monopolist, refused to support Morton and joined Republican papers in denouncing him as a "rank monopolist." Anti-Monopolists who had supported Ingersoll in 1882 turned instead to the incumbent Republican governor, J. W. Dawes. Moreover, Morton made almost no effort to attract farmers. The fusion ticket lost by over 10 percent, destroying the first incarnation of the Nebraska Farmers' Alliance and, for the time being, any hope for a viable opposition party.[7]

The Bourbon leaders of the Kansas Democratic Party acted with equal disregard for the need to broaden their base of support. A Democratic governor, George Glick, stumbled into office in 1882 when Republican John P. St. John ran for a third term against the wishes of the party's leadership. But the Democrats made no effort to build a state party and were promptly routed from office two years later. The Democrats might have attempted to cooperate with the Greenback Party, which had received almost 12 percent of the vote in 1882, but they were evidently uninterested in pursuing this option.[8]

By the mid-1880s the GOP in Kansas and Nebraska had survived both the Grange and the Greenback era with little more than a bruise or two. Conservative party leaders, however, still had to contend with antimonopolists within their ranks. During the late 1870s the Kansas GOP had taken a liberal position on questions of finance, routinely endorsing the standard Greenback demands for currency reform. In the 1880s a group of conservatives led by Republican national committeeman Cyrus Leland, Sol Miller, editor of the *Kansas Chief*, and the state's senior senator, John J. Ingalls, attempted to tighten their hold on the party and to bring it into conformity with national Republican orthodoxy.[9] The Democrats might have taken advantage of this situation by attacking the GOP's growing conservatism on economic issues, but the party's main battle cry was for the resubmission of the prohibition amendment. Given Kansas's overwhelmingly native-born electorate, this position virtually guaranteed that the Democrats would remain permanently in the minority.[10]

The important battles in Kansas politics were between the antimonopoly and probusiness factions of the GOP, and intraparty squabbling was particularly evident in the 1886 campaign. Conservatives maintained the upper hand at the state Republican convention, where they defeated a resolution to empower the state board of railroad commissioners to establish a schedule of rates.[11] Antimonopolists responded by launching a major protest against railroad domination of Kansas politics, a situation made evident when the GOP at its Concordia convention failed to nominate four-term congressman John A. Anderson to represent the fifth congressional district. The Topeka *Daily Capital* attributed Anderson's defeat to "the combined influence of the railroad corporations whom he has antagonized by his fearless and independent course." Anderson's supporters contended that the failure of several delegates to honor the instructions of county conventions invalidated the nomination of A. S. Wilson, an undistinguished railroad politician, and called a new convention at Clay Center. On the day of the convention Anderson's supporters, prefiguring Populist rallies four years later, formed a procession and carried banners bearing slogans such as "The railroads should be the servants of the people" and "Stand for clean politics."[12]

Although a Democrat was in the field, the campaign amounted to a contest between Anderson and Wilson, both of whom claimed to be the "regular" Republican. State party leaders avoided alienating the antimonopoly wing of the party by refusing to oppose the popular Anderson. Kansas's two U.S. Senators, Ingalls and Preston B. Plumb, as well as gubernatorial candidate John A. Martin, refused to stump for Wilson, and even Cy Leland's conservative organ endorsed Anderson's interpretation of the Concordia convention.[13] Anderson trounced Wilson, winning 53 percent of the vote to Wilson's 11 percent; the Democratic candidate, J. G. Lowe, received 34 percent. Although Kansas antimonopolists had not succeeded at the state convention, Anderson's victory seemed to show that they could rid the party of corrupt influences. The two factions of the Kansas GOP would coexist uneasily until the political revolution of 1890.[14]

Politics in Nebraska also centered on conflict between Republican factions. In the early eighties, Nebraska's leading conservative Republicans, John M. Thurston, counsel for the Union Pacific, and Charles Gere, editor of the *Nebraska State Journal* and spokesman for the Burlington line, made their attempt to impose national Republican orthodoxy. Conservatives had successfully forestalled meaningful reform in the legislative sessions of 1883 and 1885 by creating an essentially powerless commission, and they wanted to ensure that the next legislature did not enact railroad-reform legislation.[15] By 1886 conservatives were determined to elect a legislature that would crush antimonopolist attempts to reduce railroad rates within the state and also to deny a second term in the U.S. Senate to Charles H. Van Wyck, whose support of the Reagan interstate commerce bill and his campaign for forfeiture of unearned railroad land grants had made him anathema to the railroads.[16]

The conservative Omaha *Republican* opened the campaign with a declaration of war on Van Wyck and his ally, Rosewater of the *Omaha Bee*, men who allegedly had been fighting the Republican Party of Nebraska for the past ten years. Van Wyck's record in the Senate, the *Republican* insisted, was one of treason: He had ignored the party caucus, uttered "rabid" speeches for free trade, and had bargained with a Democratic president to secure control over patronage in Nebraska. Van Wyck was a "demagogue" who "lies to the common people" and "fattens upon the exaggeration of their misfortunes."[17] The antimonopolists responded by insisting that the Nebraska GOP had been corrupted by the railroads. For a decade, the *Bee* contended, the machinery of the GOP had been in the hands of "railroad monopoly henchmen, jobbers and barnacles," who had "controlled conventions and dictated the candidates by . . . corrupt methods." The newspaper warned that the railroads would continue to dominate Nebraska politics as long as the rank and file failed to attend party caucuses and conventions; farmers must nominate "fearless and honest law makers" who would vote for Van Wyck and support state control over the railroads.[18]

Van Wyck suffered a blow at the Republican state convention in late September. A resolution favoring abolition of the ineffectual railroad commission, which tested Van Wyck's strength, was defeated 302 to 248; Rosewater then decided not to introduce a resolution endorsing Van Wyck.[19] Evidently foreseeing that he would have trouble winning a majority when the legislature met in 1887, Van Wyck attempted to buttress his position as the choice of most Nebraskans by employing an obscure provision in the state constitution allowing for a nonbinding preferential vote for U.S. senator, which he won in November by an overwhelming margin of 46,000 to 2,000. This margin of victory lent credence to Van Wyck's claim to be the "people's candidate," but in the legislature he fell seven votes short of election.[20] The 1887 legislature, for the fourth consecutive time, also failed to establish effective state control over the railroads.[21]

With the defeat of Van Wyck and railroad reform, Nebraska's conservative Republicans in early 1887 appeared to be in a secure position on economic issues. Party managers faced some difficulties because of the GOP's identification with prohibition, a position that had cost Church Howe the election in the first congressional district (his Democratic opponent, John McShane, won); but questions of economic reform did not appear dangerous, and the state party seemed safe.[22] Having failed to form a viable third party or to achieve fusion with the Democrats in the early eighties, antimonopolists could hardly bolt the party. They had little choice but to fight the machine from within.

In the mid-1880s the configuration of the party system in Kansas and Nebraska was quite different from that in Iowa. In the Plains states the Democratic Party was not at all oriented to antimonopoly voters; almost everyone who was interested in economic reform was trying to work from within the Republican Party. In Iowa, however, the Democratic/Greenback coalition had a strong antimonopoly dimension challenging Republican supremacy, a threat from outside the Republican Party that eventually shifted the balance of power toward the antimonopoly wing of the GOP. Iowa's overall political environment of interparty competition fostered reform; the one-party political configuration in Kansas and Nebraska did not.[23]

As economic hardship deepened in the late 1880s, agrarian demands for reform took on greater urgency. Yet farmers did not rush to form a third party: "Deep-seated political habits do not vanish easily at the first hint of economic distress."[24] The symbols of the Union remained potent, and many Republicans believed that just as the GOP had destroyed slavery and fought to rid society of the evils of the saloon, so it would respond with justice for farmers and laborers. It took some time for farmers to lose this faith.

In Kansas the road to disillusionment with the GOP began with the Union Labor Party, organized in 1887 primarily at the initiative of Henry Vincent and his two brothers, Cuthbert and Leopold. Henry Vincent was born in Iowa in 1862 into a radical abolitionist family, and at the age of seventeen he launched his career as a reform journalist by founding a newspaper at Tabor. In 1886 Henry, his wife Vee, and his two brothers moved to Winfield, a small town near Wichita on the Kansas frontier, and began publishing the *American Nonconformist and Kansas Industrial Liberator*.[25] The inaugural issue of the *Nonconformist* announced the Vincents' intention to "publish such matter as will tend to the education of the laboring classes, the farmer and the producer" and gave notice that they would "endeavor to take the side of the oppressed as against the oppressor." The new journal would hardly be the standard boomtown organ. Despite the climate of optimism resulting from the rapid settlement of the region, the Vincents predicted that it would be but a "few years when more real estate in Kansas borders will be held and owned by British and Scotch capital than by actual settlers. To awaken the people to a realization of this fact is our purpose."[26]

The Vincents were deeply concerned about the growing inequality of wealth, and as Greenbackers, they attributed this tendency to the post–Civil War legislation that had contracted the supply of money. They believed that both political parties were controlled by the "money power" and were concerned that farmers and wage workers would be reduced to a condition of "slavery" if the trend continued: A society controlled by wealthy aristocrats would replace American democracy. The Vincent family's sense of social justice included political equality for women, and the *Nonconformist* advocated woman suffrage. Vee Vincent's women's column stressed that women bore a disproportionate share of the burdens of economic hardship and that since men were responsible for unjust legislation women must take a more active role in politics.[27]

The Vincents intended to form a new political party devoted to the principles of economic and social justice. One month after the organization of the national Union Labor Party at Cincinnati in February 1887, the Vincents convened a mass meeting of Cowley County citizens. This assembly, reported to include members of Farmers' Alliances, Granges, and the KOL, declared that the interests of the people had been "basely ignored by both old political parties" that always nominated men "wholly in sympathy with the capital class and against the masses of the people" and endorsed the tenets of the Union Labor platform.[28] In fall 1887 Union Laborites carried Labette County and elected sheriffs in Cowley and Linn Counties, but their strength was confined to a few sections of the state.[29]

Union Labor leaders made a particular effort to educate farmers about the "money question." The *Nonconformist* published numerous articles and editorials expounding the traditional Greenback position linking hard times to an insufficient supply of currency. A typical item attributed economic conditions—"our country is to-day bankrupted, the farmers ruined, merchants crippled, all kinds of business demoralized"—to a series of laws that had caused the post–Civil War contraction of the currency. This legislation, passed by the "Demo-Republican parties," had "fostered every trust and monopoly in the land. . . . These trusts and National banks are twin sisters and go hand in hand, and the Demo-Republican party is the foundation on which they stand." In the days of slavery, "one-half" of the country was in bondage, but now "the whole nation is enslaved by slavery tenfold worse than African slavery."[30]

To reverse the contraction of the currency, Union Labor reformers in Kansas advocated a radical plan for interest-free federal government loans on land security. This plan, which had its origins in the writings of Edward Kellogg in the 1840s, had been advanced by Greenbackers during the 1870s and 1880s and by the KOL in the 1880s. It was endorsed by the national Union Labor Party in 1888 and would become a key Populist demand as an integral part of the subtreasury plan, which the party endorsed in its Omaha platform of 1892. The land-loan proposal was designed to free producers from exorbitant interest rates and to expand the supply of currency by having the federal government issue money directly to farms through loans, thereby reversing deflation and stimulating business in general. Union Labor supporters in Kansas earnestly discussed this plan in the pages of reform newspapers and debated how to implement it.[31]

To further educate farmers on the underlying cause of economic misfortune, the central committee of the Union Labor Party printed 50,000 copies of Sarah E. V. Emery's *Seven Financial Conspiracies which Have Enslaved the American People*. First published in 1887, this remarkable work went through well over a dozen editions and was second in importance in the literature of agrarian radicalism only to William H. "Coin" Harvey's well-known free-silver work, *Coin's Financial School*, the bible of the Bryan campaign in 1896. Emery specified a series of laws passed between 1862 and 1875 that had resulted in the post–Civil War contraction of the currency and attributed this body of "class legislation" to a conspiracy initiated by English bankers. These seven conspiracies, Emery maintained, had given birth to a "more moneyed and monopolistic power than ever before cursed any civilized people." America "pays tribute to England, despite our blood-bought seal of independence."[32]

The kind of Anglophobia evident in Emery's writings permeated the political culture of the Union Labor Party in Kansas. In their inaugural issue the Vincents had hinted at an English plot to gain control of Kansas farms, and subsequent issues of the *Nonconformist* elaborated on this theme.[33] A typical item reported that a Republican had informed a Union Labor man that he could obtain all the money he wanted through a local firm lending "London money at 8%" and pointed out that if it were not for the English, "we'd have to pay our own men 24–36%." The Union Laborite responded that if England was loaning at 8 percent and farmers were making only 3 percent, "How long will it be before England will own Cowley county?" In another instance a correspondent, predicting that a wave of foreclosures by foreign moneylenders was imminent, demanded to know if farmers would "tamely give possession to those English lords and become tenants like the Irish."[34]

Notions of English conspiracy had a venerable tradition in American political thought, beginning with the need to justify revolutionary action in the 1770s: "Only 'repeated, multiplied oppressions,' placing it beyond all doubt 'that their rulers had formed settled plans to deprive them of their liberties,' could warrant the concerted resistance of the people against their government."[35] Similarly, the version of an English conspiracy espoused by the Union Labor Party in Kansas in 1888 (and later advanced by many Populists) heightened the sense of an impending crisis and made third-party action seem imperative. If foreign money lords had indeed enlisted their counterparts on Wall Street in a conspiracy to enslave the American people and had corrupted the U.S. Congress to accomplish this end, it would be futile to look to the two old parties since they too were firmly under the control of the money power. The Union Labor organs and, later, the Populist press invariably linked their references to an English conspiracy with the corruption of the two-party system. An item in the *Nonconformist*, "Jay Gould's prayer," depicted the essential unity of the English/American money power and the two-party system: "Our Father, who art in England, Rothschild be thy name. Thy kingdom come to America, and thy will be done in the United States as it is in England." After a mock confession of sin—"we know, our Father, we have done many things that were wrong. We have robbed the honest poor and brought distress to many a door"—the prayer offered an image of the servility of the two political parties: "Now, Father, thou knowest that we are above politics; that it is the same with us whether Democrats or Republicans rule, for thou knowest we are able to swing either party in our favor."[36]

Just as the conspiracy theory provided the strongest possible justification for a third party, it also offered a compelling rationale for an equal role for women in public affairs. If the party system had indeed become subservient to foreign money lords, it was imperative that women, who by virtue of their superior moral vision could more readily see the sources of economic oppression, should unmask these causes by exposing the subservience of the corrupt, male-dominated political system. It is more than a coincidence that the major propagandist for this conspiracy theory, Sarah Emery, was a woman. Indeed, this conspiratorial indictment of the two-party system linked to the oppression of women led to the remarkable public role of Emery and other Union Labor/Populist women, notably Marion Todd, author of several publications on finance, transportation, and the tariff, and Mary Elizabeth Lease, the well-known Populist orator. Lease received "wild cheers which lasted several minutes" for her address to the 1888 Kansas Union Labor Party convention.[37]

Of course, Kansas women already had a history of acting to change laws, dating from the role of the Women's Christian Temperance Union (WCTU) in securing the passage of a prohibition amendment to the state's constitution in the late 1870s and early 1880s. Kansas women had also demanded and secured the right to vote in municipal elections in 1887, when Argonia became the first U.S. municipality to elect a female mayor; over the next five years other Kansas towns elected women to the offices of mayor and city council. These female officeholders were almost all members of the WCTU and Republicans. They had won the right to a public voice, particularly on the question of prohibition, but Union Labor ideology offered a justification for women to be heard on a broader spectrum of issues.[38] Lease and Emery had been active in the WCTU and continued to advocate prohibition, but they had come to see liquor as only one aspect in an array of social problems stemming from bad laws produced by a political system that was inherently corrupt. From their perspective all political issues concerned women. The nation needed, Emery wrote, "woman's better judgment, her calm deliberation, her integrity of purpose" applied to all public affairs, not just prohibition.[39]

Although an English conspiracy provided justification for a third party at the national level, Kansas Union Labor Party leaders needed to establish a viable state party first. To demonstrate a compelling rationale for a new party at the state level, they tried to undermine the credibility of the dominant party by launching an all-out attack on the symbol of Kansas Republicanism, the flamboyant Senator Ingalls. During his fifteen years in Washington, Ingalls had developed a refined cynicism about politics and had come to relish inventing ornate epithets, referring, for instance, to civil service reformers as "canting parasites" and "political epicenes, without pride of ancestry or hope of posterity."[40] During his third term Ingalls's attacks became more vicious, and he began to express gratuitous contempt for fundamental political values. In an 1887 article in *The Forum*, "The Sixteenth Amendment," Ingalls rejected woman suffrage on the grounds that, since governmental authority ultimately rested on the ability to coerce, women as the "weaker sex" should not participate in enacting laws. Although this position was obviously unpopular with partisans of female suffrage, it hardly gave universal offense. Yet as if intending to enrage everyone, Ingalls went on to dismiss Thomas Jefferson's belief in the capacity of people for self-government and termed the Declaration of Independence "fallacious rhetoric." In politics, he defiantly proclaimed, "force was ultimately right."[41]

The *Nonconformist* gave wide coverage to the *Forum* article and to Ingalls's subsequent elaborations of his perverse political philosophy. The paper quoted his judgment that the sacred belief that "governments derive their just powers from the consent of the governed" was simply a "fallacy." Ingalls's dismissal of the "tariff question" as "a feint, a false pretense [and] an instrument for jugglery and tomfoolery," an astonishing admission that the GOP avoided essential issues, was of course precisely what Union Labor leaders wanted voters to believe. The 1888 Union Labor Party platform denounced Ingalls's recent utterances as "treason to our republic" and declared the senator "a traitor unfit to represent the state of Kansas."[42]

The Union Labor Party's focus on Ingalls perfectly bridged national and state politics. As a member of the U.S. Senate, Ingalls illustrated the corruption of national politics, and as Kansas' leading Republican his views demonstrated the insincerity of the state party's promises for reform. Third-party advocates argued that just as the national GOP used the tariff to mask a naked power struggle (true by Ingalls's own admission), so did the state party dishonestly endorse state-level reform. Thus, the *Nonconformist* dismissed the 1888 state Republican platform plank calling for a reduction in the legal rate of interest as nothing more than a "dodge" and compared it to the Iowa Republican Party's 1887 promise to reduce passenger fares when it had never intended to enact this reform at all.[43] Union Laborites, promising sincerity, contended that their platform went further, endorsing not only a reduction in the legal rate of interest but also a two-year stay of execution on foreclosed farms, and, of course, woman suffrage. As the reference to broken pledges in Iowa reveals, the Vincents were keenly aware that their position could be undermined by the example of Iowa, where the GOP had sponsored reform. Accordingly, they referred more than once to Iowa's failure to reduce passenger fares and carefully avoided mentioning the passage of the 1888 commissioner law.[44]

Many Republican leaders were concerned by the Union Labor challenge. The Republican pledge to reduce the legal rate of interest had been initiated by Republican state senator C. H. Kimball, who was facing a serious threat from the Union Labor Party in Labette County and wanted to destroy the new party before it took root. In a circular letter of July, Kimball advised delegates to the upcoming Republican state convention to adopt a platform calling for reduction of the legal rate of interest on farm mortgages to 6 percent and for other contracts to 10 percent. The Topeka *Capital* heartily concurred with this recommendation since the adoption of a reform platform "will disarm the men who preach that republican rule is the rule of the rich and strong."[45] The more liberal wing of the GOP hoped to nominate A. W. "Farmer" Smith for governor instead of Lyman U. Humphrey, a banker alleged to be the candidate of the Atchison, Topeka, and Santa Fe Railroad. Although the nomination went to Humphrey, the party platform made an unequivocal pledge for legislation "reducing the legal rate of interest upon money to 6 percent, reducing the maximum contract rate to 10 percent, prohibiting usury, and providing penalties for violations thereof."[46]

The contest of 1888 foreshadowed the emergence of populism two years later and the political turmoil that would engulf Kansas over the next decade. The campaign witnessed the political awakening of ordinary men and women, who discovered a new dignity in asserting their right to elect representatives who supported their just claim to equitable treatment. Farmers organized processions of farm wagons and entered small towns and cities to hear Union Labor speakers. Local Republican politicians were confronted by farmers from the far reaches of the hinterland in lines two miles long marching into town and displaying banners mocking GOP leaders ("Shoot the Strikers Down—A dollar a day is enough—Ben Harrison" and "The Declaration of Independence is a Fallacy—John J. Ingalls") and making unruly demands ("We Want More Money and Less Taxes," "Usury must go," "Down with Monopoly").[47] Although a few antimonopoly Republicans such as William Peffer, editor of the *Kansas Farmer*, were sympathetic to the Union Labor movement, conservative party leaders, who instinctively feared a political movement based on an appeal to economic discontent, launched a campaign to smear Union Labor leaders as anarchists. On 4 October the headline in the Winfield *Courier*, the Vincents' hometown Republican rival, read "Anarchism!" followed by a lengthy exposé of a secret organization called the Videttes, allegedly begun by the Vincents a year or more earlier. The *Courier* charged that from the beginning the Vincents' "real principles were the rankest anarchism."[48]

The *Courier*'s exposé was reprinted in Republican papers throughout the state on 19 October, the day after the explosion of a bomb at Coffeyville that seriously injured an express agent and his wife and daughter. The bomb, contained in a package, had exploded accidentally while in the temporary custody of the agent; it was unclear who had sent the package or for whom it was intended.[49] The Republicans alleged that the explosion was proof positive of violent revolutionaries in the state. The Vincents saw in the simultaneous statewide appearance of the *Courier*'s exposé and the Coffeyville explosion a plot by leading Republicans to frame them as violent anarchists.[50]

The Union Labor showing on election day proved disappointing, perhaps because the highly charged atmosphere in the aftermath of Coffeyville encouraged undecided voters to retreat to the safety of the old party banners or because farmers still believed Republican promises to enact reform. The *Nonconformist* had predicted the party would receive 65,000 to 70,000 votes, but only 38,000 ballots (just over 11 percent) were actually cast for A. J. Streeter, the party's presidential candidate; Cleveland won less than 31 percent, and Harrison easily carried Kansas with 55 percent. With a massive plurality of 80,000 and the election of an overwhelmingly Republican legislature, Republicans joyfully celebrated the "Grandest Victory in the History of the Party."[51]

"Success in 1888, however, came only by mortgaging the party's future, and the debt had to be paid in January 1889 when the legislature convened."[52] At the opening of the session an overwhelming sentiment in favor of significant reform was apparent. Outgoing Governor Martin admonished the new legislature, overwhelmingly Republican, to remain faithful to party pledges by reducing the legal rate of interest: "There is no excuse for maintaining the present excessive rates of interest. They should be materially reduced. Severe penalties should be also fixed to prevent and punish usury. . . . And as nearly all the members of the present legislature were elected on a platform which explicitly declares in favor of a reduction of existing rates of interest, and the imposition of severe penalties for usury, this subject will, no doubt, receive your early and favorable attention."[53] The Topeka *Capital-Commonwealth*, representing the broadest segment of Republican opinion, warmly approved of a reduction in interest rates to fulfill Republican pledges and was even willing to accept a two- or three-year stay-of-execution law, which would allow farmers to redeem their land after foreclosure.[54] Several leading legislators also endorsed reform and expressed confidence that significant legislation would be passed. Upon his selection as speaker of the house, Henry Booth stated that in choosing a Republican legislature, Kansas voters had shown "confidence" in the GOP and predicted that the house would honor that confidence. State senator L. P. King observed a "general sentiment among the members of both houses to fulfill party pledges" and noted that the interest rate question "is looked upon as one of the most important [matters]. It was a campaign cry in many counties where the Union Labor strength was largely developed, and at least one Senator says he owes his election to it."[55] William Peffer, who like most antimonopoly Republicans was still hoping reform could come from the party of Lincoln, expressed cautious optimism that GOP leaders would deliver on the promise to reduce interest rates, but he was much less sanguine about the prospects of a redemption law.[56]

Although the majority of Republican politicians favored reducing the maximum legal rate of interest as a matter of political necessity, bankers and other business interests feared that such legislation would cause an exodus of capital from the state, and financial interests immediately began lobbying to reverse the consensus for reform. Within a week after it had unequivocally endorsed Governor Martin's recommendations, the *Capital-Commonwealth* began to print reservations. A letter signed "V. P." cautioned that a redemption law would cause creditors to liquidate their investments and to reinvest in other states. A few days later Samuel T. Howe, president of the Kansas National Bank, warned in an interview that a reduction of the legal rate of interest would harm debtors in the western part of the state by diminishing the supply of funds. A letter signed "Iowa" admonished that a redemption law would be counterproductive because it would discourage lenders from granting extensions, thereby increasing the ultimate number of foreclosures. In the face of these gloomy forecasts, the *Capital-Common-*

wealth reversed its position. Never before in the history of Kansas, the paper solemnly observed, had there been a time "when unwise and injudicious legislation would so seriously cripple the state as now." Lowering the rate of interest, the *Capital-Commonwealth* warned, "will drive from Kansas every dealer of foreign capitol [*sic*] into other states. . . . Hundreds and thousands of mortgages would be foreclosed and as many families left hopeless because the loan companies would not renew the mortgages."[57]

In the meantime, many legislators had undergone a similar conversion and now scrambled to reconcile their new position with the party platform. Senator H. P. Wilson, for one, thought that "the party should always stand by its pledges," but he could not see "any advantage accruing to the borrower" by reducing interest rates. Surely it would be foolish for Republicans to enact their pledges if doing so injured those people whom the platform was intended to help.[58] To shield retreating legislators and to rationalize their own renunciation of party pledges, newspapers attempted to create the impression that public opinion had shifted against reform. The *Capital-Commonwealth* asserted that there had been "a very decided change of sentiment with regard to the proposed amendment of interest and redemption laws. Scores of letters are being received by members of the legislature from their constituents protesting against the proposed changes." The *Leavenworth Times* maintained that "thinking borrowers have come to the conclusion that they will be the real sufferers if any of the bills proposing radical changes . . . should be given the force of law."[59]

Although subsequent political events would demonstrate that banking and business interests had not swayed opinion in the countryside, they had clearly gained control of the legislature. The House Judiciary Committee reported in favor of postponing indefinitely all proposed alterations in the redemption law. Such changes, wrote committee chairman George L. Douglas, would be unconstitutional and contrary to the best interest of the state. A better way to improve the current situation, he informed the House, "will be to serve notice to the world that Kansas . . . is still dominated by the same high sense of legal and business obligation . . . that have ever distinguished it since its admission to the Union." The Senate Judiciary Committee reported similar legislation with no recommendation, whereupon the full body of the senate defeated it by a vote of twenty-four to eight.[60]

Recognizing that they could not avoid the issue altogether, conservatives introduced "as a compromise in the spirit of Henry Clay" the Howard bill, which technically met the requirements of the party platform by reducing the legal rate of interest from 12 to 10 percent. But the measure's light penalty, which required forfeiture only of that portion of the interest above the legal limit, rendered it essentially meaningless. Antimonopolists, quoting the Republican platform, decried the Howard bill as "a farce." "It is a very strange thing," said Sen. J. H. Mechem, the sponsor of an alternative bill making usury a misdemeanor, "if a law cannot be devised . . . to protect men from squeezing 36, 50, or 75 per cent out of the unfortunate with their bony fingers."[61]

Interest-rate reduction dominated the business of both houses from mid-February to the close of the legislative session on 3 March. Antimonopolists read constantly from the party platform, which for them had assumed the status of holy writ, and predicted that unless the party carried out "the letter and the spirit of its pledge, it would fall a great many thousand below 80,000 majority in two years." Those Republicans opposed to reform grew weary of the platform; it had served well as a fortress against the Union Labor Party the previous fall, but it had since become a millstone. Had the Union Labor Party fared better in 1888, many Republican legislators might have been more reluctant to abandon the party's promises, but in the wake of the Republican landslide, they felt little threat and considered the GOP's pledges to be nonbinding. As one senator put it, the platform had been passed only to pander to the "Union Labor howl," which had proved inconsequential.[62]

In the senate the Howard bill escaped dozens of amendments to give it strong enforcement provisions and was passed almost in its original form on 27 February.[63] The house, however, which had already passed a bill including a scale of penalties escalating with the interest rate, refused to concur in the light penalty of the Howard bill.[64] With the session drawing to a close, a joint committee agreed on a measure requiring forfeiture of interest above 10 percent and deduction of the amount of the illegal interest from the outstanding principal; the final bill was clearly a victory for proponents of a weak penalty.[65]

Antimonopolists were bitterly disillusioned; Peffer could scarcely believe that a minor reduction in the legal rate of interest had caused such "grave considerations." How could it be, he wondered, that "notwithstanding the party which elected the Legislature promised it, and notwithstanding money is now being loaned at six percent as far west as Hays City, a very large proportion of the members do not see their way clear to favor the proposed legislation. What will they say to their constituents in explanation? And what will their constituents do in reply? Send them back again? Hardly."[66] Adjournment found conservatives worn out by the strain of resisting reform and antimonopolists near to despair. The only people celebrating the outcome were the Union Laborites, who rejoiced to hear "threats of vengeance" from those people who had in the fall "voted to give the old party 'one more chance.' "[67]

The proponents of reform suffered a similar fate in Nebraska. After the defeat of the antimonopolists in the 1887 Nebraska legislature, the two factions in the Nebraska Republican Party were further polarized as economic hardship deepened. Prorailroad politicians feared that even the threat of railroad-reform legislation would exacerbate capital flight by frightening already timid investors. Antimonopoly politicians contended that greater hardship made reform all the more imperative. Moreover, antimonopolists had grown increasingly frustrated as session after session had killed meaningful reform and were even more determined to reverse the hegemony of the railroads.

Proponents of regulation blamed the railroads' corruption of the electoral and legislative process for the continual failure of their proposals. The leading antimonopolist, Edward Rosewater, expounded on the nefarious methods of the railroads before a U.S. Senate commission gathering testimony on the Union Pacific Railroad in 1887. The railroads, he reported, lubricated the political machinery of the state through the liberal use of free passes and rebates, thus allowing railroad officials to manipulate primaries and conventions. Rosewater also told the commission of secret "oil rooms" hidden in the recesses of hotels, where Union Pacific officers plied solons and delegates with whiskey and cigars during conventions and legislative sessions.[68] At one session of the legislature, Rosewater claimed, the Union Pacific had offered $5,000 to the chairman of the railroad committee to make a report favorable to the railroads. In another case a Grand Island grain dealer had complained that he was unable to obtain the same rates given to other shippers and was told "point blank, by the superintendent that he was not on their side of politics, and that he could not get their rates." This man was a Republican, Rosewater pointed out, but not a "railroad" Republican. "We are all divided here," he elaborated, "into Railroad Republicans and Antirailroad Republicans."[69]

The 1887 Republican platform reflected the continuing stalemate. It affirmed the party's abhorrence of "communists" who would divide property and "anarchists" who would destroy it but at the same time expressed the view that the "great railway corporations of this state . . . shall be fairly paid servants of the state and not its masters." It declared as "grossly unjust" that rates were higher in Nebraska than in Iowa, Minnesota, or Dakota Territory and pledged the party to enact laws "to prevent unjust discrimination and extortion in transportation rates." Antimonopolists might have desired stronger wording, but this plank clearly established a basis on which to argue for a legislatively mandated reduction.[70]

For the fifth time in a decade the Nebraska legislature of 1889 deliberated on the issue of railroad reform; more than ever before, its actions would test whether the Nebraska Republican Party was responsive to public demands.[71] Gov. John M. Thayer endorsed proposals for regulation of the railroads in his message to the legislature, affirming the right of the state to control corporations and declaring that freight and passenger rates in Nebraska should be equal to those in Iowa and Kansas; he further urged the election of railroad commissioners. Larrabee of Iowa, who a year earlier had led his successful crusade for reform, appeared before the Nebraska house to respond to the "unkind words spoken of Iowa, to the effect that we are disposed to . . . drive the roads to bankruptcy." He assured Nebraska legislators that Iowa had "no desire to cripple railroad investments." On the other hand, Larrabee insisted, "discriminations practiced against our people should not be permitted. The millionaires can take care of themselves. . . . It is the masses who need protection." Iowa's governor did not presume to prescribe specific remedies to the legislative body of a sovereign state, but his counsel that "some regulation is necessary" in Nebraska clearly strengthened the hand of reformers in the legislature.[72]

The key railroad-reform measure, introduced by Representative C. L. Hall, established a schedule of maximum freight rates. Hall and others presented evidence showing that local rates in Nebraska were 30 percent higher than in Iowa and contended that the railroads could afford to haul as cheaply in Nebraska because grades were easier and roadbeds less costly than in Iowa.[73] Conservatives attempted to forestall legislation by arguing that the railroads would retaliate against a reduction in local rates by raising through rates, which were of greater importance to farmers in the first place.[74] Although this position showed sophistication in regard to the relative economic significance of local and interstate rates, it failed to recognize that state regulation was a political demand more than an economic issue.

The Hall bill passed the house by a margin of fifty-four to thirty-three, but it was smothered in the senate, failing even to reach the floor. And a moderate resolution directing the Board of Transportation to adopt a schedule preventing discrimination was indefinitely postponed in the conservative upper house.[75] As the legislature adjourned, the *Republican* praised its wisdom in refraining from "interference with the railroad problem." The *Bee* voiced the disappointment of antimonopolists:

> The demands of the producers for relief from railroad exactions were totally ignored. It was impossible to secure even respectful consideration in

the senate. It was the graveyard of every measure affecting the corporations. The absurd claim that regulation would retard railroad building and delay the development of the western section of the state was successfully worked by the lawyers and political farmers, and a majority of the senate united in defeating every bill which directly or remotely touched their interests.[76]

Kansas, Nebraska, and Iowa experienced almost constant pressure for reform during the 1880s. Antimonopolists, acting sometimes through the Democratic Party but more often through third parties or the Republican Party, continually pressed demands to restrict the prerogatives of capital. Operating within the Republican Party, these individuals were often able to secure reform platforms and to elect a majority of legislators and perhaps a governor sympathetic to reform, but they found it difficult to pass reform laws. Conservative Republican leaders and their corporate allies took particular care to control key senate committees. The bicameral structure of state legislatures made it possible for a powerful minority (particularly in the senate) to prevent passage of reform bills.

But the political systems of these three states were not simply the instruments of capital. Reform could occur when it became politically imperative for a sufficient number of legislators. Most politicians were not doctrinaire conservatives or antimonopolists and were primarily concerned about their own political careers and the security of the party. In times of particularly intense pressure for reform, as in the late 1880s, these politicians were caught between their constituents and strong business interests. Decisions were based on the level of political risk in ignoring demands for reform. In Iowa in 1887 and early 1888 the combined threat to Republican politicians from the Democratic/Greenback opposition and the Farmers' Alliance was substantial enough that almost all Republican politicians, except for a handful of doctrinaire conservatives, found it politically impossible to back away from reform. The pressures were strong enough to produce a critical mass in favor of railroad regulation. In Kansas and Nebraska the GOP was willing to accept demands for relief at party conventions but failed to pass laws regulating capital. Even though the majority of members of both houses of the legislature favored such laws, a minority was able to forestall the fulfillment of party promises; there were enough politicians who did not perceive any real danger of political opposition and who acquiesced in the arguments of powerful bankers and railroads.

The failure of the 1889 Kansas and Nebraska legislatures to provide reform proved vital to the emergence of populism a year later. Farmers had demanded relief and had received assurances from their representatives. They closely followed the deliberations of their legislators through agricultural journals such as the *Kansas Farmer* or in the regular press. When just measures were killed in committee or voted down on the floor, farmers began to question their political allegiances. The Kansas and Nebraska Farmers' Alliances had only recently been organized and did not formally participate in the legislative debate in early 1889. But once the Alliances in the two states began to grow and to debate political strategy in late 1889 and early 1890, the lack of action in the previous legislative sessions offered a powerful argument for forming a new party.

6

In Search of "The Way Out": The Farmers' Alliance in Kansas and Nebraska

At the close of the legislative sessions in Kansas and Nebraska in spring 1889 there was little sign of the political revolution that would sweep both states eighteen months later in the fall elections of 1890. In early 1889 the Kansas and Nebraska Farmers' Alliances had organized only a handful of farmers and hardly appeared capable of becoming major political forces. Yet in late 1889 and early 1890 the Alliances in both states experienced an enormous surge in membership, and by mid-1890 they had decided to nominate their own candidates. In the fall the People's tickets in Nebraska and Kansas shattered the post–Civil War hegemony of the Republican Party and ushered in a new period of competitive state politics.

The explosive growth of the Alliance and its rapid movement toward a third party suggest an inevitability to the process, but during its initial period of growth such an outcome was by no means certain in Kansas and Nebraska. Like the Iowa Alliance, the Kansas and Nebraska Alliances were officially nonpartisan and at the outset advanced a two-part program of economic cooperation and legislative reforms. Neither aspect of this agenda necessarily entailed a third-party strategy. To obtain federal or state legislation, an Alliance could adopt a strategy to influence state and national officeholders or to elect new representatives from the two parties, or it could form a new party. Third-party formation was highly problematic and became a matter of intense debate within the Alliance leadership and among its members.

Although Kansas and Nebraska eventually became two of the strongest Farmers' Alliance states, the Alliance was slow to organize there. The Nebraska Alliance was originally formed in 1881 as an affiliate of Milton George's National Farmers' Alliance, which eventually became known as the Northern Alliance. Following its foray into politics with the Anti-Monopoly Party in 1884, the Nebraska Farmers' Alliance all but disappeared except in name. It adopted a new constitution in 1887, but as late as January 1889 the organization remained weak. Only fourteen counties sent delegates to the annual meeting held that month, and there were at most 230 local suballiances in the state with a maximum membership of 7,000 men and 1,750 women.[1]

The Northern Alliance also organized a branch in Kansas in 1881, but it fell into serious decline a year later and was not reorganized until 1888. It was absorbed in December 1889 by the Kansas affiliate of the National Farmers' Alliance and Industrial Union (NFA and IU), known as the Southern Alliance.[2] The Southern Alliance first attempted to recruit Kansas farmers in July 1887, when an organizer from the already well-established Texas Farmers' Alliance began work in Cowley, Butler, and Sumner Counties, but his efforts proved ineffective. In May 1888 W. P. Brush, a Kansan commissioned by the Texas Alliance, successfully organized the first Kansas suballiances in the southwestern part of the state, and a state organization of the NFA and IU was established in Kansas in December 1888. At that time there were perhaps 6,000 members of the Kansas branch of the Southern Alliance. By comparison, the Iowa Alliance had been a significant force in state politics for over a year, and its membership was more than double that of the Kansas or Nebraska Alliances. In general, the Alliance was stronger in much of the South, in Missouri, and in the Dakota territory.[3]

During the winter of 1889–1890, according to the best estimates, the Kansas Alliance grew dramatically, from approximately 17,500 members in August 1889 to 61,000 in March 1890. The Nebraska Alliance had about 25,000 members in January 1890; by July this figure had increased to 60,000. These numbers include an estimated one-fifth female membership.[4] Much of the rapid growth of the Alliance can be attributed to the fall in prices for agricultural products, which reached a post–Civil War low in early 1890.[5] One Alliance organizer explained the impact of hard times in simple terms: "Low prices make good listeners." In McPherson County, Kansas, much of the bumper corn crop of 1889 "went to waste as cribs, pens, and old buildings were filled, and immense piles lay uncovered on the ground." One farmer reported that he had taken a load of corn to town but had received "just two drinks and lunch" for the product of weeks of toil. Many Kansas and Nebraska farmers, short of cash, could not afford coal and were reduced to burning surplus corn as fuel. Farmers were desperate to understand the source of their problems and to find a way out of hard times.[6]

The burdens of economic hardship were particularly severe for farm women. In the nineteenth century, midwestern farm wives, with help from their daughters, had full responsibility for all the work in the home. They grew and processed the food: The typical farm wife raised a garden, churned butter, and dried fruits and vegetables in addition to cooking three meals a day. Farm women also provided for every other household need. They made candles, soap, and cloth and did the mending, washing, ironing, and cleaning. Women were also responsible for raising chickens and geese, collecting eggs, and feeding and milking cows. And of course farm women bore and cared for children. Moreover, the farm household depended upon the products of women's labor for cash income. Women sold products such as butter, eggs, cloth, and honey to obtain money for household necessities such as flour, salt, sugar, and coffee and to pay for home improvements. Women's income also contributed to relieving short- and long-term debts. Men, who worked long hours planting, growing and harvesting field crops, repairing fences and equipment, and caring for cattle and hogs, were hardly in an enviable position, but it is safe to conclude that an unequal division of labor prevailed on midwestern farms, with women carrying the larger share of the work.

During times of economic hardship women's duties increased since farm families often could not afford to hire outside labor. In such times, wives and daughters worked in the fields in addition to their usual chores. Moreover, since women were generally responsible for managing the household budget, they bore the burden of stretching fewer dollars to cover necessary expenses when prices for field crops and for their own products declined. Pressed to make interest payments in the late 1880s, Rosie Ise, a farm wife in western Kansas, economized by forbidding her children to buy candy and by rationing the amount of sugar for coffee. She accepted her role of "stingy parent" as part of her duty but not without resentment. It was during this period, her son later recalled, that Rosie, not yet thirty, began to grow tired, worn, and "angry and rebellious at what seemed her unjustly heavy share of care and responsibility."[7]

Male leaders of the Alliance encouraged women to join the organization, reasoning that women would make the meetings into interesting social gatherings, thus ensuring enthusiasm for the order. Furthermore, Alliance leaders, recognizing that "the farmer and his wife worked together as an agricultural unit," believed that it "made sense to involve both in the Alliance."[8] A few men thought women did not belong in the Alliance; some farmers grumbled that women did not know enough or that they were incapable of keeping quiet about the secret rituals of the order. Because of the resistance to female membership by a few suballiances in Kansas, the president of the state Alliance threatened to revoke the charters of those local Alliances that had refused to admit women to membership. Most men, however, accepted participation of women in the Alliance if only on fairly traditional grounds. Since it involved no extension of their accepted domestic role, it was not problematic for women to plan socials, organize glee clubs, provide literary entertainments, or even to serve as secretaries of suballiances. Only rarely, if ever, would a woman be elected president of a suballiance, however, as this would have challenged men as the ultimate source of authority.[9]

If men wanted to include women in the Alliance to enhance the vitality of what they saw as an essentially male organization, rural women had their own reasons for joining. Women did perform the traditionally feminine tasks in the organization, but they also joined in order to understand for themselves the cause of hard times and to advance remedies to alleviate their own suffering and that of their families. As women endured greater economic hardship in the late 1880s, the division between the "public" world of politics and economics and the "private" world of the domestic household economy appeared ever more artificial. Forced to economize, farm wives saw membership as an extension of their role as mothers and as an act of self-preservation to understand how the protective tariff drove up the price of sugar or how currency contraction drove down the price of eggs or grain.[10] At first, Alliance women probably thought that by understanding such matters they could then influence their husbands, sons, and other women, but as the Kansas and Nebraska Alliances moved toward becoming independent political parties, Alliance women began to make bolder claims for a public voice.

Nebraska and Kansas Alliance leaders devoted most of their attention at first to economic cooperation as a solution to the problems of the farmers. The founders of the Nebraska Alliance, recognizing the need to offer a "definite and tangible means of relief," decided to promote "some method of cooperation in selling the products of the farms, and in purchasing needed supplies." During 1889 several Nebraska suballiances instituted various forms of economic cooperation.[11] Many of them made rather ambitious plans to construct mills or elevators, financed by selling stock to members.[12] These cooperatives were often unable to raise the necessary capital to commence operation or soon failed, but several Nebraska cooperatives achieved some degree of success if not always on the grand scale originally envisioned. The Cambridge Business Association (Furnas County), organized in August 1889, reported in December that it had saved its members "many hundreds of dollars" through direct purchases of lumber and that it had almost com-

pleted construction of an elevator; by threatening to contract directly with
jobbers, it had also forced local merchants to lower their prices. An agent
for another suballiance reported that he had shipped twenty cars of corn
and two of hay and had been able to secure up to 2 cents more per bushel
for corn than the local elevator was willing to pay.[13]

Many of these efforts were opposed by merchants and other business interests. When an Alliance in Adams County arranged with an Omaha jobber to purchase goods at wholesale prices, local retailers boycotted the
Omaha firm, forcing it to cancel its Alliance contract. By spring 1890 suballiances' direct purchases of lumber had become a sufficient threat to merchants that wholesalers and retailers formed a state association to prevent
parties not engaged in the lumber trade from buying at wholesale rates.[14] Alliance efforts to market grain encountered similar opposition. One suballiance at Edgar, Nebraska, reported that after farmers had loaded ten rail
cars to be shipped to an eastern buyer, the railroads informed them that
"the road was blocked and hence the delivery direct by the Alliance people
was refused." Local grain merchants had probably pressured the railroad to
stop the Alliance initiative.[15] In another case that attracted statewide attention, the Elmwood Farmers' Alliance filed a complaint before the Nebraska
Board of Transportation charging the Missouri Pacific with discrimination
for denying track privileges to a proposed Alliance elevator. The board decided the case in favor of the Alliance, and the Nebraska Supreme Court
sustained the ruling.[16]

Besides encouraging local cooperatives, Nebraska Alliance leaders established a state "Business Association" in the summer of 1889 to consolidate
orders from local Alliances and to obtain bulk discounts from wholesalers.
The agency tried to avoid the problems of insufficient capital and indebtedness that often plagued large-scale agricultural cooperatives by requiring suballiances to make payment when they placed an order.[17] Most suballiances at
one time or another probably placed small orders for coal or binding twine
with the state agency; one of the first actions taken by the May Alliance of
Kearney County was to appoint an "alliance purchasing agricultural agent,"
who was instructed to place an order for a carload of coal.[18] The savings
gained by such purchases were an immediate benefit of Alliance membership and created an important incentive to join.

Alliance leaders in Kansas also initially emphasized economic cooperation.
Texas Alliance organizers working in Kansas in mid-1888 attempted to recruit members by explaining the advantages of cooperative purchasing and
selling. Speaking on the "objects of the Alliance" before the Cowley

County Alliance in April 1889, J. H. McDowell, vice-president of the NFA and IU, stressed the advantages of cooperation and promised savings of 25 to 40 percent on direct purchases of goods. This was a sermon to the converted: Cowley County Alliance members had established a cooperative store in February; by August it reported its total business at $24,000.[19] Although the Cowley County cooperative had been inspired by the example of the cooperative movement in Texas, the Johnson County Co-operative Association, which one Southern Alliance national organizer recommended as a model cooperative, dated from the Grange era and reported total business of $3 million since it was founded in 1876.[20]

Several other local and county Alliances in Kansas also laid plans for cooperative purchasing and marketing. The Barton County Alliance Exchange Company, for example, intended to conduct a "general mercantile business, to assist farmers in the disposal of their stock and farm products, [and] to negotiate loans." This exchange was capitalized at $100,000 with shares at $5 each. Profits were to be divided quarterly based on the amount of goods shareholders had purchased during the quarter. The Kansas Alliance's official newspaper reported the organization of several other county and local cooperatives, especially during spring and summer 1890.[21]

The first project of the Kansas Alliance was to establish a state cooperative agency. At the annual Alliance meeting in August 1889, leaders unveiled an ambitious plan of cooperative purchasing and marketing through an Alliance Exchange, which as originally envisioned would have eventually operated warehouses, stockyards, grain elevators, and packing houses. The capital stock of the exchange was $500,000 with shares at $5 each; business would begin when $10,000 had been raised.[22] Despite its lofty aspirations, the Kansas Alliance Exchange was seriously hindered by a lack of capital. In late November 1889 H. W. Sandusky, secretary of the exchange, complained that because of the failure of Alliance members to subscribe to the exchange's stock, it would not be able to market grain as originally planned. In April 1890 the exchange was still "in great want of spot cash" and had failed to receive funds promised by county Alliances; in August, Sandusky was still attempting to raise capital to begin full operations.[23] In practice the scope of the Kansas Alliance Exchange's activities was similar to the Nebraska Alliance Business Association's. The Kansas Exchange was able to purchase binding twine and coal directly from wholesalers and may have obtained some discounts on farm machinery, but it was never able to implement its plans for cooperative marketing although it did market livestock through the American Livestock Commission Company.[24]

Local and county cooperation in Kansas seldom went beyond purchasing. Kansas suballiances, unlike those in Nebraska, evidently made little effort to market their crops or to establish elevators, perhaps because they were waiting for the promised marketing operations of the state exchange to go into effect. The *Nonconformist* recognized the advanced position of the Nebraska Alliance's cooperative program by giving front-page coverage to the Nebraska Board of Transportation's decision in favor of the Elmwood Farmers' Alliance, noting that the decision would encourage Kansas farmers to establish elevators of their own.[25]

Although cooperatives were an important arena for Alliance activity, from the start members and leaders of the organization sought political solutions to their problems. Their pursuit of legislative remedies eventually led them to form independent political parties. The Alliance offered political education; each suballiance, as the secretary of the Nebraska Alliance put it, was a "school house where the members were forming new ideas of their duties as citizens and new conceptions of their privileges as sovereign voters."[26] The content of the Alliance curriculum can be glimpsed in some detail through an account written by S. M. Scott, a Kansas Alliance organizer. Scott received a commission from the Kansas state Alliance in December 1889 and on 2 January set out to organize farmers scratching out an existence on the barren, windswept plains in the northwestern part of the state. Over the next four months he endured below-zero temperatures and at least one blizzard to organize eighty-seven suballiances and played the title role in his account of this near-epic journey, "The Champion Organizer of the Northwest."[27] Scott's method of operation was to ride to a post office or a small town and to circulate an announcement of a meeting to be held that evening or the next:

STOP AND READ.

Farmers,

There will be a free lecture on the aims and objects of the Farmers Alliance and Co-operative Union of Kansas, at _____.

Come one, come all over sixteen years of age and hear a lecture you cannot afford to miss. The unparalleled growth of this order warrants us in saying that before another year rolls around we can boast of the strongest organization in America.

Ladies are especially invited. Don't forget the date.[28]

Scott typically began his lectures by quoting the Alliance's declaration of purposes: to "labor for education of the agricultural classes in the science of economical government, in a strictly non-partisan spirit." In simpler terms, Scott explained, this meant "that we are to study the science of politics." The time had come, he announced, for there to be "a school started to educate the people in the science of economical government. And this is what we have to offer you in the Alliance."[29] For the next two or three hours Scott taught a course in basic political economy—lecturing on the credit system, the monetary system, interest and commission, transportation, the beef combine, and commodity futures and offering an array of statistics on railroad stock-watering or the unfair rebates given to Chicago meatpackers.[30] He then instructed farmers about the deceptive practices of politicians:

> As a rule, when the time comes for the campaign to open, Mr. Politician steps out and sniffs the political atmosphere. . . . He comes to our homes about ten A.M., while you are in the field, drives to the house, provided he is sure your little boy is large enough to send for his papa. The first step necessary is to brag on your small boy and make his mamma think, if possible, that it is not all put on, but in nine cases out of ten this is the hardest task.
>
> The little boy and girl are soon captured by his 'ta tas' and 'lu lus,' mixed well with high colored candy, with more color than candy.
>
> The whole trouble has been 'lo these many years' that the farmers have had the power to send men who could work for them, but just because these dudes came around and made them some fine promises; we have said yaw, yaw, yaw, to everything, and we have always lost the sausage.[31]

Given the long history of politicians ignoring the legitimate demands of those people who performed honest labor, Scott asked, "How long will the people be hoodwinked? How long will the people continue to be lashed into line with the cry you will weaken your party and let the other fellows in? . . . How long will it be before we will realize that our officers are our servants rather than masters?"[32]

Scott appealed to farmers to join the new organization because it would allow farmers once more to become free citizens of a democratic republic. Each farmer who joined the Alliance could say, "For myself I shall be a free man and cast my vote on the side of justice, and once more our laws shall be for the people, of the people and by the people." This did not mean, however, that those individuals who became members of the Alliance would be joining a new political party; Scott indeed urged the Alliance to be cautious about its future political course.[33] The appeal was directed to fundamental political values. Like most ordinary nineteenth-century Americans, Scott's rural audiences believed as the basic premise of their democratic creed that the people had the right to elect representatives who would enact laws to ensure the common good. There was no question in the minds of farmers that proper legislation could remedy their difficulties.

During 1889 and early 1890, the initial period of Alliance growth, Alliance members and leaders searched for legislative solutions to their problems; they certainly found no shortage of available explanations or possible reforms to discuss. The official newspaper of the Kansas Alliance identified several questions to be considered at Alliance meetings. The first of these concerned state legislation:

1. Do the state laws of assessment and taxation bear equally on all its citizens?
2. Are the present rates of interest as fixed by law in harmony with the agricultural and other business interests of the country?
3. Is the present penalty for taking usury by money loaners of sufficient severity?

The remaining issues implied national solutions:

4. How does the contraction of the currency effect [sic] the farmers, wage-laborers, and commercial interests of the country?
5. How does gambling in futures of farm products effect [sic] the price of grain in the hands of producers, and the cost to consumers?
6. What favors, privileges and powers does the National banking law confer upon National banks?
7. Are the present high protective tariff laws beneficial to farmers?
8. Is the acquirement by Aliens of large tracts of land in the United States dangerous and wrong?
9. In what way do trusts and combines effect [sic] commerce and trade?[34]

Alliance leaders saw state-level reform as the logical starting place. Peffer's *Kansas Farmer* observed that immediate relief "must come from State Legislatures"; Jay Burrows, leader of the Nebraska Farmers' Alliance, also counseled farmers to "attend to matters of serious concern right at home first," such as assessment, taxation, and lower freight rates.[35] But Alliance leaders, regarding monetary contraction as the basic cause of hard times, also recognized that the solution to farmers' problems ultimately would require national remedies. In early January 1889 Burrows penned a "memorial" to Congress that attributed the agricultural depression to the contraction of the currency and requested Congress to enact the land-loan plan calling for federal government loans at a low rate of interest on land security. This memorial was adopted by the Northern Alliance at its annual meeting the same year.[36] As he began publication of the Alliance newspaper in June, Burrows identified money as "the great issue" and wrote a series of articles on Greenback monetary theory, in which he explained that money had no intrinsic value and was the creation of government by law. Burrows informed farmers that the contraction of the currency over the past twenty years had caused a decline in prices that injured debtors by increasing their interest obligations. The remedy, he said, was for the federal government to loan money directly to farmers at a low rate of interest; this move would inflate the currency, increase prices, and allow farmers access to credit at a low rate of interest.[37]

In Kansas Peffer was also considering various economic solutions. During mid-1889 the *Kansas Farmer* solicited its readers' opinions on the cause of hard times and received dozens of replies, ranging from national banks to trusts, cattle syndicates, middle men, and inequitable taxation of mortgages.[38] Moreover, Peffer allowed space for a plan put forward by W. V. Marshall to abolish trusts through graduated taxation and for another proposal by the future Populist congressman John Davis for currency expansion through government redemption of foreclosed mortgages.[39] Having allowed other men their say, in late 1889 Peffer unveiled his own solution in a series of articles, "The Way Out," which formed the core of his later book, *The Farmers' Side*. Because monetary contraction was at the root of the sufferings of farmers and workers, Peffer proposed the creation of a federal "loan bureau" under the Treasury Department that would establish several local branches to loan money at 1 percent per annum with 9 percent of the principal payable each year. To extend the appeal of the land-loan plan to urban dwellers, he added a provision whereby loans would be offered to people in towns and cities on the security of lots.[40]

Unlike the Vincents, who were attempting to recruit farmers to a new political party, Peffer and Burrows did not explain currency contraction in conspiratorial terms. Burrows wrote that state and national legislation enacted since 1861 had created two classes, "the very rich and the very poor," but he was uncertain whether this had been done "consciously or unconsciously." Peffer attributed the passage of laws responsible for currency contraction simply to the notion that most congressmen had been schooled in the "old ideas" about political economy and therefore believed the doctrines of hard money.[41]

Burrows and Peffer did not believe that their endorsement of Greenback monetary theory and the land-loan plan necessarily required a third-party strategy. During the early period of Alliance growth Peffer remained uncertain about the wisdom of such a course of action and as late as April 1890 held open the possibility that the Alliance could achieve reform through the two parties.[42] Burrows had particularly strong reservations about a third party, undoubtedly because he had witnessed the rapid disintegration of the Nebraska Alliance following the rout of the Anti-Monopoly Party in 1884. In an address to the Northern Alliance in January 1889 Burrows termed the Nebraska Alliance's earlier foray into independent politics a "fatal mistake" and vowed that the Alliance would not become "a political party, until the time comes when a new party is organized based on living issues." He hoped that this time was "not far distant," but meanwhile the Alliance should not go into third-party politics.[43]

Other Alliance leaders, however, argued from the outset for the creation of a new party. In October 1889 Stephen McLallin, editor of the *Advocate*, the Kansas Alliance's official organ, contended that the "old parties have been tried in the years past and found wanting," offering as evidence the proposition that "the circulating medium had been contracted until it is insufficient for the business of the country." But could not the old parties reverse this situation? No, replied McLallin, because currency contraction had occurred "in pursuance of a preconceived purpose, as announced in the infamous Hazzard Circular, and the scheme has been abetted and faithfully sustained by these old parties." As any student of Emery's *Seven Financial Conspiracies* would have known, the "Hazzard Circular" was the key document purporting to reveal the conspiracy initiated by the English money power during the Civil War.[44] Had currency contraction taken place through any means short of a conspiracy, the parties might be reformable, McLallin implied; only a conspiracy provided ample justification for rejecting the existing parties.

Kansas and Nebraska Alliance leaders advocated other economic reforms through national legislation. They endorsed government ownership of railroads, although they did not give this reform the same attention they devoted to monetary issues.[45] Schooled in Greenback monetary theory, Alliance leaders believed that an ample supply of money ultimately required paper-money issue and regarded free coinage of silver as only a partial remedy to the money shortage.[46] Silver became a divisive issue among Populists in 1895–1896 when midroad members contended that fusion with the Democrats would destroy any hope of achieving the comprehensive reforms of the 1892 Omaha platform and that free silver by itself would do nothing to help farmers. But in 1890 Kansas Alliance leaders wholeheartedly endorsed free silver from the pragmatic standpoint that it would bring real, albeit limited, benefits. "So long as we must be afflicted with the nonsense of a metallic currency," the *Nonconformist* explained, "we favor all we can get, so by all means give us free coinage of silver."[47]

Furthermore, Alliance leaders sometimes blurred the distinction between legal-tender paper and silver coinage altogether. In early 1890, with Congress seriously considering free coinage, Alliance leaders lobbied for this reform as if it were a panacea. During February 1890 the columns of the Topeka *Advocate* were filled with the words of national advocates of free silver, one of whom promised that free coinage would bring a 35 percent increase in the price of wheat. The Lincoln *Alliance* distributed free-silver literature and printed a petition favoring "free and unlimited coinage of silver" to be circulated among Nebraska farmers and sent to Congress.[48]

The Alliances of Kansas and Nebraska learned of another important national reform at a meeting of the Southern and Northern Alliances at St. Louis in December 1889 when Charles W. Macune of the Texas Alliance introduced his subtreasury plan. This proposal, which Macune had devised following the failure of the Texas Alliance Exchange, was intended to remedy chronic problems in the short-term credit system of southern agriculture. Macune's proposal called for the establishment of "subtreasuries," warehouses and elevators where farmers would deposit crops and receive a certificate of deposit. Farmers could use these certificates to obtain government loans at 1 percent interest, payable in legal-tender notes; the certificates would be redeemed and the loans repaid within one year. Macune's subtreasury plan was intended to stabilize the annual fluctuations in commodity prices and to provide farmers with low-interest short-term loans. It was not intended, in contrast to the land-loan plan already espoused by Kansas and Nebraska Alliance leaders, to inflate the overall supply of currency.[49]

Following the adoption of the subtreasury plan by the Southern Alliance at the St. Louis meeting, McLallin of the *Advocate*, observing wide differences of opinion on the causes and remedies for the depression, urged all reformers to unite behind the Southern Alliance's St. Louis platform in order to obtain a "harmony of purpose and effort."[50] The *Advocate* ran several articles explaining the subtreasury proposal, and the lecturer of the state Alliance instructed suballiance lecturers to introduce the subtreasury plan to members as soon as possible. William Peffer endorsed the plan as a valuable complement to the land-loan measure.[51]

Some Alliance leaders were decidedly skeptical about Macune's proposal, however. Benjamin H. Clover, president of the Kansas Alliance, objected that the subtreasury "so inflates and contracts the currency . . . that the money power can get a vast amount of it in its possession during the period of inflation."[52] Although other Kansas Alliance leaders generally endorsed the subtreasury, if for no other reason than that they were affiliated with the NFA and IU, Nebraska Alliance leaders felt little obligation to follow the Southern Alliance. Burrows of Nebraska regretted the adoption of this "unwise and unjust proposition" as it was bound to bring "ridicule" on the Alliance. A scheme proposing to contract and expand the currency by over a billion dollars twice a year, Burrows exclaimed, "is too hair-brained [sic] for even patient criticism. Such propositions tend to make one conservative, and inspire a healthy dread of revolutions."[53]

Despite these disagreements, Alliance leaders in Kansas and Nebraska were beginning to bring into focus a comprehensive program of "economic collectivism." Drawing on a Greenback heritage, Alliance leaders were developing a critique of American capitalism that rooted the concentration of economic power in trusts and powerful railroad corporations in the post–Civil War policy of currency contraction. They were also articulating an inclusive program of reform, starting first with particular remedies at the state level but ultimately moving to the national level. They had put forward numerous proposals—particularly the land-loan plan but also government ownership of railroads and, in Kansas, the subtreasury, which entailed an active use of government power to ensure the common good. This synthesis went further than antimonopolism, which advocated piecemeal solutions such as government regulation of railroads or trusts.[54]

Describing the content of the Alliance curriculum as set forth by Alliance leaders is less difficult than knowing the minds of their pupils, the ordinary Alliance members. Suballiances were free to debate questions or to engage in any activities, and ordinary farmers sometimes pursued their own course of action without any apparent guidance from their leaders. Desperate farmers lashed out against the most visible, proximate targets they could identify as sources of their oppression. Several suballiances in Kansas determined to withhold all information pertaining to crops from county assessors, who routinely collected agricultural data from farmers for the state Bureau of Agriculture. The statistical report of the state bureau, in the words of one suballiance, was "a source of information to the money combines of the east [who] are enabled to dictate the prices of grain and live-stock."[55] Another grass-roots rebellion was instigated by 200 farmers who gathered at Hiawatha, Kansas, to protest a trust that controlled the price of binder twine. One farmer compared the "present oppression" to the Boston Tea

Party and declared that "if we would pay the trust prices we would be un-
worthy sons of worthy sires." Two weeks later the Cowley County Alliance
resolved to boycott twine in order to crush "that heinous and outrageous
monster, the binding trust."⁵⁶ Alliances also resolved to boycott sugar since
its price was artificially inflated by a trust.⁵⁷

Suballiances discussed broader economic issues as well. The May Alliance in Nebraska debated the proposition, "Resolved that the rail[road] has
caused more distress to the people [than] the Banking sistem [sic]." On another evening the members considered whether "usery [sic] is more of a
curse to the western people than liccar [sic]."⁵⁸ The either/or phrasing of
such questions revealed a probable tendency for farmers to think in terms of
a single remedy, but framing questions in mutually exclusive terms allowed
them to improve their understanding of these issues.

Through hearing lectures, reading the Alliance press, and discussing issues among themselves, farmers began to grasp the causes of their problems
and to see a way out. In one suballiance a member reported, "We are beginning to find out that among the great inventions of man is money. . . . that
a delegated government under the modern regime is not a government of
the people, but a government of, for and by the monied classes."⁵⁹ Given
their mounting burdens of mortgage indebtedness, Kansas and Nebraska
farmers responded enthusiastically to the land-loan plan, which promised
higher prices and lower interest. Suballiances carefully considered this measure and in some cases modified its provisions as they saw fit. The Good
Will Union of Reno County, Kansas, determined that the government
should loan exactly $1 billion in paper money and set 3 percent as the ap-
propriate rate of interest and then proposed that the interest proceeds from
the loans be used to buy gold and silver, coin it, and loan it once again on
land security. Eventually enough gold and silver would be in circulation
that it would no longer be necessary to issue paper money. Through their
own deliberations these farmer-citizens had arrived at a creative synthesis of
Greenback and hard-money ideas and had solved the money question all at
once. The Sunny Valley Alliance of Kansas, having discussed some possible
objections to the land-loan plan, endorsed the measure but added a list of
safeguards against speculators.⁶⁰

The land-loan plan, in one form or another, was popular. In spring 1890
dozens of suballiances in Kansas and Nebraska penned resolutions supporting the proposal, most groups endorsing a version of the plan contained in a
bill before Congress sponsored by Sen. Leland Stanford of California.⁶¹
Many suballiances realized that the Stanford land-loan plan could provide
immediate relief, making a new political party unnecessary. F. M. Scott,

president of Kansas suballiance no. 318 wrote, "We cannot wait to revolutionize the politics of our country. We must have help, and have it now. . . . A measure has already been introduced in the Senate by Mr. Stanford, of California, which would give the people immediate relief."[62]

Although several Kansas suballiances endorsed Macune's subtreasury plan, significant opposition to it surfaced among ordinary farmers in Kansas. The Oak Grove Alliance of Nortonville heartily endorsed free coinage of silver but unanimously denounced the subtreasury as "detrimental to the farmers and industrial classes." The president of this suballiance explained that the subtreasury was "class legislation" and therefore violated the Alliance motto, "Equal rights to all and special privileges to none." The Culvert Alliance objected that the subtreasury would encourage speculation and suggested that long-term storage of grain was impractical. Even after the Kansas Alliance became a new political party, little enthusiasm existed within the organization for the subtreasury. During a visit to Kansas in March 1891, Macune was alarmed to hear alliance members saying that his plan was a "very good thing for the cotton and tobacco growers in the south, but it would not work so well in the wheat growing districts."[63]

Some farmers may have achieved a fairly sophisticated understanding of the Greenback monetary theory undergirding the land-loan plan, but most ordinary members of the Alliance (and even many leaders) probably had an incomplete grasp of the money question. The president of the Dry Creek Alliance of Kansas, for example, urging farmers to hold their crops sixty to ninety days for higher prices, showed little understanding of Greenback doctrine. "Those who can't hold out," he said, should go to their banker, who will "help you for that length of time." We must "knock out the eye of the middle man," he proclaimed, "he is the man who is hurting us at present."[64] This focus on middle men, although a commonplace in rural American culture, was, within the logic of Greenback analysis, entirely misplaced. Greenback theory implied that the problem per se was not that grain merchants held prices down or pocketed excessive profits on the transaction between buyer and seller; problems such as middle men gouging farmers were symptoms of the underlying condition of insufficient currency. Moreover, the Dry Creek Alliance president's advice to farmers to turn to bankers ignored the fundamental Greenback proposition that interest was the mechanism by which the nonproductive classes (bankers and financial speculators) accumulated wealth from the labor of farmers and other producers.

Few ordinary members understood the subtle distinctions within Greenback monetary theory between money issued by government fiat (greenbacks) and money based on a notion of intrinsic value (free silver), a point that was not always made clear by Alliance leaders. Farmers often looked upon free silver as the simplest and most direct means to increase the money supply and to raise prices. A typical suballiance in Kansas, affirming that "the present financial depression is caused by an insufficient amount of money in circulation," resolved in favor of free and unlimited silver coinage at the earliest possible date, evidently without realizing any of the possible limitations of free silver.[65]

The Alliance created a new community of farmers. Through the weekly meeting of the suballiance, farmers overcame rural isolation and shared a variety of experiences while working together to achieve a common purpose.[66] Meetings regularly included singing, speech making, and literary exercises, activities that encouraged individual expression and helped bind members together. Although some of the activities of the suballiance were meant simply to entertain—for example, the Lone Tree Alliance debated whether or not "fire is a more destructive agent than water"—most meetings had a political dimension. Singing Alliance songs expressed solidarity within a political movement:

> Farmer, now, stand by your vow,
> Stick fast unto your farm and plow;
> Monopolies we must put down,
> And then we're bound to win the crown.
> For equal rights we do implore:
> That's all we ask, and nothing more.[67]

The suballiance attempted to put democratic ideals into practice in its everyday affairs, with the local structured to encourage maximum participation. Meetings were conducted according to parliamentary procedure, allowing members to introduce and debate motions on any subject at almost any time.[68] This democratic format invited each member to participate in the decisions affecting the organization. The concept of a self-governing body was also enhanced through providing almost all members with the opportunity to hold an office in the organization. Offices rotated frequently, and they expanded in number to accommodate growth in membership. The May Alliance of Nebraska included not only the expected president, vice-president, secretary, treasurer, and lecturer but also an assistant lecturer, a sergeant-at-arms, a doorkeeper, and an assistant doorkeeper.[69] One suspects that the group could have functioned without an assistant doorkeeper, but holding office allowed members to have a sense of their own importance to the community, and it served as a model in helping farmers to participate in political life.

Any mass political movement requires a coherent justification for its challenge to the existing economic and political order. The Alliance drew upon rich traditions to give its members a sense of belonging to a righteous cause, one of which was evangelical religion. When observed superficially, the religious-like enthusiasm of the movement can reinforce a picture of Populists as backward-looking or irrational, but such a conclusion misses the point: The Alliance/Populist movement transformed religious traditions for its own political purposes. Like the contemporary social-gospel movement, the Alliance used Christian principles to critique social injustice in its message that Christ had "fed the hungry, healed the sick, and clothed the naked, but the nation ignored His example." Since economic injustice resulted from the sins of selfishness and greed, people must learn to obey the Decalogue and to heed the Golden Rule. But the Alliance did not rely upon people voluntarily to adopt Christian precepts; they looked to the state to establish the conditions necessary for economic justice.[70]

The tradition of the "producer ethic" also provided the Alliance with legitimacy. This ethic, deeply rooted in American political culture, was based on a labor theory of value and saw society as divided into two classes: a class of "producers," including farmers, artisans, wage workers, and small businessmen, and a predatory class of speculators, bankers, and lawyers, who performed no socially useful function. The producer ethic was embedded in the democratic doctrine of popular sovereignty, which held that the government drew its authority from "the people," defined as the producing classes. An unjust economic order, therefore, resulted from the illegitimate activities of nonproducers both in the marketplace and in the institutions of government. From this perspective, then, the Alliance saw itself as a movement of the people exercising their natural right to self-government in opposition to an illegitimate class of nonproducers who had unjustly usurped sovereignty.[71]

The traditions of Christianity and the producer ethic fused to give the Alliance a substantial fund of moral capital and a boundless supply of optimism. Protestant millennialism encouraged a sense that salvation from monopoly and the establishment of Christ's kingdom on earth was imminent. Popular democratic beliefs also allowed a sense of immediacy, for there had once been a time, perhaps at the nation's Founding or during the era of Jackson or Lincoln, when the people had controlled their own affairs.

Given their numerical superiority and once they were aroused, it would not be difficult for the people to reestablish their lost sovereignty.

The Alliance encompassed the entire family as men, women, and children attended meetings and social gatherings.[72] Although the Alliance did not cause a revolution in the family, its democratic "movement culture" did lead to some changes in the traditional roles of women and children. In keeping with accepted customs, farm wives prepared the food at Alliance gatherings—and cleaned up after—but they also debated measures of economic and social reform at the meetings and occasionally occupied positions of leadership, particularly as suballiance lecturers. Women and men who welcomed women's nontraditional public activities justified them in terms of domestic ideology. Annie L. Diggs, one of the leading women in the Kansas Alliance, rejected the notion that "women should cook and gossip, rock cradles, and darn socks—merely these and nothing more" and contended that "women should watch and work in all things which shape and mold the home, whether 'money,' 'land' or 'transportation.' So now Alliance women should look at politics and trace the swift relation to the home—their special sphere." An editorial in the *Advocate* instructed women members never to think that "the questions of political economy are out of your sphere. They bear with terrible directness upon your God-given kingdom of home."[73]

Economic crisis made the connection between politics and the home particularly apparent. In the event of foreclosure, as the *Advocate* observed, "the calamity of homelessness falls as heavily upon the women as upon the men. If low prices for farm products create the necessity for pinching economy, the brunt of managing falls upon woman." Since women bore the burden of unjust legislation, reasoned the *Advocate*, they should "take part in the program of open meetings." This did not mean that they should speak on "Flower Culture on the Farm"; farm women should address hard questions of political economy: "The Sub-Treasury Bill" or "Cumulative Taxation." The sense of crisis within the Alliance community clearly justified an otherwise problematic reconceptualization of women's domestic work to justify a voice in public debate on political issues. Just as "our dauntless revolutionary foremothers" had acted heroically in the "days of '76," the *Advocate* urged women to "play the same high part that true womanhood has ever played in times of struggle and of danger. . . . Our warfare is one of contending principles and ideas, but just as surely do we need the qualities of heroism, of courage, of strong devotion and ardent zeal, as we would if our battle was one of bullets and bayonets. . . . It is only needed that women should be fully informed as to the gravity of the situation for them to rise to the full measure of past heroism."[74]

It was one thing for women to claim the right to speak out about public affairs during a period of crisis, but should they have the vote on a permanent basis? To some extent the answer to this question was related to the issue of whether the Alliance should go into third party politics. For Vee Vincent, woman suffrage was a corollary of the third-party proposition that male-dominated politics had become inherently corrupt: "If we must live under the law of the land, we want a voice in choosing the law makers. We have left it too long to the male half of the citizens, and they in turn have chosen as law makers men who work for the money power, and against the people as a whole." Another proponent of female suffrage contended that if "women had been in partnership with men in law-making things would never have been in the muddle they now are"; reform of national affairs was a matter of "national housekeeping." In the past "no woman's hand has been there to adjust and regulate, no woman's penetrating eye to search out dark and hidden corners, where moth and rust corrupt, and thieves hide away to steal."[75]

Other women, however, used domestic metaphors to argue against female enfranchisement. In an address to the Chase County Alliance (Kansas), Mrs. M. E. Carpenter urged women to "be man's help, comfort and sweetest, purest joy" in his fight against "monopolies, trusts, [and] combines," but when women "want to vote or dabble in politics I think of my little girl in her white dress playing in a puddle of water; she pleases herself, raises a commotion, soils her dress, and does no good at all." Woman's work was "infinitely greater than this—teaching her boys how to vote."[76] Although Carpenter's views on the desirability of a third party are not known, her position that women should teach their sons how to vote hinted that traditional two-party politics could be effective and perhaps obviated the need for a third party. Certainly it was theoretically possible for someone to uphold woman suffrage and not advocate a third party, and vice versa, but a correspondence was clear between the arguments for a third party and for woman suffrage.

The Alliance also had an impact on the political awareness of children, who, judging from their letters to the children's column in the *Nonconformist*, often grasped fundamental teachings of the Alliance school. Thirteen-year-old Theodosia Page of Thayer, Kansas, had four brothers, an aunt and uncle, and both parents in the Alliance—she had learned that "if the great Money King don't loosen his grip a little it will come to the bayonet, and that pretty soon, too, if we don't get some relief." Another girl of ten may not have had the answer, but she knew "something" should be done to "bring about better prices for things the farmers have to sell."[77]

Through the Alliance, men, women, and children took pride in their position as hard-working producers, and farmers displayed their newly discovered sense of self-worth through Alliance processions. A typical Alliance picnic at Valley Falls, Kansas, in October 1889, brought over 3,000 farmers to town in a procession consisting of nearly 200 farm wagons. The Blue Mound Alliance carried banners, undoubtedly made by the women, protesting injustices: "Two bushels of corn for one pound of coffee" and "Money Trusts; Fat Capitalists and lean Farmers." The Swabville Alliance had "eight young ladies in costume of white and blue" on a "handsomely decorated wagon"; the procession was "an imposing sight, one that powerfully demonstrated the strength of the Alliance in this section of Kansas." Another procession of 4,000 to 5,000 farmers in McPherson County was led by a steam thresher and a band playing atop a separator. "This day," wrote S. M. Scott, was remembered "as the date when the farmers of McPherson County spoke to the world that they were equal to the occasion. From this day on the farmers seemed proud of their occupation."[78]

During late 1889 and early 1890 the Alliance mobilized tens of thousands of farmers desperate to find a way out of hard times. In schoolrooms across Kansas and Nebraska, farmers sensed that they could determine their destiny. Through hearing the words of their leaders and by discussing and debating various proposals among themselves, they could arrive at a solution to economic injustice. United farmers could then assert their democratic right to choose representatives and to restore government to the hands of the people; a responsive government would regulate economic affairs and recreate equality of opportunity. In these schoolrooms the Alliance created a political community.

Some leaders and members were committed to a third-party strategy early on, and a few prescient individuals may have foreseen the probability that the Alliance would soon nominate its own candidates independent of any existing party, but most Alliance members probably expected the organization to remain true to its constitutional commitment to nonpartisanship. Yet as farmers considered the "science of economical government," they developed new views of the existing political system. Alliance farmers in Kansas and Nebraska began to take stock of the record of the two parties, particularly the Republican Party in their own states. Economic hardship was the proximate cause of the Alliance's rapid growth, but the future direction of the organization would depend upon an assessment of political conditions.

7

From Schoolroom to Political Party: Third-Party Formation in Kansas and Nebraska

The Kansas and Nebraska Farmers' Alliances were dedicated to pursuing the political interests of farmers in a "strictly non-partisan spirit."[1] As the Alliance grew rapidly in winter 1889–1890, however, members and leaders were increasingly drawn into a debate about the political future of the Alliance, with the immediate issue centering on state-level political strategy. Even those advocates of a third party who perceived the necessity for national legislation understood that forming a new party at the state level was a necessary prelude to organizing a national party. Accordingly, the context of state politics provided a backdrop for this debate and was a critical element in shaping its resolution. Although the Alliance evaluated the party system at both the national and the state level in considering an appropriate strategy, the organization's experience with state politics shaped its general perceptions of political possibilities at both levels.

The unresponsiveness of the Republican Party in the Kansas and Nebraska legislative sessions of 1889 was strong evidence of corporate control of state politics and argued powerfully for a third party; the GOP's rejection of agrarian demands in late 1889 and early 1890 provided further proof of its intransigence. With the Democrats so far removed from power and the Republicans unwilling to yield, each state's party system clearly was incapable of responding to farmers' pleas. The failure of the GOP to make even modest concessions tipped the scales toward forming a new state party and at the same time increased the strength of the position that monopoly controlled the two national parties.

For reasons that are not entirely clear, Kansas and Nebraska Alliance leaders made little effort to influence their legislatures in early 1889. William Peffer's *Kansas Farmer* gave extensive coverage to the Kansas legislative sessions, but neither he nor other Kansas Alliance leaders attempted to mobilize farmers to lobby the legislature. Jay Burrows of the Nebraska Alliance was evidently uninterested in pursuing state railroad reform in early 1889 and instead devoted his efforts to securing the Nebraska legislature's endorsement of the Northern Alliance's memorial to Congress in favor of the land-loan plan. To "get rid of Burrows," a chagrined solon later confessed, the Nebraska legislature approved the memorial, but when national newspapers broadcast its assertion that the amount of outstanding mortgages in the state was an astonishing $150 million, the embarrassed legislature, fearing that the state's reputation had been permanently besmirched, rushed a new resolution to Washington repudiating the charge that the Cornhusker state did not flow with milk and honey.[2] Following this episode, Burrows continued to advocate the land-loan plan, but he began to counsel that state-level reform should precede national reform.[3]

The approach of a new round of politicking in fall 1889 initiated a lively discussion of political strategy in the columns of the Alliance press. Charles Wooster, farmer and editor, advised that the true policy of the farmer is to "work within the old party lines." If in the past the parties had failed to represent the people, Wooster argued, it was the fault of the people for neglecting to "turn out to the primaries EN MASSE to choose faithful and efficient men to represent them in party councils." Others disparaged this approach. John Long thought that Wooster "means all right, but . . . he has not got all the moss off yet." If farmers remained in the old parties, Long contended, "they will keep us fighting over the bloody shirt, or tariff and free trade. . . . Monopoly wants us in the old parties, for there they can control us." A third correspondent offered a compromise: "Let us try the old part[ies] once more and see that good men are put up for office." But if the parties could not be purified, "we will and must form a third party."[4] Some of the strongest voices against a third party came from proponents of economic cooperation. The leadership of the Kansas State Alliance Exchange, fearing that politics would divert the Alliance from its cooperative endeavors, opposed any "discussion of partisan politics within the Alliance" as this would create "discord in our order." On the other hand, those people who favored third-party action counseled farmers against forming local cooperatives since these would antagonize local merchants, whose support would be necessary to build a broadly based party.[5]

Although the majority in the Kansas and Nebraska Alliances in 1889 favored a wait-and-see approach, some county Alliances did support Independent tickets in the fall. In Kansas third-party activity was closely linked to the Union Labor Party. In Cowley County, the Independents made their move when several Union Labor men attended the Republican county convention in September. When regular Republicans controlled the convention and nominated their candidates, the Union Laborites, who had probably anticipated defeat, bolted the convention, denounced the "Winfield office trust," and called upon Republican farmers to support a "People's Ticket."[6] With support from Kansas Alliance president Benjamin Clover, himself a resident of Cowley County, the new ticket swept to victory in November. The local Republican organ attributed the result to the Farmers' Alliance: "The cause of the 'disturbance' is plainly shown by reference to the table of returns. In every locality where the Alliance was strong, the People's ticket had large majorities, and in every township where there was no Alliance, the usual vote was cast."[7] People's, Independent, or Union Labor tickets also appeared in Bourbon, Anderson, Montgomery, Harper, and Chautauqua Counties among others, but the majority of Kansas Alliances stayed clear of independent politics.[8]

In Nebraska, where the Union Labor Party was weaker, the scope of independent political activity was more limited. Led by Omer M. Kem, Union Labor candidate for university regent, the Custer County Alliance formally nominated a slate of candidates in September. The response of the Alliance leadership to this move clarified their opposition to a third-party strategy: The executive committee of the state Alliance ruled the action of the Custer County farmers in violation of the order's constitution and denounced them for deceiving those people who had joined the Alliance under the belief that it was a nonpartisan organization. In explaining the leadership's censure Burrows conceded that it might be necessary to organize a temporary local third party under exceptional circumstances, but in such cases, it would be better to call a "people's convention, in which all the citizens could join." This move would achieve the same results, and "members who did not coincide in such action [would] be left free, and not feel that they had been deceived when they joined." Beyond this, however, Burrows cautioned against third parties in general:

> Every effort either in county or state, to transform the Alliance into a political party has been disastrous . . . . The State Alliance formed the antimonopoly party [in 1882]. It elected Mr. Sturtevant [sic] state treasurer, a democrat—and he was the only state officer it ever elected. But it destroyed the Alliance, and it took years to restore it to its present position. If the Alliance at that time had simply used the agencies at its hand, through the principle of a balance of power, it could have placed reliable Alliance men in every state office, and controlled the legislature. . . . It is

a hundred times easier to elect our men through one of [the existing two parties] than to do so by forming a new party.[9]

Burrows's nonpartisan approach presumed that access to party power was open and that farmers could gain control of party machinery simply by exercising their numerical superiority. Nevertheless, although some Alliances had achieved success within the party system, as in Furnas County where the Republicans had nominated an Alliance member for county treasurer over an "ardent admirer of Jay Gould," events at the Republican state convention demonstrated that railroads held a tight grip on political power in Nebraska. Prior to the convention there had been little doubt that the Republicans would renominate Judge M. B. Reese for supreme court justice. Although Reese was hardly a wild-eyed radical, he was identified with the antimonopoly wing of the party, and the railroads did not trust him. Through the liberal distribution of free passes and a vigorous smear campaign on the eve of the convention, the railroads defeated Reese on the first ballot. According to one observer, the convention was an undisguised display of railroad aggression: "Railroad attorneys were on hand in unusual numbers, and the customary policy of keeping these paid agents of the roads as much as possible out of sight was abandoned. It seemed as if the roads wished to give the politicians of the state and judges of the courts an intimidating object lesson in the power of the corporations to control a convention."[10] Burrows saw the convention's actions as another deed in a long series of Republican betrayals: "Again we witness the political machinery of the dominant party used to defeat the will of the people. Again we see combined monopolies seize that which should be the agency of free government and prostitute it to the base purpose of retiring a judge whose only fault is that he would not be their tool, and elevating in his stead a man whom they think they can use." Outraged, Burrows called for an independent state convention to nominate Reese "and thus make a square issue between the people and the corporations."[11] Local Alliances were also angry about the railroads' blatant defeat of Reese. An officer of a suballiance in Lamar wrote to Burrows, "Having read of the defeat of Reese in our paper, I want to say . . . that the indignation of the citizens of our neighborhood at the proceedings of the railroad monopoly know no bounds, and they declare they will not vote for a railroad nominee and unless the Democrats put up a straight man who will stand firm for the people, we urge you to use all influence in your power to have Reese . . . run independent. . . . We cannot and will no longer be ruled by this infernal B & M gang."[12]

The corporations struck another blow on 15 October when a Republican convention nominated Gilbert Laws to fill the vacant congressional seat in the second district. The *Alliance* reported Laws's nomination "with feelings of profound sorrow." Although Laws himself was a "courteous gentleman," the "prominent fact stands out in all its nakedness, that a corporation, an artificial creation of the law . . . with no soul and no patriotism . . . steps into the political arena with the people who created it, and within a week dictates to them who shall wear the judicial ermine in their highest court, and who shall sit in the highest place among their makers of laws."[13] Other independent papers denounced Laws as "another tool of the B & M railroad." Reviewing the "glaring outrages" that had been committed during the fall conventions, the *York Times* hinted at bolting the Republican ticket. The *Ulysses Dispatch* asked had the GOP "come to that point where anybody can be a congressman if agreeable to the railroads? Are the republicans compelled to vote the ticket and thereby place a premium upon such unjust and disgraceful nominations?" The answer was clear: "In the language of 'Old Hickory' Jackson, 'by the eternal' no!"[14]

Although nothing came of the talk of independent politics, the events of October strengthened the argument for a new party. The scales had not yet tipped in the direction of third-party action, but the belligerence of the railroads provided further evidence of the corruption of the Nebraska party system and added more weight to the third-party side of the debate over political strategy. The victory of the Custer County Alliance by a two-to-one margin along with the success of a "Farmers' and Laborer's Ticket" in Antelope County was proof that such independence could be effective, Burrows's fears notwithstanding.[15] But Burrows's outburst and his call for an independent convention following Reese's defeat did not last; by December he was again urging "all the gentlemen who have resolutions in their breast pocket making the Alliance a political party to remember that it has once been utterly destroyed in this state by such action."[16] Yet the fuse was growing shorter. Nonpartisanship would remain a viable position only if it could gain results.

In the cruel winter of 1889–1890, farmers cried out for immediate relief, demanding that their state governments take emergency measures. Kansas farmers initiated a petition campaign requesting the governor to call an extra session of the legislature to reconsider the two-year redemption and stay-of-execution laws it had rejected in the spring.[17] In a circular letter to all Alliance members, G. W. Roberts, chairman of a grass-roots committee, acknowledged that such legislation "is but a small fraction of the legislation needed to dispel the dark clouds that intervene between us and relief"; still, it was more important than "anything else within our immediate reach." Roberts assured the farmers that Governor Humphrey "is willing to hear us; that he is in sympathy with us; that he stands ready to do all in his power to extricate us from impending peril."[18] But those people already convinced of the futility of nonpartisanship opposed a special session. The "only result of a special session of the political confidence men, sharks, and lickspittles elected by the party of great moral ideas," predicted the *Nonconformist*, "would be unprecedented corruption and great increase of taxation."[19] On the other hand, although Peffer agreed that reform from a special session was unlikely, the bearded sage gave his wholehearted support to the campaign for a new session if only because it was "a rebuke to the Legislature and the party which controlled it" and would help "the authorities to understand that the voters are in earnest."[20]

Governor Humphrey replied to the deluge of petitions by expressing his deepest sympathy for distressed farmers and vowed to give their entreaties his "earnest consideration."[21] Some Republican politicians, primarily concerned with the safety of the party, urged Humphrey to call a special session. Samuel S. Dix, a wealthy non-Alliance farmer, informed the governor that "local politicians are scared, two of them said to me today 'We believe the Republicans will [lose] the legislature.'" A special session, Dix believed, "will quiet everything," but if the governor ignored the farmers, "we're gone. I don't think there is any question about it, almost every farmer belongs to the Alliance and they are red hot."[22]

Other voices also sought the governor's ear. From Albany, New York, the president of the R. J. Waddell Investment Company informed Humphrey that any law damaging creditors "would result in a great injury to the State at large in making every lender call his funds in as fast as due." George Peck of the Atchison, Topeka & Santa Fe could "conceive of nothing which would be as disastrous to the welfare of our State" as calling a special session. "Already," he wrote, "the demagogues and howlers are seriously injuring our credit in the East, and an extra session of the Legislature would be the finishing nail in the coffin." But what of the political risks in ignoring the farmers' petitions? Edward Russell, a mortgage broker in Lawrence, Kansas, reminded Humphrey that the Grange had "spent itself in a short time" and assured him that although the Alliance leaders were "very noisy," they were "only political wrecks." Like grasshoppers, he assured Humphrey, "they cannot be measured by their capacity for noise, but need only to be pointed out to see how little we need worry as to them or the mischief they can work."[23]

In a futile attempt to please all sides the governor appealed to the state's railroads to grant a temporary rate reduction on grain shipped to the East.

The railroads, Humphrey evidently reasoned, fearing that the threat of legis-lation against creditors would diminish the value of Kansas railroad invest-ments, would lower rates to avoid a special session. Taking note of the farmers' campaign, Humphrey urged railroad officials in late January to give farmers an "emergency rate [to] tide them over the present emergency," a re-sponse that would do much to promote "that good will which should ever characterize the relation between railroads and the people."[24] Although the railroads contended that a rate reduction would only depress prices further by throwing more grain on the market, they did recognize the political ne-cessity to make some concession and agreed in early February to reduce their rate to Chicago by 10 percent.[25] Peffer regarded the economic benefits of this reduction as inconsequential, but the decision of the railroads was a valuable step, he wrote, because it showed "the power of the people." Other observers, however, were more cynical. One suballiance claimed that the railroads had initiated the petition drive themselves so that they could "win an easy victory over the universal demand for lower, a great deal lower, rates."[26]

Although the governor did not formally reject a special session, by mid-February he was quietly making it known that the legislators would not be summoned to Topeka. To the chairman of the Riley County Republican central committee Humphrey indicated that stay and redemption laws would be "in violation of the Constitution of the United States, which pro-vides that no State shall pass a law impairing the obligations on contracts. The Legislature, at its session one year ago, considered this very question and determined the same as I have suggested."[27] The Republican press un-derlined the point that laws impairing contracts would be unconstitutional and would destroy the state's credit. For the *Capital* there was "but one hon-est way out of the situation—and that is to pay [the debts] as contracted."[28] Yet this was not an option for cash-poor farmers facing foreclosure, and it seemed to those struggling to meet their obligations that the state's chief ex-ecutive had ignored the suffering majority for the sake of a powerful minor-ity.

Any legitimacy the Kansas GOP still possessed disappeared in the face of the contemptuous attitude shown toward the Alliance by Senator Ingalls, Kansas' leading Republican. In early February Peffer requested that Ingalls state his recommendations for relieving the depressed condition of agricul-ture; specifically, he asked if the senator favored an increase in the volume of money in circulation, reformation of the national banking system, and free coinage of silver.[29] Based on Ingalls's past utterances, his response was un-likely to satisfy the Alliance. Indeed, only a month before, the senator had written that the conditions facing farmers were caused by factors "which leg-islation does not produce and which statutes cannot cure."[30] Ingalls did not even give Peffer the courtesy of a response; instead he mocked the ideals of political reformers, the Farmers' Alliance included, in an April interview with the *New York World* in which he characterized the "purification of poli-tics" as "an iridescent dream" and lectured naive reformers that "govern-ment is force [and] politics is a battle for supremacy." This "modern cant about the corruption of politics," Ingalls sighed, "is fatiguing in the ex-treme."[31] As late as early April Peffer was still hoping the GOP would re-spond to the farmers. "Alliance members," he informed party politicians, "expect to vote for persons friendly to their demands, and they hope to find them in the ranks of their own parties." But Ingalls's cynical defense of polit-ical corruption solidified Peffer's growing alienation from the dominant party. Three months having elapsed since his query to Ingalls and having re-ceived no reply, Peffer had little choice; in mid-May he announced he would not support Ingalls's reelection. The editor of the most influential agricul-tural paper in the state was at last ready to wash his hands of the Grand Old Party.[32]

In Nebraska desperate farmers staked their hopes for relief on railroad rate reductions. "Notwithstanding the enormous corn crop of 1889," the *Bee* ob-served in January 1890, "the farmers of the state will scarcely realize enough to pay for the labor involved. In the river counties the prices obtained are barely profitable, while in the interior counties the crop is a loss." To meet this crisis Gov. John Milton Thayer begged the railroads to lower the inter-state rate on grain by 5 cents per 100 pounds as such a reduction would cause an immediate rise in the price of corn and would also promote a "bet-ter feeling between the producers and the transportation companies."[33] At the same time the state Board of Transportation, at the initiative of Attor-ney General William Leese, adopted a resolution condemning Nebraska's lo-cal rates for being "unjust and unreasonable" since they were "from 50 to 350 per cent higher" than rates in Iowa. Within a few days, however, the other four members of the board rescinded this resolution as "it would be unwise" to take a hostile position toward the roads when they were consid-ering a voluntary reduction.[34]

The railroad managers were reluctant to comply with Thayer's request. Thomas L. Kimball of the Union Pacific protested that if rates were cut in Nebraska, the railroads would have to give farmers in surrounding states a similar reduction, further glutting the market and lowering prices. But a spe-cial delegation of Nebraska government officials journeyed to Chicago in early February to plead for an emergency rate, and the railroad managers were forced to yield, if only slightly. Instead of reducing rates by 5 cents, as Thayer had requested, the railroads granted a reduction of only 10 percent, which amounted to 2 cents per 100 pounds.[35]

This paltry reduction gave little satisfaction; Leese stated flatly that the new rate would not help farmers at all and called for a reduction of 10 cents, not 10 percent. The other members of the board defended the railroads' refusal to grant a greater reduction by pointing out that rates had fallen substantially since 1875.[36] Although technically true, this argument missed the point entirely. Farmers could not see why wealthy railroads should not shoulder a fair share of the burden by slashing rates by as much as one half. Several suballiances condemned the small reduction as a "bait to catch the farmer's vote" and praised Leese's stance.[37] The farmers of the Palestine Alliance of Platte County demanded "that the state railroad commission . . . take steps to compell [sic] all the Railroads to reduce the freight rates in the state of Neb. at least 50 percent. not only on corn, wheat, Oats, etc., but also on Merchandise of every discription [sic]." If the board refused, the governor should call a special session of the legislature, and if "the farmers & labouring men cannot get Justice from the present addminestration [sic]," the Palestine Alliance wished "to impress upon their minds that November will soon role [sic] around."[38]

Over the next few months, Republican antimonopolists (led by Rosewater and Leese) and the Farmers' Alliance fought to obtain rates for Nebraska as low as those in Iowa. At meetings of the Board of Transportation Leese introduced resolution after resolution requiring that Nebraska roads adopt the Iowa schedule of rates, but these were inevitably defeated.[39] Conservative papers such as the *Nebraska State Journal* contended that Iowa farmers had gained nothing through lower local rates since these had nothing to do with the interstate rates on which most farm produce was shipped to market and argued that a reduction in local rates in Nebraska would reduce railroad earnings, making it less likely that the roads would grant further voluntary concessions on the far more important through rates to Chicago.[40] Antimonopolists and farmers responded by advancing the common although erroneous view that through rates consisted of the sum of the locals and that reducing local rates would therefore have an immediate and direct impact on interstate rates.[41]

In the meantime Governor Thayer intensified his effort to convince the railroads to make further voluntary reductions. In a letter to the Central Traffic Association of Missouri in March he accused the railroads of having made the earlier insignificant reduction knowing full well that it would result in a corresponding decline in prices. When prices did fall, those critics who had predicted the decline "were enabled to say 'I told you so.'" Thayer contended, however, that if the roads had made a reduction of 5 cents, as he had originally requested, speculators would have been unable to depress prices. The railroads, the governor continued, were prosperous, and the condition of farmers was growing worse. "The farmers of Nebraska are aroused now as they never were before. They demand justice and just treatment and will not cease that demand till they get it."[42]

As the Board of Transportation and the railroads remained resolutely opposed to further concessions, farmers began a petition campaign for a special session of the legislature in early April.[43] Yet for many members in the Alliance, it was too late to hope for reform from the existing political system. Indeed, the Nebraska Republican Party was showing signs of cracking under the stress of grievances too long suppressed and reforms too long denied. On 21 March former senator Charles Van Wyck announced that he was leaving the GOP.[44] A meeting of Republican antimonopolists on 26 March protested "the domination of corporate power in the republican party" and called for a mass convention of antimonopoly Republicans to be held in two months.[45] In early May Burrows advised the Alliance to "see to it that the members of the next legislature are selected from its own members" by nominating candidates through one of the two parties or by running "independent candidates if you prefer," a message that represented a significant softening in his attitude toward independent politics. Although he cautioned against "any premature step by a few extremists" to form a state party, clearly the moment for such an effort might be near: "Time is doing good work. The seeds are being planted. The air is full of moral dynamite that will explode in the fullness of time."[46]

Sometime in spring 1890 the scales tilted, and most Alliance leaders and members determined to strike out on their own. The continued unresponsiveness of the GOP during early 1890 underscored the party's previous record of broken promises and its submission to financial and corporate interests; a nonpartisan strategy was no longer tenable given the opposition to agrarian demands. Although third-party formation occurred in the context of state politics, Alliance members and leaders were aware of the ultimate necessity of securing national legislation. Suballiances petitioned Congress in early 1890 to adopt the land-loan plan and to free coinage of silver. During spring and early summer, it appeared that free-coinage legislation would pass Congress, but the situation at the national level was ambiguous and offered no clear guidance to those observers who were trying to decide whether the two parties were beyond hope.[47] The evidence from the state party system, however, was obvious and was even more persuasive as it was close to home. Moreover, since the fall campaign would be a state campaign, the initial question for the Alliance in early 1890 was whether or not to form a state party. Although third-party advocates indicted the national party system and hoped eventually for a national third party, their immediate objective, given the decentralized structure of political parties in a federal state, was perforce to organize a state party. The question of organizing a national party in Kansas or Nebraska in early 1890 was never raised.

That the state political environment was the primary context for third-party formation is evidenced in the farmers' expressions of political alienation. The Grant Alliance of Nemaha County, Nebraska, for example, observed that through "attorneys and paid political agents who are located in every county [and] the free pass system," corporations had "manipulate[d] primaries, and county, and state conventions [and] . . . have controlled the legislation of our State." The Bunker Hill Alliance of Ellsworth County, Kansas, deplored the "pretentious, sham legislature of the last session . . . on the interest question" and stated its intention to support only those candidates who had "identified themselves with the agricultural and laboring classes."[48] Although these resolutions did not call directly for a new party—suballiances were awaiting the action of state leaders on this question—farmers certainly weighed political action in light of state politics.

The centrality of state politics to the debate on political tactics is further illustrated by the fact that the effectiveness of the Iowa Alliance's nonpartisan strategy was an issue. One apostle of a new party in Kansas advised against nonpartisanship since it was proving to be a failure in Iowa, where Alliance legislators were being "whipped into party caucus, and forced to vote for [Senator] Allison." Burrows gave an alternative evaluation of the Iowa Alliance's success in politics when he wistfully observed that the Iowa Alliance "seems to have complete control" of the legislature and predicted that it would pass legislation against usury and to tax mortgages.[49]

The formal organization of a new party began in Kansas with a special meeting of county Alliance presidents in Topeka on 25 March, and the resolutions they adopted document the Kansas Alliance's priorities at this crucial moment. Several resolutions concerned national legislation, the most prominent demanding the enactment of a land-loan law "similar to that proposed by Senator Leland Stanford," which would offer the "greatest and most permanent relief." The county presidents also called on the federal government to use the treasury surplus to employ idle labor on public works and further demanded government construction of a "double track line of railroad" from the Midwest to the Atlantic seaboard. These resolutions gave evidence of the careful consideration and discussion of "the way out" that had occurred over the previous several months. Proposals for state-level reform were more numerous. Applying their understanding of the money question creatively, the county presidents demanded a law reducing the face value of mortgages in proportion to the rate of deflation from the time of the original contract. They further requested the election of railroad commissioners with "plenary powers to regulate [rates] as is now the law in the State of Iowa" and that a "cumulative system of taxation be levied on lands, held for speculative purposes." The county presidents especially desired the stay-of-execution and redemption laws that had been denied by the Republican Party and demanded a state constitutional amendment to circumvent objections to the constitutionality of such measures. Observing that the "last legislature was elected on demands that were in the interest of the farmers" but that its actions "were adverse in their effects to the farmers interests," they resolved against convening a special session of the legislature. This indictment of the state party system logically led to a statement of political intentions: "We will no longer divide on party lines and will only cast our votes for candidates of the people, for the people, and by the people." Spelling out the implications of this general principle, the meeting declared its opposition to the reelection of Senator Ingalls and agreed to organize a "People's State Central Committee" consisting of an Alliance leader from each congressional district to be appointed by President Clover.[50]

The final step in formal party organization occurred at a "convention of industrial organizations" on 12 June, which consisted of forty-one delegates from the Farmers' Alliance, ten from the Farmers' Mutual Benefit Association, seven from the Grange, twenty-eight from the Knights of Labor, and four from Single Tax clubs. This gathering unanimously agreed that the "name 'People's Party' is adopted as the title under which we will base our political action" and set 13 August as the date for a state convention to nominate a state ticket.[51] Although the Kansas People's Party was largely a movement of farmers, the presence of the KOL at the founding convention indicates that many labor leaders supported the new party. Populists hoped to gain the support of workingmen, but conditions were unfavorable for the mobilization of labor. In Kansas City the KOL had captured the local Republican Party in 1886, electing an Irish-Catholic stonemason, Thomas F. Hannan, as mayor. As a result of the formation of a Republican/Labor coalition, the Union Labor Party chose not to run a slate of candidates in Wyandotte County in 1888. The Knights declined in the late 1880s and had lost much of their political power by 1890, but the fact that the Republicans and Democrats had learned to appeal to working-class voters in Kansas City would make it difficult for Populists to gain inroads there. Moreover, the Populists' identification with prohibition and woman suffrage would hinder their effort to attract urban wage earners in larger cities.[52]

In Nebraska the process of formal party organization differed only in details. A meeting of the officers of the state Alliance in May considered whether to organize a new party. Even at this late hour many state leaders opposed such a radical course, believing it would be best to continue "the educational features of the organization." But under mounting pressure from third-party proponents, the leadership decided to circulate petitions calling for a "People's Independent Convention"; if a sufficient number of people signed the petitions, state leaders would call for a convention.[53] As the petitions circulated, antimonopoly Republicans sought to keep Republican farmers within a revitalized GOP. At a mass meeting held on 20 May Leese, Rosewater, and other antimonopolists expressed alarm over the "intense discontent" among the Republican voters, demanded that the railroad corporations "stop interference with our conventions and legislatures," and called for the Republican Party to hold a convention as early as the second week in July. An early convention, the antimonopolists evidently hoped, would encourage Republican farmers to participate in local conventions and stay within the party.[54] Although many farmers looked favorably on Leese and Rosewater, their efforts came too late; farmers had abandoned the notion that the GOP could be reformed.

On 23 May Governor Thayer made a desperate bid to keep Alliance farmers from bolting, startling the state by calling the legislature into special session on 5 June in order to enact a law establishing maximum freight rates. It was far too late for this maneuver, and in any event, Thayer quickly reversed himself when stunned GOP and business leaders denounced his reckless proclamation. One prominent person in Lincoln dismissed the governor's move as "political buncombe," and another predicted that the enactment of a maximum-rate law would not only lead to "ruin" of the railroads but would also destroy the "industrial, the commercial, the intellectual, and the moral advancement of the state." This fiasco clinched the case against the GOP. Burrows attributed Thayer's reversal to the influence of George W. Holrege of the B & M and wrote that "the circus of the past few months, coupled with the recall of the Governor's proclamation," had "plainly manifested" the "domination of railroad influence" in the state. The only way to "SMASH THESE MACHINES," Burrows concluded, would be to convene independent and county conventions. In the meantime, with 15,000 farmers having signed the petition for a new party, state Alliance leaders called for an independent convention on 29 July to create a state party organization and to nominate candidates.[55]

The conventions to nominate representatives of the people in summer 1890 met in an atmosphere of profound crisis. An address "to the people" issued by the Kansas People's Party state central committee declared that "a crisis is approaching in the affairs of our government that calls for prompt and united action on the part of her intelligent and patriotic citizens, if we are to maintain our independence as a people, and our liberties and equality as citizens of a great republic." At stake was nothing less than the salvation of republican government from the conspiratorial designs of monarchy:

> Monarchy has watched with jealous eye the strides of the young republic, as it developed into a mighty nation, ever seeking to plant in her free institutions the seed of destruction and death. Monarchy is . . . accomplishing through a money system what she failed to accomplish by the force of arms, the subjugation of American citizenship. . . . The perpetuation of the republic is at stake in this issue. . . . London, through New York, rules our nation of 60,000,000 people and governs us through party prejudice and a "solid north and a solid south." . . . Let us lay aside party prejudice and earnestly appeal to every patriot who values his country above party, to unite in a people's movement upon the question of money, transportation and land, and redeem our fair land from the withering blight of monopoly rule.

Just as the Founding Fathers had fought for freedom, so now was it necessary for the people to rise as one to defeat tyranny: "We are in a greater engagement than that of Valley Forge. Corporations are arrayed upon one side and the people upon the other. Stand firm, we beseech you."[56]

Burrows drew on similar themes in explaining that a new party was necessary because "the whole system" under which people had labored for a generation "is a lie and an imposture." Reviewing the past twenty-four years of statehood, he found a pattern of cries for deliverance answered by stony silence. "Two dozen times . . . have the farmers petitioned the railroads for redress," but the railroads had "insolently spurned their petitions and grasped them with a firmer grip in their merciless coils." This "cold and cruel process" had gone on "year after year. . . . Like Pharaoh of old, the monopolist rulers hardened their hearts to the appeals of the people until the state has become a veritable Egypt, and the Great God of justice and mercy has thundered forth as he did to the Egyptian monarch, 'Let my people go.' "[57]

At the independent conventions farmers were determined to pass over politicians in favor of leaders of their own movement. Despite his unblemished record as a foe of monopoly, Van Wyck was rejected for governor—he was a professional politician. Instead, they chose "Honest Farmer" John Powers, a man of "mild manners," who was "happily ignorant of the politician's arts." Powers had enlisted as a private in the Civil War and homesteaded in Nebraska in 1873; he now lived on a modest farm and was president of the Nebraska Farmers' Alliance. Although the independent convention was dominated by farmers, several delegates from the Knights of Labor were present. They proposed a platform plank for the eight-hour day, which was adopted with an amendment exempting agricultural labor. The KOL also secured the nomination of one of its members, William H. Dech, for lieutenant governor.[58]

In Kansas, Democrats seized the moment and tried to convince the Populists to nominate Charles Robinson, the state's first governor, a Republican turned Democrat because of his opposition to prohibition. But the delegates revealed their contempt for cooperation with any party, even if it would aid in the noble cause of defeating the Republicans, by nominating John F. Willits, a lifelong Republican farmer, by a wide margin over Robinson. The People's Party attempted to induce black voters to leave the party of Lincoln by nominating B. F. Foster, the pastor of the African Methodist Episcopal Church in Topeka, for auditor. In recognition of the importance of women in the movement, the convention nominated Fannie McCormick for state superintendent of public instruction.[59]

Most Republicans recognized the potential of the agrarian uprising to end Republican dominance in the two states. Church Howe opened the Nebraska Republican state convention by warning that "a slight mistake might end the old republican party." The "old ship is leaking badly," he declared, "and men are wanted at the pumps who can work them successfully." In this emergency the conservative Howe joined his old enemy Rosewater to patch the sinking Republican ship with an antimonopoly platform in favor of free coinage of silver, reduction of freight rates, and more stringent usury laws. But the nomination for governor of Lucius D. Richards, a banker and real estate promoter with connections to the regular wing of the party, and the failure to nominate any of the antimonopoly leaders for the other offices demonstrated that conservatives controlled the convention.[60]

Kansas Republicans also rushed to stem the flight of farmers by embracing economic reform. GOP state and congressional district conventions expressed an ardent desire for free silver coinage, reform of the national banking system, and lower freight rates. Conservative party leader Sol Miller, regarding these resolutions as madness, cried, "O, Lord, send us some backbone. We would like to see a genuine, straight out Republican platform adopted by some republican convention in Kansas this year." Apparently, Miller's prayers were heard when it came time to select candidates; Humphrey, along with most members of Kansas' congressional delegation, easily secured renomination.[61]

Once it became clear that friendly overtures would not lure grateful farmers back to the fold, Republicans took up the party lash to drive them into submission. One GOP tactic was to ridicule the leadership of the independent movement. The *Nebraska State Journal* accused the Populist candidates, "shiftless, lazy and improvident" men, of mortgaging their homesteads in order to live off the loan, fully intending to deed their land to the mortgagee, yet all the while "peddling out the slander that the farmers are starving and that the state is bankrupt." Such "demagogues" were to Nebraska "what a herd of hogs would be in the parlor of a careful housekeeper, and however carefully they are kicked out in November the filth they have scattered broadcast will leave its traces on our housekeeping for many months to come."[62] Republicans further insinuated that Populist leaders were anarchists and communists. A correspondent to the *Capital* alleged that one Independent had told an Alliance audience that "there was more virtue in the red flag than in the stars and stripes" and had referred ominously to a "noted communist community" in the area. Another Republican claimed that Populist congressional candidate Jerry Simpson had once "publicly asserted that he loved the anarchists' red flag better than the stars and stripes." Coming just two years after the Coffeyville explosion, these allegations were intended to frighten voters by linking the People's Party to violence.[63]

The GOP also unfurled the tattered bloody shirt. The arrival of Southern Alliance president Leonidas L. Polk of North Carolina gave the Republican press the opportunity to paint the Populist movement as a "southern democratic sideshow" and to revile Polk as a "pusillanimous confederate soldier." In another instance of bloody-shirt politics, Republican congressional candidate Col. James R. Hallowell questioned the Civil War record of his opponent, Jerry Simpson. Although Simpson had spent three months in a camp in Illinois, this did not count: He "never saw an armed rebel, never smelled rebel powder or heard the rebel yell in the bayonet charge." Simpson responded by dubbing Hallowell "Prince Hal" and accusing him of wearing silk stockings. Victor Murdock, the editor of the *Wichita Eagle*, countered

that Simpson wore no stockings at all, thus bestowing upon him the nick-
name "Sockless Jerry."[64]

Democrats generally avoided alienating the independent movement and
concentrated their fire on the Republicans. Nebraska Democrats, acting on
their own initiative in the second congressional district, endorsed the Populist candidate, William A. McKeighan, and in the first district tried without
success to convince Populists to endorse William Jennings Bryan. Kansas
Democrats decided against nominating candidates to oppose Populist congressional candidates Clover, Simpson, and John G. Otis and endorsed the
People's candidate for attorney general, J. N. Ives. As in Nebraska, Democrats made the overtures, and though Populists were pleased when Democrats offered no opposition, they did not actively seek Democratic support.[65]
In later election campaigns when professional politicians had assumed a
more prominent position in the People's Party and it had grown more desperate for electoral gains, fusion became a more attractive option; but in
1890 the Independents saw themselves as a popular uprising, a movement
opposing the corruption of both parties. To seek Democratic assistance
would be to bargain with the devil.

Whether they looked upon the political situation with trepidation or as a
moment of opportunity, observers agreed they were witnessing a political
revolution. On 26 July an astonished Republican correspondent observed
farmers gather for an Alliance picnic in Osage County, Kansas. "I watched
the procession as it paraded from the city to the picnic ground. It was immense. By careful computation we found it required just about fifty-five
minutes of time for streams of teams to pass a given point." This procession
was nothing less than a sign of a new political order: "Nothing like it has
happened since 1856, when the old Whig party disintegrated and voted for
the old pathfinder Fremont."[66] Such scenes were repeated countless times in
the hamlets, towns, and cities of Kansas and Nebraska, and the sheer numbers were impressive. A Knights of Labor/Alliance procession in Boone
County, Nebraska, was two-and-one-half miles long. An Alliance celebration brought 974 wagons to Parsons, Kansas. When 6,000 people gathered
in Nuckolls County, Nebraska, everyone was astonished at the "uprising of
the industrial classes" and asked, "Where did they come from?" The Morris
County, Kansas, suballiances gathered at their local meeting places in the
early morning and started for a central point. From the "high elevation just
before going down into the valley of Munkre's creek," an observer reported,
one could "look to the north and south and east, and west, and see the lines
full of people until your sight would be lost in the blue distance." According
to this witness, exactly 1,153 "vehicles" were in this "grand procession."[67]

The Populist processions were at once a sober protest against past injustice and a joyful celebration of independence and the prospect of a better future. Populist men and women displayed banners demanding "Free Coinage of Silver," "Special Privileges to None," or simply, "We Demand Our Rights." Other banners proclaimed solidarity: "United We Stand, Divided We Fall" and "In Union is Strength."[68] Many banners mocked politicians and monopolists. Heading a procession in Nebraska's capital city was a large banner inspired by Church Howe's statement to the Republican state convention that showed a leaking ship and the inscription "Wall Street Ship, Full of Holes. Help! Help! Pump! Pump!" On the other side of the banner was another ship under full sail with the words "Independent Ship of State—Full crew and no leaks." Later in the procession there was a man on horseback appearing to weigh 1,000 pounds, who was identified as "Bloated Bond Holder." Bringing up the rear of another procession was a dilapidated old riding plow identified as the "g. o. p."[69] The processions also demonstrated pride in rural life. Families decorated their wagons with symbols of their productivity—sunflowers, sheaves of grain, baskets of peaches— thereby rebuking the Republicans' attribution of agrarian discontent to laziness. The presence of numerous American flags, along with the "Goddess of Liberty" surrounded by forty-four young girls dressed in white representing the states, showed the patriotism of the farmers and visibly linked the demands of the movement to republican traditions of freedom and civic virtue.[70]

The processions were followed by speeches. One of the major themes of Populist orators was the paradox of hardship in the midst of plenty. Jerry Simpson was incredulous that despite "improvements in wealth producing machinery, we find the farmer in worse condition than twenty years ago." How had such a state of affairs come to exist, he asked, and he offered the answers: insufficient currency, railroad robbery, and England's growing control of American land.[71] No one spoke more forcefully on economic inequality than Mary Lease, who made as many as 160 appearances during the campaign of 1890. For two hours or more Lease held her audiences enrapt as she "hurl[ed] thunderbolts" against the injustices of a world turned upside down.[72] "This is a nation of inconsistencies," she began. Americans had fought England for their liberty, but had "put chains on four millions of blacks." During the Civil War, "we wiped out slavery" but at the same time "by our tariff laws and national banks began a system of white wage slavery worse than the first." Now, she claimed, "Wall Street owns the country. It is no longer a government of the people, by the people and for the people, but a government of Wall Street, by Wall Street and for Wall Street." Things

were exactly the reverse of what they ought to be: The system "clothes ras-
cals in robes and honesty in rags." Politicians had told farmers to "go to
work and raise a big crop," but "what came of it? Eight-cent corn, ten-cent
oats, two-cent beef and no price at all for butter and eggs." Then the politicians had countered that low prices were from overproduction. Lease scoffed
at this explanation: "Over-production, when 10,000 little children . . .
starve to death every year in the United States, and over 100,000 shop-girls
in New York are forced to sell their virtue for the bread their niggardly wages
deny them." Although Lease probably did not actually call upon farmers to
"raise less corn and more hell," as has often been said, the slogan is consistent with her overall theme, for it was legitimate for farmers to right an up-
side-down world even if to do so meant abandoning their calling of tilling
the land.[73]

Others women orators included the more soft-spoken Annie Diggs, who
wrote for the *Advocate*, and Fanny Randolph Vickery, a woman of "Quaker-
Abolitionist-Greenback ancestry."[74] The prominent place of women orators
and writers in the Populist campaign, particularly in Kansas, was a conse-
quence of populism's self-justification and was an essential part of the movement. Prior to populism western women had claimed the right to pronounce
upon public affairs through the WCTU's crusade against the saloon. Many
female Populist leaders had been active in the temperance movement and
had since extended their social critique to include all aspects of political
economy. As a third-party movement, populism expanded political space for
women because its central legitimizing principle was a devastating critique of
the male-dominated political order. Through this opening, women asserted
their superior moral vision as wives and mothers and "named men's political
hegemony as a major cause of civilization's decline."[75] Having discovered
that they, too, had been disfranchised by the two-party system, male farmers
responded enthusiastically to women orators calling for the nation to be
cleansed.

Perhaps because women led the Populists' denunciation of traditional politics, Republicans were particularly abusive to women orators. The *Welling-
ton Monitor* described Lease as a "miserable caricature upon womanhood,
hideously ugly in feature and foul of tongue."[76] Later, William Allen White,
editor of the *Emporia Gazette*, ridiculed the Populists for sending "three or
four harpies out lecturing, telling the people that Kansas is raising hell and
letting the corn go to weeds."[77] White's identification of the movement with
the foolishness of women not only rejected a public role for women, it also
dismissed populism for its irresponsibility toward public affairs, as evidenced

by its sanction of female orators, and therefore reaffirmed traditional male politics.

The campaign of 1890 marked the farmers' graduation from the Alliance school. In Alliance meetings farmers had discussed the causes of their troubles, sought relief through their representatives, and had then been rebuffed. They had learned their lesson and learned it well: They were now going to wrest control of the government from the grasp of monopoly and bring it back into the hands of the "plain people." The act of severing their ties of loyalty to an old party and joining a new political movement meant embracing a new set of beliefs about the political universe. Before, Republican farmers had accepted appeals to the memory of the Civil War or had believed in the promise of a protective tariff to bring prosperity; Democratic farmers had responded to Jacksonian rhetoric against government or had accepted the promise of prosperity through free trade. But farmers now understood that both parties were firmly in the grasp of wealthy and powerful financiers and corporations, and they joined in singing the Populist anthem, "Good-bye, My Party, Good-bye":

It was no more than a year ago,
    Good-bye, old party, good-bye.
That I was in love with my party so,
    Good-bye, old party, good-bye.
To hear aught else I never would go,
    Good-bye, old party, good-bye.
Like all the rest I made a great blow,
    Good-bye, old party, good-bye.

I was raised up in the kind of school,
    Good-bye, old party, good-bye.
That taught to bow to money rule,
    Good-bye, old party, good-bye.
And it made of me a "Kansas Fool,"
    Good-bye, old party, good-bye.
When they found I was a willing tool,
    Good-bye, old party, good-bye.[78]

By bidding farewell to their old party, Populists were not merely joining another party but were participating in a new kind of political movement, one of "democratic promise." Populism was a "spirit of egalitarian hope expressed . . . not in the prose of a platform, however creative, and not ultimately even in the third party, but in a self-generated culture of collective dignity and individual longing."[79] Yet there were elements in the movement culture of populism that those students who look to it as a model for democratic possibilities in America may find troubling. Populists were in a situation of economic and political crisis. To legitimize an action they regarded as desperate, severing ties of party loyalty, many Populists embraced the conspiratorial view of political history as taught by Sarah Emery and the Vincents. The experience of those people who accepted this view was akin to receiving enlightenment or to undergoing a religious conversion. One Kansas Alliance organizer reported that he had been lecturing three nights a week on the "scheme hatched in 1859 to bring about the rebellion and institute the English system of robbing the people north, south, east and west." Farmers used to reject his talk, he said, but now they "want me to repeat what I told them then. They say the scales are falling from their mental vision."[80] A lecturer from a suballiance in Olathe, Kansas, wrote that he had recently discovered that thirty years before, "while the unsuspecting marched on to battle, the rogues with selfish greed, conspired with English capitalists to get possession of this wonderfully productive American nation." He urged his listeners to consider these truths: "Even if you have been converted to the new faith," he said, "you will find that the longer and deeper this matter is examined the greater will be the rottenness unearthed."[81] Even in Nebraska, where there was little word of the English conspiracy in early 1890, Populists employed the rhetoric of conspiracy once an independent course had been decided upon. On the eve of the election, the *Alliance* reported that the state Banker's Association had issued a secret circular urging its members to use their influence to defeat the Populist ticket. This story was hardly far-fetched; more remarkable was the paper's casual comparison of the document to the "Hazzard Circular," which supposedly documented the initial conspiracy to contract the currency and was evidently a matter of common knowledge.[82]

The belief in an English conspiracy and the general atmosphere of crisis allowed some ugly expressions to surface. A member of a suballiance in Crestline, Kansas, castigated the men "who bow to the will of the money lords [of] Wall Street—paid agents of a set of hawk billed Jews (who represent the London money power) on Lombard and Threadneedle Streets, London." This instance of blatant anti-Semitism was isolated, but it illustrates how reactionary sentiments could attach themselves to the Anglophobic dimension of Populist thought.[83] Any mass movement arising suddenly in response to economic crisis is likely to contain some contradictory ideological tendencies. To destroy strong political identities, Populists had to create a compelling justification for independent action and so seized upon a republican tradition that had justified heroic action when liberty had been threatened in the past; in so doing they were following the path of the revolutionaries of the 1770s. Although the belief in an English conspiracy was traditional, it did not carry reactionary implications. The Populists' embrace of this ideology did not lead to misguided attacks on other oppressed groups but toward democratization, cooperation with labor, and reform of the national system of finance and transportation.

The results of the 1890 election were "a Waterloo to the Republican Party."[84] The Populist accomplishment was particularly impressive as it had been achieved without any overtures to the Democrats. In Nebraska the Populists lost the governorship by only 1,000 votes but won both houses of the legislature and two of the state's three congressional races. The Kansas People's Party also fell short in a close race for governor, but the Populists secured five of the state's seven congressional seats. The Populists gained control of the Kansas legislature and proved, by retiring Ingalls from the Senate and electing Peffer in his stead, that the "purification of politics" was no mere dream.[85] In one analysis of the 1890 People's Party vote in Kansas, former Republicans provided 36 percent of the total Populist vote, former Democrats constituted 31 percent, former Union Laborites 29 percent, and former prohibitionists 4 percent. There is no reason to doubt that these figures accurately convey a general sense of the sources of the Populist vote, but it should be stressed that these and similar estimates may suggest a misleading impression that the strength of former Republicans in the coalition was less than it actually was. Almost all the Union Laborites of 1888 had at one time been Republicans; thus, the bulk of support for the People's Party in 1890 came from voters who had left the GOP—if not between 1888 and 1890 then sometime before.[86] That the Populist revolt consisted, for the most part, of disgruntled Republicans underscores the importance of the failure of the Republican Party in Kansas and Nebraska to respond to the demands of mostly Republican farmers. Historians of Kansas populism have observed that the GOP's rejection of Alliance demands played a pivotal role in the process of third-party formation, but why was the GOP so completely unresponsive?[87] The comparison with Iowa, where the threat from the Democratic/Greenback antimonopoly coalition forced the Republican Party to embrace reform, indicates that the crucial variable was party competition. In Kansas and Nebraska, where there appeared to be little threat to the GOP's dominance, Republican politicians spurned the Alliance. Given that Kansas and Nebraska had always been bastions of Republicanism, the Republicans' calculation that there was little risk in ignoring the Alliance was reasonable, but it ultimately failed to recognize that the people's patience was limited.

The Independents had done well in their first battle and were optimistic about soon repeating their achievement nationally. Yet the Populists did not fully appreciate the problems they would face. It would prove hard enough for them to win elections and to enact legislation in their own states and to survive the inevitable problems that would arise as the movement became more like a political party. Even more difficult would be the creation of Populist movements in other states, a task essential to maintaining momentum.

8
Party Competition and the Incorporation of the Iowa Farmers' Alliance

Just as third-party formation in Kansas and Nebraska was related to the failure of state-level reform, the failure of populism in Iowa was closely linked to the Iowa Alliance's successful campaign for railroad reform in 1888. The Iowa Alliance had entered the state political system and was strongly committed to nonpartisan politics; during the next few years it continued to pursue the opportunities for state-level reform. Iowa's competitive party system incorporated much of the movement's leadership although substantial support for radical reform remained at the grass-roots level, and many farmers continued to manifest discontent with the GOP by responding to the Democrats on economic issues. Many middle-level IFA leaders showed signs of willingness to support a third party, but the top leadership became more conservative. Not wanting to jeopardize the positions they had won within the party system, they limited the Alliance's agenda and steered the movement away from independent politics.

Like their counterparts in Kansas and Nebraska, Iowa farmers in the Alliance sought to secure redress through economic cooperation, and the Grange movement of the 1870s had provided them with specific blueprints. Iowa Granges had instituted a program of making direct purchases from wholesalers and manufacturers, bringing significant savings. In 1872 the Iowa State Grange appointed an agent to coordinate purchases by local Granges, and the movement also established creameries, elevators, and packing plants. An effort by the state organization to manufacture farm machinery was a disaster, however, and contributed to the Grange's decline. Although there is little evidence of continuity between the Iowa Grange and the Alliance leadership, it is reasonable to assume that Alliance members and leaders were aware of the Grange's cooperative activities and tried to implement its more successful aspects.[1]

Shortly after the organization of the Iowa Farmers' Alliance in 1886, sub-alliances began to organize cooperatives. In July 1887 the Advance Alliance of Shelby County reported that it had saved $3 per 1,000 pounds on lumber through bulk orders and was in the process of organizing a mutual insurance company. From mid-1887 to mid-1888 the Sac County Alliance purchasing agent bought forty-six corn cultivators at $13 each ($7 less than the retail price) and obtained similar discounts on coal, rock salt, binding twine, flour, and barbed wire. The Audubon County Alliance reported savings of 30 percent on direct purchases from local retailers. In Neola merchants were "feeling a little hard towards the Alliance" because farmers were buying flour and groceries elsewhere.[2] By September 1888 the number of local and county Alliances engaged in direct purchasing warranted a state purchasing agency to coordinate buying, and it began operating in early 1889.[3] Suballiances reported substantial savings on twine, farm machinery, coal, and flour through the state agency; for the year ending October 1891 the state agency's business totaled $107,000.[4] Three separate complaints filed before the Iowa Board of Railroad Commissioners in 1890, charging railroad lines with refusing to allow suballiances to erect coal houses, further indicate widespread cooperative activity. Other suballiances started cooperative creameries and mutual insurance companies and even attempted to market grain. From 1886 through 1892 Iowa Alliances organized twenty-two elevators; fourteen of these were still operational in 1892.[5]

In contrast to the Kansas and Nebraska Alliances, which became more oriented toward national reform as they failed to gain power at the state level, the Iowa Alliance's successful entry into the state political system encouraged the leadership to emphasize state over national reform. After their victory in 1888, Iowa Alliance leaders sought to shore up previous gains and to advance new state-level measures to address specific grievances. The 1889 IFA platform was silent about national issues but called for numerous state reforms: extending the railroad commission's rates to cover shipments made over two or more lines, reducing passenger rates from 3 to 2 cents per mile, reforming state taxation, reducing the legal rate of interest on mortgages from 10 to 8 percent, adopting a uniform textbook law, and making "entering into" trusts or "trade conspiracies" a criminal offense. Although these reforms did not promise to reverse the fundamental problems of agriculture in one stroke, they did offer meaningful changes. The IFA's proposals for tax reform, in particular, extended significant benefits to farmers by removing flagrant inequities in property assessment that favored personal property over real property and by requiring that mortgagees, rather than mortgagors, pay the tax on the value of mortgages.[6]

Given the success of its nonpartisan political strategy in 1888, there was little question that the IFA would continue to pursue its program within the party system. After the adjournment of the 1888 legislature the most important item on the Alliance's political calendar was the election of railroad commissioners in the fall. Because the commission was empowered to set rates, it was vital for farmers to elect men committed to low maximum rates. In July the *Homestead* warned farmers of a "very grave danger" that the railroads would take advantage of an inevitable "relaxation of vigilance" by fabricating an "alleged public demand for repeal" of the maximum rates set by the commission in compliance with the law of 1888. Thus, the *Homestead* urged Alliance members to remain active in politics to ensure the reelection of the incumbent commissioners. All three commissioners—two Republicans and one Democrat—were reelected.[7]

In other races the GOP made its best showing since 1880. The Republican state party chairman had expressed alarm that the loss of railroad support would prove damaging, but his fear proved groundless. Benjamin Harrison carried the Hawkeye state by a comfortable margin of almost 8 percent over Grover Cleveland. The Democrats' lone congressional victory was in the heavily partisan second district. Republicans were particularly gratified to defeat two fusion incumbents, Albert Anderson, Hepburn's traducer two years earlier, and the "arch demagogue" James B. Weaver. For the moment John F. Lacey, the man whose "belt is now adorned with the gory scalp of J. B. Weaver," was the party's hero.[8]

But even as Iowa fell safely into the Republican column in the national election of 1888, conservative leaders remained deeply disturbed by the antimonopoly element in the party. Iowa seemed safer than it had in some time, but the Regency was uncertain that political success was worth the price of hostility to capital. Furthermore, in early 1889 when President Harrison offered Allison the position of secretary of the treasury, the Regency feared that the legislature would probably choose the hated Larrabee to fill the vacant seat. With this in mind, Allison's closest associates, railroad men like Charles Perkins and Nathaniel Hubbard, strongly urged Allison to turn down the cabinet position.[9] Allison's acceptance of this counsel kept Larrabee in Iowa for the time being, but many observers felt that the governor would probably contest Allison's bid for reelection when the General Assembly met in 1890. As early as January 1889, one adviser had warned Allison that the antimonopolist state senator George Finn had been "talking against your reelection, and telling how the Alliance will be opposed to you, because you have never expressed any sympathy with the people on . . . the R. R. question." It was uncertain if Larrabee would run, but "he has a stronghold on the popular strength at present, and should he be in the field, will be a formidable competitor."[10]

The primary goal of conservative Republicans as they approached the election of 1889 was to neutralize the antimonopoly wing of the party without making undesirable concessions. The Regency intended to accept the 1888 legislation as an accomplished fact, thus defusing this issue, and then to secure the nomination of conservative men. Observing that some Republican papers were attempting to "create dissension" in the party over the railroad question, the *Register* argued that this issue had no more to do with the campaign than "the purchase of Alaska or the Chinese question"; it assured the state that all candidates for governor "would maintain the accepted policy of state control of railroads" and affirmed the GOP's commitment to give the 1888 legislation a "fair trial." In a similar vein the Regency's preferred candidate for governor, John A. T. Hull, denied allegations that he was a prorailroad candidate by pointing to his previous support for an elective commission and for a law "controlling all trusts and combines." Hull reaffirmed his commitment to "legislative control" although he cautioned against going too far: "When we correct the evils of railroad management we should stop. . . . To build up a great prosperous commonwealth, all great interests should work together in harmony."[11]

Despite these assurances, the Farmers' Alliance was not prepared to entrust the governorship to a candidate acceptable to the Regency. Although the IFA made no official endorsement, Alliance leaders and members favored Hiram C. Wheeler, a Sac County farmer and three-term president of the Iowa Agricultural Society.[12] Alliance members also took an active role in local Republican conventions to secure the nomination of legislative candidates supporting Larrabee for the Senate. Hull informed Senator Allison that Republicans in Lucas County had nominated "a great Larrabee man" for representative and passed on further intelligence that "Larrabee men are very active" in Taylor and Sac Counties. The editor of the regular Republican newspaper in Adair County, C. B. Hunt, told Allison of a "Larrabee Senatorial boom." Although this boom could not "possibly amount to much," Hunt wrote, "in these days of Granger excitement and such extreme radical views bordering upon cranky notions," one could never be sure. Less than two weeks later, Hunt's fears were realized when Adair County Republicans nominated for representative a "farmer, a very radical anti railroad man, and a great *Larrabee* man." Other correspondents apprised Allison of similar disturbing developments elsewhere.[13]

The GOP state convention provided a test of the relative strength of the antimonopoly and conservative factions. With conservatives supporting the 1888 legislation and antimonopolists deciding not to place any new items on the agenda, an unusual degree of consensus on the platform prevailed. The convention endorsed the Harrison administration, generous pensions, and the "American system of protection." On state matters the platform reaffirmed "the principle and policy of State railway regulation," endorsed legislation to "punish trade conspiracies, trusts and combines," and called for arbitration of labor disputes. The delegates agreed that prohibition was "the settled policy of the State" and resolved that there "should be no backward step" in enforcing the law. The platform was adopted without dissent, but the selection of candidates was another matter. On the first ballot Hull and Wheeler showed almost equal strength but fell short of a majority, as about one-fifth of the delegates favored Joseph G. Hutchison, an attorney and two-term state senator. Twenty-one additional ballots brought little change, and the convention adjourned for the night. The next morning the convention once again deadlocked, but on the twenty-fourth ballot Hutchison showed sudden gains at the expense of Wheeler. The next ballot concluded the "most protracted contest" in the history of Iowa Republicanism as a sufficient number of Hull and Wheeler delegates went over to Hutchison to give him the nomination.[14] The Regency was pleased with the outcome. Ret Clarkson rejoiced that the "failure to get Wheeler nominated for Governor" had "broken [Larrabee's] back." The *Register* praised Hutchison as a "conservative man" and exulted that his nomination marked the "effectual extinguishment" of the party's "guerilla element." Now that the "enemies" had been vanquished, the *Register* predicted, the Republican majority in the fall would easily reach 25,000.[15]

The triumph of the regulars along with the continued ascendancy of the "drys" in the GOP gave the Democrats two weak points to exploit: prohibition and antimonopoly. Democrats had made significant gains in 1887 among antiprohibition voters who opposed Larrabee's policy of vigorous enforcement of prohibition, and they hoped to capitalize further on mounting discontent with the prohibition law among foreign-born voters and urban "jugwumps" who objected to prohibition because it raised taxes and hindered economic growth. In addition, although the Democratic/Greenback coalition had fallen apart in 1887, Democrats had not forgotten the gains they had made on economic issues in the mid-eighties. Now that the Regency had regained the upper hand, the Democrats hoped once again to attract farmers and others who objected to corporate control of the Republican Party.

Immediately following the Republican convention, the *Leader* declared that a counterrevolution had taken place in the GOP. One editorial, "Here is the Record," reminded readers that after the passage of the Granger Law in 1874 the railroads had taken over the GOP and repealed the law. Although antimonopolists had regained control of the party and enacted the 1888 legislation, the *Leader* contended that, once again, "reaction is setting in," as clearly manifested by Hutchison's nomination. The *Leader* alleged that in the 1888 session Hutchison had "favored the adoption of every amendment which looked to delaying and weakening the pending bills." Hutchison had voted for the final bill, the *Leader* acknowledged, but only because he recognized that its passage was a foregone conclusion.[16]

Democrats were unified as seldom before at the 1889 state convention. In the past the party had frequently squabbled over the question of high versus low license. But with the scent of victory in the air, the Democrats unanimously adopted a platform calling for local option with a minimum license of $500. The platform also opposed the protective tariff, as it "lays its heaviest burden on the farmer, the mechanic and the day-laborer," and affirmed the "doctrine of state and national regulation of railroads and other corporations." The selection of Horace Boies, a Waterloo attorney, to lead the ticket demonstrated the Democrats' pragmatic determination to attract the widest possible constituency on the prohibition question. Although Boies was not a major figure in state politics, he possessed several assets. He had been a "zealous member" of the Republican Party until the early 1880s when he broke with the GOP over the tariff and prohibition. He was personally a temperate man but believed that Iowa's prohibition law violated property rights because it did not provide compensation for lost investment in the liquor trade. Boies also objected to sumptuary legislation as an encroachment upon the rights of the individual. Prohibition, Boies believed, was "a dangerous innovation in the fundamental principle upon which our system of government is founded—the largest possible liberty of the individual consistent with the welfare of the whole." The former Republican would attract many voters who would find a Bourbon candidate unacceptable.[17] Although Boies's candidacy was designed primarily to preserve the saloon, Democrats recognized that every vote would count and saw the imperative of winning over the farmers on economic issues. Accordingly, Boies affirmed his support for further railroad regulation and also challenged Republican tariff policy. "Year after year under this beneficent system of protection," Boies declared, the farmer "has been compelled to face the unpleasant fact that the market value of all the products of the farm is growing less. Will he not sometime realize that his only hope of relief is in a more extended foreign market?" Thus free trade would bring farmers relief from low prices.[18]

The main objective of the IFA leadership in the campaign of 1889 was defensive: to ensure that the gains won the year before would not be lost. After the two parties had held their conventions, the Alliance state secretary, August M. Post, asked the candidates for state office to give their "views" on four issues:

1. The retention of an elective railway commission
2. The maintenance of the present railway law in its integrity, with such amendments as may be needed to make it more restrictive and efficient
3. The enlargement of the powers of the railroad commission and making the necessary amendments in the law to enable them to make and enforce joint rates within the state
4. The enforcement of the entire law in letter and spirit

These issues were remarkably ill-designed for the task of helping voters distinguish between Hutchison and Boies. With the exception of the minor point about joint rates across two or more lines, Post's request did not require the candidates to take a position on any further reform. They simply had to affirm their support for the present law in appropriately stern language, a task well suited to their skills as politicians. Not surprisingly, their replies were much the same.[19]

One main difference separated the candidates: Hutchison had a record. Democrats charged that although Hutchison pretended to be a great friend of the people, his record in the state senate showed that he was really the ally of corporations. An exposé of Hutchison's voting record written by Alliance lecturer Newton B. Ashby enhanced the credibility of this allegation. Appearing in early October, Ashby's article received maximum publicity in the Democratic press as the authoritative position of the IFA. The *Leader* portrayed Ashby as a loyal Republican, who "with the utmost reluctance" had been compelled to oppose Hutchison in light of the facts. The influential Republican antimonopoly organ, the *Cedar Rapids Gazette*, also published Ashby's critique and called upon Hutchison to withdraw from the race.[20]

This eleventh-hour attack scored a direct hit. Conservative Republicans scrambled to repair the damage by smearing Ashby. The *Register* objected that the Alliance had not authorized the state lecturer to speak on its behalf and rejected the *Leader*'s claim that Ashby was a Republican. Like the "guerilla papers," Ashby has "pretended at times to be a Republican," but the

Register insisted that he was really "a breeder of strife, a chronic kicker and disorganizer." Another Republican newspaper alleged that Ashby had been a Democrat all along and falsely asserted that he had recently been expelled from the Alliance when it had been discovered that he had joined the Alliance "for the money he could make out of it."[21]

After attacking Ashby, conservatives endeavored to obtain counterendorsements from leading Republican antimonopolists. They entreated Larrabee—for the sake of the party and its holy war against the saloon—to issue a statement for Hutchison. Larrabee affirmed the accuracy of Ashby's characterization of Hutchison's record, but he did offer an endorsement, nonetheless, deeming Hutchison's "record of the past, as compared with his present views and opinions, of small importance indeed." Hutchison, the governor recalled, had "labored hard" during the 1888 legislative assembly "to secure the adoption of the best features of our law" and had since assured Larrabee of his support for the commissioner's rates. Republicans also obtained two valuable statements from Alliance officials. IFA secretary August Post interviewed Hutchison and was satisfied with his expressions of assurance on the railroad question. Alliance president J. B. Furrow went even further, not only stamping Hutchison's record with his seal of approval but informing farmers that their interests would be "advanced by the continued triumph of Republican principles." Furrow insisted that the farmer "must secure a home market that will make a demand for his products" and declared that he could not "endure the Democratic position on the saloon question. The quiet Iowa farmer who loves his sons and desires them to grow to noble manhood, cannot in the honesty of his heart desire the return of this great evil."[22]

Despite these last-moment endorsements of Hutchison, Boies was elected as Iowa's first Democratic governor since the 1850s by the narrow margin of just under 7,000 votes. Six years earlier John Dolliver had proclaimed that Iowa would go Democratic only when hell went Methodist; now that hell had gone Methodist, Dolliver's metaphor seemed completely upside down, at least according to a report of a Democratic victory celebration near LeMars. Hundreds of men, according to one Republican observer, were "wild with liquor and young boys were given free access to it and scores of them were carried home dead drunk. The scenes in the hills where the beer was passed out resembled the scrambling of hogs for swill and were too revolting for description."[23] Boies's triumph occasioned an anguished debate among Republicans on the causes of the catastrophe. Foes of the saloon refused to concede that prohibition had had anything to do with the Republican defeat and blamed the outcome on Hutchison's poor railroad record. Other observers suggested that although prohibition had hurt the GOP, the party might have survived the loss of the river counties had it chosen a candidate and run a campaign "calculated to arouse the enthusiasm of the farmers." The *Register* disputed this assessment and blamed the outcome on dissatisfaction with the party's unyielding position on the saloon.[24] If the ship was sinking, the Regency would far prefer to jettison prohibition than to concede that its stand on economic issues had cost the GOP its lead among farmers.

It would be simplistic to attribute the Democratic victory to any single cause. Regression-based estimates show that Democratic gains from 1887 to 1889 increased among antiprohibition voters and farmers. The estimated percentage of the electorate with antiprohibition proclivities who voted Democratic increased from 58 percent in 1887 to 62 percent in 1889; at the same time, the estimated percentage of farmers voting Democratic also increased from 29 percent in 1887 to 34 percent in 1889. Republicans made slight gains among farmers (from 49 percent in 1887 to 51 percent in 1889), but the Democratic gains were greater. These estimates indicate that although the electorate showed strong cleavages along ethnocultural lines, the farm vote was critical to Boies's margin of victory. Boies did not gain the support of a majority of Iowa farmers, but the increase in his share of their vote helped tip the scales.[25]

In addition to capturing the statehouse the Democrats made strong gains in the legislature. In the house, there were fifty Republicans, forty-five Democrats, and five Independents; if the opposition united, its strength would be equal to that of the Republicans. In the senate, the Republicans held twenty-eight seats, the Democrats twenty, and the Independents two.[26] Although Republicans had a majority in both houses, it was possible that a coalition of Democrats, Independents, and antimonopoly Republicans might form behind Larrabee or some other antimonopoly candidate for U.S. senator, such as Iowa supreme court justice James H. Rothrock.[27]

In the weeks before the opening of the legislative session, Allison's informants apprised him of strong grass-roots opposition to his reelection. "The Iowa Cyclone has left an awful wreck," lamented C. B. Hunt in a letter to Allison following the November debacle. Hunt warned Allison that "the Farmers Alliance are largely opposed to you and now they are going to do their most and if you do not look out they will surely defeat you." Gilbert Pray, a clerk in the Iowa Supreme Court, had also "heard some things with reference to the Farmers Alliance movement" and promised Allison to "use all means at my command to create a favorable impression among that class of people for you." Ret Clarkson was certain who was "at the bottom of all the mischief toward you"; Larrabee, he affirmed, "is the storm centre, and the heart of all the opposition. . . . His implacable hostility to you is a mystery to me."[28] Several key legislators seemed likely to oppose Allison. One informant wrote that "Senator Finn and other 'kindred spirits'" had been "hob-knobing with Gov Larabee [sic]. Finn thought he could not possibly vote for you for Senator."[29] Others expressed doubts about Senator Smith, an "independent Republican" who had won in the thirty-seventh district.[30]

To court reluctant supporters and to gather intelligence, Allison wrote to numerous legislators, asking their views; their replies were scarcely reassuring. Republican senator D. B. Davidson indicated a hesitance to vote for Allison because of popular unrest: "The people are alive to the fact that something has deprived them of once prosperous times and are on the look out for the cause. Trusts and monopolies have grown up that are enriching themselves rapidly while the producing class [is] receiving less for their produce each year. And the Republican Party is charged with a good share of the fault." Another Republican senator, A. F. Meservey, wrote Allison that he was "not unfriendly" to him, "but I represent an agricultural district that seems to be uneasy and dissatisfied with the present condition of things and are anxious for a change." Although Meservey would not presume to "dictate" the "changes to be made," thus indicating he would not oppose Allison at least for the moment, he did not wish "to hamper myself with any pledges now."[31]

Allison's reelection would require careful planning and the full use of the senator's resources. By early December Iowa secretary of state Frank Jackson, who shared responsibility for the management of Allison's reelection effort with Gilbert Pray, had already convened several "informal caucuses" with key Allison supporters. "All of us," he assured Allison, "are wide awake and determined to have our forces well drilled and in good order for the contest." Despite Jackson's use of a military metaphor, Allison's lieutenants proceeded more in the fashion of a diplomatic corps than an army. The moment required flattery and gifts. Allison's friends arranged to keep a Democratic postmaster in office in exchange for assistance from Sen. James H. Barnett. As an Independent, Barnett could not openly support Allison, but he agreed to vote against Allison's "principal competitor," undoubtedly Larrabee.[32] Particularly vital was the support of George Finn, the foremost antimonopolist in the state senate. Although conservatives for years had scorned Finn as a demagogue, they agreed to overlook their differences if it would help Allison. G. L. Godfrey informed Allison that Finn "intended to support you if left alone, that is, if the republicans stopped their abuse of him." Richard Clarkson, the *Register*'s editor since his brother Ret's departure to Washington, agreed to have the paper "do all it can to reconcile Mr. Finn." Nathaniel Hubbard of the Chicago and Northwestern informed Allison that he and Joseph W. Blythe of the CB&Q had met with Finn on separate occasions; in a veiled reference to a quid pro quo possibly involving a committee chairmanship, Hubbard related that Finn "has agreed positively, and we have accepted all his suggestions."[33]

Other cases required subtle coercion. Having learned that Senator Davidson was in a tight financial situation—he was driving a dray at $1.25 per day—and desperately needed an unspecific "favor" that could be provided only by John W. Near, Jackson moved to obtain a pledge from Davidson in exchange for Near's appointment to the position of supervisor of the census. The pressure could not be too direct, the deal overtly transparent. Allison was to request Congressman John P. Dolliver to write Near that "his chances are good." According to the plan, Near would then appeal to Davidson, who "will pledge himself to you to save Near." Two weeks later, Jackson conveyed to Allison the good news that "Mr Davidson will give you his support" and reminded him not to "loose [sic] sight of Friend Near but see that he secures this appointment when the time comes." A consummate politician such as Allison did not overlook such matters, nor did he lack the power to deliver—in due time Near became one of Iowa's four census supervisors.[34]

Allison had an especially valuable ally in "Tama Jim" Wilson, a professor at the Iowa State College of Agriculture and Mechanical Arts who had strong ties to the IFA and to agrarian legislators. Wilson personally wrote to twenty members of the legislature and used his contacts in the Alliance on Allison's behalf, in one case hinting to an official of a county Alliance that Allison might provide a favor. If this man "cant have what he wants," Wilson requested Allison to "write me a nice letter that I can send him, saying pleasant things." Tama Jim also served as Allison's eyes and ears in agrarian circles. "Will see Wallace next week at Breeders Meeting," he reported; "if there is any plans a making I will get a hint of them."[35]

As the legislature convened, the IFA served notice of its intention to defeat Iowa's senior senator. On 15 January a meeting of sixty-seven Alliance delegates voted for a resolution demanding the election of Larrabee "as United States senator by the Iowa legislature." As if timed to coincide with the Alliance declaration, Larrabee stated his opposition to Allison publicly for the first time on the grounds that the incumbent lacked sympathy with the movement for railroad reform. His subservience to the railroads, Larrabee declared, showed that the senator "hasn't the courage of a mouse." Although Larrabee did not formally offer himself as an alternative, the man who had boldly stood up to the corporations clearly was available.[36]

Normally the vote for senator could be expected to occur within two weeks of the opening of the legislative session.[37] But the Twenty-third Iowa General Assembly would not be an ordinary session. The house was immediately thrown into a deadlock when the five Independents joined the forty-five Democrats in the Democratic caucus. With both party caucuses consisting of fifty members, it was two weeks before the house agreed on a temporary speaker, and it was not until a month later that the house was finally organized.[38]

At first Allison's campaign managers thought the stalemate in the house would have a salutary effect on Allison's chances, since the fight to organize the house appeared to be strengthening party loyalty among Republican legislators. But as the delay lengthened, Larrabee's friends were able to mobilize grass-roots support. In early February several suballiances sent resolutions to the state senate demanding that Allison not be reelected. The Knights of Labor added to the opposition by indicting Allison as a "monopolist" and demanding his defeat.[39] By mid-February Allison's lieutenants were close to a state of panic. An intelligence report from Gilbert Pray to Allison arrived on 14 February: "I hardly know what to write to you. I am more disgusted and discouraged than at any time. The fact is I feel that there is some subtle influence at work that I am unable to fathom." Pray had thought he had reached an agreement to organize the house by giving the Democrats all the offices except speaker; in the afternoon, however, Larrabee (who remained governor as long as the house deadlock prevented the inauguration of Boies) had decided to file his annual message to the legislature. Since then, Pray complained, "no Dem will talk at all." Pray feared that the Democrats "are now going to claim that they are organized & that the Gov has recognized them as organized by sending in his message." The success of this ploy would depend upon the agreement of the Republican state auditor, a man whom Pray believed would be "cool & level headed enough not to give away anything." Still, Pray had lost control of events—anything could happen. The main problem, he explained, was that "the Dems & farmers alliances crowd are flooding the State with petitions . . . for Larrabee who is furnishing the music for all the fun." No one was yet "inclined to leave you," Pray felt assured, "but this strain, and the petition business is having an effect and I can see some of our best men are worrying about it." Although Pray was not explicit about the entire range of possibilities, his chief fear, apparently, was that Larrabee's supporters in the house, bolstered by public senti-

ment, might have cut a deal with the Democrats to organize the house on
their terms in exchange for Democratic support of Larrabee.[40]

Given the unpredictability of the situation, Allison's managers determined that the safest course of action was to organize the house as quickly
as possible, even if it meant giving the speaker to the Democrats. On 18 February Pray wrote Allison, "I hope I may be able [to] telegraph you the news
of organization tomorrow or very soon at least. I assure you it is very humili-
ating . . . to see the rep's give up the speaker but we must organize even if we
put our 'mouths in the dust' and all other schemes have failed." An agreement was reached the next day. Democrats would have the speaker and Republicans would have their choice of the chairs of five of the ten most important committees. Most important, although it was not part of the formal
agreement, Allison's supporters, having forestalled any agreement between
antimonopoly Republicans and Democrats, could now elect their man. The
balloting on 4 March revealed little about the intense battle between Allison and Larrabee that had been waged over the past several months: Allison
received seventy-nine votes; S. L. Bestow, a Democrat who had never been a
serious contender, received sixty-three; and only eight antimonopolists remained true to Larrabee. The Allison organization's superior resources had
enabled the incumbent to gain the active or passive support of enough potential Larrabee backers to ensure that the Larrabee movement did not develop a critical mass.[41]

Although strong support for Larrabee existed among ordinary members
of the Farmers' Alliance, the 1890 senatorial campaign showed a growing di-
vergence between the goals of members and leaders. In the closing days of
the legislature A. L. Stuntz, the IFA's official lobbyist at the General Assembly, had bolstered Allison's cause through his active support. Stuntz's primary responsibility was to lobby for the reforms specified in the Alliance
platform of September 1889. While the house was deadlocked, Stuntz had
little to do except "get acquainted with the members and lay plans for the
future." As he made his rounds at the capitol, Stuntz soon learned that
many solons wanted assurance that the Alliance was not "in politics,"
meaning that the Alliance should not pursue controversial measures that
would array the two parties against one another or aggravate factional
strife.[42] Given these concerns Stuntz concluded that a crusade for Larrabee
would do little to allay fears that the Alliance was "in politics" and might
easily jeopardize broad legislative support for Alliance measures. After Allison's reelection, Stuntz congratulated the senator and reported that he had
given him "all the influence in my power." Stuntz regretted that "a few Sore-
headed 'hangers-on-to-the-Alliance' Farmers" had demanded the election of

Larrabee, for this action had "injured the Farmers Alliance" by making the organization appear to be "in politics." Throughout the session, Stuntz wrote, "the only thing I could do was to contend that the Farmers Alliance as an organization was not in Politics. We were law abiding citizens and had cast our 'ballot' for U.S. Senator when we voted for our Representatives."[43] Stuntz's efforts to avoid the appearance that the Alliance was "in politics" represented a significant narrowing of the meaning of nonpartisan political action. In 1887 the Alliance had been willing to exploit factional and inter-party competition by selective candidate endorsement, but by Stuntz's definition, nonpartisanship was now limited to pursuing goals that could obtain consensus.

Following Allison's reelection, Alliance legislators introduced several bills on a variety of subjects: further railroad reform, regulation of insurance companies, taxation of mortgages, and reduction of the legal rate of interest. A correspondent to the Omaha *Bee* reported that the "lower house had been literally swept off its feet by the number and character of bills introduced in that body. The corporation cappers seem to be completely dazed at the turn of affairs." Many antimonopoly bills were indefinitely postponed, but the legislature did pass a law to make the railroad commission's schedule of rates applicable to shipments across two or more lines, a law to reduce the legal rate of interest from 10 to 8 percent, and an antitrust law. It was not without justification that Stuntz felt the session had been a resounding success.[44]

By early 1890 the IFA's orientation to the political system had changed significantly from its position in 1887 and early 1888. Before, the Alliance had pressured the political system from outside by threatening to defeat candidates who did not support Alliance demands. But the success of this strategy began to draw the leadership of the IFA into the party system. Alliance leaders established ties with party politicians, particularly in the antimonopoly wing of the GOP but also among regular Republicans and Democrats, and they formed an alliance with the state's jobbers. These connections obligated Alliance leaders to support those politicians who had responded to its demands and to maintain good relations with nonagricultural interests. Furthermore, Iowa's competitive political environment required politicians to gain the support of key Alliance officials and the Alliance's legislative allies. Candidates in Kansas and Nebraska never thought to entreat Alliance officials for an endorsement, but Iowa politicians coveted the blessing of an Ashby, a Furrow, or a Post. Ingalls assumed he had the luxury of ignoring reformers and even mocking them, but Allison was compelled to dispatch emissaries to bargain and to persuade. IFA leaders undoubtedly believed they were fulfilling their duties by influencing the political process on behalf of farmers, but as they became enmeshed in the web of obligations constituting the existing party system, they were losing their ability to act independently.

The ultimate effect of nonpartisanship in a competitive party system was to reinforce existing party loyalties. Since most Alliance leaders had always been Republicans, the GOP in the long run stood to benefit from the IFA's nonpartisan strategy. Once political pressure from the Alliance had succeeded in producing a political consensus on railroad regulation, other issues, which reinforced traditional party loyalties, became more salient. In the election of 1889 with both parties pledged to uphold the 1888 law and actively competing for the farm vote, many Republican Alliance leaders perceived little difference between the two parties on antimonopoly issues. Perhaps doubts about Hutchison's record hovered, but his endorsement of the 1888 maximum-rate law could be considered credible. For many Iowa Alliance leaders prohibition became the important question, and there was little doubt which party was on the right side of this issue. An election in which the saloon was paramount activated traditional party loyalties based on cultural cleavages between "drys" and "wets"; President Furrow's declaration of his abhorrence of the Democratic Party's position on the saloon in the 1889 campaign illustrates this point perfectly. Had the Republicans' record and position on railroad reform been entirely unsatisfactory, someone such as Furrow might have bolted the party for the Democrats or for a third party. But with the GOP position at least somewhat acceptable, prohibition overrode any lingering doubts about Hutchison's record. It is noteworthy that in 1890 Furrow openly campaigned for the Republicans in the eleventh congressional district.[45]

As the Alliance leaders were drawn into the party system, many of them (although not all) embraced a more cautious approach to reform and moved toward an ideology of consensus that narrowed the definition of acceptable political action. In the campaign for railroad reform Alliance leaders had frequently employed radical antimonopoly rhetoric and had directly confronted their political opponents. At the same time, however, leaders such as Henry Wallace had justified demands for railroad regulation in broad cross-class terms stressing the interests of farmers, merchants, and manufacturers vis-à-vis railroad corporations. Once the 1888 legislation passed, this rationale for reform bound the Alliance to certain standards of "reasonableness," thereby narrowing the meaning of the pursuit of nonpartisan politics. Having met with success through appealing to a broad coalition of interests,

IFA leaders counseled the organization to advocate only measures that all Iowans would regard as beneficial and to reject any form of "class legislation" that might appear to favor farmers and injure another group. Thus in late 1888 state secretary Post warned that the Alliance "cannot afford to demand unreasonable and unjust things or measures which, enacted into law, would deprive any other class of any rights or privileges they enjoy." Recognizing that "success in a country where the majority must always rule" required continued support from other classes, Post advised "conservatism in the formulation of plans of action as will surely enlist public opinion in our behalf."[46] Wallace voiced the same sentiment in writing that the Alliance could ill afford to listen "to socialistic or anarchical sophisteries [sic]. They can safely advocate only such measures as are just and right in themselves and which they can defend successfully before the highest intelligence of a civilized age."[47]

A strategy based upon a search for consensus posed little threat to the existing political system. The parties themselves would be allowed to define for the Alliance the boundaries of admissability since the Alliance's criterion allowed the parties to reject any measure threatening the interests of any segment of their constituency as "class legislation." Once inside the party system, Alliance leaders had given up the right to advance any measures unacceptable to the corporations—and these entities continued to possess substantial political power. Accordingly, the agenda Henry Wallace considered appropriate was fairly narrow: the Conger lard bill to tax compounds of cottonseed oil and lard, the Butterworth antioption bill to prohibit "gambling" in grain futures, government "control" (but not ownership) of telegraphs (but not railroads), postal savings banks, and compulsory arbitration of labor disputes. Despite Wallace's disclaimer that none of these propositions was "in any degree partisan," even these moderate measures encountered strong opposition. The Chicago Board of Trade fought restrictions on its speculative operations, and southern farmers vigorously opposed the Conger lard bill.[48]

The leadership's support for the Conger bill demonstrated the costs of Wallace's policy of consensual nonpartisanship. Although all interests in Iowa—not only hog farmers but merchants, bankers, and railroad managers—could accept a measure to protect the market for one of Iowa's major products, the price of achieving an intrastate unanimity of interests was to destroy the possibility of national unity among farmers. The Conger lard bill was one of many obstacles blocking a proposed merger between the Northern and Southern Alliances in St. Louis in December 1889.[49] Moreover, the Alliance leaders' efforts to protect pure lard illustrate the point that the Alliance's agenda usually depended upon working through the GOP. Post and Stuntz worked closely with Allison on the Conger bill, named for its sponsor Edwin H. Conger (R-Iowa), and both men traveled to Washington to lobby for its passage. Hoping to cash in on his investment in Allison's reelection, Stuntz urged Allison to "do all you can" for the measure and reminded him that the "agricultural classes ought to have some Legislation very soon and I with many others would like to see the Republican Party take the lead in this matter."[50] The IFA leadership's commitment to interclass cooperation validated basic tenets of orthodox Republicanism. No one preached the doctrine of social harmony more enthusiastically than Iowa's conservative Republicans, who envisioned Iowa's interests—agriculture, labor, finance, railroads—working together to build a prosperous state. A cardinal economic doctrine of the conservatives held that if farmers passed injurious regulatory legislation or if labor struck against corporations, everyone would be harmed since prosperity depended upon a favorable climate for investment. Republican tariff doctrine was built upon a similar concept: protective tariffs would build up industry, thus raising wages and providing a home market for the products of the farm. In accepting the necessity of interclass consensus, many Iowa Alliance leaders gave subtle confirmation to this conservative Republican view.

The pursuit of consensus led Henry Wallace to seek ways for improving the farmer's position that were outside the political arena entirely. In 1887 and early 1888 Wallace had stressed political solutions to farmers' problems, but after achieving the goal of railroad regulation, he increasingly emphasized the importance of education in improved farming methods. Wallace's disengagement from politics was partly because of pressure from the owner of the Homestead, J. M. Pierce, who advised his editor in 1889 that since "we have won our fight" on the railroad question, "it might be well to let the matter rest a while until the excitement quiets down." By 1890 Wallace was counseling the Alliance that "the education of the farmers in the direct line of his business as a producer" should be the organization's top priority. Once the farmer had become "an earnest and effective thinker in the line of his business," then he could proceed to an intelligent discussion of public policy.[51] Wallace's pedagogical approach thus contrasted sharply with that of the leaders of the Kansas and Nebraska Alliances, who, as they moved toward a third party, taught the need for radical restructuring of economic and political institutions to meet the immediate crisis. Wallace, on the other hand, envisioned a gradual process of education, one that would discourage farmers from challenging the structures of power. The effect of Alliance education, as prescribed by Wallace, would shift the responsibility for the problems of agriculture onto the shoulders of farmers themselves; to enhance profitability farmers must practice better methods of crop rotation or improve the quality of their livestock. Like Republican politicians, Uncle Henry was telling farmers that legislation was at most a partial remedy for economic hardship.

Wallace represented the increasingly conservative tendencies of most Alliance leaders, but one state official, lecturer Newton B. Ashby, advocated a much broader agenda for reform in a work published in 1890, *The Riddle of the Sphinx*. Ashby carefully rejected any measure that smacked of being "class legislation"; for him, this criterion excluded the subtreasury and the land-loan plan, but it did admit government ownership of railroads and free coinage of silver. Ashby also advocated an interesting plan to inflate the currency by reducing taxation and issuing greenbacks to meet government obligations, similar in intent to modern deficit spending. This proposal, according to Ashby, would accomplish the same purpose as the land-loan plan but without violating the Alliance injunction against special privileges. Ashby, the only state Alliance official to advocate currency inflation, was after 1888 also alone in challenging the GOP as he did by attacking Hutchison's record in 1889.[52]

Ashby's attention to issues such as the subtreasury and the land-loan plan indicates that the Iowa Alliance was exposed, at least to some extent, to the ideas of the more radical Kansas and Nebraska Alliances. With prices so low that the *Register* was entreating farmers to burn corn in place of coal, the IFA grew rapidly during the winter of 1889–1890, its male membership almost doubling from 20,000 in September 1889 to 38,000 in October 1890.[53] These hard-pressed farmers undoubtedly were receptive to some of the ideas that were circulating among their neighbors to the west. Considering that no one in the Iowa Alliance leadership, not even Ashby, endorsed the land-loan plan, it is remarkable that the Iowa delegation to the annual meeting of the National Farmers' Alliance in January 1891, which included many middle-level leaders, voted eleven to six in favor of the plan.[54] Moreover, two farmers responding to the Iowa Commissioner of Labor Statistics survey in 1890 urged the government to loan money on real estate security and several others called for increasing the level of currency, an indication of the presence of radicalism at the grass roots.[55]

The resolutions passed at the IFA's 1890 annual meeting provide further evidence of some degree of radicalism among the membership and middle-level leaders. The platforms of 1888 and 1889 had consisted of piecemeal state-level reforms, but the platform of 1890 addressed a wide array of na-

tional reforms. In addition to the Conger lard bill and the Butterworth option bill, the convention expressed support for a graduated income tax, government ownership of railroads, free coinage of silver, "issue of all money by
the government without the intervention of national banks," prohibition of
alien ownership of land, the Australian ballot, and direct election of U.S.
senators. With the notable exception of the subtreasury and the land-loan
plan, the IFA platform endorsed most of the provisions that would be found
in the Populists' Omaha platform two years later. The impetus for an expanded platform seems to have come from the membership or from local
leaders rather than from the state leadership.[56]

Although the leadership of the Alliance was becoming more closely connected to the GOP, ordinary farmers continued to be restless with Republican economic policy. In the 1890 election Democratic congressional candidates capitalized on farmers' disgust with the GOP for passing the heavily
protective McKinley Tariff bill in the so-called "Billion-Dollar Congress."
For the first time in the post–Civil War era Democrats won the majority of
Iowa's congressional seats. Regression-based estimates indicate that the
Democrats obtained the votes of 38 percent of eligible farmers (47 percent
voted Republican, 3 percent Independent, and 12 percent did not vote).
Even though most farmers remained Republican, the Democrats had the
support of a greater percentage of farmers than at any time in the 1880s, a
significant achievement in view of the strong party loyalties binding farmers
to the party of Lincoln.[57] The election of 1890 in Iowa was not a revolution
as it was in Kansas and Nebraska, but it was nonetheless a repudiation of
the GOP and a sign, albeit more subtle, of agrarian unrest.

Iowa farmers were clearly more radical in 1890 than their leaders, but the
movement as a whole was certainly less so than the Alliance in Kansas and
Nebraska. The members of the Iowa Alliance were antimonopolists, but unlike their counterparts in Kansas and Nebraska, they had not embraced a
comprehensive program of economic collectivism. Nor had the Iowa Alliance movement as a whole arrived at a substantial critique of the existing
political order. Iowa farmers recognized that corporations manipulated political processes, but they had not developed an ideology of political corruption as farmers in Kansas and Nebraska had done by 1890. Not having experienced a political crisis, the Iowa Alliance did not become a movement with
tendencies for broader social reform. In Kansas and Nebraska the political
crisis had created space for women to assert a new political role, but in the
Iowa Alliance, where traditional politics had been effective, even if to a limited extent, there was little or no space for women to claim a voice in public
affairs, and they remained on the margins of the movement.[58] The Iowa Alli-

ance may have remained relatively moderate because economic hardship in Iowa was less severe than it was in some parts of Kansas and Nebraska. But the Iowa political environment clearly played a major role in shaping the Iowa Alliance's development, particularly at the leadership level, where it functioned to blunt much of the Alliance's potential for insurgency. Had the Iowa Alliance's leadership become alienated from the dominant party, as it did in Kansas and Nebraska, quite probably the IFA would have organized and supported a third party.

By late 1890 the leadership of the Iowa Alliance was firmly integrated within the existing party system, but the political upheaval to the west suddenly created a new challenge to the Alliance's stated policy of political neutrality. Kansas and Nebraska Populists would need to colonize the Iowa Alliance to create a national movement. No one knew for sure if the prairie fire to the west would spread to Iowa in 1891 or 1892. There was certainly sufficient tinder—low prices, mortgages, and high freight rates—to allow the flames to expand eastward. There were also political leaders in Iowa who had been recently isolated from the center of Iowa politics—men like "Widow" Weaver or "Calamity" Weller—and who were eager to lead a revolt.

9
Why Was There No Populism in Iowa?

The national farmers' movement reached an important crossroads in late 1890. Farmers' Alliances in Kansas, Nebraska, South Dakota, and Minnesota had formed state parties, and Alliance leaders in these states were confident they could launch a successful national third party even though they faced significant obstacles. The Alliance movement remained sectionally divided following the failure of a proposed merger between the NFA and IU (the Southern Alliance) and the NFA (the Northern Alliance) at St. Louis in December 1889. Southerners had made concessions to meet the NFA's objections to their exclusion of blacks and their requirement of secrecy, but the weaker NFA feared being swallowed by a movement that remained committed to working within the Democratic Party. In 1890 the NFA's sponsorship of legislation placing punitive taxes on lard products made with cottonseed oil further aggravated tensions. Republican and Democratic politicians had made a living prolonging sectional hatred and would exploit these sentiments whenever possible.[1]

Third-party strategists faced a serious political problem: The independent movements of 1890 had arisen in Republican strongholds, but in most southern states the Alliance had achieved some success in capturing the Democratic Party and thus had not moved toward independent action. In Missouri, Alliance delegates led by state lecturer Uriel S. Hall controlled the Democratic state convention of 1890, securing the nomination of the Alliance president for railroad commissioner and the adoption of a platform virtually identical to the Southern Alliance platform, with the notable omission of the subtreasury. Having captured the Democratic Party in Missouri, Hall became one of the leading opponents within the NFA and IU of the radicals' campaign to use the subtreasury as a wedge to split farmers from the Democrats. Leonidas Livingston, the Georgia state Alliance president, was another influential Alliance leader who resolutely opposed leaving the "party of the fathers."[2]

It was imperative that the third party make some gains in the South; otherwise, the GOP's charge that the independent movement was merely a creature of the Democratic Party would gain plausibility. Thus, at the annual convention of the NFA and IU at Ocala, Florida, in December 1890, a group of Kansans led by Benjamin Clover, John H. Rice, John Willits, and Stephen McLallin attempted to convince the delegates to endorse a new national political party. The Kansans found support from the radical wing of the Texas and Arkansas Alliances and from the South Dakota Alliance, which had defected from the Northern to the Southern Alliance in 1890. But most delegates from the southern states opposed a new party. During the 1890 campaign southern Alliances had achieved striking success by pledging candidates to "measure up" to an "Alliance yardstick" consisting of the Southern Alliance's 1889 St. Louis platform and other state-specific demands; through this strategy they had elected hundreds of legislators across the South. Now that Democratic legislators were pledged to support the Alliance, southerners could hardly turn their backs on the Democratic Party. As a compromise Charles Macune proposed that the convention postpone consideration of a third party until February 1892. The Kansans could do nothing to further a third party until then anyway, and the southerners would by then know if the new Democratic legislatures had been faithful to their promises. The convention adopted Macune's plan, but third-party advocates were impatient with the compromise. Even as the Ocala convention was preparing to adjourn, the Vincent brothers of Kansas and C. A. Power of Indiana issued a call for a national convention of all agricultural, industrial, and reform organizations to be held in early 1891.[3]

The question of a national third party also surfaced at the NFA's annual convention held at Omaha in January 1891. National lecturer Ashby of Iowa advised the delegates to "keep out of politics, for if we enter the swim we are bound to become corrupt." But Burrows of Nebraska urged the northerners to adopt a platform "upon which honest men cannot differ" and to publish it in the form of a declaration. This, he predicted, would enable the Alliance to "sweep the country in 1892." The convention, dominated by the Nebraska delegation, followed Burrows's advice and resolved to hold a preliminary convention in February 1892 that would then arrange a nominating convention. Although the rationale for this date was not made explicit, the northerners clearly were aware that the southerners had decided to meet then and hoped that both Alliances, beneath the banner of a new party, could transcend sectional animosities.[4]

Despite the NFA's apparent move toward a third party, apart from Minnesota and Nebraska there was little enthusiasm for independent politics in the Midwest. The IFA leadership was firmly nonpartisan. In Michigan a faction of the Patrons of Industry, the largest farm organization in the state, had decided to support a third-party movement, but instead of cooperating with the Union Labor or Greenback factions had captured the Prohibition Party, a tactic that had severely divided the agrarian movement. The NFA was weak in Ohio, Wisconsin, Michigan, Illinois, and Indiana. In the latter two states the much stronger Farmers' Mutual Benefit Association had achieved some success within the party system, and its leaders generally opposed a third party.[5]

The IFA leadership watched with alarm as Kansas and Nebraska farmers bade the old parties farewell in 1890. As the *Homestead* saw it, "scheming, corrupt, and selfish" men as well as "flighty, theoretical fellows" threatened to gain control of the Farmers' Alliance and lead it onto the disastrous path of a third party. The *Homestead* warned farmers that because they lacked "training and skill in organizing and conducting political campaigns," they would lose their enthusiasm, the new party would be defeated, and "then from both the old parties goes up the exultant shout, 'I told you so!' 'What fools these farmers are!' 'The old story of the Grange!' " The "true policy" of the Alliance, the *Homestead* instructed, should be for farmers to seek to control both parties' nominations: "Use your political birthright as a republican or a democrat, and name your man. Swear him to fidelity to Alliance principles. If he fails you, put him on the black list, bury him in a political grave wide and deep, and let his monument be a stake driven through the centre of the grave." To the argument that nonpartisan politics were ineffective, the *Homestead* turned to the history of Iowa. Prior to 1885 no state had been "more completely under the control of corporations," but Iowa had passed "the best railroad law in the Union." This had not come about because of a "third-party anti-monopoly movement," but it had been accomplished by "farmers going to the primaries in their own party and defeating any and every member of either party who was on record in 1885 as voting against the Alliance measures." For the *Homestead*, there were two roads: One was a "clear open pathway . . . lit up with the halo of past successes" and the other a "rocky road, above which false lights gleam, but which is strewn with wrecks of noble men and well-meant plans—the pathway of a third, or farmers' or Alliance party. There will be new wrecks along it next November."[6]

The *Homestead*'s defense of nonpartisanship was coupled with an attack on the NFA and IU. After the abortive attempt at a merger by the two national Alliances in St. Louis in 1889, the *Homestead* had minimized the differences between the two agricultural organizations, declaring both to be "practically a unit upon the great industrial questions of the day." But in mid-1890 the *Homestead* suddenly discovered that the Southern Alliance was a suspiciously centralized, secretive organization advocating a dangerous scheme—the subtreasury—that would surely encourage a speculative fever and "leave the West in a state of boom-stricken collapse." Moreover, the Southern Alliance had a "marked tendency . . . to form third party movements."[7]

As the spectacular Populist campaigns of 1890 came to a close in Kansas and Nebraska, the IFA held its annual meeting. Speaker after speaker exhorted the membership to remain true to the principle of nonpartisan politics. Henry Wallace encouraged the members to "keep on" in the policy of nonpartisanship since the "Iowa Alliance can to-day point to greater success than any Alliance in the United States," and H. H. Haaff "advised the Texas fellows to go back home and put their own state right before they [come] up here." Lecturer Will N. Sargent urged the delegates to "freeze" the ambitions of "demagogic" men who "flock to the Alliance; and they are not within the fold a month until they think the whole Alliance was made for their benefit, and although the organization is a pledged non-partisan one, they straightway advise and urge that we make a political party of it."[8] The IFA leadership's defensive response to the perceived threat of a third party restricted the scope of its action and led to depoliticization. President Furrow's address to the convention revealed that he had nothing to offer farmers eager for an improvement in their economic position. Furrow realized that Iowa farmers were discouraged because of low prices, but in an astonishing admission for the head of an organization formed primarily to secure legislative reform, Furrow confessed he knew of nothing that could be done except to "hang to the willows and fight it out on the line of better farming, better breeding, and better feeding." The major battlefront was not in the halls of legislation but on the fields and in the feedlots. "A little less kid-glove gentry and a little more practical and operative farming," Furrow lectured, would go a long way to remedy the problems of farmers.[9]

Although the IFA leadership opposed third-party politics, some middle-level figures favored independent action. One of these radicals, A. J. Westfall, ran for Congress in 1890 on the Union Labor ticket in the eleventh congressional district in northwestern Iowa, receiving 13 percent of the vote. After being appointed to confer on the best method to organize a new party at the Northern Alliance's January 1891 meeting, Westfall convened a meeting of Northern Alliance representatives from Iowa, Minnesota, Nebraska, and North Dakota in Sioux City for the purpose of inaugurating a third party; a majority of those members in attendance opposed this plan.[10] But the most ambitious attempt to create a Populist Party in Iowa originated outside the IFA and was led by James Baird Weaver, the most experienced and capable radical politician in Iowa. After the collapse of the statewide Democratic/Greenback coalition in 1887 and his defeat as a fusion candidate for Congress the next year, Weaver was politically isolated. He had lost much of his influence within the Democratic Party, and the Union Labor Party, the successor to the Greenback Party, was seriously demoralized after its poor showing in 1887. Many third-party politicians had returned to the old parties. Henry S. Wilcox informed L. H. Weller that he saw little hope that a new party could succeed for at least another decade. Meanwhile, Wilcox wrote, "I shall strive to benefit my country through the caucus of the strongest party in my legislative and congressional district i.e. the republican party." KOL leader James R. Sovereign had supported the Union Labor ticket in 1887, but realizing that a third party afforded limited opportunities, he began to operate within the Democratic Party; his approach paid a dividend when Governor Boies appointed him commissioner of labor statistics in 1890.[11]

Those individuals who remained in the Union Labor Party were bitterly divided over the perennial question of fusion. A letter to the antifusionist Weller, which characterized "office-seekers" such as Weaver as "a greater curse to Labor than all the monopolists this side of Hadies [sic]," revealed the depths of feeling provoked by this issue. At the Union Labor Party's 1889 convention Weller won a resolution against fusion. Yet if consorting with the Democrats was unprincipled, remaining pure brought few concrete rewards: The party's candidate for governor, S. B. Downing, received under 2 percent of the total vote.[12] With the Union Labor Party obviously irrelevant in Iowa politics, Weaver sought to create a new base; setting his sights on a different political course, he declined the Union Labor congressional nomination and a likely Democratic endorsement in the seventh district in 1890. Watching the political revolution to the west, the general saw brighter prospects in the Farmers' Alliance.[13]

From 1887 through 1890 Weaver had had little to do with the IFA. In 1890 he may have considered the tactic of burrowing within the IFA in order to steer it toward a third party, but he apparently judged that it would be more effective to encourage the formation of a branch of the NFA and IU in Iowa. This branch, he may have reasoned, would provide a vehicle for an eventual merger with the IFA, and he could then direct a new combined Alliance toward a third party. In any case, with Weaver's encouragement the NFA and IU organized an Iowa branch at Creston in March 1891. Leonidas L. Polk of North Carolina, president of the NFA and IU, presided over the meeting. He was accompanied by national lecturer John F. Willits, the Kansas People's Party's gubernatorial candidate the previous fall, congressman-elect John G. Otis of Kansas, and Alonzo F. Wardall of the South Dakota Alliance. The convention chose J. M. Joseph as president, Daniel Campbell as vice-president, G. B. Lang as secretary, and L. H. Griffith as lecturer, all of whom had been associated with third-party movements in the past. Although Weaver did not play a conspicuous role in the proceedings, he was clearly the most prominent figure associated with the new movement.[14]

Having formed a new Alliance, third-party advocates moved immediately to organize a political party in time for the fall campaign, calling for an independent state convention to be held in early June. Heralding a "new era in the politics of Iowa," the *Tribune* predicted that the "Independent success of Kansas last year" would be "duplicated in Iowa this year." In fact, the newspaper contended, conditions were more auspicious in Iowa, where both parties were evenly divided, than in Kansas, where there had been a huge Republican majority to overcome. This assessment accurately identified state party systems as an important influence on the chances of a third party but reversed the actual consequences of one-party dominance and two-party competition. The *Tribune* justified a third party on the grounds that the two parties had been unresponsive to the concerns of producers, citing the recent refusal of the bipartisan state executive committee to increase the rate of assessment on railroad property and the GOP's determination to reelect the unpopular Allison, but it was much more difficult to persuade voters of the need to reject the two parties when, under the pressures of party competition, the system had achieved some reforms, even if these were limited in scope.[15]

The *Tribune* glowed with optimism, but third-party leaders were more realistic behind closed doors. Jonathan Shearer, chairman of the independent convention committee, wrote to Weller in late April that the "Farmers' Alliance in Iowa is in the worst shape imaginable. The Industrial Union and the Iowa Alliance are about locking horns and the result for the immediate future certainly seems to me to be deplorable."[16] As Shearer recognized, a successful third-party movement in Iowa would require unity between the two Alliances, but the old Alliance was hardly playing the role of gracious host. The *Homestead* continued its assault on the methods and purposes of the NFA and IU, which was "striving by hook or by crook, to gain a foothold" in Iowa; it charged that although organizers of the new Alliance publicly professed friendship to the old Alliance, in private, they "breathe all manner of slander and backbiting concerning everything and everybody connected with the Iowa Farmers' Alliance." Organizers of the new Alliance had deceitfully posed as organizers commissioned by the old Alliance in order to enroll farmers under false pretenses, and they had even attempted to bribe organizers of the old Alliance.[17] These efforts were part of the NFA and IU's plot to create a "gigantic cotton trust, which by controlling the product of the American cotton belt, should virtually control the cotton market of the world." The Southern Alliance's advocacy of the subtreasury—a blatant case of "class legislation"—demonstrated beyond doubt that the organization was in the service of "corporate interests," and it had repeatedly "strangled" all measures of "genuine reform" such as the Conger lard bill. The *Homestead* neglected to explain why producers of cottonseed oil should have regarded a measure intended to preserve hog producers' monopoly on lard products as a "genuine reform."[18]

To meet the threat of the new Alliance, the leadership of the old Alliance moved to tighten its control by organizing congressional district Alliances, a plan originally adopted in late 1890 to promote the organization's financial health. Although the Iowa Alliance had grown rapidly during the winter of 1889–1890, many members had been unable to pay their annual dues of 50 cents; cash-poor farmers simply could not afford to part with a sum amounting to two and one-half bushels of corn. The IFA commissioned district organizers to strengthen existing suballiances and to organize new suballiances where possible; they would be paid a portion of the dues they collected and a per diem of $2.00 plus expenses for arranging county Alliance meetings.[19]

Once the Southern Alliance began operating in Iowa, the IFA leadership, in a classic illustration of the "iron law of oligarchy," turned to the system of district organizers to centralize their control over the organization and thereby resist the threat the NFA and IU posed.[20] During early summer 1891 congressional district Alliances were organized in most of Iowa's districts. The proceedings of the organizational meeting of the third congressional district Alliance at Waterloo clearly show that the main purpose of these groups was to ensure nonpartisanship. J. H. Sanders, the district organizer, called the meeting to order and was made temporary chairman; he then appointed a committee to draft a constitution and by-laws. While this committee retired to fulfill its assignment, President Furrow and Lecturer Sargent, both strong opponents of a third party, addressed the assembly. The committee then returned with a document containing an affirmation that "this Alliance is strictly non-partisan in its methods"; this declaration, as the

Homestead's reporter noted, was the "only article of special interest in the document."[21]

This systematic restructuring of the organization effectively created a cadre devoted to the policy of nonpartisanship; there were a few hitches, however. Even though IFA leadership undoubtedly made every effort to appoint district organizers who opposed independent politics, they could not exclude members who desired to devote themselves to the work simply because they harbored third-party sympathies. Thus, although A. J. Westfall had run as an Independent for Congress in 1890, the state leadership could not deny him a commission as a district organizer in the eleventh district since excluding "independents" would be partisan. Nor could the old Alliance prevent Westfall from leading the eleventh district into the Weaver Alliance in protest against "Emperor" Furrow and "Czar" Post, as he did in September 1891. This incident, however, was the only instance of mass defection.[22]

The Alliance even gave a commission to that old third-party warrior, "Calamity" Weller, in the fourth congressional district. Perhaps the Alliance leaders were so desperate for funds that they opened their doors to such a well-known friend of third parties, but they may have known that Weller would stay clear of the Weaver-dominated Southern Alliance. "The FA & IU in Iowa," Sargent informed Weller shortly after his appointment," is "J.B.W.'s order." That fact, he confided, "is sufficient to explain why silence will break their neck for they are bound to hang themselves inside of the next 6 months." Weller may have nodded in assent, but just to be sure that he toed the line, Sargent took the unusual precaution of appointing a second district organizer in Weller's district, a Republican named William T. Diller.[23]

Evidently, Weller's strategy was to work within the old Alliance in order to effect a merger with the new Alliance. If he could manage this plan, he would perhaps be in the dominant position in a new consolidated Alliance, but to work within the new Alliance would leave him subordinate to Weaver. From these premises, apparently, Weller rejected the advice of H. L. Loucks, president of the NFA and IU–affiliated South Dakota Alliance, who urged Weller to join with his order as it was "more aggressive [sic] politically in Iowa than the N.F.A."[24] Weller's moment came in October when the state organizations of both Alliances met separately in Des Moines. As a delegate to the IFA convention, Weller offered numerous resolutions and motions designed to consolidate the two orders; their defeat dashed his hopes of leading the IFA out of the wilderness of nonpartisanship.[25]

Conditions, then, were scarcely auspicious for the success of a new party in Iowa. The original Farmers' Alliance of Henry Wallace and August Post still held the allegiance of the majority of Iowa's farmers. IFA leaders were entrenched in their opposition to third-party politics, and they had established the effective mechanism of congressional district Alliances to ensure their control over the organization. Partisans of a third party were weak and divided. Some potential leaders of a new party had found their way back into the two-party system in the wake of the demoralization of the Greenback/Union Labor movement. The two most capable radicals in the state—Weaver and Weller—were barely on speaking terms, and although they both looked to a harvest of farmers for a third party, they were tilling separate fields at a moment requiring cooperation.

The Iowa People's Party was born on 3 June 1891 at the Grand Opera House of Des Moines. The hall was decked with banners denouncing economic inequality ("Our plutocracy must be downed or crowned" and "3,000 millionaires, 3,000,000 tramps, 9,000,000 mortgages.") and expressing faith in the prospects of a political revolution in Iowa ("The storm center is moving Eastward"). Congressman John Otis of Kansas informed the delegates that his state was "watching Iowa with intense interest and hopes for your success this fall." Otis's hopes were high because the current situation was similar to the 1850s—Iowa had been antislavery then and was "anti-slavery now, when it involves the freedom of 45,000,000 Industrial slaves." The convention nominated A. J. Westfall for governor and Walter S. Scott, Iowa president of the United Mine Workers, for lieutenant governor. The platform endorsed the national platform of the People's Party adopted at Cincinnati and indicted the two major parties' records in Iowa, condemning the failure of the state executive committee to increase the assessment on railroad property and denouncing the two previous legislatures for defeating the Australian ballot law, the 2-cent passenger fare, uniform schoolbooks, and taxation of mortgages. On labor issues the platform endorsed the eight-hour day, weekly pay for miners, and the repeal of an objectionable provision that had been added to a recently passed law designed to ensure that the method of screening coal provided fair compensation to coal miners.[26]

Conservative Republicans dismissed the new party as nothing more than the same old wine in a new wineskin. The *Register* scoffed at the notion that the convention was a "popular uprising of the people"; the new party "is composed of the same men who years ago started out to reform the world under the Greenback banner and later as the Union Labor party." The platform was "made up of such discordant planks that [it] is hard to see how it can hold together until November." The newspaper predicted that the leaders of the new party would "form a coalition with the Democrats before the campaign is over," just as they had often done in the past.[27]

Conservative Republicans probably were not worried that the Iowa People's Party would replicate the accomplishment of the Kansas and Nebraska Populists the previous fall. They were, however, concerned that the new party would cost them the upcoming election by attracting Republican farmers. Republicans already faced an uphill battle to unseat the popular Boies; they could not afford to lose a single Republican vote. Looking ahead to the national election of 1892, a third party that could draw even 5 or 10 percent of the vote might give Iowa to the Democrats. The situation required the utmost caution. The GOP avoided direct attacks on the leaders of the Iowa People's Party, instead sounding the alarm against an invasion of Kansans. The Burlington *Saturday Evening Post* reported that "Kansas third party orators will be brought across the Big Muddy in shoals and turned loose to board around among the farm houses on the Iowa prairies. There will be such a mussing up of spare bedrooms and antique china as has not been known in the country since the first settlements."[28] The *Register*, announcing the imminent arrival of "a whole swarm of Kansas grasshopper politicians," warned them that "Iowa is not ready to be devastated by political cyclones of the Kansas kind that leave nothing but crippled industries and wrecked commercial credit behind them. Iowa people do not believe in turning everything topsy turvy in hope of accomplishing some visionary reforms." The *Register* admitted that farming in Iowa "has not been as profitable as some other lines of business for several years past," but if this state of affairs was due to legislation, Iowa farmers could easily find relief. The *Register* assured farmers that any laws that would benefit them, "without destroying other interests, will be gladly conceded them by the old parties."[29]

The GOP soon hoisted the venerable banner of sectionalism to wave beside the flag of state patriotism. The *Register* informed any Republican farmers and laboring men "who have been invited to join the people's party movement" that it "was originated and is being operated by the Southern Alliance entirely in the interest of the Democratic party, and that while the Southern Alliance is pushing the 'people's' party stool pigeon scheme in the Northern states it is insisting that 'the South must remain solidly Democratic!' "[30] The *Register*'s contention that the People's Party would benefit the Democrats was entirely plausible given the situation at the state and national level. Leaders of the Iowa Populist movement had a history of cooperation with the Democrats; Populist/Democratic fusion was certainly a possibility. Moreover, at the national level the Alliance movement did seem to be operating in the interests of the Democratic Party. In the Democratic South the Alliance had remained nonpartisan, but in Kansas and Nebraska the Alliance had formed a third party and brought down the GOP. Republicans may have been mistaken in attributing this pattern to a sinister design, but there was no mystery about which party stood to gain by it.

Iowa Democrats adopted a friendlier disposition toward the People's Party, recognizing that although it might draw the votes of some Democratic farmers and workingmen, it would, as the Des Moines *Leader* observed, "prove a very serviceable haven for a large number of republicans who have renounced their own party, but cannot persuade themselves to work with [the] democracy." Yet the *Leader* distanced itself from the People's Party, contending that little in the platform would appeal to "workingmen, farmers and anti-monopolists generally" and dismissing the "main feature" of the new party, the subtreasury, as a "paternalistic idea" and a "gigantic and barefaced" case of "class legislation."[31]

The Democrats hoped that they, not the Populists, would reap the benefit of discontent with the GOP. Following Boies's election in 1889 the Iowa Democratic Party had begun to envision itself as leading the national party to triumph in the traditionally Republican Midwest. Campaigning against protection in Iowa in the elections of 1889 and 1890, Horace Boies had become convinced that midwestern farmers would respond favorably to the message of a tariff for revenue only, and on 23 December 1890 he became a national apostle for the doctrine of free trade. In a speech before the Tariff Reform Club in New York City, Boies cited figures from the Iowa Commissioner of Labor Statistics showing that Iowa farmers had been producing corn at a loss for the previous five years. Under these conditions, Boies argued, it was unfair for the GOP to demand that farmers pay a "tax" on manufactured goods and at the same time exclude their products from foreign markets. Nor was it equitable to ask farmers to wait for a home market to "grow up around them that is large enough to consume the enormous surplus they annually produce." Farmers wanted "relief for themselves and not for generations unborn."[32]

Boies's New York speech catapulted him into national prominence—he would become a leading contender for the Democratic presidential nomination in 1892 and 1896—and it defined much of the terrain for the election of 1891 in Iowa. The *Register* immediately pounced upon the speech as a lie, the work of a demagogue, a slander against the farmers of Iowa and gravely predicted that homeseekers and investors would bypass the Hawkeye state since "Blunder" Boies had maligned its productive fields as a poverty-stricken wasteland.[33] As the campaign opened, the *Register* reminded Iowans that Boies had "steadily traduced the name and fame" of their state and had "grossly slandered its chief business interests and most numerous class of citizens." The *Register* reprinted Boies's "New York Beer garden speech," serving notice that the document would be a vital issue in the upcoming contest.[34]

Democrats did not regard Boies's speech as a liability and insisted that the governor had courageously spoken the truth. Addressing the Democratic state convention, Walter H. Butler pointed out that the labor of farmers "is not fairly rewarded" because they "sell their products at too low a price, and pay too much for that which they must buy." This, Butler declared, "is not a new truth"; it had been evident to farmers themselves for several years. The innovation was that "in the very home of monopoly, the truth was declared with glorious courage, and the legitimate demands of the agricultural west, asserted by that grand old tribune of the people, Governor Horace Boies, of Iowa." The Democratic platform, written by a committee chaired by the *Leader*'s editor, Henry Stivers, indicted the McKinley bill and demanded free coinage of silver, equality of taxation, antitrust legislation, prohibition of alien ownership of land, public employment agencies, the Australian ballot, and direct election of U.S. senators. As in years past, the platform called for a high license on saloons of $500. This platform indicated the persistence of the strategy the Democrats had been employing successfully since the mid-1880s: appealing to antimonopoly voters on economic issues and at the same time avoiding alienating such voters, who were often sympathetic toward prohibition, by endorsing at least some restrictions on saloons.[35]

Republican Party managers realized how vulnerable they were. The party's support for prohibition remained a substantial liability. Although a vocal minority of "wets" at the convention tried to convince the delegates to abandon the party's suicidal commitment to prohibition, the "drys" had the numbers and soundly defeated a local-option plank.[36] From the standpoint of conservative party managers, the only possible hope for Republican victory, given the albatross of prohibition, was to recapture some of the farmers they had lost to the Democrats in 1889. This task would be difficult since farmers were scarcely enthusiastic about the McKinley tariff bill, passed in 1890. Conservative Republicans determined that their only course of action was to embrace Hiram Wheeler, the man they had spurned two years earlier. "Farmer Wheeler," the *Register* announced after the convention had nominated him virtually by consent, "is not a political demagogue, is not a slanderer of his own state or a self convicted liar . . . [and] never classes the farmers of the state as fools and paupers." On the other hand, "Blunder Boies represents retrogression, free whiskey, free trade, calamity, and general ruin."[37]

As never before, the Regency extended the hand of fellowship to Iowa farmers, inviting them to full participation in the affairs of the party. Sounding much like the *Homestead* during the campaign for railroad regulation in 1887, the *Register* urged farmers to participate in local Republican conventions. Since farmers "have the power to select at least 90 percent of the delegates to the state conventions of their party," they could "make the party just what they desire it to be."[38] The *Register* was particularly solicitous of the IFA. Again like the *Homestead*, the *Register* drew a sharp distinction between the "Southern Alliance," which it characterized as "merely a stool pigeon trap, baited with demagogues, and operated in the interests of the Democracy," and the "National Farmers' Alliance," an organization of "real farmers" who were not "repudiators" or "visionary schemers or reckless demagogues" but were "the real strength and main stay of honest government."[39] As if Uncle Henry had suddenly assumed control of its editorial page, the *Register* praised the original Alliance for its past successes in securing beneficial legislation and expressed confidence that the Alliance could obtain any needed legislation through its wise nonpartisan policy.[40] Although Wallace may have welcomed this belated endorsement of the Iowa Alliance's involvement in politics, he detected more than a little opportunism in the *Register*'s sudden conversion to the cause of the farmer, and the *Homestead* chastised the *Register* for "kissing the granger's toe."[41] Despite lingering tensions between Wallace and conservative Republicans, the political situation had changed greatly since 1887–1888. The Iowa Alliance leadership, having moderated its rhetoric and narrowed the scope of nonpartisanship, had become far less dangerous to GOP managers. Given the shared threat from the People's Party, the IFA and the Regency had become political allies even if they might not have cared to admit it.

Fears of an invasion of Kansas Populists never materialized. Although Kansas Populists, who had taken the lead in organizing a national party in 1891, ideally would have sent dozens of organizers into every state of the Midwest and the South, the scarcity of personnel, time, and money forced them to make painful choices. In order to deprive the Republican Party of its major argument that independent politics would result in a national Democratic triumph, Kansas Populists made the conversion of southern farmers to the third party their highest priority; and they focused their efforts in the Midwest on Ohio where they hoped to unseat Sen. John Sherman, who for many Populists was the very incarnation of the "money power." Although Kansas Populists helped organize the Populist movement in Iowa, the Hawkeye state was not at the top of their agenda. When Peffer did campaign in Iowa for two weeks in August and September, he was discouraged to find little enthusiasm for the new party. The tireless Mary E. Lease spoke in Iowa during the closing week of the campaign, but a concerted effort by Kansas Populists to saturate Iowa never materialized; their resources were simply stretched too thin.[42]

The Nebraska Populists made no attempt to organize in Iowa or elsewhere in 1891. Indeed, most Nebraska Independents were ambivalent about the national People's Party, primarily because they were suspicious of the NFA and IU and its subtreasury plan. Prior to the Nebraska People's Party state convention of 1891, the *Alliance* urged the delegates to refrain from endorsing the subtreasury, flatly predicting that a "national party that would adopt so wild and chimerical a proposition would not endure three months." The *Alliance* buttressed its position by quoting an article written by an old Greenbacker, Col. S. F. Norton, editor of the *Chicago Sentinel*, lamenting the Cincinnati convention's recent adoption of the subtreasury plan. There was no chance that the subtreasury would ever become law, Norton was relieved to say, but the problem was that "its fall may take with it the grand and useful scheme of government loans on real estate to men who want to procure for themselves homes of their own." Although Burrows eventually endorsed the subtreasury plan in 1892, evidently for the sake of party unity, in the crucial organizing year of 1891, the Nebraskans (with the exception of Van Wyck) remained at home.[43]

Even if Kansas and Nebraska Populists had been able to unite and to concentrate their resources exclusively on organizing Iowa, it is doubtful they would have encountered much success since the political situation there was so unfavorable to a new party. The leadership of the third-party movement bore the scars of past conflict over fusion and was deeply divided, and the leadership of the IFA opposed a third party and possessed significant resources allowing it to resist. Furthermore, party competition worked against a third party by providing farmers with options to express their grievances. For farmers who had always been Democrats or who had become alienated by the Republican Party, the Democratic Party's attacks on the McKinley bill and its support for free silver provided a viable means for the expression of political discontent and the desire for reform. Such voters might have been willing to support a third party under some circumstances, but since the Iowa People's Party seemed to have little chance of winning and the Democrats appeared quite likely to prevail, it made more sense to cast a ballot for the Democrats, especially as the party appeared to be, at least to some extent, an antimonopoly party. On the other hand, the GOP remained a viable choice for many Republican farmers. Although the party had rejected Wheeler in 1889, farmers had prevailed and secured his nomination in 1891.

Moreover, farmers had been able to influence the GOP in the past; the 1888 railroad legislation continued to testify to the efficacy of working within the two-party system. Although farmers had not achieved everything they had wished since, they had obtained some reforms and could plausibly hope for further success. To vote for the People's Party, as IFA and Republican Party leaders cautioned, would only help the Democratic Party and would destroy the IFA by dragging it into third-party politics.

Ultimately, the election of 1891 was a battle between the Democrats and the Republicans. The People's Party was relevant to the outcome only because in such a close contest the defection of even a small percentage of voters could affect the result. Iowa Populists gained only slightly over 3 percent of the total vote. Boies was reelected, winning 49.4 percent to Wheeler's 47.5 percent; Wheeler proved no more successful at attracting farmers than Hutchison had two years before. Although turnout among farmers increased from 1889 to 1891 (from an estimated 88 percent to a remarkably high 94 percent) both major parties gained about equally over the two elections. Once again, Democrats were successful in 1891 in attracting a substantial number of farmers. This achievement, combined with the anger of "wets" toward the GOP's unyielding stance on prohibition, gave the Democrats another victory.[44] The 1891 election was truly the decisive test of whether Iowa would produce a viable People's Party movement; the poor showing clearly revealed that the Hawkeye state would not be fertile ground for Populism in 1892, no matter who headed the ticket.

Despite his prediction in August 1892 that the Populist fire would spread eastward, James Weaver probably knew that he would be an unhonored prophet in his native state.[45] That Iowa knew Weaver so well was not necessarily an advantage. Familiarity may not have bred universal contempt, but it had undoubtedly produced a widespread skepticism about the general's motives. By 1892 Weaver had been maneuvering within the world of Iowa politics for several years. Although his initial break with the GOP in the late 1870s could be seen as principled and his adoption of fusion in the early and mid-1880s as a justified accommodation to political reality, Weaver's return to third-party politics cost him much of his credibility and left him more vulnerable than ever to the charge of political opportunism. The prophet had become too much the politician.

The obstacles that Iowa Populists had faced in 1891 were if anything more formidable in 1892. A national campaign worked against the People's Party in states where the party had not already become viable. In a state where no independent movement had emerged, the Populists might not mount any showing at all, making it especially difficult for them to counter the argument that a Populist vote was a wasted vote or an indirect vote for the least preferred (or most hated) candidate of the two major parties. This logic was salient in any election but particularly so in a national one when the stakes were high. Moreover, in a national election the entire resources of the two major parties would be available, and both would now be fully alert to the danger of the People's Party. The Farmers' Alliance in Kansas and Nebraska might have caught the GOP off guard in 1890, but it would be quite another matter for a national third-party movement to make advances in hostile territory in a national election with both parties prepared to meet the challenge. Finally, although the national People's Party had become better organized since 1891, its resources were still meager and would be stretched even thinner in a national campaign. Populist leaders undoubtedly would have been elated to saturate Iowa with orators and organizers, but the Hawkeye state was a relatively low priority. The People's Party's major objective was to build upon its strength in areas where significant independent movements had already emerged (the Rocky Mountain, Far Western, and Plains states) and to break the solid South. Accordingly, Weaver began his ambitious campaign in the Rocky Mountains and the Far West, then turned to the South, and finally ventured to the Midwest, concentrating his efforts primarily on states such as Kansas and Nebraska that had earlier developed strong independent parties. In August Weaver had made a twenty-four-hour rest stop in Iowa on his way from Cheyenne, Wyoming, to Moberly, Missouri, and returning from the South, where he and Mary Lease had endured the abuse of egg-throwing Democrats, Weaver spent five days in Iowa in mid-October, finding the crowds friendlier but smaller.[46] It was understandable that Weaver could not devote more attention to Iowa, but Iowa Populists were aggravated that the party's national committee was unable to provide other orators. The only speaker of national renown to campaign in Iowa was Hamlin Garland, and the Populist National Committee reneged on its promise to dispatch Marion Todd to Iowa, instead sending her to work elsewhere.[47]

Republicans, too, seemed to sense that the Populists were doomed in Iowa and decided they could afford to ignore them. In June the *Register* announced that it would not "take issue with any of the things done or said" by the Populists, and apart from an occasional attack the Republican press generally adhered to the policy of silently condemning Weaver and the Populists to irrelevance.[48] The GOP's attention instead was devoted exclusively to the mission of redeeming Iowa from the horrors of Democratic governance; to accomplish this the Regency's strategists were determined to focus solely on national issues—particularly the tariff—and to avoid the divisive question of prohibition. Conservative party managers won a significant battle at the Iowa Republican state convention in March when they defeated a resolution endorsing prohibition. During the campaign this move enabled Republicans to respond to Democratic demands that they take a stand on the saloon question by airily dismissing the issue as irrelevant to the "present canvass."[49] The Regency's strategy of emphasizing the tariff probably did not gain them many votes among discontented farmers, but the Democrats, having nominated Grover Cleveland, a staunch partisan of the gold standard, were poorly positioned to take advantage of the GOP's vulnerability. In the election both parties won about the same proportion of the farm vote as they had in 1891. Important to the Republican victory was the GOP's ability to attract a small percentage of antiprohibition voters: Estimated turnout among such voters increased from 64 to 72 percent; the estimated percentage voting Democratic remained the same (64 percent), but the estimated percentage of antiprohibitionists voting Republican increased from zero in 1891 to 8 percent in 1892. Apparently some antiprohibition voters who had been alienated by the GOP's policy and had not voted in 1891 were willing to vote for the Republicans once the party had distanced itself from prohibition.[50] By allowing even a minority of antiprohibition voters to return to the fold, the GOP's jettisoning of prohibition helped give Republican Benjamin Harrison the consolation of carrying Weaver's home state even as Weaver denied Harrison the traditional Republican strongholds of Colorado and Kansas.[51]

Near the close of the campaign , in an announcement that revealed much about the unfavorable climate for populism in Iowa, Albert Anderson, the antimonopoly candidate who had defeated the conservative William Hepburn in 1886, stated that he would support Benjamin Harrison. Anderson remained in favor of a reduction of the tariff and the free and unlimited coinage of silver, and he acknowledged that General Weaver was "sound on these questions." The problem, though, was that Weaver "does not stand a chance of an election," and to vote for him would be to "contribute to the support of Cleveland, . . . a result to which I do not intend to be a party."[52] Under other circumstances, Anderson and many other Iowans might have become Populists. Party loyalties were strong in Iowa, as they were everywhere, but they were constantly being considered, reevaluated, and adjusted according to changing political situations. Had the Iowa Farmers' Alliance failed to obtain any of its demands, and had it then moved toward independent political action, thus providing a strong organizational base for populism, the calculations of antimonopolists such as Anderson surely would have been different, as they would have been for countless Iowa farmers.

The Populists justified a third party through two arguments. They began from the premise of substantial economic distress, as the Omaha platform stated: "Business [is] prostrated; our homes [are] covered with mortgages; labor [is] impoverished; and the land [is] concentrating in the hands of the capitalists." Farmers everywhere in the Midwest could accept this proposition. Second, Populists contended that the existing parties were incapable of remedying this situation: "We charge that the controlling influences dominating both these parties have permitted the existing dreadful conditions to develop without serious effort to prevent or restrain them. Neither do they now promise us any substantial reform."⁵³ This rationale for a third party was compelling in Kansas and Nebraska, but in Iowa potential Populists remained unpersuaded to follow a course of action they regarded as unnecessary and dangerous.

The leadership of the IFA was able to save Iowa from the Populists, but in so doing they took steps that blunted the organization's momentum and eventually proved fatal. The IFA's program of congressional district organization, adopted to counter the threat from the new branch of the NFA and IU, proved costly. During the year ending 1 October 1890 the Iowa Alliance paid district organizers $660 and county and local organizers $1,644. After the adoption of the policy of district organization, the Iowa Alliance's expenditures increased significantly. For the year ending 1 October 1891 the Iowa Alliance paid district organizers $4,307 and county organizers $994; the total cost of organizing had increased by $2,997. The IFA had originally envisioned that district organizers would form new suballiances, thus increasing the total dues paid to the state organization, but instead district organizers concentrated mainly on fostering ideological conformity by incorporating existing suballiances into district Alliances. Consequently, the IFA's revenues from dues increased by only $932 (from $9,018 for the year ending 1 October 1890 to $9,950 for the year ending 1 October 1891). The costs of employing an army of district organizers were so great that the leadership abruptly suspended district-level work shortly after most districts had been organized in summer 1891.⁵⁴

Although district-level organization had proven effective in minimizing the defections of suballiances to the local branch of the NFA and IU and to the People's Party, the solidification of oligarchy proved counterproductive by sapping resources that might have gone into organizing new suballiances. Furthermore, the sudden decision of the Alliance leadership to suspend the work in summer 1891 undoubtedly demoralized organizers, many of whom probably were not paid in full for their efforts. The abrupt halt in district-level organization marked the end of the growth of the Iowa Alliance. From July through October only twenty-three new suballiances were organized, and apparently few, if any, new suballiances were organized thereafter.[55] Moreover, the IFA's drive to counter the rival branch of the NFA and IU led it to adopt a more defensive posture, in the long run contributing to its decline. By late 1890 the leadership had become so concerned with the threat of the new Alliance that it neglected to emphasize any positive program. The old Alliance, zealous to protect Iowa farmers from heretical proposals such as the subtreasury and the false political god of a third party, focused almost exclusively on its past successes and stopped telling farmers of the benefits they might gain from membership in the organization. There remained some grass-roots pressure from within the IFA for significant reform—the 1891 and 1892 conventions embraced a fairly radical platform.[56] Secretary Post continued to lobby Congress for pure-food and antioption legislation, and he was appointed by a Republican governor to the 1893 Iowa State Revenue Commission, which rejected as "unwise and illogical" an agrarian proposal for tax exemption of mortgaged property.[57] Post's efforts often failed to involve ordinary members, however, and the IFA leadership never advanced a new agenda to reawaken the dying enthusiasm of its membership.

Gradually farmers left the Iowa Alliance. At the 1892 annual meeting President J. H. Sanders acknowledged a "decrease in membership during the past year owing to several unfortunate conditions which are to be deplored." Still, Sanders maintained, the organization "stands to-day on a firmer basis of success" than ever before. One year later, however, Sanders lamented the fact that so many members had become inactive. By 1894 the Alliance was so weak that it evidently failed to hold an annual convention.[58] A further indication of its decline was the shrinking *Homestead* subscription list. From 1891 to 1894 Wallace lost about 5,000 of his 16,000 paid subscribers, and the *Homestead* in 1895 declared an "urgent need" for a revival of the IFA, but by then the Alliance had spent its energy and was no longer a meaningful expression of farmers' grievances and aspirations.[59]

Iowa's competitive party system eventually incorporated the leadership of the IFA. Indicative of this process, several Alliance leaders eventually sought and in many cases obtained political rewards for their work on behalf of one of the two parties. Secretary Post proudly assumed the position of sergeant-at-arms at the 1896 Republican National Convention; an adherent of McKinleyism, he went on to organize a national bank in his hometown of Moulton in 1900. "Tama Jim" Wilson, who had been closely identified with the Alliance and had played a crucial role in the reelection of Senator Allison in 1890, became secretary of agriculture in the McKinley administration. J. B. Furrow, Alliance president and Republican campaigner during the crucial years from 1889 through 1891, unsuccessfully sought a position from Republican governor Francis M. Drake as state commissioner of labor statistics in 1896, his supporters claiming that he had prevented the Alliance from going over to the Populists. The Democrats rewarded Ashby for his assistance in the 1889 campaign by appointing him to a position in the Dublin consulate early in the Cleveland administration.[60] Although rumors of political ambition swirled around Henry Wallace, he never sought to obtain an elective or an appointive position; he remained concerned about corporate influence in the Republican Party but was unwilling to launch a new crusade against the Regency. Through the pages of the *Homestead*, and after 1895, *Wallaces' Farmer*, he instructed farmers on how to improve their position through better feeding and breeding. In 1896 Wallace supported McKinley.[61]

Late nineteenth-century politics, at least before the Populist era, have often been characterized as offering voters little choice. The astute English observer of American politics in the Gilded Age, Lord James Bryce, concluded: "Neither party has anything definite to say on [the] issues; neither party has any principles, any distinctive tenets. Both have traditions. Both claim to have tendencies. Both have certainly war cries, organizations, interests enlisted in their support. But those interests are in the main the interests of getting or keeping the patronage of the government. Tenets and policies, points of political doctrine and points of political practice, have all but vanished."[62] Many historians have challenged this view, showing that the national political parties presented voters with meaningful options, particularly on social policy, an area in which the parties differed significantly over issues of moral reform.[63] Other scholars have shown that the parties' positions on the tariff represented real economic interests and were not just a device to obscure more pressing issues.[64]

At the level of state politics an even greater complexity of two-party political conflict existed over both social and economic issues. Iowa's party system contained a wide array of political positions represented by various parties and factions. There was the Greenback element, itself divided by issues of prohibition and fusion, a Democratic Party, far from the stereotypical image of a conservative Bourbon party with its strong antimonopoly wing, and the Iowa Republican Party, consisting of antimonopolists, conservative advocates of laissez-faire, and "drys" and "wets." An equally diverse array of political positions could be found in Kansas and Nebraska politics, but party competition made Iowa unique. This dynamic compelled each party to respond to voters' demands and to the strategy of their opponents. It is possible to see Iowa's party system as an example of a "healthy" two-party system: It provided voters with options and proved more responsive to popular demands than the one-party system in Kansas and in Nebraska. Yet even though Iowa politics appeared democratic, there were significant limits to popular influence. The dynamics of party competition allowed farmers to capture political power for a moment in 1888, but once they had broken through, the two-party system functioned to close political space for ordinary farmers. Party elites quickly regained dominance, and the party system easily absorbed Alliance leaders. Farmers continued to have some political options, but the boundaries of permissible actions were defined from above.[65]

10
The Fate of Populism

One year after Weaver's defeat, Frederick Jackson Turner stood before the American Historical Association in Chicago to explain the "significance of the frontier in American history." Historians should study the frontier, Turner contended, in part because from colonial times it had been the site of episodes of agrarian radicalism. The "recent Populist agitation," Turner indicated, was another manifestation of this typical frontier phenomenon.

A frontier society, according to Turner, was "primitive," and as such, could "hardly be expected to show the intelligent appreciation of the complexity of business interests in a developed society." If this view was an apology for the Populists—the heroic individualists of the frontier could be excused for such naive excesses as favoring currency expansion—Turner's identification of populism with the frontier also assured his audience of easterners that the uncivilized Grangers of the West posed no real threat. Safely isolated on the frontier, populism had as much chance of spreading eastward as the Sioux Indians had of conquering Turner's native Wisconsin.[1]

Ultimately, Turner proved prophetic. In 1894, even as the nation was gripped by the deepest depression in its history, the Populist Party failed to build significant support east of the Missouri River.[2] Desperate for an electoral victory, the majority of Populist leaders found it necessary to limit their platform to free silver and to support the Democratic Party in 1896. William Jennings Bryan won Kansas, Nebraska, and South Dakota—states where a strong independent movement had taken root in 1890—but he was beaten elsewhere in crucial midwestern states. In Iowa, Minnesota, Wisconsin, Illinois, and Michigan, William McKinley won in a rout; only in Ohio and Indiana did Bryan even come close.[3] Turner's prediction was on target, but the final defeat of populism was not because the movement's potential was limited to the frontier.

In July 1896 a Republican farmer with a substantial mortgage informed the proprietor of a small bank in Rock Rapids, Iowa, that he planned to vote Democratic in the fall. The nervous banker wrote his Republican congressman that he was "unable to formulate any argument that would convince him that he would not be benefitted thereby, being only a debtor and a seller of agricultural products as he is. His case will apply to thousands of others throughout Iowa."[4] This unusually frank acknowledgment that free silver would ease the burdens of debtors suggested that Iowa Republicans might be in for a difficult time in the fall even though the GOP had recovered its position as the dominant party in Iowa four years earlier. In August the chairman of the Iowa Republican state central committee thought that the political situation "really looked threatening." Informal polling indicated that "from twenty to twenty-five percent of the republican farmers of Iowa were inclined to free silver, and unsettled as to how they would vote on election day." In many counties "the free silver craze had taken the form of an epidemic."[5] As late as September Mark Hanna, McKinley's campaign manager, judged that Bryan stood a good chance of carrying Iowa and other midwestern states.[6]

McKinley prevailed in Iowa, then, not because "the steady advance of the cow and the hog" had immunized farmers against radicalism—they had embraced free silver at the beginning of the campaign—but because they changed their minds.[7] Political mobilization is a complex process involving not only voters' sentiments but the ability of parties to build an organization and to articulate issues. To a large extent Bryan was at a severe disadvantage in Iowa simply because the Democratic Party was weak and badly divided. Ironically, the Democrats' frailty in 1896 stemmed from their vitality earlier in the nineties. Because Iowa Democrats had won control of the governorship they were able to gain patronage from a national Democratic Party eager to make inroads in the Midwest, thus tying Iowa's Democratic Party closely to the Cleveland administration. But their identification with Cleveland proved to be a major liability after the Panic of 1893. Before this catastrophe, Governor Boies, who supported the administration but was necessarily sensitive to western interests, had straddled the silver issue, cautiously endorsing "bimetallic coinage" under certain conditions and urging free-silver Democrats to "go slow." After the panic, Boies, running for a third term as governor, endorsed Cleveland's repeal of the Sherman Silver Purchase Act and was promptly thrown out of office. Rather than shift toward free silver, Boies and other Iowa Democrats continued to retain close ties to the eastern wing of the Democratic Party and defeated a free-silver plank at the 1895 state convention. Free-silver Democrats finally gained control of the Iowa party in 1896, but this last-moment triumph split the party down the middle, and Iowa Democrats entered the election badly divided. With almost no Populist presence and a weak Democratic Party, no organizational basis existed to sustain the free-silver movement.[8] At the same time, the Iowa GOP, having healed its internal divisions over prohibition in 1892, entered the 1896 campaign united. Despite the initial outpouring of enthusiasm for free silver among Iowa farmers, the GOP's far superior organizational resources eventually prevailed. Furthermore, the national Republican Party spent between $3 million and $4 million in 1896, a sum unprecedented in the history of U.S. elections and much in excess of the amount the Democrats could command. Some of these dollars found their way to places such as Rock Rapids, Iowa.[9]

The situation differed in Kansas and Nebraska. In the early 1890s the Democrats in the Plains states were weak, and with few exceptions, they never became closely attached to Cleveland's national administration. From the outset, Kansas and Nebraska Democrats took advantage of the political opportunity afforded by a strong Populist Party and advocated free silver as the basis for cooperation. Although the Populists initially responded to Democratic overtures by indignantly proclaiming their intention to remain uncorrupted by association with the old parties, by 1892 many Populist politicians, calculating that political success demanded cooperation, openly sought fusion. Despite antagonisms between the Populists and the Democrats and divisions within each party over political tactics, by 1896 the party systems of Kansas and Nebraska had undergone a realignment from the Republican-dominated configuration of the 1880s, and the GOP faced a well-organized challenge from a Populist/Democratic free-silver coalition. This coalition was the basis for Bryan's successful fusion campaign in 1896. The pattern of support for free silver across the three states thus depended significantly on whether political developments had encouraged the emergence of an organization capable of mobilizing voters on behalf of that issue. Such a summary, of course, overlooks many of the complexities of politics in the three states from 1890 to 1896, but even a brief comparison highlights the crucial role of state party systems in affecting political outcomes.[10]

Turner's emphasis on frontier conditions as the source of political behavior overlooked the contingency of politics. The history of populism—the mobilization of farmers by the Alliance, the politicization of the Alliance, the formation of state People's Parties, the drive for national success, the tragedy of fusion, and Bryan's defeat—was not simply the story of a direct response to material conditions, frontier or otherwise. The fate of populism depended in large measure on what one historian has called the "wars of maneuver" that occurred in numerous states throughout the country in the late eighties and early nineties.[11] The way that politicians dealt with the emergence of agrarian radicalism and the Alliance's reactions to politicians' responses were crucial tactical maneuvers and countermaneuvers in determining where populism would succeed and where it would not. Had the People's Party been able to make substantially greater inroads into the Midwest or the South or both by 1892, the trajectory of the movement undoubtedly would have been much different. At the very least the People's Party might have been able to establish a critical threshold of viability, thus allowing it to preserve its identity as a third party and to fight seriously for the Omaha platform beyond 1896.

The Populists themselves saw 1892 as the beginning of their fight to reclaim the nation, but in the final analysis it is difficult to avoid concluding that even before the party met in Omaha on 4 July 1892 the crucial developments in the movement's history had already taken place. Although the failure of populism to take advantage of the depression of 1893 by building a strong farmer/labor coalition in the industrializing Midwest was neither politically nor economically inevitable, the fact that strong independent political movements had not emerged in those states before the depression seriously diminished the odds that such movements would develop. At Omaha in 1892, neither the Populists nor their enemies could have realized it, but in retrospect it seems that the cards had already been dealt, that the movement's fate would be to play a losing hand.

Comparison of Kansas and Nebraska with Iowa demonstrates that the presence or absence of party competition at the state level could be a crucial factor in shaping the wars of maneuver. Whether party competition was as important in determining party-system responses to the Alliance in other states requires further study. The fact that strong agrarian movements emerged but remained nonpartisan in Missouri, Illinois, and Indiana, states where the Democrats and Republicans were closely matched, suggests that the dynamics of party competition that were so important in Iowa may have operated in these states, too. It is possible that other factors may explain why Populism failed in those states; in Illinois, for example, the presence of one of the strongest urban labor movements in the nation obviously complicated matters. Clearly, though, the weakness of midwestern populism cannot be explained in simple economic terms; politics must be taken into account.[12] As for generalizing from the cases of Kansas and Nebraska, one-party nonresponsiveness may help explain the emergence of independent politics in some states—South Dakota is a likely candidate[13]—but in many Rocky Mountain states, for example, populism apparently emerged more because of the weakness of the incompletely developed party systems in those states rather than because of one-party dominance per se, even though the GOP was the leading party.[14] Moreover, one-party dominance did not always lead to third-party formation, as the Democratic South illustrated. It might be fruitful, however, to determine the extent to which differences in the degree of competition among Democratic Party factions in southern states would explain varying degrees of responsiveness to the Alliance and, hence, different levels of support for populism.[15]

The extent of party competition may or may not be decisive everywhere, but in one way or another, state politics provided the crucial matrix for agrarian radicalism. In the end, the national party system and the emerging corporate order it supported proved resilient to the challenge of the People's Party. Hit hard by the surge of agrarian radicalism in the late 1880s, the major parties collapsed in a few places, but elsewhere they maneuvered and adjusted. As time went on the party system as a whole accommodated and eventually absorbed the threat from a grass-roots movement demanding economic and political democracy. The two-party system operating within a federal structure gave it flexibility in the face of the challenge.

Ultimately, the Populists might have fared better had they seen more clearly the obstacles in their path. Convinced of the justice of their cause, they understandably believed that the moment was at hand to "restore the government of the Republic to the hands of 'the plain people.'"[16] The only requirement was for the veil to fall from the people's eyes—then they would see that party loyalties were chains enslaving them to plutocratic masters. The problem, though, was that all people everywhere would not realize this at once. Had the Populists had a more realistic sense of their chances for a quick breakthrough, they might have created a more enduring organization with greater staying power. But such realism may be too much to ask—of the Populists or of other third parties in America's past or future. Only once has a third party succeeded in American history, and social stresses at that moment were severe enough to cause civil war. Movements contemplating becoming third parties in the future should be clear about the odds if they wish to maximize their chances by creating organizations capable of enduring over a long period of time or by concentrating their efforts in certain geographical areas. Still, short of changing the underlying constitutional structure of federalism that determines the odds, a path that risks creating unforeseeable political dangers, even the most brilliantly constructed third party is likely to be a long shot in the United States. Yet in "a nation brought to the verge of moral, political, and material ruin," cold calculations of probability may give way, as they did in 1892, to the demands of hope.[17]

Appendix A
Farmers' Alliance Membership

Scholars have often repeated Farmers' Alliance membership figures without recognizing that state Alliances had an incentive to overstate their strength, especially as they began to contend for power in the political arena. In spring 1890 the Kansas Alliance claimed as many as 100,000 members; the Nebraska Alliance claimed 90,000 in October 1890.[1] Arriving at realistic figures for the number of members requires making two estimates: first, the number of suballiances in existence at a given time and second, the average number of members per suballiance.

One must exercise caution when encountering figures in the Alliance press for the number of suballiances in existence at a given time, as these figures appear to be based on the practice of the consecutive numbering of suballiances, which can be misleading. It does not necessarily follow, in other words, that when charter number 2,000 was issued to a particular suballiance, there were 2,000 suballiances. First, the numbering scheme began with the number 100, meaning there would have been at most (in this example) 1,900 suballiances. Furthermore, over the course of the organization and reorganization of state Alliances in the 1880s, numerous charters were issued to suballiances that later disbanded. To illustrate that relying on charter numbers can be misleading, the Kansas Alliance secretary reported 470 suballiances in August 1889, yet charter number 723 had been issued five months earlier.[2] To obtain the best possible estimate of the number of suballiances, I have used other means to determine the number of suballiances when possible, such as direct statements of the number of suballiances organized over a particular period. The problem of estimating the number of suballiances is further complicated because even after reorganization in the late 1880s, some suballiances probably ceased to exist. This was undoubtedly more of a problem in the Iowa Alliance than in the Kansas and Nebraska Alliances because the Iowa Alliance grew more slowly over a longer period of time, thus increasing the probability of dropout. I have made a somewhat crude attempt to adjust for this factor by using a lower estimate of the average number of members per suballiance for the Iowa Alliance.

Scott McNall has reasonably concluded that the average number of voting-age male members per suballiance was about thirty.[3] I have used the same figure for Nebraska. Although reports from ninety-one suballiances in the *Homestead* show an average of 39.8 male members, this figure would be too high for an average since only strong suballiances probably would have taken the initiative to write the *Homestead*.[4] To adjust for the dropout factor resulting from the Iowa Alliance's comparatively slow growth, I have assumed an average of 25 members, an estimate that, if anything, understates the numerical strength of the Iowa Alliance with respect to the Alliance in the other two states.

According to the records of the Nebraska Alliance, about 12 percent of the membership in January 1890 were women. Quarterly reports from seventy-seven suballiances in 1893 indicate that the proportion of women in the Nebraska Alliance by then was much higher—about 34 percent.[5] Based on her work in these records, MaryJo Wagner contends that the 1893 quarterly reports truly reflect the sexual composition of the Alliance and that the earlier reports failed to list women; she concludes that more than one-third of the Alliance membership in Kansas and Nebraska consisted of women. Wagner offers no reason to suspect that the earlier records were inaccurate, however.[6] It is much more plausible to believe that the proportion of women in the Alliance increased as it was eclipsed by the People's Party beginning in 1891, since males (as voters) were able to participate directly in the new People's Party organizations and dropped out of the Alliance (overall membership declined substantially from 1891 to 1893); women, unable to vote, maintained their membership.

The only other evidence for the number of women members was given by William Peffer, who stated in July 1890, during the period of third-party formation, that 20 percent of the Kansas Alliance's members were women.[7] Since the process of radicalization opened up space for Alliance women to claim a more public role both as participants and as leaders, it is possible that during the rapid growth of the Alliance in Kansas and Nebraska in early 1890 the proportion of women who were joining was actually higher than it had been earlier and that this would explain why Peffer's figure is higher than the one for January 1890 from the Nebraska Alliance records. On the other hand, it may be that the Nebraska records do understate female membership in January 1890, or that the Nebraska Alliance had a lower percentage of women than Kansas, or that Peffer's figure is too high.

Of the two possible figures for female membership—Peffer's 20 percent or the Nebraska Alliance's 12 percent—I have used the more liberal figure. I have found little information that would allow a realistic estimate of the number of women in the Iowa Alliance. Of 238 reports in the *Homestead* listing names of members, only 10 have names that are obviously female, and the total female membership is less than 1 percent. Yet as most names on these lists give only first initials, it is possible that the number of women listed is much higher. It makes sense to think that the percentage of women in the Iowa Alliance was lower than in Kansas and Nebraska because the political situation in Iowa, where the Alliance was directing its political activity within the two-party system, did not open political space for women. Because of the paucity of evidence, I have not made estimates for the number of women in the Iowa Alliance.

TABLE A-1. Kansas Farmers' Alliance Membership, 1888–1891

	Number of Suballiances	Estimated Membership		
		Male	Female	Total
December 1888		5,000[a]	1,250	6,250
August 1889	470[b]	14,000	3,500	17,500
March 1890	1,645[c]	49,000	12,250	61,250
July 1890	2,410[c]	72,000	18,000	90,000
April 1891	2,630[c]	79,000	20,000	99,000

[a]Robert C. McMath, "Preface to Populism," *Kansas Historical Quarterly* 42 (Spring 1976): 58.
[b]*Advocate* (Meriden, Kans.), 17 August 1889. At this time, the most recently issued charter was about number 830, based on dividing the difference between two known charters, 723 issued in March 1889 and 935 issued in November 1889. There was then a gap of about 360 between the actual number of suballiances and the current charter number; *Nonconformist* (Winfield, Kans.), 7 March 1889, 30 January 1890.
[c]Based upon subtracting 360 (see above) from the current charter numbers; for March 1890 from the Lone Tree Alliance Minutes, Kansas State Historical Society, Topeka; for July 1890 from the *Kansas Farmer* (Topeka), 6 July 1890; for April 1891 from the *Advocate* (Topeka), 1 April 1891.

TABLE A-2. Nebraska Farmers' Alliance Membership, 1889–1891

	Number of Suballiances	Estimated Membership		
		Male	Female	Total
January 1889	230	7,000	1,750	8,750
January 1890	670	20,000	5,000	25,000
July 1890	1,604	48,000	12,000	60,000
January 1891	1,849	55,500	13,875	69,375

Source: Membership Journal, Nebraska Farmers' Alliance Papers, Nebraska Historical Society, Lincoln.

TABLE A-3. Iowa Farmers' Alliance Membership, 1886–1891

	Number of Suballiances	Estimated Membership
September 1886	100[a]	2,500
September 1887	350[b]	9,000
September 1888	540[b]	13,500
September 1889	806[b]	20,000
October 1890	1,490[b]	38,000
October 1891	1,835[c]	46,500[d]

[a]Based upon the conservative assumption that 100 of the 300 suballiances that had received charters from 1881 to September 1886 remained in existence. The 300 figure is obtained by subtracting the 440 known suballiances organized from September 1886 to September 1888 from 840, the current charter as of September 1888 (see below), less 100, which is assumed to be the number of the first charter.
[b]Based upon annual reports by the IFA secretary of suballiances organized; Western Rural (Chicago), 17 September 1887; Homestead (Des Moines), 21 September 1888, 13 September 1889; Proceedings of the Iowa Farmers' Alliance, . . . 1890 (Des Moines, 1890), 23.
[c]Based upon 495 new charters issued from October 1890 to October 1891 as reported by the IFA secretary with the subtraction of an estimated 150 suballiances joining the Iowa branch of the NFA and IU; Homestead, 16 October 1891.
[d]Total gain of 8,475 from October 1890 to October 1891 reported by the IFA secretary; Homestead, 16 October 1891.

Appendix B
Regression-based Estimates for Iowa Elections, 1880–1892

In making regression-based estimates for Iowa elections from 1880 to 1892, I have generally followed the procedures outlined by J. Morgan Kousser.[1] Ecological regression is based on the assumption that voting behavior of groups was consistent within the counties of a state or that any variation in behavior was random. This is a difficult assumption to verify. Accordingly, the regression percentages presented should be treated in themselves only as general estimates. These estimates are particularly useful for sensing the shift of voters across pairs or over a series of elections. Even small shifts from one election to another should be an accurate indicator of the general tendencies of a particular group of the electorate although the actual figures may not be precise.

I have made two different sets of estimates: one by nativity (antiprohibition, other foreign-born, and native-born) and one by occupation (farmers and nonfarmers). For the first set, approximately 17 percent of the electorate were antiprohibition voters, 13 percent were other-foreign-born voters, and 70 percent were native-born voters. These percentages remained constant from 1880 to 1892. For the second set, approximately 56 percent of the electorate were farmers in 1880 (leaving 44 percent nonfarmers); by 1892, the ratio was about fifty-fifty.

The Iowa estimates for groups by nativity are unweighted. In estimating percentages for farmers for Iowa elections, I found it necessary to adjust for the potential disparity in voting behavior of farmers according to nativity by making estimates for two separate groups of Iowa counties: those with more than 15 percent of the voters born in countries likely to oppose prohibition and those with under 15 percent. In order to adjust further for the disproportionate impact of counties having small populations with a high percentage of farmers, I weighted the cases in the two groups by the square root of the total population of voting-age males. In cases where the regression equa-

185

tion yielded logically impossible negative values, the value was considered as zero and the other results in the row were adjusted accordingly. Votes for minor parties receiving less than 1 percent of the total vote were included in the "not voting" category. Because of rounding, the figures in the rows in some cases add up to 99 or 101 (rather than to 100).

Because of the lack of county-level data on religious affiliation in the 1880s, it was impossible to make use of this criterion in determining the number of antiprohibition voters. I considered those voters born in Germany, Austria, Belgium, Bohemia, France, Ireland, Italy, Poland, and Russia as antiprohibition, an observation that is confirmed by the estimates showing that 68 percent of these voters opposed the 1882 prohibition referendum, with 32 percent not voting, and zero percent favoring the referendum. A sensitivity to religious distinctions within these groups would have been desirable, but it is doubtful that a refined typology would have yielded any different view of the movement of these voters in the elections analyzed. A small percentage of foreign-born males of voting age were not eligible to vote and were included in the eligible electorate, but this number was quite small and did not alter the estimates.[2]

To estimate the number of farmers eligible to vote at each election, it was necessary to calculate a ratio of farmers (including farm laborers) to farms for each county from the 1895 census since neither the 1880 or 1890 national censuses nor the 1885 Iowa census has data on the number of farmers per farm. I used the 1895 ratio along with data on the number of farms per county in 1880, 1885, and 1890 to estimate the number of farmers per county in those years.[3]

I used the highest office at stake in each election. Thus, the 1880, 1884, 1888, and 1892 estimates are for president; the 1881, 1883, 1885, 1887, 1889, and 1891 estimates are for governor; and the 1882, 1886, and 1890 estimates are for the congressional races.

Election returns and population data for the 1880 and 1890 censuses used in calculating regression estimates were made available by the Inter-University Consortium for Political and Social Research. These data were supplemented by population data in the Iowa state census.[4]

TABLE B-1. Regression Estimates for Iowa Elections, 1880–1892

1880

	D	R	G	NV
AP	41	15	0	44
OFB	1	56	15	43
NB	23	45	15	17
F	21	56	8	15
NF	29	25	5	41

1881

	D	R	G	NV
AP	38	10	0	52
OFB	0	52	0	48
NB	14	32	14	40
F	12	44	8	35
NF	22	12	3	62

1882 (Prohibition Referendum)

	N	Y	NV
AP	68	0	32
OFB	0	30	70
NB	24	46	30
F	15	60	25
NF	36	16	49

1882 (General Election)

	D	R	G	NV
AP	53	9	0	38
OFB	8	46	0	46
NB	19	34	18	29
F	19	45	10	27
NF	34	14	3	49

1883

	D	R	G	NV
AP	51	5	0	44
OFB	2	53	0	45
NB	29	41	12	18
F	27	52	8	13
NF	33	15	1	50

1884

	DG	R	G	NV
AP	55	13	0	32
OFB	4	57	0	39
NB	39	48	1	12
F	37	54	1	8
NF	33	33	0	34

1885

	DG	R	NV
AP	47	7	46
OFB	2	48	50
NB	39	44	17
F	36	51	13
NF	33	21	46

1886

	DG	R	L	NV
AP	0	45	0	55
OFB	41	41	0	19
NB	32	49	0	19
F	37	51	0	13
NF	31	21	7	41

1887

	D	R	UL	NV
AP	58	3	0	39
OFB	2	47	0	51
NB	30	41	6	23
F	29	50	3	18
NF	32	18	3	47

1888

	D	R	UL	NV
AP	62	10	0	28
OFB	4	58	0	38
NB	35	49	4	12
F	34	54	3	9
NF	33	15	1	50

1889

	D	R	UL	NV
AP	62	0	0	38
OFB	0	47	0	44
NB	34	43	3	20
F	34	51	3	12
NF	36	17	1	47

1890

	D	R	I	NV
AP	55	3	0	42
OFB	0	34	0	66
NB	41	46	1	12
F	38	47	3	12
NF	36	25	0	40

1891

	D	R	P	NV
AP	64	0	0	36
OFB	5	47	1	47
NB	39	47	5	9
F	37	53	5	6
NF	41	23	0	36

1892

	D	R	P	NV
AP	64	8	0	28
OFB	7	58	1	34
NB	34	47	8	10
F	35	53	6	5
NF	38	29	1	31

Key to Symbols:
AP = Antiprohibition voters
OFB = Other foreign-born voters
NB = Native-born voters
F = Farmers
NF = Nonfarmers

D = Democrat
DG = Democrat/Greenback
G = Greenback
I = Independent
L = Labor
N = No (on prohibition)
NV = Not voting
P = People's

R = Republican
UL = Union Labor
Y = Yes (on prohibition)

Notes

CHAPTER 1. INSURGENCY AND ITS LIMITS

1. *National Economist* (Washington, D.C.), 27 August and 13 August 1892.
2. Congressional Quarterly, *Congressional Quarterly's Guide to U.S. Elections*, 2d ed. (Washington, D.C., 1985), 343.
3. Werner Sombart, *Why Is There No Socialism in the United States?* (1906; reprint, White Plains, N.Y., 1976), 106.
4. Frederick Jackson Turner, *The Frontier in American History* (New York, 1920), 32, and John D. Hicks, *The Populist Revolt: A History of the Farmers' Alliance* (Minneapolis, Minn., 1931; reprint, Lincoln, Nebr., 1961), 268–69.
5. Richard Hofstadter, *The Age of Reform: From Bryan to F.D.R.* (New York, 1955), 99–100.
6. Robert Wiebe, *The Search for Order, 1877–1920* (New York, 1967), 85, and Samuel P. Hays, *The Response to Industrialism* (Chicago, 1957), 27–28.
7. Michael P. Rogin, *The Intellectuals and McCarthy: The Radical Specter* (Cambridge, Mass., 1967), 188–89; Walter T. K. Nugent, *The Tolerant Populists: Kansas Populism and Nativism* (Chicago, 1963), 54–58; and Allan G. Bogue, *From Prairie to Corn Belt: Farming on the Illinois and Iowa Prairies in the Nineteenth Century* (Chicago, 1963), 283–85. James Turner, "Understanding the Populists," *Journal of American History* 67 (September 1980): 354–73, rejects economic determinism but through a perspective informed by modernization retains the view that the appeal of populism was limited to areas where farmers were socially and culturally isolated.
8. Lawrence Goodwyn, *Democratic Promise: The Populist Moment in America* (New York, 1976), quotation on p. 314. I discuss these problems in later chapters.
9. Peter H. Argersinger, *Populism and Politics: William Alfred Peffer and the People's Party* (Lexington, Ky., 1974), and James Edward Wright, *The Politics of Populism: Dissent in Colorado* (New Haven, Conn., 1974), 4. Other studies of midwestern populism include Stanley B. Parsons, *The Populist Context: Rural versus Urban Power on a Great Plains Frontier* (Westport, Conn., 1973); Robert W. Cherny, *Populism, Progressivism, and the Transformation of Nebraska Politics, 1885–1915* (Lincoln, Nebr., 1981); David S. Trask, "Nebraska Populism as a Response to Environmental and Political Problems," in *The Great Plains: Environment and Culture*, ed. Brian W. Blouet and Frederick C. Luebke (Lincoln, Nebr., 1979); Worth Robert Miller, *Oklahoma Populism: A History of the People's Party in the Okla-*

homa Territory (Norman, Okla., 1987); and Scott G. McNall, *The Road to Rebellion: Class Formation and Kansas Populism, 1865–1900* (Chicago, 1988). The literature on populism since 1970 is too extensive to be cited in full, but useful bibliographical essays can be found in Gene Clanton, *Populism: The Humane Preference in America, 1890–1900* (Boston, 1991), 186–91, and William F. Holmes, "Populism: In Search of Context," *Agricultural History* 64 (Fall 1990): 26–58.

10. Although most state studies have made generalizations appropriate to their scale, studies such as McNall's *Road to Rebellion* that seek to explain the failure of the movement nationally are flawed at the outset because it is impossible for a study of a state where populism was strong to explain why populism failed outside its area of strength.

11. Marc Bloch, "Pour une histoire comparée des sociétés européenes," *Revue de synthèse historique* 46 (1925): 15–50; translated as "Toward a Comparative History of European Societies," in *Enterprise and Secular Change*, ed. Frederic C. Lane and Jelle C. Riemersma (Homewood, Ill., 1953), 494–521. See also William H. Sewell, Jr., "Marc Bloch and the Logic of Comparative History," *History and Theory* 6 (1967): 208–18.

12. I have estimated that the Iowa Alliance had about 46,000 members at its peak compared to about 99,000 members for Kansas and 69,000 for Nebraska. For a detailed discussion of these estimates, see Appendix A; for the agrarian movement in other midwestern states, see Roy V. Scott, "The Rise of the Farmers' Mutual Benefit Association in Illinois, 1883–1891," *Agricultural History* 32 (January 1958): 49, and Homer Clevenger, "The Farmers' Alliance in Missouri," *Missouri Historical Review* 39 (October 1944): 24–44.

13. J. Craig Jenkins, "Resource Mobilization Theory and the Study of Social Movements," *Annual Review of Sociology* 9 (1983): 527–53. See also John D. McCarthy and Mayer N. Zald, "Resource Mobilization and Social Movements: A Partial Theory," in *Social Movements in an Organizational Society*, ed. McCarthy and Zald (New Brunswick, N.J., 1987); Anthony Oberschall, "Theories of Social Conflict," *Annual Review of Sociology* 4 (1978): 291–315; and Charles Tilly, *From Mobilization to Revolution* (New York, 1978). Works on the Farmers' Alliance and populism that employ social-movement theory include Michael Schwartz, *Radical Protest and Social Structure: The Southern Farmers' Alliance and Cotton Tenancy, 1880–1890* (New York, 1976); Donna A. Barnes, *Farmers in Rebellion: The Rise and Fall of the Southern Farmer's Alliance and People's Party in Texas* (Austin, Tex., 1984); and McNall, *Road to Rebellion*. As applied in these works, resource-mobilization theory can focus excessively either on weakness within the movement or on the capacity of larger structures to weaken or co-opt the movement. My approach instead focuses on how larger structures defeated the movement by preventing it from spreading outside its areas of initial strength.

14. James Bryce, *The American Commonwealth*, 3d ed., 2 vols. (New York, 1904), 1:425. See also Morton Keller, *Affairs of State: Public Life in Late Nineteenth Century America* (Cambridge, Mass., 1977), 319–30, 409–38; Stephen Skowronek, *Building a New American State: The Expansion of National Administrative Capacities, 1877–1920* (Cambridge, Mass., 1982), 23; Loren Beth, *The Development of the American Constitution, 1877–1917* (New York, 1971), 72–73; Samuel H. Beer, "The Modernization of American Federalism," *Publius* 3 (Fall 1973): 69; William R. Brock, *Investigation and Responsibility: Public Responsibility in the United States* (Cambridge, Mass., 1984), 19; Ballard C. Campbell, *Representative Democracy: Public Policy and Midwestern Legislatures in the Late Nineteenth Century* (Cambridge, Mass., 1980), 2; and Theodore J. Lowi, "Why Is There No

Socialism in the United States? A Federal Analysis," in *Why Is There No Socialism in the United States?* ed. Jean Heffer and Jeanine Rovet (Paris, 1988), 69–85.

15. E. E. Schattschneider, *Party Government* (New York, 1942), 132–33. The importance of state-level politics in the disintegration of the second American party system is stressed in William E. Gienapp, *The Origins of the Republican Party, 1852–1856* (New York, 1987), and Michael Holt, *The Political Crisis of the 1850s* (New York, 1978).

16. On the theme of federalism and the structure of politics, see Frank J. Sorauf, *Political Parties in the American System* (Boston, 1964), 39–40; David J. Rothman, "The Structure of State Politics" in *Political Parties in American History*, ed. Felice A. Bonadio, 3 vols. (New York, 1974), 2:815–39; David B. Truman, "Federalism and the Party System," in *Politics and Social Life: An Introduction to Political Behavior*, ed. Nelson W. Polsby, Robert A. Dentler, and Paul A. Smith (Boston, 1963); Theodore J. Lowi, "Party, Policy, and Constitution in America," in *The American Party Systems*, ed. William N. Chambers and Walter Dean Burnham (New York, 1974), 253–54; Herbert Jacob, "State Political Systems," in *Politics in the American States: A Comparative Analysis*, ed. Herbert Jacob and Kenneth N. Vines (Boston, 1965), 3; and Daniel J. Elazar, *American Federalism: A View from the States*, 2d ed. (New York, 1972), 45.

17. Richard M. Valelly, *Radicalism in the States: The Minnesota Farmer-Labor Party and the American Political Economy* (Chicago, 1989), 9–10, observes that prior to the New Deal, federalism provided significant "incentives" for state-level radicalism.

18. Richard Franklin Bensel, *Sectionalism and American Political Development, 1880–1980* (Madison, Wis., 1984), 60–73, stresses the importance of pension outlays in maintaining the allegiance of the West to the Republican Party. On the origins of Republican ideology, see Eric Foner, *Free Soil, Free Labor, Free Men: The Ideology of the Republican Party before the Civil War* (New York, 1970).

19. Eric Foner, *Reconstruction: America's Unfinished Revolution, 1863–1877* (New York, 1988), 484–87; Keller, *Affairs of State*, 251–56, 558–64; George H. Mayer, *The Republican Party 1854–1964* (New York, 1964), 171–220; and David J. Rothman, *Politics and Power: The United States Senate, 1869–1901* (Cambridge, Mass., 1966), 159–90.

20. Paul Kleppner, *The Third Electoral System, 1853–1892: Parties, Voters, and Political Cultures* (Chapel Hill, N.C., 1979), 125–31.

21. Historians have only recently recognized the importance of fusion in preserving the viability of third parties in the late nineteenth century. See Peter H. Argersinger, "'A Place on the Ballot': Fusion Politics and Antifusion Laws," *American Historical Review* 85 (April 1980): 287–306, and Howard A. Scarrow, "Duverger's Law, Fusion and the Decline of American 'Third' Parties," *Western Political Quarterly* 39 (December 1986): 634–47. On opportunistic Democratic/Greenback fusion in the Midwest in the late 1870s, see Horace Samuel Merrill, *Bourbon Democracy of the Middle West, 1865–1896* (Baton Rouge, La., 1953), 128–33.

22. Charles Moore, *History of Michigan*, 4 vols. (Chicago, 1915), 1:561; Harriette M. Dilla, *The Politics of Michigan, 1865–1878* (New York, 1912), 252; Homer Clevenger, "Missouri Becomes a Doubtful State," *Mississippi Valley Historical Review* 29 (March 1943): 545–48; and David P. Thelen, *Paths of Resistance: Tradition and Dignity in Industrializing Missouri* (New York, 1986), 211. For Iowa politics, see chapter 3.

23. Melvyn Hammarberg, *The Indiana Voter: The Historical Dynamics of Party Allegiance during the 1870s* (Chicago, 1977), 19; Eugene Roseboom and Francis Weisenburger, *A History of Ohio* (New York, 1934), 340–47; John Moses, *Illinois: Historical and Statistical,*

2 vols. (Chicago, 1889–1892), 2:876; Robert C. Nesbit, *The History of Wisconsin: Volume 3; Urbanization and Industrialization, 1873–1893* (Madison, Wis., 1985), 579–93; Willis Frederick Dunbar, *Michigan: A History of the Wolverine State*, 2d ed. (Grand Rapids, Mich., 1970), 529; and Clevenger, "Missouri Becomes a Doubtful State," 541–56. Minnesota defies easy classification as the Republicans were clearly dominant until 1886, when they lost three of five congressional elections and narrowly lost the governorship. See Martin Ridge, *Ignatius Donnelly: The Portrait of a Politician* (Chicago, 1962), 252. For Iowa politics, see chapter 3; for politics in Kansas and Nebraska, see chapter 5.

24. My ideas about party competition are partly inspired by V. O. Key, Jr., *Southern Politics in State and Nation* (New York, 1949). I agree with Key that interparty competition can be conducive to reform but stress that the political process may narrow the potential scope of reform as well as lead to cooptation of the social movement advocating reform. Holt (*Political Crisis*, 219–59) shows the importance of state-level party competition in explaining why some southern states supported secession in 1860 while others opposed this move.

25. For a comprehensive discussion of the barriers to third-party success in the United States, see Schattschneider, *Party Government*, chapter 4. See also Seymour Martin Lipset, "Radicalism in North America: A Comparative View of the Party Systems in Canada and the United States," *Transactions of the Royal Society of Canada*, 4th ser., 14 (1976): 19–55.

26. See Theodore Saloutos, "Radicalism and the Agrarian Tradition," in *Failure of a Dream? Essays in the History of American Socialism*, ed. John H. M. Laslett and Seymour Martin Lipset, rev. ed. (Berkeley and Los Angeles, 1984), 52–64; Leon Fink, *Workingmen's Democracy: The Knights of Labor and American Politics* (Urbana, Ill., 1983), 32–33; and Martin Shefter, "Trade Unions and Political Machines: The Organization and Disorganization of the American Working Class in the Late Nineteenth Century," in *Working-Class Formation: Nineteenth-Century Patterns in Western Europe and the United States*, ed. Ira Katznelson and Aristide R. Zolberg (Princeton, N.J., 1986), 258. The attempt to establish a farmer/labor coalition in Chicago is detailed by Chester McArthur Destler, "The Labor-Populist Alliance of Illinois in the Election of 1894," in his *American Radicalism, 1865–1901* (New London, Conn., 1946; reprint, Chicago, 1966), 175–211.

CHAPTER 2. DEFLATION AND THE GEOGRAPHY OF ECONOMIC HARDSHIP

1. U.S. Senate, *Wholesale Prices, Wages, and Transportation*, 52d Cong., 2d sess., 1893, S. Rept. 1394, pt. 2, 62–63, and George F. Warren and Frank A. Pearson, *Prices* (New York, 1933), 26.

2. Kirk H. Porter and Donald B. Johnson, eds., *National Party Platforms, 1840–1964* (Urbana, Ill., 1966), 90.

3. William A. Peffer, *The Farmers' Side: His Troubles and Their Remedy* (New York, 1891), 226.

4. David A. Wells, *Recent Economic Changes and Their Effect on the Production and Distribution of Wealth and Well-Being of Society* (New York, 1893), 447.

5. John D. Hicks, *The Populist Revolt: A History of the Farmers' Alliance* (Minneapolis, Minn., 1931; reprint, Lincoln. Nebr., 1961), 54–95, and Lawrence Goodwyn, *Democratic Promise: The Populist Moment in America* (New York, 1976), 10–15, 26–31. See also C.

Vann Woodward, *Origins of the New South, 1877–1913* (Baton Rouge, La., 1951), 180–88, and Norman Pollack, *The Populist Response to Industrial America: Midwestern Populist Thought* (Cambridge, Mass., 1962), 17. Despite Richard Hofstadter's critical interpretation of the Populists, he did regard their economic grievances as genuine in the context of falling prices. See *The Age of Reform: From Bryan to F.D.R.* (New York, 1955), 50, 99.

6. For general summaries of the revisionist viewpoint, see Douglass C. North, *Growth and General Welfare in the American Past*, 2d ed. (Englewood Cliffs, N.J., 1974), 131–37; Susan P. Lee and Peter Passell, *A New Economic View of American History* (New York, 1979), 294–300; Robert Higgs, *The Transformation of the American Economy, 1865–1914* (New York, 1971), 86–102; and Robert William Fogel and Jack L. Rutner, "The Efficiency Effects of Federal Land Policy, 1850–1900: A Report of Some Provisional Findings," in *The Dimensions of Quantitative Research in History*, ed. William O. Aydelotte, Allan G. Bogue, and Robert William Fogel (Princeton, N.J., 1972), 390–418. Studies that generally accept the revisionist viewpoint but seek to explain farmers' grievances in more specific terms of economic uncertainty, short-term price fluctuations, or increasing commercialization include John D. Bowman, "An Economic Analysis of Midwestern Farm Land Values and Farm Land Incomes, 1860–1900," *Yale Economic Essays* 5 (Fall 1965): 317–20; John D. Bowman and Richard H. Keehn, "Agricultural Terms of Trade in Four Midwestern States, 1870–1900," *Journal of Economic History* 34 (September 1974): 592–609; Robert A. McGuire, "Economic Causes of Late-Nineteenth Century Agrarian Unrest: New Evidence," *Journal of Economic History* 41 (December 1981): 835–52; Anne Mayhew, "A Reappraisal of the Causes of Farm Protest in the United States, 1870–1900," *Journal of Economic History* 32 (June 1972): 464–75; and James H. Stock, "Real Estate Mortgages, Foreclosures, and Midwestern Agrarian Unrest, 1865–1920," *Journal of Economic History* 44 (March 1983): 89–105.

7. Agricultural prices declined by 57.8 percent from 1864–1868 to 1894–1898, and the prices of all commodities fell over the same period by 60.0 percent. Warren and Pearson, *Prices*, 26–27. On transportation rates, revenue per ton mile declined by 51 percent from 1867 to 1890 (William Z. Ripley, *Railroads, Rates and Regulation* [New York, 1912], 412), which was similar to the decline of 46.6 percent for agricultural prices (Warren and Pearson, *Prices*, 26–27). See also Robert Higgs, "Railroad Rates and the Populist Uprising," *Agricultural History* 44 (July 1970): 291–97.

8. The figures include Ohio, Indiana, Illinois, Wisconsin, Iowa, Missouri, Minnesota, Kansas, and Nebraska; see U.S. Census Office, *Report on Farms and Homes: Proprietorship and Indebtedness in the United States at the Eleventh Census: 1890* (Washington, D.C., 1896), table 93.

9. Robert F. Severson, Jr., Frank F. Niss, and Richard D. Winkelman, "Mortgage Borrowing as a Frontier Developed: A Study of Farm Mortgages in Champaign County, Illinois, 1836–1895," *Journal of Economic History* 26 (June 1966): 157; David Rozman, "Land Credit in Walnut Grove Township, Knox County, Illinois," *Journal of Land and Public Utility Economics* 4 (August 1928): 306; David Rozman, "Land Credit in the Town of Newton, Manitowoc County, Wisconsin, 1824–1926," *Journal of Land and Public Utility Economics* 3 (November 1927): 374; William G. Murray, *An Economic Analysis of Farm Mortgages in Story County, Iowa, 1854–1931*, Iowa Agricultural Experiment Station Research Bulletin 156 (Ames, Iowa, 1933), 396; George S. Pease, *Patriarch of the Prairie: The Story of the Equitable of Iowa, 1867–1967* (New York, 1967); Eleanor Hinman and J. O. Rankin, *Farm Mortgage History of Eleven Southeastern Nebraska Townships, 1870–1932*, Ne-

braska Agricultural Experiment Station Research Bulletin 67 (Lincoln, Nebr., 1933), 44; Allan G. Bogue, *Money at Interest: The Farm Mortgage on the Middle Border* (Ithaca, N.Y., 1955); D. M. Frederiksen, "Mortgage Banking in America," *Journal of Political Economy* 2 (March 1894): 203–34; New York Banking Department, *Annual Report of the Superintendent . . . Relative to Foreign Mortgage Loan, Investment, and Trust Companies, 1891* (Albany, N.Y., 1891); and Massachusetts Commissioner of Foreign Mortgage Corporations, *Annual Report, 1895* (Boston, 1895). Larry McFarlane, "British Investment in Midwestern Farm Mortgages and Land, 1875–1900: A Comparison of Iowa and Kansas," *Agricultural History* 48 (January 1974): 196–97, argues that British capital played a fairly small role in financing farm mortgages.

·10. Ivan Wright, *Bank Credit and Agriculture under the National and Federal Reserve Banking Systems* (New York, 1922), 46; Howard H. Preston, *History of Banking in Iowa* (Iowa City, Iowa, 1922), 277–78; and Jesse E. Pope, "Agricultural Credit in the United States," *Quarterly Journal of Economics* 28 (August 1914): 726.

11. U.S. Census Office, *Report on Real Estate Mortgages in the United States at the Eleventh Census: 1890* (Washington, D.C., 1895), 286–89.

12. These were the typical terms for a farm mortgage loan in the 1880s and 1890s. See William G. Murray, *Agricultural Finance: Principles and Practice of Farm Credit* (Ames, Iowa, 1941), 99.

13. North, *Growth and General Welfare*, 133. Agricultural prices fell by 25 percent or more from 1868 to 1873, 1873 to 1878, 1874 to 1879, 1882 to 1887, and 1891 to 1896; see Warren and Pearson, *Prices*, 26–27.

14. Lee and Passell, *New Economic View*, 300.

15. Severson, Niss, and Winkelman, "Mortgage Borrowing," 152; Rozman, "Walnut Grove," 308; Rozman, "Newton," 378; Murray, *Economic Analysis*, 396; Alan G. Bogue, *From Prairie to Corn Belt: Farming on the Illinois and Iowa Prairies in the Nineteenth Century* (Chicago, 1963), 178; Hinman and Rankin, *Farm Mortgage History*, 25; and Bogue, *Money at Interest*, 230, 255.

16. Severson, Niss, and Winkelman, "Mortgage Borrowing," 147–68; Howard J. Houk, *A Century of Indiana Farm Prices, 1841 to 1941*, Purdue University Agricultural Experiment Station Bulletin 476 (Lafayette, Ind., 1943), 8–9. The Severson study is the best of the many similar studies because it includes a relatively large number of mortgages and provides mean interest rates on an annual basis for the entire post–Civil War period, which allows a more refined sense of interest-rate movements; other studies summarize interest-rate movements by decade or do not cover the entire period. Comparing the movement of Illinois interest rates with Indiana prices does not present a problem as there is no reason to believe that the rate of decline of prices in Indiana and Illinois varied to any significant degree.

17. The equation for the real interest rate is $r = n - i$ where r is the real rate of interest, n is the nominal rate of interest, and i is the annual rate of inflation. The real interest rates in Table 2.1 assume the following: annual payment of interest, principal due upon maturity of the loan, and the principal valued at the average price level over the duration of the loan. The tendency for interest rates to lag behind inflationary or deflationary trends was observed by Irving Fisher, *The Theory of Interest* (New York, 1930), 43. See also Lawrence H. Summers, "The Nonadjustment of Nominal Interest Rates: A Study of the Fisher Effect," in *Macroeconomics, Prices and Quantities*, ed. James Tobin (Washington,

D.C., 1983), 201–41; and Barry Eichengreen, "Mortgage Interest Rates in the Populist Era," *American Economic Review* 74 (December 1984): 998.

18. Severson, Niss, and Winkelman, "Mortgage Borrowing," 154; Rozman, "Walnut Grove," 308; Murray, *Economic Analysis*, 400; and Murray, *Agricultural Finance*, 99.

19. Murray, *Economic Analysis*, 383–84.

20. The J. B. Watkins Land Mortgage Company was offering loans in Kansas at 7 percent with a 4 percent cash commission in 1884. In 1886 and 1887 in Kansas, farmers with "good security" could obtain loans for 6 to 7 percent. Commissions increased the total costs of these loans to 8 to 9 percent; see Bogue, *Money at Interest*, 139, 143. James W. Gleed, "Western Mortgages," *Century* 9 (March 1890): 95–96, states that commissions received by mortgage companies in major midwestern cities were as high as 15 percent for a five-year loan. (Gleed was a Kansas attorney and professor of law at the University of Kansas.) For insurance requirements, see J. P. Dunn, Jr., "The Mortgage Evil," *Political Science Quarterly* 5 (March 1890): 80, and Pease, *Patriarch*, 38–45.

21. Gleed, "Western Mortgages," 96–97, and Edward N. Darrow, *A Treatise on Mortgage Investments* (Minneapolis, Minn., 1892), 40. The *United States Investor* (Boston), 5 August 1893, a journal of information and advice for eastern investors, informed its readers that Kansas tax certificates, carrying a rate of 24 percent per annum, were a "splendid investment." For rates on Iowa tax certificates in the late eighties and nineties, see Robert P. Swierenga, *Acres for Cents: Delinquent Tax Auctions in Frontier Iowa* (Westport, Conn., 1976), 93, 115.

22. John Ise, *Sod and Stubble: The Story of a Kansas Homestead* (New York, 1936), 183. On the onerous southern lien system, see Alex M. Arnett, *The Populist Movement in Georgia* (New York, 1922), 49–64; Thomas D. Clark, "The Furnishing and Supply System in Southern Agriculture since 1865," *Journal of Southern History* 12 (February 1946): 24–44; and Matthew B. Hammond, *The Cotton Industry: An Essay in American Economic History* (New York, 1897), 141–65.

23. Illinois Bureau of Labor Statistics, *Biennial Report, 1888* (Springfield, 1888), xlvii, and *Biennial Report, 1890* (Springfield, 1890), 206, 212, 252; Nebraska Bureau of Labor and Industrial Statistics, *Biennial Report, 1895–96* (Lincoln, Nebr., 1896), 248–49; and Kansas Bureau of Labor and Industrial Statistics, *Annual Report, 1893* (Topeka, 1893), 702. George K. Holmes, a census-bureau statistician, estimated that in 1910 in the United States the total personal indebtedness was for chattel mortgages, $700 million; for crop liens (other than cotton), $400 million; for cotton-crop liens, $390 million; and for unsecured loans, $660 million. See Clara Eliot, *The Farmers' Campaign for Credit* (New York, 1927), 98.

24. Iowa Commissioner of Labor Statistics, *Biennial Report, 1890–91* (Des Moines, 1891), 69; Ise, *Sod and Stubble*, 183.

25. *American Nonconformist* (Winfield, Kans.), 11 July 1889, 27 February 1890; *Farmers' Alliance* (Lincoln, Nebr.), 30 August 1890; *Iowa Tribune* (Des Moines), 6 February 1884.

26. Bogue, *Money at Interest*, 263–72.

27. Preston, *History of Banking in Iowa*, 277–78; Wright, *Bank Credit*, 48–59; Pope, "Agricultural Credit," 726; and V. N. Valgren and Elmer N. Engelbert, *Bank Loans to Farmers on Personal and Collateral Security*, U.S. Department of Agriculture Bulletin 1048 (Washington, D.C., 1922), 1–2. For further discussion of the barriers to entry for na-

tional banks prior to 1900, see Richard Eugene Sylla, *The American Capital Market, 1846-1914: A Study of Public Policy on Economic Development* (New York, 1975), 47-70.

28. Wright, *Bank Credit*, 60-61. Wright observes that the impact of the lowering of capital requirements had a less dramatic effect in Iowa as it had a more highly developed banking structure than other midwestern states. Preston, *History of Banking in Iowa*, 171, gives the number of national banks in Iowa at 172 in 1899 and 221 in 1901.

29. These issues are discussed in James Livingston, *Origins of the Federal Reserve System: Money, Class, and Corporate Capitalism, 1890-1913* (Ithaca, N.Y., 1986), 71-78, 129-44.

30. Indianapolis Commission of the Indianapolis Monetary Conference, *Report* (Chicago, 1898), 309-32, 369-75.

31. Edwin W. Kemmerer, *Seasonal Variations in the Relative Demand for Money and Capital in the United States*, 61st Cong., 2d sess., 1910, S. Doc. 588, 15, 18, 20, 31, 153, 173, 217.

32. U.S. Country Life Commission, *Report*, 60th Cong., 2d sess., 1909, S. Doc. 705, 14-15.

33. U.S. Congress, *Hearings before the Subcommittee of the Joint Committee on Rural Credits*, 64th Cong., 1st sess., 1915, 17; U.S. Census Office, *Report on Farms and Homes*, table 107.

34. The reductions of capital requirements for national banks in 1900, which expanded the activity of national banks in rural areas, would have increased competition primarily for short-term loans. The prohibition on national bank loans on real estate security remained in effect. See Wright, *Bank Credit*, 60-61.

35. T. B. McPherson, "Cattle as Mortgage Security," *Proceedings of the Second Annual Convention of the National Livestock Association, January 24-27, 1899* (Denver, Colo., 1899), 168.

36. Kansas Bureau of Labor and Industrial Statistics, *Annual Report, 1887* (Topeka, 1887), 99, 106; "Governor John A. Martin, Biennial Address to the State Legislature," 8 January 1889, Kansas Governor's Office, Letter Press Books, box 24, no. 85 A, Kansas State Historical Society, Topeka.

37. *Iowa Tribune*, 6 February 1884, and *Western Rural and American Stockman* (Chicago), 17 September 1887. Another local Alliance officer estimated in 1889 that the prevailing rate for short-term loans in the state was 18 percent per annum. L. H. Griffith to L. H. Weller, 16 September 1889, Luman H. Weller Papers, Wisconsin State Historical Society, Madison.

38. John R. Hopkins, Jr., *Economic History of the Production of Beef Cattle in Iowa* (Iowa City, Iowa, 1928), 144; James W. Whitaker, *Feedlot Empire: Beef Cattle Feeding in Illinois and Iowa, 1840-1900* (Ames, Iowa, 1975), 65; and Mildred Throne, "A History of Agriculture in Southern Iowa, 1833-1890," Ph.D. diss., State University of Iowa, 1946, 232-33.

39. Gatch's and Head's comments are in the *Iowa State Register* (Des Moines), 18, 19 March 1890.

40. U.S. Census Office, *Report on Farms and Homes*, 286; U.S. Census Office, *Agriculture*, pt. 1, "Farms, Livestock, and Animal Products" (Washington, D.C., 1902), lxix; Donald L. Winters, *Farmers without Farms: Agricultural Tenancy in Nineteenth-Century Iowa* (Westport, Conn., 1978), 20-25; Margaret B. Bogue, *Patterns from the Sod: Land Use and Tenure in the Grand Prairie, 1850-1900* (Springfield, Ill., 1959), 154-62; and Seddie

Cogswell, Jr., *Tenure, Nativity and Age as Factors in Iowa Agriculture, 1850–1880* (Ames, Iowa, 1975), 41.

41. Winters, *Farmers without Farms*, 59; M. Bogue, *Patterns from the Sod*, 167–68, notes that in eight Illinois counties there was a similar trend: The percentage of cash rents increased from 19 percent in 1880 to 44 percent in 1900. Winters (pp. 59–60) and Bogue (pp. 171–72) both assume that the tendency toward increased cash rents was the result of tenants and landlords bargaining on equal terms and perceiving mutual advantages to cash rent, but neither explains why cash rents would be mutually advantageous. If, however, one accepts the implication of increasing competition among tenants for leases (a development Winters and Bogue amply document), it becomes clear that tenants and landlords did not bargain on equal terms. Considering that cash rents favored landlords in a deflationary economy, it is apparent why rents shifted from share to cash.

42. Paul W. Gates, *Frontier Landlords and Pioneer Tenants* (Ithaca, N.Y., 1945), 47–50, 43, 56.

43. *Sioux City Journal*, 1 January 1896; *Onawa Weekly Democrat*, 16 January 1896.

44. For a more positive evaluation of conditions in the corn belt in the late nineteenth century, see A. Bogue's indispensable *Prairie to Corn Belt*.

45. In Kansas and Nebraska, voting for the Independent gubernatorial candidates in the election of 1890 is the best index of Populist voting strength because this election was a genuine three-way contest. In subsequent elections Populist/Democratic fusion obscured the core Populist vote. For Iowa and Missouri the Populist vote shown is for the election of 1892, as there was not yet an Independent Party in those states in 1890. The election data are found in Kansas Secretary of State, *Biennial Report, 1888–90* (Topeka, 1890), 85–86; Nebraska Legislative Reference Council, *Nebraska Blue Book and Historical Register, 1918* (Lincoln, Nebr., 1918), 451–52; Iowa Secretary of State, *Official Register for the State of Iowa, 1893* (Des Moines, 1893), 119–92; and Missouri State Department, *Official Manual of the State of Missouri, 1893–94* (Jefferson City, 1893), 19.

46. C. Warren Thornwaite, "The Climate of North America According to a New Classification," *Geographical Review* 21 (October 1931): 633–55, especially the map facing p. 654. See also Walter Prescott Webb, *The Great Plains* (New York, 1931), 17–26.

47. Hicks, *Populist Revolt*, 1–35, provides a vivid description of the Great Plains boom and its collapse. See also James C. Olson, *History of Nebraska* (Lincoln, Nebr., 1955), 195–208; Richard Sheridan, *Economic Development in South Central Kansas*, part 1A, *An Economic History, 1500–1900* (Lawrence, Kans., 1956), 126–233; James C. Malin, "The Kinsley Boom of the Late Eighties," *Kansas Historical Quarterly* 4 (February–March 1935): 23–49, 164–87; and Craig Miner, *West of Wichita: Settling the High Plains of Kansas, 1865–1890* (Lawrence, Kans., 1986), 212–29. For an eloquent statement of the mythology of the Great Plains as desert and garden, see Henry Nash Smith, *Virgin Land: The American West as Symbol and Myth* (New York, 1950), 201–26.

48. Scholars of populism in Kansas and Nebraska have often implied that it had little support in the eastern sections of those states. Robert W. Cherny, *Populism, Progressivism, and the Transformation of Nebraska Politics, 1895–1915* (Lincoln, Nebr., 1981), 37, for example, states that the "Independents cut a broad swathe across central Nebraska but were weak in the east and in the panhandle." In the absence of actual voting figures, one is left with the impression that there was little support for populism in eastern Nebraska. Similar statements with no voting data are found in Peter H. Argersinger, *Populism and Politics: William Alfred Peffer and the People's Party* (Lexington, Ky., 1974), 64; Raymond

C. Miller, "The Populist Party in Kansas," Ph.D. diss., University of Chicago, 1928, 142; Louise E. Rickard, "The Impact of Populism on Electoral Patterns in Kansas, 1880-1900: A Quantitative Analysis," Ph.D. diss., University of Kansas, 1974, 102; Walter T. K. Nugent, *The Tolerant Populists: Kansas Populism and Nativism* (Chicago, 1963), 57; and John D. Barnhart, "The History of the Farmers' Alliance and of the People's Party in Nebraska," Ph.D. diss., Harvard University, 1930, 238-39. Stanley B. Parsons, *The Populist Context: Rural versus Urban Power on a Great Plains Frontier* (Westport, Conn., 1973), 85-90, also implies that populism was weak in eastern Nebraska, although he does provide voting data suggesting the contrary.

49. Populism in the eastern counties remained strong in the 1892 presidential election. In Nebraska, where there were three tickets in the field, the average Populist percentage in the eastern counties was 37.7. In a two-way election in Kansas, the presidential fusion ticket carried seventeen of the thirty-three eastern counties; the mean fusion percentage was 49.2. Data for the 1892 elections for Kansas and Nebraska was provided by the Inter-University Consortium for Political and Social Research (ICPSR), Ann Arbor, Mich.

50. *Daily Capital* (Topeka), 6 November 1890, and *Daily Nebraska State Journal* (Lincoln, Nebr.), 10 November 1890.

51. Snowden D. Flora, "Climate of Kansas," *Report of the Kansas State Board of Agriculture, June 1948* (Topeka, Kans., 1948), 10.

52. On the rapid pace of settlement following the Civil War, see William F. Zornow, *Kansas: A History of the Jayhawk State* (Norman, Okla., 1957), 161-63; and Olson, *Nebraska*, 161-75. Population figures are from U.S. Census Office, *Statistics of Population of the United States at the Tenth Census* (Washington, D.C., 1883), table 2.

53. Clarence L. Petrowsky, "Kansas Agriculture before 1900," Ph.D. diss., University of Oklahoma, 1968, 139, 149; Olson, *Nebraska*, 205-6; and Earle D. Ross, *Iowa Agriculture: An Historical Survey* (Iowa City, Iowa, 1951), 72-75, 82. Keach Johnson, "Iowa Dairying at the Turn of the Century," *Agricultural History* 45 (April 1971): 95-110, dates the surge in dairying in northeastern Iowa to the depression of the 1890s.

54. See Seymour Martin Lipset, *Agrarian Socialism: The Cooperative Commonwealth Federation in Saskatchewan* (New York, 1968), 24; Michael P. Rogin, *The Intellectuals and McCarthy: The Radical Specter* (Cambridge, Mass., 1967), 188-89; Hofstadter, *Age of Reform*, 100; Samuel P. Hays, *The Response to Industrialism* (Chicago, 1957), 28; and Robert Wiebe, *The Search for Order, 1877-1920* (New York, 1967), 85. In the sixty-three counties of western Nebraska and Kansas, the average county had only 6 percent of its improved acres in wheat at the 1890 census, but 22 percent of its acreage in corn. Farmers in the seventy-two counties of central Kansas and Nebraska planted 8 percent of improved acres in wheat compared to 34 percent for corn. See U.S. Census Office, *Report on the Statistics of Agriculture in the United States at the Eleventh Census: 1890* (Washington, D.C., 1895), tables 6, 14. James C. Malin, *Winter Wheat in the Golden Belt of Kansas: A Study in the Adaptation to Subhumid Geographical Environment* (Lawrence, Kans., 1944), 157, provides annual statistics for Kansas showing that wheat production did not expand until 1891-1892. Works that have recognized the minimal role of wheat in the Populist revolt include Argersinger, *Populism and Politics*, 71-72, and Parsons, *Populist Context*, 126.

55. Hicks, *Populist Revolt*, 31; Nugent, *Tolerant Populists*, 55; Chester McArthur Destler, "Agricultural Readjustment and Agrarian Unrest in Illinois, 1880-1896," *Agricul-*

tural History 21 (April 1947): 104; and John D. Barnhart, "Rainfall and the Populist Party in Nebraska," *American Political Science Review* 19 (August 1925): 527–40.

56. *Iowa State Register*, 18 March 1888; Iowa State Improved Stock Breeders' Association, *Proceedings of the Seventeenth Annual Meeting, December 3–5, 1890* (Des Moines, Iowa, 1891), 32–34.

57. U.S. Department of Agriculture, Bureau of Statistics, *Corn Crops of the United States, 1866–1906*, Bulletin 56 (Washington, D.C., 1907), 15–20.

58. Ibid.; U.S. Department of Agriculture, *Report of the Statistician* 80 (December 1890): 601.

59. Kansas State Board of Agriculture, *Monthly Report, September 30, 1890* (Topeka, Kans., 1890), 12–14.

60. Hicks, *Populist Revolt*, 268–69; Hallie Farmer, "The Railroads and Frontier Populism," *Mississippi Valley Historical Review* 13 (December 1926): 387–97; and Higgs, "Railroad Rates," 296.

61. These distinctions are made clear in the Kansas Board of Railroad Commissioners, *Annual Report, 1890* (Topeka, Kans., 1890), 110–18. The Iowa Board of Railroad Commissioners, *Annual Report, 1892* (Des Moines, Iowa, 1892), 20, estimated that about a quarter of all freight originating in the state was local. The percentage of specifically agricultural freight shipped within state boundaries was almost certainly lower.

62. Ripley, *Railroads*, 85–86, 102–3, 113–32.

63. Ibid., 126–32, 354–79; U.S. Interstate Commerce Commission, *Interstate Commerce Reports*, vol. 3 (Rochester, N.Y., 1893), 94. Shipments from Topeka could also be routed through Chicago and billed at the Topeka-Chicago plus the Chicago-New York rate, which was about the same as the rate through St. Louis.

64. These rates are from tariff schedules in U.S. Department of Agriculture, *Report of the Statistician* 59 (January–February, 1889), except rates from interior points in Kansas and Nebraska, which are found in U.S. Interstate Commerce Commission, *Railways in the United States in 1902*, pt. 2, "A Forty Year Review of Changes in Freight Tariffs" (Washington, D.C., 1903), 107, 110. Rates cited for interior points are for Central City, Nebraska, and Abilene, Kansas. Wheat rates were identical to corn rates in trunk-line territory and 5 cents higher west of the Mississippi.

65. U.S. Interstate Commerce Commission, *Interstate Commerce Reports*, vol. 3, 95.

66. Ibid.

67. USDA, Bureau of Statistics, *Corn Crops*, 15–20; *Iowa State Register*, 18 January 1890. Some evidence indicates that there was a slightly wider disparity between rates in Iowa and rates in interior points of Kansas and Nebraska earlier in the 1880s; however, rates at these interior points fell rapidly between 1887 and 1888, and there was less disparity between rates at these points and rates at the Missouri River and in Iowa. Rates can be examined in USDA, *Report of the Statistician*, 1884–1891; U.S. Interstate Commerce Commission, *Railways in the United States*; and Nebraska Board of Transportation, *Annual Report, 1890* (Lincoln, Nebr., 1890), chart. On the impact of the railroad construction boom in spurring competition in Kansas, see Joseph M. Trojanowski, "The Stability of Freight Rate Agreements at Minor Railroad Junctions in Iowa and Kansas, 1880–1910," Ph.D. diss., Yale University, 1980, 20–21.

68. U.S. Census Office, *Report on Farms and Homes*, table 94.

69. Eichengreen, "Mortgage Interest Rates," 996, observes that "an acre of farmland

is an asset, and its price contains information about the market's assessment of risk and expected returns to farming."

70. Because farms were slightly larger in the eastern parts of Kansas and Nebraska (160 acres per farm) than in Iowa (151 acres per farm), the average value of an acre of farmland (improved and unimproved acreage) was a little more in the latter ($28.12) compared to the former ($26.14).

71. The total annual debt obligation is determined by adding one-fifth of the value of the mortgage (this assumes a five-year term for loans) and the per annum interest on the value of the mortgage. For example, on a mortgage of $2,000 with an interest rate of 8 percent on a farm valued at $5,000, the annual debt obligation would be $400 (one-fifth of $2,000) added to $160 (8 percent of $2,000) for a total of $560. The ratio of the annual debt obligation to the value of mortgaged property would be 11.2 percent.

72. Confirmation for this geographical division is found in the pattern of foreclosure rates in Nebraska using data from 1890, 1892, 1894, and 1895. According to these data, the twenty-six eastern Nebraska counties had a foreclosure rate of only 1.1 percent per annum; the remaining sixty-three western and central Nebraska counties had a foreclosure rate of 5.2 percent. See Nebraska Bureau of Labor and Industrial Statistics, *Biennial Report, 1889-90* (Lincoln, 1890), 309-10; *Biennial Report, 1891-92* (Lincoln, 1892), 137-40; *Biennial Report, 1893-94* (Lincoln, 1894), 146-48; and *Biennial Report, 1895-96* (Lincoln, 1896), 248-49.

73. Iowa Commissioner of Labor Statistics, *Biennial Report, 1890-91*, 55-57.

74. Undoubtedly only a few highly capitalized farming operations relied entirely on hog production. Although most corn was fed to livestock, a significant percentage was marketed. Figures for 1888-1890 show that between 20 and 25 percent of the corn crop in Iowa was shipped out of the county where it was grown. U.S. Department of Agriculture, *Report of the Statistician* 60 (March 1889): 55; *Report of the Statistician* 71 (March 1890): 71; and *Report of the Statistician* 82 (March 1891): 62.

75. Iowa Commissioner of Labor Statistics, *Biennial Report, 1890-91*, 49-50; Murray, *Economic Analysis*, 417-18; and A. Bogue, *Prairie to Corn Belt*, 179.

76. Iowa Commissioner of Labor Statistics, *Biennial Report, 1890-91*, 69, 89.

77. Ibid., 61, 89.

CHAPTER 3. ANTIMONOPOLY AND THE EMERGENCE OF PARTY COMPETITION IN IOWA

1. Congressional Quarterly, *Congressional Quarterly's Guide to U.S. Elections*, 2d ed. (Washington, D.C., 1985), 337, 772.

2. Robert J. Cook, "Puritans, Pragmatists, and Progress: The Republican Coalition in Iowa, 1854-1878," Ph.D. diss., Oxford University, 1986, 57, and Leland L. Sage, *William Boyd Allison: A Study in Practical Politics* (Iowa City, Iowa, 1956), 71-75.

3. Sage, *Allison*, 91-118; Cook, "Puritans," 52-53; and Robert Dykstra, "Iowa: 'Bright Radical Star,' " in *Radical Republicans in the North: State Politics during Reconstruction*, ed. James C. Mohr (Baltimore, 1976), 188.

4. Solon Justus Buck, *The Granger Movement: A Study of Agricultural Organization and Its Political, Economic, and Social Manifestations, 1870-1880* (Cambridge, Mass., 1913), 50, and chart between pp. 58-59.

5. Mildred Throne, "The Grange in Iowa, 1868-1875," *Iowa Journal of History* 47 (Oc-

tober 1949): 306, 312–16; Throne, "The Anti-Monopoly Party in Iowa, 1873–1874," *Iowa Journal of History* 52 (October 1954): 291–307; and Horace Samuel Merrill, *Bourbon Democracy of the Middle West, 1865–1896* (Baton Rouge, La., 1953), 84.

6. Sage, *Allison*, 123–26; Throne, "Anti-Monopoly Party," 310–12; Mildred Throne, *Cyrus Clay Carpenter and Iowa Politics, 1854–1898* (Iowa City, Iowa, 1974), 154–72; and Congressional Quarterly, *Guide*, 500.

7. *Iowa State Register*, 30 October 1873, quoted in Cook, "Republican Coalition," 85. One of the central themes of Cook's excellent study is that Republican Party leaders, though eager to promote economic growth, had to make compromises with antimonopoly public opinion in order to stay in office (see especially 75–87). On the 1874 legislative session, see Throne, *Carpenter*, 173–80. George H. Miller, *Railroads and the Granger Laws* (Madison, Wis., 1971), 102–14, attributes the 1874 legislation to the efforts of Mississippi River jobbers to obtain lower rates to enable them to compete with Chicago jobbers. Although it is true that the final legislation was shaped by jobbers, it seems evident that the threat from agrarian agitation created the political conditions favorable for regulatory legislation.

8. Cook, "Puritans," 90–92; and Mildred Throne, "The Repeal of the Iowa Granger Law, 1878," *Iowa Journal of History* 51 (April 1953): 118–24.

9. Fred Emory Haynes, *James Baird Weaver* (Iowa City, Iowa, 1919), 74.

10. Haynes, *Weaver*, 77–95; Thomas Burnell Colbert, "Disgruntled 'Chronic Office Seeker' or Man of Political Integrity: James Baird Weaver and the Republican Party in Iowa, 1857–1877," *Annals of Iowa* 49 (Winter/Spring 1988): 187–207; and Herbert Quick, *The Hawkeye* (Indianapolis, Ind., 1923), 298.

11. Throne, "Repeal," 120, and Haynes, *Weaver*, 106.

12. Congressional Quarterly, *Guide*, 500.

13. Haynes, *Weaver*, 101–6.

14. Ibid., 156–57; Congressional Quarterly, *Guide*, 340, 500.

15. Thomas Richard Ross, *Jonathan Prentiss Dolliver: A Study in Political Integrity and Independence* (Iowa City, Iowa, 1958), 65.

16. John D. Denison, *Iowa Democracy: A History of the Politics and Personalities of the Democratic Party*, 4 vols. (Des Moines, Iowa, 1939), 1:299, 302.

17. Sage, *Allison*, 203, and George Mills, "The Fighting Clarksons," *Palimpsest* 30 (September 1949): 283–89.

18. Sage, *Allison*, 276.

19. Dan Elbert Clark, "The History of Liquor Legislation in Iowa, 1861–1878," *Iowa Journal of History and Politics* 6 (July 1908): 366–68, and Clark, "The History of Liquor Legislation in Iowa, 1878–1908," *Iowa Journal of History and Politics* 6 (October 1908): 505–12. See also Richard Jensen, *The Winning of the Midwest: Social and Political Conflict, 1886–96* (Chicago, 1971), 91–93.

20. Clark, "Liquor Legislation, 1878–1908," 525.

21. The Republican vote declined from 56.7 percent in 1881 to 50.1 percent in 1883; see Congressional Quarterly, *Guide*, 500. County-level election data are from the Inter-University Consortium for Political and Social Research (ICPSR), Ann Arbor, Mich. Reviews of the ethnocultural interpretation of nineteenth-century politics can be found in Peter H. Argersinger and John W. Jeffries, "American Electoral History: Party Systems and Voting Behavior," in *Research in Micropolitics: Voting Behavior*, ed. Samuel Long, 2 vols. (Greenwich, Conn., 1986), 1:1–33; Richard L. McCormick, "Ethno-Cultural Inter-

pretations of Nineteenth-Century American Voting Behavior," *Political Science Quarterly* 89 (June 1974): 351-77; Allan J. Lichtman, "Political Realignment and 'Ethnocultural' Voting in Late Nineteenth Century America," *Journal of Social History* 16 (Spring 1983): 55-77; and Allan G. Bogue, "The New Political History in the 1970s," in *The Past before Us: Contemporary Historical Writing in the United States*, ed. Michael Kammen (Ithaca, N.Y., 1980), 231-51. The most important ethnocultural studies of the Midwest are Paul Kleppner, *The Cross of Culture: A Social Analysis of Midwestern Politics, 1850-1900* (New York, 1970); Kleppner, *The Third Electoral System, 1853-1892: Parties, Voters, and Political Cultures* (Chapel Hill, N.C., 1979); Jensen, *Winning of the Midwest*; and Frederick C. Luebke, *Immigrants and Politics: The Germans of Nebraska, 1880-1900* (Lincoln, Nebr., 1969). Ethnocultural interpretations of Iowa politics in the 1880s can be found in Jensen, *Winning of the Midwest*, 89-121; Kleppner, *Third Electoral System*, 298-356; and Ballard C. Campbell, "Did Democracy Work? Prohibition in Late Nineteenth-Century Iowa: A Test Case," *Journal of Interdisciplinary History* 8 (Summer 1977): 97. For a similar view of Iowa politics in the 1890s, see Bruce Gunn Kelley, "Ethnocultural Voting Trends in Rural Iowa, 1890-1898," *Annals of Iowa* 44 (Fall 1978): 441-61.

22. Henry S. Fairall, *Fairall's Manual of Iowa Politics, 1884* (Iowa City, Iowa, 1884), 5, and Sage, *Allison*, 193.

23. Fairall, *Manual. 1884*, 9-12, and Sage, *Allison*, 194.

24. These and all other estimates in this book are based upon ecological regression. The election data are from the ICPSR; population data are from the Iowa Secretary of State, *Census of Iowa for the Year 1885* (Des Moines, Iowa, 1885), table 3, and Iowa Secretary of State, *Census of Iowa for the Year 1895* (Des Moines, Iowa, 1896), tables 32, 46. Regression-based estimates rest on assumptions that are difficult to verify and should be treated only as general estimates. For the purposes of this analysis, however, these estimates are particularly useful for sensing the shift of voters across pairs or over a series of elections. For a discussion of the methodology used in making these estimates, see Appendix B.

25. These antiprohibitionist groups had opposed the referendum of 1882 solidly. An estimated 68 percent were in opposition, with none in favor and 32 percent not voting (see Appendix B).

26. Since the categories of native-born voters and farmers overlap, it is impossible to estimate a percentage of native-born farmers. It is relevant to note, however, that the estimated percentage of farmers voting Democratic increased by only slightly more in counties with high concentrations of foreign-born antiprohibition voters. In those counties with over 15 percent of voting-age males of national origin likely to oppose prohibition, the estimated percentage of Democratic farmers increased from 12 to 29 percent. In all other counties the estimated percentages were almost identical: 12 percent in 1881 and 26 percent in 1883.

27. Denison, *Iowa Democracy*, 1:325; Henry S. Fairall, *Fairall's Manual of Iowa Politics, 1885* (Iowa City, Iowa, 1886), 26.

28. Haynes, *Weaver*, 206; Congressional Quarterly, *Guide*, 802.

29. *Iowa State Register*, 20, 27, 29 August, 4 September 1884.

30. *Des Moines Leader*, 8 October, 30 September, 1 November 1884.

31. Ibid., 8 October 1884.

32. Ibid., 25 October 1884. For the 1883 Republican state platform, see Henry S. Fairall, *Fairall's Manual of Iowa Politics, 1883* (Iowa City, Iowa, 1883), 45-46.

33. Congressional Quarterly, *Guide*, 806, 340–41.

34. *Des Moines Leader*, 14 August, 30 July 1885.

35. Ibid., 19, 20 August 1885; Denison, *Iowa Democracy*, 1:341.

36. Quoted in *Des Moines Leader*, 22 August 1885.

37. Quoted in Ross, *Dolliver*, 64.

38. David B. Henderson to James S. Clarkson, 5 January 1885, James S. Clarkson Papers, Library of Congress, Washington, D.C.

39. *Iowa State Register*, 28 August 1885. For biographical information on Larrabee, see J. Brooke Workman, "Governor Larrabee and Railroad Reform," *Iowa Journal of History* 57 (July 1959): 231–66.

40. *Iowa State Register*, 9, 27 September 1885.

41. Ibid., 18, 5 September 1885.

42. *Des Moines Leader*, 6 October, 26 September, 2 October 1885.

43. Ibid., 11 October 1885.

44. *Iowa State Register*, 29 September 1885.

45. *Des Moines Leader*, 30 October 1885.

46. Ibid., 29 October 1885.

47. Ibid., 3 November 1885.

48. John P. Dolliver to James S. Clarkson, 9 November 1885, Clarkson Papers.

49. See Appendix B.

50. Shelton Stromquist, *A Generation of Boomers: The Pattern of Railroad Labor Conflict in Nineteenth-Century America* (Urbana, Ill., 1987), 63–66, and Ralph Scharnau, "Workers and Politics: The Knights of Labor in Dubuque, Iowa, 1885–1890," *Annals of Iowa* 48 (Winter/Spring 1987): 353–77.

51. Beef cattle decreased from $4.72 per 100 lbs. to $3.65 (23 percent); hogs declined from $6.08 per 100 lbs. to $3.43 (44 percent); corn fell from 56 cents per bushel to 25 cents (55 percent). See Norman V. Strand, *Prices of Farm Products in Iowa, 1851–1940*, Iowa State Agricultural Experiment Station Bulletin 303 (Ames, Iowa, 1942), 937–39.

52. The NFA, later known as the Northern or Northwestern Alliance, was organized in 1880 by Milton George, editor of a Chicago farm paper, the *Western Rural*. In 1881 there was an NFA organization in Iowa along with another small competing Alliance, organized by Coker F. Clarkson and Henry Wallace; these two alliances merged on 11 January 1882. August Post was elected secretary and Jesse Kennedy president. The consolidated Alliance remained affiliated with the NFA. See Roy V. Scott, "Milton George and the Farmers' Alliance Movement," *Mississippi Valley Historical Review* 45 (June 1958): 90–109, and Judith A. Gildner, "An Organizational History of the Iowa Farmers' Alliance, 1881–1890," Master's thesis, Drake University, 1972, 12–49.

53. *Homestead* (Des Moines, Iowa), 20 August 1886. No record of this meeting has been found, although it clearly took place as it was referred to at the 1887 annual meeting summarized in the *Western Rural* (Chicago), 17 September 1887.

54. U.S. Senate, *Report of the Senate Select Committee on Interstate Commerce*, 49th Cong., 1st sess., 1886, S. Rept. 46, pt. 2, 1002–3.

55. The Senate Committee on Mines and Mining recommended that the Cassatt mining bill be indefinitely postponed. Later in the session the senate amended a similar bill passed in the house beyond recognition, but antimonopolists in the house stood firm against any watered-down substitute and rejected the senate version. See Iowa Senate, *Journal, 1886* (Des Moines, Iowa, 1886), 343–44, 491, 507, and Iowa House, *Journal, 1886*

(Des Moines, Iowa, 1886), 421–22, 755. A bill to make the Iowa commission elective passed the house seventy to sixteen but died in the senate. See Iowa House, *Journal, 1886* 442–43, and Iowa Senate, *Journal, 1886*, 534, 656. On the KOL's "labor protection bill," see Scharnau, "Workers and Politics," 362–63.

56. Charles Beardsley to William B. Allison, 17 April, 15 July 1886, William Boyd Allison Papers, State Historical Society of Iowa, Des Moines.

57. Stephen Skowronek, *Building a New American State: The Expansion of National Administrative Capacities, 1877–1920* (Cambridge, Mass., 1982), 145–49.

58. J. C. Clarke to William B. Allison, 8 January 1885, and Charles E. Perkins to William B. Allison, 20 May 1886, Allison Papers.

59. *Homestead*, 20 August 1886.

60. *Des Moines Leader*, 12 July 1886. For Hepburn's biography, see John E. Briggs, *William Peters Hepburn* (Iowa City, Iowa, 1919).

61. *Des Moines Leader*, 13 July 1886. The platform also favored free coinage of silver, liberal pensions to soldiers, and arbitration of labor disputes.

62. *Iowa State Register*, 28 August 1886.

63. Ibid., 23 July 1886.

64. The first debate was held 18 September at Centerville and reported in ibid., 19 September 1886. The third debate was held at Leon and reported in ibid., 3 October 1886. A ninth joint debate took place at Corning as reported in ibid., 26 October 1886.

65. Ibid., 10 October 1886.

66. Ibid., 3 October 1886.

67. Ibid., 19 September 1886.

68. Ibid., 10 October 1886.

69. Ibid., 20 October and 10 October 1886.

70. Ibid., 24 September 1886; *Homestead*, 29 October 1886; *Des Moines Leader*, 29 October 1886.

71. *Homestead*, 29 October 1886.

72. *Des Moines Leader*, August–October 1886, 14 October, 2 November 1886.

73. *Iowa State Register*, 24 September 1886.

74. *Congressional Quarterly, Guide*, 810.

75. William P. Hepburn to James S. Clarkson, 5 November 1886, Clarkson Papers.

76. James W. McDill to William B. Allison, 22 November 1886, Allison Papers. The sponsor of the Cullom bill, Sen. Shelby Cullom of Illinois, feared Hepburn's defeat would frighten western congressmen into supporting the Reagan bill. See James W. Neilson, *Shelby M. Cullom: Prairie State Republican* (Urbana, Ill., 1962), 113.

CHAPTER 4. THE IOWA FARMERS' ALLIANCE AND THE POLITICS OF RAILROAD REFORM

1. Henry S. Fairall, *Fairall's Manual of Iowa Politics, 1883* (Iowa City, Iowa, 1883), 45, and Fairall, *Fairall's Manual of Iowa Politics, 1885* (Iowa City, Iowa, 1886), 46–47.

2. *Weekly Bee* (Omaha), 11 April 1888, and Iowa House, *Journal, 1886* (Des Moines, Iowa, 1886), 419–20.

3. *Cedar Rapids Evening Gazette*, quoted in the *Des Moines Leader*, 22 August 1885. The *Gazette*, 23 August 1887, claimed to have been the "first to voice the general desire for 'a two cent fare' in Iowa" several months earlier.

4. Richard Jensen, *The Winning of the Midwest: Social and Political Conflict, 1886-96* (Chicago, 1971), 98-99; Dan Elbert Clark, "The History of Liquor Legislation in Iowa, 1878-1908," *Iowa Journal of History and Politics* 6 (October 1908): 551-63; and Cyrenus Cole, *A History of the People of Iowa* (Cedar Rapids, Iowa, 1921), 464-65. William Larrabee to G. B. Kuyendall, 25 June 1886, Governor's Letter Books, vol. 59, Iowa State Archives, Des Moines.

5. *Iowa State Register*, 24 September 1886.

6. William Larrabee published his views in *The Railroad Question: A Historical and Practical Treatise in Railroads, and Remedies for their Abuses* (Chicago, 1893). The history of regulation in Iowa is also told in Frank H. Dixon, *State Railroad Control with a History of Its Development in Iowa* (New York, 1896), and J. Brooke Workman, "Governor Larrabee and Railroad Reform," *Iowa Journal of History* 57 (July 1959): 231-66.

7. William Larrabee to Board of Railroad Commissioners, 6 December 1886, William Larrabee Papers, State Historical Society of Iowa, Clermont.

8. Iowa Board of Railroad Commissioners, *Annual Report, 1887* (Des Moines, Iowa, 1887), 625-26.

9. William Larrabee to E. G. Morgan (secretary of the Iowa Board of Railroad Commissioners), 4 January 1887, Larrabee Papers.

10. Larrabee to Board of Railroad Commissioners, 7 March 1887, Larrabee Papers.

11. *Homestead* (Des Moines, Iowa), 29 April 1887.

12. Iowa Board of Railroad Commissioners, *Annual Report, 1887*, 671 (emphasis in original).

13. Ibid., 670-75, quotation, 670.

14. *Homestead*, 13 May 1887; Marshalltown *Weekly Times-Republican*, 2 June 1887, quoted in Workman, "Larrabee," 250; and *Iowa State Register*, 8 May 1887.

15. James S. Clarkson to William B. Allison, 24 March 1887, Allison Papers.

16. William Larrabee to N. M. Hubbard, 4 October 1889, Larrabee Papers.

17. *Western Rural* (Chicago), 17 September 1887. For estimates of the membership of the Iowa Farmers' Alliance, see Appendix A.

18. Judith A. Gildner, "An Organizational History of the Iowa Farmers' Alliance, 1881-1890," Master's thesis, Drake University, 1972, 57-58.

19. Roy V. Scott, "Milton George and the Farmers' Alliance Movement," *Mississippi Valley Historical Review* 45 (June 1958): 93-95.

20. *Homestead*, 1 July 1887.

21. *Iowa State Register*, 1 July 1887.

22. Iowa Board of Railroad Commissioners, *Annual Report, 1885* (Des Moines, Iowa, 1885), 45-47, 536-40, and Iowa Board of Railroad Commissioners, *Annual Report, 1886* (Des Moines, Iowa, 1886), 31. See also Dixon, *State Railroad Control*, 67-76.

23. *Homestead*, 6 May 1887.

24. Ibid., 29 July 1887.

25. On the ubiquity of factionalism at the local level, see Patrick F. Palmero, "The Rules of the Game: Local Republican Political Culture in the Gilded Age," *Historian* 47 (August 1985): 480-81. Herbert Quick, *The Hawkeye* (Indianapolis, 1923), 137ff., contains a rich fictionalized account of rivals among "ins" and "outs" at the county level.

26. *Ft. Dodge Messenger*, quoted in *Iowa State Register*, 13 August 1887.

27. *Clarinda* [Iowa] *Herald*, 19 October, 2 November 1887.

28. *Winterset* [Iowa] *Madisonian*, 8, 15 September 1887.

29. *Cedar Rapids Gazette*, 22 July, 19 August 1887.

30. *Lake City* [Iowa] *Graphic*, 13 August 1887.

31. *Iowa State Register*, 23 August 1887.

32. Ibid., 24 August and 13 August 1887.

33. *Sioux City Journal*, quoted in ibid., 21 August 1887.

34. *Cedar Rapids Gazette*, 23 August 1887.

35. Ibid., 25 August, 29 July 1887; *Iowa State Register*, 25 August 1887.

36. The *Iowa State Register*, 16 February 1888, quoted the transportation plank of the platform and elucidated Clarkson's authorship.

37. *Des Moines Leader*, 10 August, 2 September 1887; John D. Denison, *Iowa Democracy*, 4 vols. (Des Moines, Iowa, 1939) 1:361; and *Iowa State Register*, 3 September, 8 October 1887. The *Des Moines Leader*, 30 August 1887, favored S. L. Bestow, "a farmer and an anti-monopolist," for the nomination.

38. *Iowa State Register*, 10 June 1887, and *Iowa Tribune* (Des Moines), 15 June 1887.

39. H. S. Wilcox, quoted in the *Iowa Tribune*, 10 August 1887.

40. Ibid., 20 July, 7 September, 2 November 1887.

41. *Des Moines Leader*, 21, 29 October 1887.

42. The estimated percentage of antiprohibition voters voting Democratic increased from 47 in 1885 to 58 in 1887; turnout increased from 54 to 61 percent, suggesting a greater interest in the election among this group. The estimated percentage of native-born voters voting Democrat fell from 39 to 30 percent. Larrabee gained almost no support from antiprohibition voters (an estimated 3 percent) in 1887, but he won an estimated 47 percent of foreign-born voters for prohibition; the Democrats won only 2 percent (the remaining 50 percent did not vote). See Appendix B. Larrabee won 50.1 percent of the total vote; Anderson 45.4; Cain 4.2. Congressional Quarterly, *Congressional Quarterly's Guide to U.S. Elections*, 2d ed. (Washington, D.C., 1985), 500.

43. The estimated percentage of all voting-age farmers who voted Republican changed from 51 percent in 1885 to 50 percent in 1887, and the estimated percentage voting Democrat fell from 39 to 30 percent. Turnout declined from 83 percent to 77 percent. An estimated 3 percent of farmers voted Union Labor in 1887; see Appendix B. The reason for the decline in turnout among farmers in 1887 is unclear although it may have been because some farmers protested the GOP's failure to adopt an antimonopoly platform and the Democrats' nomination of Anderson.

44. *Cedar Rapids Gazette*, 6, 19 September 1887.

45. Russell Lord, *The Wallaces of Iowa* (Boston, 1947), 103, and *Iowa State Register*, 4 November 1887. Unfortunately, because issues of the *Homestead* from August through December 1887 are missing, it is impossible to verify Lord's figures, which are based on Wallace's recollections. But the *Register*'s constant stream of invective toward Wallace makes it clear that he was conducting a wide-ranging campaign against prorailroad candidates.

46. See the letter dated 24 October 1887 by T. J. Caldwell, Republican nominee for state senator from the seventeenth district (Audubon, Dallas, and Guthrie Counties), replying to a request from the Pioneer Alliance in the *Homestead*, 23 March 1888.

47. *Iowa State Register*, 17 September, 25 October 1887.

48. Ibid., 2 November 1887.

49. Lord, *Wallaces*, 103, and Frank S. Stork and Cynthia A. Clingan, *The Iowa General Assembly: Our Legislative Heritage, 1846–1980* (Des Moines, Iowa, 1980), 6, 11.

50. *Iowa State Register*, 13 November 1887; J. S. Clarkson to William Larrabee, 17 January 188[8], Larrabee Papers.

51. Benjamin F. Shambaugh, comp. and ed., *The Messages and Proclamations of the Governors of Iowa*, 7 vols. (Iowa City, Iowa, 1903-1905), 6:91.

52. Ibid., 6:94-95.

53. Ibid., 6:97.

54. Ibid., 6:98-99.

55. Ibid., 6:103, 106. Larrabee had outlined his specific legislative proposals to abolish free passes, to reduce passenger fares to 2 cents per mile, and to establish maximum freight rates one day earlier in a separate biennial message. Although not specifically recommending election of commissioners, he stated that "such legislation will not meet with any opposition at my hands"; see ibid., 6:73-74.

56. J. S. Clarkson to William B. Allison, 13 January 1888, and C. E. Perkins to William B. Allison, 17 January 1888, Allison Papers.

57. *Iowa State Register*, 25, 26 January 1888. Cummins was nominated as an "independent Republican" from Polk County in 1887 with Democratic support on a platform favoring repeal of prohibition, a position that earned him the label "jugwump." His opponents charged his candidacy was a railroad-initiated subterfuge to defeat an antimonopoly candidate. See *Register*, 4 November 1887, and *Daily Inter-Ocean* (Chicago), 18 October 1887. Antimonopolists saw the Cummins bill as the continuation of Cummins's prorailroad activities; see *Weekly Bee*, 1 February 1888, and *Homestead*, 3 February 1888.

58. Under the existing commission law there was no requirement of senate consent.

59. *Iowa State Register*, 26 January 1888. By 1888 there were substantial wholesaling interests in Des Moines and to a lesser degree in other interior points, as evidenced by the presence of a large number of wholesalers and manufacturers from Des Moines and other interior cities at the January meeting. Iowa wholesalers and manufacturers shared the same interest in securing lower local rates to compete with their major rivals in Chicago. In 1895 (the only year for which data are available) Des Moines (with 11 firms and 146 employees) and Ottumwa (with 13 firms and 214 employees) were well-developed wholesaling centers; Cedar Rapids, Waterloo, and Oskaloosa had between 50 and 100 employees. See Iowa Commissioner of Labor Statistics, *Biennial Report, 1895-96* (Des Moines, Iowa, 1897), 19-55.

60. *Homestead*, 3, 10 February 1888.

61. Ibid., 24 February 1888.

62. Ibid., 10 February, 16 March 1888. The *Homestead* printed dozens of similar resolutions in February and March.

63. Larrabee, *Railroad Question*, 340, and *Iowa State Register*, 29 February 1888. Although the Alliance probably had no more than 10,000 to 12,000 members in early 1888 (see Appendix A), Kennedy's figure was probably not exaggerated since many nonmember farmers were probably sympathetic to the Alliance's position.

64. James W. McDill to William B. Allison, 22 February 1888, and J. H. Sweeney to William B. Allison, 24 February 1888, Allison Papers.

65. *Iowa State Register*, 21 February, 17 March 1888.

66. Ibid., 8 March 1888.

67. On this same day the house also indefinitely postponed the Cummins bill; see Iowa House, *Journal, 1888* (Des Moines, Iowa, 1888), 510.

68. Ibid., 435. The provisions of HF 373, which (with minor changes) eventually be-

came law, are summarized in the Iowa Board of Railroad Commissioners, *Annual Report,*
1888 (Des Moines, Iowa, 1888), 31–33.

69. Iowa House, *Journal,* 1888, 826, 835, and Iowa Senate, *Journal, 1888* (Des Moines,
Iowa, 1888), 672, 828, 835. By relying solely on the final vote, Ballard C. Campbell, *Rep-*
resentative Democracy: Public Policy and Midwestern Legislatures in the Late Nineteenth Cen-
tury (Cambridge, Mass., 1980), 159, fails to detect the significant political conflict over
railroad reform in Iowa.

70. *Homestead,* 20 April 1888.

71. A comparison of the Iowa and Illinois schedules (and other midwestern and western states) is in the Nebraska Board of Transportation, *Annual Report, 1890* (Lincoln,
Nebr., 1890), 184–91.

72. Iowa Board of Railroad Commissioners, *Annual Report, 1888,* 36, and Dixon,
State Railroad Control, 148–55.

73. J. S. Clarkson to William Larrabee, 17 January 188[8], Larrabee Papers.

74. Allan G. Bogue, "The New Political History in the 1970s," in *The Past before Us:*
Contemporary Historical Writing in The United States, ed. Michael Kammen (Ithaca, N.Y.,
1980), 251. Peter H. Argersinger, "The Value of the Vote: Political Representation in the
Gilded Age," *Journal of American History* 76 (June 1989): 59–60, also discusses this issue.

75. V. O. Key, Jr., *Southern Politics in State and Nation* (New York, 1949). For summaries of the literature testing Key's hypothesis, see Duane Lockard, "State Party Systems
and Policy Outputs," in *Political Research and Political Theory,* ed. Oliver Garceau (Cambridge, Mass., 1968), and Richard E. Dawson, "Social Development, Party Competition,
and Policy," *The American Party Systems,* ed. William N. Chambers and Walter Dean
Burnham, 2d ed. (New York, 1975).

76. The Iowa Board of Railroad Commissioners, *Annual Report, 1892* (Des Moines,
1892), 20, estimated that about 20 to 25 percent of all freight originating in the state was
local. The percentage of agricultural freight was probably lower.

77. Michael Schwartz, *Radical Protest and Social Structure: The Southern Farmers' Alli-*
ance and Cotton Tenancy, 1880–1890 (New York, 1976), 150–51, makes the important distinction between the wide variety of protest actions that are rational given the level of
knowledge of those enduring economic hardship and the very limited number of strategies that actually address determinative socioeconomic structures.

78. *Homestead,* 21 September 1888.

79. Ibid., 29 June 1888.

80. Ibid., 21 September 1888.

CHAPTER 5. BASTIONS OF REPUBLICANISM

1. Kenneth S. Davis, *Kansas: A Bicentennial History* (New York, 1976), 81–82.

2. Solon Justus Buck, *The Granger Movement: A Study of Agricultural Organization and*
Its Political, Economic, and Social Manifestations, 1870–1880 (Cambridge, Mass., 1913), see
chart between 58–59.

3. Ibid., 92–93, 196–97, and Frank H. Dixon, "Railroad Control in Nebraska," *Politi-*
cal Science Quarterly 13 (December 1898): 620–22.

4. Congressional Quarterly, *Congressional Quarterly's Guide to U.S. Elections,* 2d ed.
(Washington, D.C., 1985), 501, 513.

5. Ibid., 501, 513, 340.

6. James C. Olson, *J. Sterling Morton* (Lincoln, Nebr., 1942), 267-69; Stanley B. Parsons, *The Populist Context* (Westport, Conn., 1973), 14-18; Addison Erwin Sheldon, *Nebraska: The Land and the People*, 3 vols. (Chicago, 1931), 1:603-8, 621; John D. Barnhart, "The History of the Farmers' Alliance and of the People's Party in Nebraska," (Ph.D. diss., Harvard University, 1930), 130-31, 155-63; Roy V. Scott, "Milton George and the Farmers' Alliance Movement," *Mississippi Valley Historical Review* 45 (June 1958): 98-100; and J. M. Thompson, "The Farmers' Alliance in Nebraska: Something of Its Origin, Growth, and Influence," *Proceedings and Collections of the Nebraska State Historical Society* 10 (1902): 199.

7. Sheldon, *Nebraska*, 1:623-24, and Olson, *Morton*, 304-13, quotation on 308.

8. William Frank Zornow, *Kansas: A History of the Jayhawk State* (Norman, Okla., 1957), 192-94.

9. Peter H. Argersinger, *Populism and Politics: William Alfred Peffer and the People's Party* (Lexington, Ky., 1974), 2-3; and Raymond Curtis Miller, "The Populist Party in Kansas" (Ph.D. diss., University of Chicago, 1928), 42-43.

10. *Daily Capital* (Topeka), 5 August, 21 October 1886. The Republicans won the governorship in 1886 in Kansas by a margin of 54.7 to 42.3 percent (see Congressional Quarterly, *Guide*, 501). In Kansas only an estimated 10 percent of the voting-age population at the 1890 census were of national origins likely to oppose prohibition compared to 17 percent in Iowa and 18 percent in Nebraska (individuals born in Austria, Belgium, Bohemia, France, Germany, Ireland, Italy, Poland, and Russia are considered antiprohibition voters). The estimates assume that the percentage of the entire population of each national group is identical to that of the voting-age population. See U.S. Census Office, *Report on the Population of the United States at the Eleventh Census: 1890*, pt. 1 (Washington, D.C., 1895), tables 32, 77.

11. *Capital*, 8, 9 July 1886.

12. Ibid., 2, 30 July 1886. The *Capital*, located in the fourth congressional district, gave prominent coverage to the fifth district controversy as a matter of statewide importance.

13. Ibid., 16 October 1886; *Troy Chief*, n.d., quoted in ibid., 16 July 1886.

14. Congressional Quarterly, *Guide*, 810.

15. Eva May Fosbury, "Biography of John Mellon Thurston," Master's thesis, University of Nebraska, 1920, 10-24; Parsons, *Populist Context*, 5-7; and Dixon, "Railroad Control in Nebraska," 623-26.

16. For a summary of Van Wyck's Senate career, see Marie V. Harmer and James L. Sellers, "Charles H. Van Wyck—Soldier and Statesman," *Nebraska History* 12 (October-December 1929): 324-35.

17. *Republican* (Omaha), 21 September 1886.

18. *Weekly Bee* (Omaha), 7 July, 8 September 1886.

19. *Republican*, 30 September 1886.

20. *Weekly Bee*, 18 August 1886; Sheldon, *Nebraska*, 1:638, 644; *Republican*, 19, 20, 21, January 1887. Algernon S. Paddock was elected.

21. A comprehensive reform measure passed the house, but the senate removed the bill's maximum-rate clause, leaving only an empty shell; see *Republican*, 26 February, 31 March 1887, and Dixon, "Railroad Control in Nebraska," 627-28.

22. Although the convention that nominated McShane favored the Reagan bill, ap-

parently neither this nor other economic issues defined the campaign. McShane's victory resulted largely because Howe made an ill-advised attempt to make prohibition the main issue. See *Weekly Bee*, 29 September, 10 November 1886.

23. It is not entirely clear why Kansas and Nebraska remained one-party states and Iowa became competitive; two plausible explanations can be dismissed, however. First, differences in the ethnocultural composition of the electorates in the respective states might explain the political divergences. Yet although the Iowa electorate was culturally more inclined toward the Democratic Party than the Kansas electorate, it was slightly less inclined than the Nebraska electorate (see n. 10, this chapter). As Frederick C. Luebke, *Immigrants and Politics: The Germans of Nebraska, 1880-1900* (Lincoln, Nebr., 1969), 114–41, points out, Democrats in Nebraska did succeed in attracting foreign-born antiprohibition voters, but there were not enough voters in this group to make the Democrats competitive. A second possibility—that Iowa's party system became competitive because its electorate had a larger labor element, which would have been Democratically inclined—can also be rejected. The percentage of employed males over the age of ten years in mining, manufacturing, or transportation was 26.5 in Iowa, 30.2 in Nebraska, and 23.6 in Kansas. See U.S. Census Office, *Report on Population of the United States at the Eleventh Census: 1890*, pt. 2 (Washington, D.C., 1897), table 79.

24. Lawrence Goodwyn, *Democratic Promise: The Populist Moment in America* (New York, 1976), 97.

25. Harold Piehler, "Henry Vincent: Kansas Populist and Radical-Reform Journalist," *Kansas History* 2 (Spring 1979): 15, and Goodwyn, *Democratic Promise*, 99. After moving the *American Nonconformist* to Indianapolis as a national Populist journal in 1891, Henry Vincent returned in 1907 to Girard, Kansas, the home of Julius Wayland's influential socialist newspaper, *Appeal to Reason*, and served as Kansas district secretary for the Socialist Party. See Piehler, "Henry Vincent," 24-25.

26. *American Nonconformist and Kansas and Industrial Liberator* (Winfield, Kans.), 7 October 1886.

27. Ibid., passim. For an example of Vee Vincent's column for women, see ibid., 21 June 1888.

28. The Union Labor Party, centered in the Midwest, rejected Henry George's single-tax plan and was separate from George's United Labor Party. John R. Commons et al., *History of Labour in the United States*, 4 vols. (New York, 1918-1919), 2:464–65. The mass meeting was reported in the *Nonconformist*, 24 March 1887. It is doubtful that many members of the Farmers' Alliance (or any other agricultural organization) attended this meeting since the first efforts to organize local Alliances in Kansas did not occur until July (see chapter 6). It is more plausible that some members of the Knights were in Cowley County and nearby counties at this time. Although there is no record of Kansas KOL assemblies in 1886 or early 1887, it is clear that the strikes against Jay Gould's Southwestern system in 1885 had galvanized the Knights in Kansas, and evidence exists of assemblies in southeastern, south-central, and western Kansas in September 1887. The *Nonconformist*, 29 September 1887, listed the places of twenty-six assemblies in fourteen counties, mostly in southeastern, south-central, and western Kansas.

29. *Nonconformist*, 17 November 1887.

30. Ibid., 16 August 1888. For discussions of Greenback monetary theory and political ideology, see Irwin Unger, *The Greenback Era: A Social and Political History of Ameri-*

can Finance, 1865-1879 (Princeton, N.J., 1964), 68-119, and Walter T. K. Nugent, Money and American Society, 1865-1880 (New York, 1968), 37-43, 202-4.

31. Chester M. Destler, American Radicalism, 1865-1901 (New London, Conn., 1946; reprint, Chicago, 1966), 7-8, 50-55, 60-69; Nonconformist, 13 September, 11 October 1888. The "subtreasury plan of the Farmers' Alliance" in the 1892 Omaha platform included both the land-loan plan and a plan developed in 1889 by Charles W. Macune of the Texas Farmers' Alliance for a system of subtreasuries that would issue negotiable certificates of deposit on the security of stored crops. See William A. Peffer, The Farmers' Side: His Troubles and Their Remedy (New York, 1891), 241-56; S. M. Scott, The Sub-Treasury Plan and Land and Loan System (Topeka, Kans., 1891); and Harry Tracy, "The Subtreasury Plan," in James H. Davis, A Political Revelation (Dallas, Tex., 1894).

32. Nonconformist, 7 June 1888. Sarah E. V. Emery, Seven Financial Conspiracies which Have Enslaved the American People (Lansing, Mich., 1892), 57-58, 66, 52-53. This edition quotes John W. Briedenthal, chairman of the central committee of the Kansas Union Labor Party, who claimed that the party distributed 50,000 copies of the work in its 1888 campaign, p. 107. By 1896, 400,000 copies had been sold, according to William D. P. Bliss, Encyclopedia of Social Reform (New York, 1897), 1246.

33. Nonconformist, 7 October 1886. Larry McFarlane, "British Investment in Midwestern Farm Mortgages and Land, 1875-1900," Agricultural History 48 (January 1974): 196-97, shows that British capital played a minor role in financing farm mortgages.

34. Nonconformist, 19, 26 July 1888. Because of his radical views, this correspondent proudly added, "I am dubbed an anarchist, and our place of business is called the Haymarket Square."

35. Gordon S. Wood, The Creation of the American Republic: 1776-1787 (New York, 1972), 40. On the theme of conspiracy in revolutionary thought, see also Bernard Bailyn, The Ideological Origins of the American Revolution (Cambridge, Mass., 1967), 144-59, and for further discussion of conspiracy, see Richard Hofstadter, The Paranoid Style in American Politics and Other Essays (New York, 1965); David Brion Davis, The Slave Power Conspiracy and the Paranoid Style (Baton Rouge, La., 1969); David Brion Davis, ed., The Fear of Conspiracy: Images of Un-American Subversion from the Revolution to the Present (Ithaca, N.Y., 1971); and William E. Gienapp, "The Republican Party and the Slave Power," in New Perspectives on Race and Slavery in America: Essays in Honor of Kenneth M. Stampp, ed. Robert H. Abzug and Stephen E. Maizlish (Lexington, Ky., 1986), 51-78.

36. The prayer's conclusion beseeched deliverance from strikers and the Knights of Labor, "and thus shall we have the kingdom, bonds, interest, power and Gold until the Republic shall end" (Nonconformist, 12 April 1888).

37. Biographical information about these three Populists can be found in Pauline Adams and Emma S. Thornton, A Populist Assault: Sarah E. Van De Vort Emery on American Democracy, 1862-1895 (Bowling Green, Ohio, 1982); Dorothy R. Blumberg, "Mary Elizabeth Lease: Populist Campaigner," unpublished manuscript, Kansas State Historical Society, Topeka; and Paul L. Murphy, "Marion Marsh Todd," in Notable American Women, 1607-1905, ed. Edward T. James et al., 3 vols. (Cambridge, Mass., 1971), 3:469-70. For the reaction to Lease's speech, see the Nonconformist, 6 September 1888.

38. Robert Smith Bader, Prohibition in Kansas: A History (Lawrence, Kans., 1986), 58-60, and Lorraine A. Gehring, "Women Officeholders in Kansas, 1872-1912," Kansas History 9 (Summer 1986): 48-57.

39. Blumberg, "Lease," 3, and Adams and Thornton, *Populist Assault*, 61-67, quotation on 67.

40. Quoted in Burton J. Williams, *Senator John James Ingalls: Kansas' Iridescent Republican* (Lawrence, Kans., 1972), 108-9.

41. Quoted in ibid., 111-12.

42. *Nonconformist*, 18 October 1888, 12 July, 30 August 1888.

43. *Capital*, 27 July 1888; *Nonconformist*, 9 August 1888.

44. *Nonconformist*, 30 August 1888, 19 April, 24 May 1888.

45. *Capital*, 22, 25 July 1888. Kimball narrowly defeated the Union Labor candidate in the fall. See *Populist Handbook for Kansas: A Compilation from Official Sources of Some Facts for Use in Succeeding Political Campaigns* (Indianapolis, Ind., 1891), 94.

46. *Capital*, 14, 18, 27 July 1888. The 6 percent figure was meant to apply to loans for which no rate was specified; the 10 percent applied to loans for which interest was stated and was thus the maximum legal rate of interest. See text of the law as eventually passed in the successor to the *Capital*, the *Capital-Commonwealth* (Topeka), 2 March 1889.

47. See accounts of processions at Clay Center and at an unidentified town in Sumner County in the *Nonconformist*, 13, 20 September 1888.

48. Argersinger, *Populism and Politics*, 13, and *Daily Courier* (Winfield, Kans.), 4 October 1888, quoted in the *Nonconformist*, 4 October 1888. Henry Vincent stated that there was an organization of the Videttes in Winfield at one time and that the *Nonconformist* had printed its secret work but that neither he nor his brother Leo had been members; see *Nonconformist*, 4 October 1888. Goodwyn, *Democratic Promise*, 101, 630, suggests the Vincents had joined the Videttes, a secret organization originating in Texas to promote a labor/farmer third party although his evidence does not clearly establish this. In any case, membership in the Videttes hardly entailed a devotion to anarchism since the organization existed to promote reform through the ballot. The Vincents were among the few voices in Kansas that denounced as "judicial murder" the impending executions of those people convicted in the Haymarket bombing, but their objection was a protestation of the innocence of the convicted rather than an endorsement of anarchist methods. See *Nonconformist*, 22 September 1887, quoted in Kansas Legislature, *Proceedings of the Joint Committee of the Legislature . . . to Investigate the Explosion which Occurred at Coffeyville, Kansas, October 18, 1888* (Topeka, Kans., 1891), 613.

49. A full account of this incident can be found in *Proceedings to Investigate the Explosion*, which noted the widespread publication of the *Courier's* charges in Republican papers on October 19 (p. 615). See also *The Plot Unfolded! or a History of the Famous Coffeyville Dynamite Outrage* (Winfield, Kans., 1889) in People's Party Pamphlets, Kansas State Historical Society, Topeka.

50. *Nonconformist*, 25 October 1888; *Courier*, n.d., quoted in the *Capital*, 27 October 1888.

51. *Nonconformist*, 8 November 1888; Congressional Quarterly, *Guide*, 342; and *Capital-Commonwealth*, 8 November 1888. The Union Labor ticket achieved support primarily in rural areas but found none among workers in Kansas City, where the KOL had become enmeshed within the local Republican Party. See Leon Fink, *Workingmen's Democracy* (Urbana, Ill., 1983), 135.

52. Argersinger, *Populism and Politics*, 15.

53. Gov. John A. Martin, "Biennial Address to the Legislature, January 8, 1889," Governor's Letter Press Books, box 24, no. 85A, Kansas State Historical Society, To-

peka. The legislature had only six Democrats in the house and one in the senate. See *Capital-Commonwealth*, 9, 12 January 1889.

54. *Capital-Commonwealth*, 6 January 1889.

55. Ibid., 9 January 1889.

56. *Kansas Farmer* (Topeka, Kans.), 17, 24 January 1889.

57. *Capital-Commonwealth*, 13, 18, 19 January 1889.

58. Senators O. S. Woodward and John K. Wright also made similar statements; see ibid., 20 January 1889.

59. Ibid., 29 January 1889; *Leavenworth Times*, n.d., quoted in ibid., 30 January 1889.

60. *Kansas Farmer*, 7 February 1889; *Capital-Commonwealth*, 13 February 1889.

61. *Capital-Commonwealth*, 15 February 1889.

62. Ibid., 19, 26 February 1889.

63. Ibid., 16, 20, 26, 28 February 1889.

64. The house bill required forfeiture of two times the excess interest on loans of 10 to 12 percent; forfeiture of all interest on loans between 12 and 15 percent; forfeiture of all interest and one-half the principal on loans from 15 to 20 percent; and on loans over 20 percent, forfeiture of all principal and interest. See ibid., 19 February 1889.

65. Ibid., 1 March 1889.

66. *Kansas Farmer*, 28 February 1889.

67. *Nonconformist*, 21 March 1889.

68. U.S. Senate, *Testimony Taken by the United States Pacific Railway Commission*, Vol. 3, 50th Cong., 1st sess., 1888, S. Ex. Doc. 51, pt. 4, 1336, 1339. On free passes, see also George W. Berge, *The Free Pass Bribery System* (Lincoln, Nebr., 1905).

69. Senate, *Pacific Railway Commission*, 1339, 1344. In his cross-examination of Rosewater, Andrew Jackson Poppelton, an attorney for the Union Pacific, did not attempt to refute Rosewater's testimony; instead he insinuated that Rosewater had been a Confederate spy (see pp. 1419–22). In an interview, George W. Holrege, general manager of the Burlington lines west of the Missouri River in the late 1880s, conceded the validity of charges of railroad corruption in Nebraska politics, defending the necessity of such methods because of "the unreasonable attacks of the people and politicians in the legislature." See Barnhart, "Farmers' Alliance and People's Party," 197.

70. *Weekly Bee*, 12 October 1887.

71. The Nebraska house had seventy-nine Republicans, twenty Democrats, and one member of the Union Labor Party. The senate consisted of twenty-seven Republicans and six Democrats. See Nebraska House, *Journal, 1889* (Omaha, Nebr., 1889), 4–6, and Nebraska Senate, *Journal, 1889* (Lincoln, Nebr., 1889), iii–iv.

72. *Weekly Bee*, 9 January 1889; *Republican*, 4 January 1889.

73. *Weekly Bee*, 16, 30 January 1889; *Republican*, 12 February 1889. This argument was also made by Nebraska's antimonopoly attorney general, William Leese, in Nebraska Attorney General, *Biennial Report, 1889–90* (Omaha, 1890), 9.

74. *Weekly Bee*, 20 February 1889.

75. Ibid., 3 April 1889. The legislature failed to pass any other antimonopoly measures. A strong bill requiring forfeiture of principal on all loans drawing illegal interest failed to pass even the house. The legislature did pass the Ransom bill requiring fire insurance companies to pay the full value of the policy and the Keckley antitrust bill, but these were minor reforms. See ibid., 6, 13 March, 3 April 1889.

76. *Republican*, 1 April 1889; *Weekly Bee*, 3 April 1889.

CHAPTER 6. IN SEARCH OF "THE WAY OUT"

1. J. M. Thompson, "The Farmers' Alliance in Nebraska," *Proceedings and Collections of the Nebraska State Historical Society* 10 (1902): 199–201; and Roy V. Scott, "Milton George and the Farmers' Alliance Movement," *Mississippi Valley Historical Review* 45 (June 1958): 98–100. Membership figures are from Appendix A.

2. Scott, "Milton George," 98–100; Robert C. McMath, Jr., "Preface to Populism: The Origin and Economic Development of the 'Southern' Farmers' Alliance in Kansas," *Kansas Historical Quarterly* 42 (Spring 1976): 55–56; and *Advocate* (Topeka, Kans.), 9 January 1890.

3. *Nonconformist* (Winfield, Kans.), 28 July 1887, and McMath, "Preface to Populism," 56. McMath effectively points out the problems in an account of the Kansas Farmers' Alliance origins by a Populist leader, W. F. Rightmire, "The Alliance Movement in Kansas—Origin of the People's Party," *Transactions of the Kansas State Historical Society* 9 (1905–1906): 1–8. The origins of the Kansas Alliance are also discussed in Gene Clanton, *Populism: The Humane Preference in America, 1890–1900* (Boston, 1991), 25–27. Estimates of membership for the Iowa, Kansas, and Nebraska Alliances are in Appendix A. By late 1888/early 1889 there were already strong Alliances in most of the states that had formed the Confederacy as well as in Missouri and Dakota Territory. See Lawrence Goodwyn, *Democratic Promise: The Populist Moment in America* (New York, 1976), 91; Homer Clevenger, "The Farmers' Alliance in Missouri," *Missouri Historical Review* 39 (October 1944): 27; and report of H. D. Loucks of South Dakota in the *Homestead* (Des Moines), 18 January 1889.

4. See Appendix A.

5. January 1890 New York prices on spring and winter wheat and corn were lower than in any previous January since the Civil War; the January 1890 price for hogs was the lowest except for January 1879, and cattle had been lower only in January 1889. See U.S. Senate, *Wholesale Prices, Wages, and Transportation*, 52d Cong., 2d sess., 1893, S. Rept. 1394, 7–10, 25–26, 28–29, 60–64.

6. *Nonconformist*, 29 August 1889; Clarence L. Petrowsky, "Kansas Agriculture before 1900" (Ph.D. diss., University of Oklahoma, 1968), 191–92; and *Alliance* (Lincoln), 7 December 1889.

7. Dorothy Schwieder, "Labor and Economic Roles of Iowa Farm Wives, 1840–1880," in *Farmers, Bureaucrats and Middlemen: Historical Perspectives on American Agriculture*, ed. Trudy Huskamp Peterson (Washington, D.C., 1980), 153–60; Deborah Fink, *Open Country, Iowa: Rural Women, Tradition and Change* (Albany, N.Y., 1986), 32–37, and Fink, *Agrarian Women: Wives and Mothers in Rural Nebraska, 1880–1940* (Chapel Hill, N.C.. 1992), 62; Glenda Riley, *Frontierswomen: The Iowa Experience* (Ames, Iowa, 1981), 29, 58–69; John Mack Faragher, *Sugar Creek: Life on the Illinois Prairie* (New Haven, Conn., 1986), 101–5, 118; Carolyn E. Sachs, *The Invisible Farmers: Women in Agricultural Production* (Totowa, N.J., 1983), xii, 20; MaryJo Wagner, "Farms, Families, and Reform: Women in the Farmers' Alliance and Populist Party," Ph.D. diss., University of Oregon, 1986, 144; and John Ise, *Sod and Stubble: The Story of a Kansas Homestead* (New York, 1936), 207.

8. Julie Roy Jeffrey, "Women in the Southern Farmers' Alliance: A Reconsideration of the Role and Status of Women in the Late Nineteenth-Century South," *Feminist Studies* 3 (Fall 1975): 79.

9. *Kansas Farmer* (Topeka), 16 April, 14 May 1890, and *Advocate*, 9 January, 19 November 1890. An examination of officers from seventy-seven suballiances in Nebraska in 1893 shows twenty-two recognizable male names for the office of president and no recognizable female names; the rest are identified only by initials or left blank. For secretary, on the other hand, there are twenty-three male names, thirteen female names, and again the rest are identified by initials or left blank. See quarterly reports for the quarters ending 30 June and 30 September 1893 in Nebraska Farmers' Alliance Papers (microfilm edition), Nebraska State Historical Society, Lincoln.

10. Wagner, "Farms, Families, and Reform," 107.

11. *Alliance*, 18 January 1890, 3, 17, 24, 31 July 1889.

12. The Phillips Farmers' Alliance Business Association, incorporated with a capital stock of $15,000, intended to bypass local grain dealers and ship grain directly to market, probably by constructing an elevator; see ibid., 21 August 1889. Large cooperatives with relatively high levels of capitalization were apparently common, judging from the advice given by the *Alliance*, 1 March 1890, that farmers should start cooperative stores rather than enterprises such as mills and elevators since the capital requirements were lower.

13. Ibid., 7 December 1889, 1 February 1890.

14. Ibid., 21 August 1889, 5 April 1890.

15. Ibid., 7 December 1889.

16. A similar case was initiated by the Farmers' Co-operative Grain and Elevator Company of Osceola; see Nebraska Board of Transportation, *Annual Report, 1890* (Lincoln, 1890), 58–89. The Nebraska Supreme Court's decision is reported in the *Daily Nebraska State Journal* (Lincoln), 14 May 1890.

17. The Nebraska Alliance Business Association was soliciting business as early as June 1889; see *Alliance*, 12 June 1889. The rationale for the association and details of its operation are fully discussed in ibid., 8 November 1890. This type of cooperative was different from the Rochdale plan, widely adopted by the Grange, which sold goods at retail prices and paid a dividend on members' shares.

18. Minutes of May Alliance no. 1772, Kearney Co., 23 October 1890, Nebraska Farmers' Alliance Papers. From December 1889 to December 1890 the Nebraska Alliance Business Association reported a total volume of business of $39,500. See *Alliance*, 27 December 1890.

19. McMath, "Preface to Populism," 60, and *Nonconformist*, 11 April, 7 February, 15 August 1889.

20. *Kansas Farmer*, 23 April 1890.

21. Barton County Alliance Exchange Company, *Rules of the Barton County Alliance Exchange Company* (Great Bend, Kans., 1890), vol. 5, People's Party Pamphlets, Kansas State Historical Society, Topeka. Other reports of the organization of county and local exchanges, business agencies, and stores are in the *Advocate*, 6, 13 March, 2, 16 April, 14 May, 4 June, 9 July 1890, and the *Kansas Farmer*, 26 February 1890. Scott G. McNall, *The Road to Rebellion: Class Formation and Kansas Populism, 1865–1900* (Chicago, 1988), 245, finds that no alliances or cooperatives filed articles of incorporation with the Kansas secretary of state from 1887 to 1889. In 1890, 101 charters were issued; in 1891, 54; in 1892, 19; in 1893, 10; in 1894, 7; and in 1895, 9. Stanley B. Parsons et al., "The Role of Cooperatives in the Development of the Movement Culture of Populism," *Journal of American History* 69 (March 1983): 877, estimates that there were about thirty cooperatives in Kansas in 1889 and seventy in 1891.

22. *Advocate*, 17 August 1889.

23. Ibid., 29 November 1889, 9 April, 13 August 1890.

24. Ibid., 28 May 1890; *Kansas Farmer*, 13 November 1889. On the American Livestock Commission Company, see the *Advocate*, 6 March 1890, and *Alliance-Tribune* (Topeka, Kans.), 23 October 1890.

25. *Nonconformist*, 9 January 1890. In the several accounts of Kansas Alliance cooperatives reported in the *Kansas Farmer*, the *Nonconformist*, and the *Advocate* I have found only one mention of a plan to build an elevator (*Advocate*, 2 April 1890) and no evidence of any other attempt to implement cooperative marketing. This account of Kansas and Nebraska cooperatives points out a serious empirical flaw in the position of Goodwyn, *Democratic Promise*, 104-6, 182-85, 194-97, 209-10, 260-62, 388-401, that the Nebraska Alliance's ignorance of economic cooperation led it to join the "shadow movement" for free silver but that the Kansas Alliance's understanding of cooperation led to the emergence of a genuine form of populism. See also Robert W. Cherny, "Lawrence Goodwyn and Nebraska Populism: A Review Essay," *Great Plains Quarterly* 1 (Summer 1981): 188, and Parsons et al., "Role of Cooperatives," 866-85.

26. Thompson, "Farmers' Alliance in Nebraska," 202. See also Theodore R. Mitchell's book, *Political Education in the Southern Farmers' Alliance, 1887-1900* (Madison, Wis., 1987).

27. S. M. Scott, *The Champion Organizer of the Northwest, or My First Sixty Days Work as an Organizer* (McPherson, Kans., 1890). A list of the suballiances Scott organized is found on pp. 191-92.

28. Ibid., 14.

29. Ibid., 66-67, 72.

30. A typical lecture at Gaylord lasted almost three hours. See ibid., 89.

31. Ibid., 71-72.

32. Ibid., 84-85.

33. Ibid., 85, 124-25.

34. *Advocate*, 20 December 1889.

35. *Kansas Farmer*, 27 December 1888, and *Alliance*, 14 August 1889.

36. *Alliance*, 12 June 1889. This document is cited by Chester M. Destler, *American Radicalism, 1865-1901* (New London, Conn., 1946, reprint, Chicago, 1966), 69-70, as an example of one of the numerous variants of the land-loan proposal stemming from the writings of Edward Kellogg in the 1840s. Goodwyn, *Democratic Promise*, 180-81, 202-8, 585-87, is particularly critical of Burrows and mistakenly asserts that he and other Nebraska Alliance leaders were unaware of Greenback monetary theory.

37. See *Alliance*, 26 June 1889, and articles from June through October 1889.

38. *Kansas Farmer*, 17, 24, 31 July, 7, 21 August, 18 September 1889.

39. Ibid., 23, 30 October 1889. See also William V. Marshall, *Cumulative Taxation* (Winfield, Kans., 1890).

40. William A. Peffer, *The Farmers' Side: His Troubles and Their Remedy* (New York, 1891), 167, 247-56. The first installment of "The Way Out" appeared in the *Kansas Farmer*, 25 December 1889.

41. *Alliance*, 6 September 1890, and Peffer, *Farmers' Side*, 168-69.

42. *Kansas Farmer*, 2 April 1890, and Peter H. Argersinger, *Populism and Politics: William Alfred Peffer and the People's Party* (Lexington, Ky., 1974), 29-31.

43. *Homestead*, 18 January 1889.

44. *Advocate*, 5 October 1889, and Sarah E. V. Emery, *Seven Financial Conspiracies which Have Enslaved the American People* (Lansing, Mich., 1892), 57–58.

45. *Alliance*, 21 September, 12 October 1889.

46. Ibid., 23 November 1889.

47. *Nonconformist*, 14 November 1889.

48. Speech of Thomas W. Fitch of Nevada before the National Silver Convention of December 1889, quoted in the *Advocate*, 13 February 1890, and *Alliance*, 15, 22 February 1890. The reemergence of free silver as a national issue in 1889 and 1890 can be traced in Fred Wellborn, "The Influence of the Silver Republican Senators, 1889–1891," *Mississippi Valley Historical Review* 14 (March 1928): 462–68, and Max Silverman, "A Political and Intellectual History of the Silver Movement in the United States, 1886–1896," Ph.D. diss., New York University, 1986, 63–66.

49. On the background to Macune's development of the subtreasury and his presentation of the plan at the St. Louis meeting, see Goodwyn, *Democratic Promise*, 149–53, 166–69. Contemporary explanations are in Harry Tracy, "The Sub-treasury Plan," in James H. Davis, *A Political Revelation* (Dallas, Tex., 1894), and S. M. Scott, *The Sub-Treasury Plan and the Land and Loan System* (Topeka, Kans., 1891). See also John D. Hicks, "The Sub-Treasury: A Forgotten Plan for the Relief of Agriculture," *Mississippi Valley Historical Review* 15 (June 1928–March 1929): 355–73.

50. *Advocate*, 9, 16 January 1890.

51. Ibid., 16 January, 27 February, 13 March 1890, and *Kansas Farmer*, 5 March 1890.

52. *Advocate*, 30 January 1890.

53. *Alliance*, 4 January 1890. At the same time Burrows was writing, the *New York Times*, 6 January 1890, mocked the "cranks" at the St. Louis convention who would "plaster the country with a paper currency based upon stored pumpkins, potatoes, corn, cider, peanuts, and watermelons, and all become rich out of the abundant supply of 'cheap money.'"

54. Destler, *American Radicalism*, 19.

55. *Advocate*, 13 March 1890.

56. *Nonconformist*, 28 March, 11 April 1889. On the National Cordage Company, which exerted monopoly control over prices from 1887 through 1893, see U.S. Industrial Commission, *Report* (Washington, D.C., 1901), 13: 127–34. The binder-twine boycott was similar to the Southern Alliance's boycott of the trust that manufactured jute, used as cotton bagging.

57. Resolutions of Morehead Alliance (no. 363) in the *Nonconformist*, 21 November 1889. Agreements among sugar refiners initially made in 1887 succeeded in holding the price of sugar above competitive prices through 1898. See Jeremiah W. Jenks, "Industrial Combinations and Prices," in *Preliminary Report on Trusts and Industrial Combinations*, U.S. Industrial Commission (Washington, D.C., 1900), 40–46, and Eliot Jones, *The Trust Problem in the United States* (New York, 1921), 40.

58. May Alliance Minutes, 10 December, 20 November 1890, Nebraska Farmers' Alliance Papers.

59. *Alliance*, 3 July 1889.

60. *Advocate*, 16 January, 28 May 1890.

61. Stanford introduced a resolution in the Senate on 10 March 1890 that called for loans to be made by the government "upon mortgages deposited with it upon real estate . . . the government to receive some small rate of interest (from 1 to 2 per cent)." See Hu-

bert Howe Bancroft, *History of the Life of Leland Stanford: A Character Study* (Oakland, Calif., 1952), 182–83. Two months later Stanford introduced a bill "to provide for making loans by the Government and securing the same by liens upon land." The Senate Committee on Finance reported against the bill; in the financial centers of the East Stanford's "sanity was questioned." See George T. Clark, *Leland Stanford: War Governor of California, Railroad Builder, and Founder of Stanford University* (Stanford, Calif., 1931), 461.

62. *Advocate*, 30 April 1890. Other resolutions favoring the land-loan plan in general or the Stanford bill in particular are found in ibid., 13, 20 March, 16 April, 21, 28 May 1890; *Kansas Farmer*, 14 May 1890; *Alliance*, 29 March, 5, 12 April, 3, 31 May, 7, 21 June 1890.

63. *Advocate*, 28 May 1890; *Kansas Farmer*, 23 April 1890; *Advocate*, 18 March 1891. In Nebraska, where the subtreasury was not a matter of Alliance doctrine, less discussion of the measure occurred in suballiances, although the Star Alliance of Custer County resolved against the subtreasury, "believing it would turn out a gamboling [sic] ring and leave the farmers and laboring class entirely at the mercy of monopoly." See *Alliance*, 21 June 1890.

64. *Nonconformist*, 9 January 1890.

65. *Advocate*, 27 February 1890.

66. The best discussion of community in the Alliance is in Robert C. McMath, Jr., *Populist Vanguard: A History of the Southern Farmers' Alliance* (Chapel Hill, N.C., 1975), especially chapter 5.

67. Minutes of the Lone Tree Alliance, 27 November 1890, Kansas State Historical Society, Topeka; "Alliance Song," in *The Alliance and Labor Songster*, comp. Leopold Vincent (Indianapolis, Ind., 1891; reprint, New York, 1975), 28.

68. Scott, *Champion Organizer*, 160–64.

69. May Alliance Minutes, Nebraska Farmers' Alliance Papers.

70. Robert C. McMath, Jr., "Populist Base Communities: The Evangelical Roots of Farm Protest in Texas," *Locus* 1 (Fall 1988): 53–63; Norman Pollack, *The Just Polity: Populism, Law, and Human Welfare* (Urbana, Ill., 1987), 11; and Peter H. Argersinger, "Religion, the Farmers' Alliance, and the Gospel of Populism," *Kansas Quarterly* 1 (Fall 1969): 24–35, quotation on 30.

71. Marvin Meyers, *The Jacksonian Persuasion: Politics and Belief* (New York, 1960), 21–24; Bruce Laurie, *Working People of Philadelphia, 1800–1850* (Philadelphia, 1980), 75–77; Eric Foner, *Free Soil, Free Labor, Free Men: The Ideology of the Republican Party before the Civil War* (New York, 1970), 15–18; and Destler, *American Radicalism*, 25–26.

72. Only recently have scholars recognized the family dimension of the Farmers' Alliance. See McNall, *Road to Rebellion*, 195, and Wagner, "Farms, Families, and Reform," 152ff.

73. Annie L. Diggs, "The Women in the Alliance Movement," *Arena* 6 (June 1892): 165, and *Advocate*, 30 April 1890.

74. *Advocate*, 30 April 1890. The impact of crisis on the household also justified a limited expansion of the accepted place of women in society at earlier moments. See Linda K. Kerber, *Women of the Republic: Intellect and Ideology in Revolutionary America* (Chapel Hill, N.C., 1980), and Mary P. Ryan, *Women in Public: Between Banners and Ballots, 1825–1880* (Baltimore, 1990), 104–7, 146–52.

75. *Nonconformist*, 25 September 1890, 19 July 1888.

76. *Kansas Farmer*, 30 April 1890.

77. *Nonconformist*, 28 March 1890, 9 January 1890.

78. *Advocate*, 19 October 1889; Scott, *Champion Organizer*, 8.

CHAPTER 7. FROM SCHOOLROOM TO POLITICAL PARTY

1. Nebraska Farmers' Alliance "declaration of principles," quoted in J. M. Thompson, "The Farmers' Alliance in Nebraska," *Proceedings and Collections of the Nebraska State Historical Society* 10 (1902): 200, and Kansas Farmers' Alliance "declaration of purposes," quoted in *Kansas Farmer* (Topeka), 25 June 1890.

2. *Kansas Farmer*, 28 February 1889; *Alliance* (Lincoln), 12 June 1889; *Republican* (Omaha), 10, 30 March 1889. The 1890 census reported the value of mortgages on Nebraska farms to be $48 million; see U.S. Census Office, *Report on Farms and Homes* (Washington, D.C., 1896), table 102.

3. *Alliance*, 14 August 1889.

4. Ibid., 31 July, 14, 21 August 1889. There was a similar debate in Kansas prior to the 1889 elections; see the *Advocate* (Meriden, Kans.), 5 October 1889.

5. *Advocate*, 5 October 1889, 16 April 1890.

6. Harold Piehler, "Henry Vincent," *Kansas History* 2 (Spring 1979): 19; Elizabeth N. Barr, "The Populist Uprising," in *A Standard History of Kansas and Kansans*, comp. William P. Connelley, 2 vols. (Chicago, 1919), 2:1142–43; *Nonconformist* (Winfield, Kans.), 26 September 1889.

7. *Winfield Courier*, quoted in Barr, "Populist Uprising," 1143.

8. *Nonconformist*, 19, 26 September, 17 October, 14 November 1889.

9. *Alliance*, 21, 28 September 1889, and Addison E. Sheldon, *Nebraska*, 3 vols. (Chicago, 1931), 1:661.

10. *Alliance*, 21 September 1889; Samuel Chapman to Samuel Maxwell, 12 October 1889, Samuel Maxwell Papers, microfilm edition, Nebraska State Historical Society, Lincoln; *Republican*, 9 August 1889; A. G. Warner, "Railroad Problems in a Western State," *Political Science Quarterly* 6 (March 1891): 86–87.

11. *Alliance*, 12 October 1889. The objection was not so much to T. L. Norval, the man who defeated Reese, whom the *Weekly Bee* (Omaha), 16 October 1889, described as "a man of unimpeachable character," but the "underhand[ed] methods" used to nominate him.

12. *Alliance*, 19 October 1889.

13. Ibid.

14. *Schuyler Quill, York Times, Ulysses Dispatch*, quoted in *Weekly Bee*, 23 October 1889.

15. Stanley B. Parsons, *The Populist Context: Rural versus Urban Power on a Great Plains Frontier* (Westport, Conn, 1973), 77, and *Alliance*, 16 November 1889.

16. *Alliance*, 28 December 1889.

17. There are petitions for these demands from Farmers' Alliances representing thirty-five counties in box 14 of the Governor Lyman U. Humphrey Papers, Kansas State Historical Society, Topeka.

18. Circular letter signed G. W. Roberts (Bed Rock Alliance), 20 December 1889, box 14, folder 3, Humphrey Papers.

19. *Nonconformist*, 13 February 1890.

20. *Kansas Farmer*, 12 February 1890.

21. Lyman U. Humphrey to L. A. Simpson, 25 January 1890, box 26, vol. 92, Kansas Governor's Office, Letter Press Books, Kansas State Historical Society, Topeka.

22. Samuel S. Dix to Lyman U. Humphrey, 15 February 1890, box 14, folder 17, Humphrey Papers.

23. R. J. Waddell to Lyman U. Humphrey, 6 February 1890, George Peck to Lyman U. Humphrey, 10 March 1890, Edward Russell to Lyman U. Humphrey, 5 February 1890, box 13, Humphrey Papers.

24. Lyman U. Humphrey to A. A. Robinson (general manager of the Atchison, Topeka & Santa Fe), 25 January 1890, box 26, vol. 92, Kansas Governor's Office, Letter Press Books.

25. Thomas L. Kimball (vice-president, Union Pacific) to Lyman U. Humphrey, 4 February 1890, George R. Peck et al. to Lyman U. Humphrey, 8 February 1890, box 15, folder 12, Humphrey Papers.

26. *Kansas Farmer*, 12 February 1890, emphasis in original.

27. Lyman U. Humphrey to J. Crans, 14 February 1890, box 26, vol. 93, Kansas Governor's Office, Letter Press Books.

28. *Daily Capital* (Topeka), 20 February 1890.

29. William Peffer to John J. Ingalls, 10 February 1890, quoted in *Kansas Farmer*, 26 February 1890.

30. John J. Ingalls to Eli Sherman, 4 January 1890, quoted in *Advocate*, 13 February 1890.

31. *New York World*, 30 April 1890, quoted in *Kansas Farmer*, 21 May 1890.

32. *Kansas Farmer*, 2 April, 14 May 1890.

33. *Weekly Bee*, 1 January 1890, and *Daily Nebraska State Journal* (Lincoln), 17 January 1890.

34. *Journal*, 23, 28 January 1890. There are instances of discrepancies on tariffs for merchandise of the magnitude indicated by Leese, but the local-distance tariff on cattle and grain was more on the order of 20 to 30 percent lower in Iowa than in Nebraska. See Nebraska Board of Transportation, *Annual Report, 1890* (Lincoln, 1890), 184–91.

35. Ibid., 5, 6, 7 February 1890.

36. Ibid., 8, 9 February 1890.

37. Resolutions of the Ote County Alliance quoted in *Alliance*, 1 March 1890.

38. Petition of the Palestine Farmers' Alliance, 15 February 1890, to John Milton Thayer, box 5, folder 51, Governor John Milton Thayer Papers, Nebraska State Historical Society, Lincoln.

39. *Journal*, 28 February, 4 March, 3 April 1890.

40. Ibid., 23, 27 March 1890.

41. The *Weekly Bee*, 26 February 1890, claimed that a reduction of local rates to the Missouri River by 5 cents would reduce the interstate rate to New York by the same amount. One of the secretaries of the Board of Transportation correctly explained that through rates were established independently of local rates. See *Journal*, 30 March 1890.

42. John Milton Thayer to the Central Traffic Association of Missouri, 14 March 1890, box 10, Thayer Papers.

43. *Alliance*, 5 April 1890.

44. Parsons, *Populist Context*, 79.

45. *Alliance*, 5 April 1890.

46. Ibid., 3 May 1890.

47. By the time Congress adopted the compromise Sherman Silver Purchase Act in July, the decision to form a third party had already been taken. See Fred Wellborn, "The Influence of the Silver Republican Senators, 1889–1891" *Mississippi Valley Historical Review* 14 (March 1928): 462–80.

48. *Alliance*, 3 May 1890, and *Advocate*, 16 April 1890.

49. *Nonconformist*, 1 May 1890, and *Alliance*, 8 March 1890.

50. *Advocate*, 2 April 1890.

51. Ibid., 18 June 1890.

52. Leon Fink, *Workingmen's Democracy: The Knights of Labor and American Politics* (Urbana, Ill., 1983), 123–39.

53. Thompson, "Farmers' Alliance in Nebraska," 203.

54. *Journal*, 21 May 1890.

55. Ibid., 25 May, 2 June 1890; *Alliance*, 7 June, 2 August 1890; Thompson, "Farmers' Alliance in Nebraska," 203.

56. *Advocate*, 16 July 1890.

57. *Alliance*, 6 September, 2 August 1890.

58. The other nominees were Charles N. Mayberry, a well-to-do farmer and Union Labor politician, for secretary of state; Jacob V. Wolfe, a breeder of hogs and cattle, for treasurer; Joseph W. Edgerton, an attorney and Union Labor politician, for attorney general; W. F. Wright, an orchardist and an Alliance lecturer, for commissioner of public lands; and A. D'Allemand, a German-born farmer/teacher and president of the Furnas County Alliance, for superintendent of public instruction. See *Alliance*, 2, 9 August 1890.

59. Peter H. Argersinger, *Populism and Politics: William Alfred Peffer and the People's Party* (Lexington, Ky., 1974), 36–38, and *Advocate*, 20 August 1890. The other nominees were John N. Ives, a former Democrat, for attorney general; Albert C. Shinn, a stock raiser, for lieutenant governor; and Russell S. Osborn, a Congregational minister and farmer, for secretary of state. See O. Gene Clanton, *Kansas Populism: Ideas and Men* (Lawrence, Kans., 1969), 60. Fleeing oppression and violence in the South after the withdrawal of the federal presence during Reconstruction, thousands of "Exodusters" came to Kansas in the late 1870s. In 1890, 3.3 percent of voting-age adult males in Kansas were black. See Nell Irwin Painter, *Exodusters: Black Migration to Kansas after Reconstruction* (New York, 1977), and U.S. Census Office, *Report on the Population . . . at the Eleventh Census: 1890* (Washington D.C., 1895–1897), pt. 1, table 77. Blacks in Topeka became increasingly disenchanted with the GOP in the 1880s, and some black leaders supported the Populists in the 1890s. See Thomas C. Cox, *Blacks in Topeka, Kansas, 1865–1915* (Baton Rouge, La., 1982), 120–30.

60. *Journal*, 24 July 1890; Sheldon, *Nebraska*, 1:684–85; Parsons, *Populist Context*, 85.

61. *Capital*, 25 June, 31 July, 28 August, 5 September 1890; *Goodland News*, quoted in Raymond C. Miller, "The Populist Party in Kansas (Ph.D. diss., University of Chicago, 1928)," 135; and Argersinger, *Populism and Politics*, 42.

62. *Journal*, 14 September 1890, quoted in Sheldon, *Nebraska*, 1:690.

63. *Capital*, 12 October, 23 August 1890.

64. Ibid., 1 August 1890, and Miller, "Populist Party," 127–28.

65. Robert W. Cherny, *Populism, Progressivism, and the Transformation of Nebraska Poli-*

tics, 1885–1915 (Lincoln, Nebr., 1981), 36; Argersinger, *Populism and Politics*, 40–41; and *Capital*, 11 September 1890.

66. *Capital*, 3 August 1890.

67. *Alliance*, 6 September 1890; *Nonconformist*, 10 July 1890; *Alliance*, 12 July 1890; and *Advocate*, 20 August 1890.

68. These banners were carried in a procession in Emporia, Kansas, described by the *Emporia Republican*, quoted in *Nonconformist*, 10 July 1890.

69. *Alliance*, 6 September, 12 July 1890.

70. *Nonconformist*, 10 July 1890, and *Alliance*, 6 September 1890.

71. *Nonconformist*, 18 September 1890.

72. Dorothy R. Blumberg, "Mary Elizabeth Lease," unpublished manuscript, Kansas State Historical Society, Topeka, 7, and Annie L. Diggs, "The Women in the Alliance Movement," *Arena* 6 (June 1892): 166.

73. Quoted in Barr, "Populist Uprising," 1150. According to Clanton, *Kansas Populism*, 76, this speech was delivered in March 1891 and was distilled in the *Star* (Kansas City), 1 April 1891. The *Nonconformist*, 25 September 1890, reported that one of Lease's speeches lasted two-and-one-half hours.

74. Clanton, *Kansas Populism*, 79–80, and Diggs, "Women in the Alliance," 169.

75. Mari Jo Buhle, *Women and American Socialism, 1870–1920* (Urbana, Ill., 1981), 87.

76. Quoted in Clanton, *Kansas Populism*, 76.

77. William Allen White, "What's the Matter with Kansas?" *Emporia Gazette*, 25 August 1896, in United States History Collection of Pamphlets, vol. 25, New York Public Library.

78. Leopold Vincent, comp., *The Alliance and Labor Songster* (Indianapolis, Ind., 1891; reprint, New York, 1975), 60.

79. Lawrence Goodwyn, *Democratic Promise: The Populist Moment in America* (New York, 1976), 542.

80. *Advocate*, 6 March 1890.

81. Ibid., 6 August 1890.

82. *Alliance*, 11 October 1890.

83. *Advocate*, 13 August 1890.

84. *Star*, 5 November 1890, quoted in Peter H. Argersinger, "Road to a Republican Waterloo: The Farmers' Alliance and the Election of 1890 in Kansas," *Kansas Historical Quarterly* 33 (Winter 1967): 467.

85. Nebraska Legislative Reference Council, *Nebraska Blue Book and Historical Register, 1918* (Lincoln, 1918), 451–52; Sheldon, *Nebraska*, 1:693, 696; Kansas Secretary of State, *Biennial Report, 1888–90* (Topeka, 1890), 85–86; and *Populist Handbook for Kansas* (Indianapolis, Ind., 1891), 187, 279–82.

86. Argersinger, *Populism and Politics*, 73. See also D. Scott Barton, "Party Switching and Kansas Populism," *Historian* 52 (May 1990): 459–61. William A. Peffer, *Populism: Its Rise and Fall*, ed. and with an introduction by Peter H. Argersinger (Lawrence, Kans., 1992), 69, indicates the Republican antecedents of Union Laborites.

87. Argersinger, *Populism and Politics*, 20–21.

CHAPTER 8. PARTY COMPETITION AND THE INCORPORATION OF THE IOWA FARMERS' ALLIANCE

1. Mildred Throne, "The Grange in Iowa, 1868–1875," *Iowa Journal of History* 51 (April, 1953): 305–10.

2. *Homestead* (Des Moines), 15 July 1887, 31 August, 27 January, 3 August 1888.

3. Ibid., 21 September, 1888, 1 February 1889.

4. Ibid., 29 March, 3 May, 27 December 1889, 21 February, 28 March, 9 May, 27 June 1890; Minutes of the Hartford Center Farmers' Alliance, 1 October 1890, State Historical Society of Iowa, Iowa City; *Homestead*, 23 October 1891.

5. Iowa Board of Railroad Commissioners, *Annual Report, 1890* (Des Moines, Iowa, 1890), 911-12, 943; Iowa Board of Railroad Commissioners, *Annual Report, 1891* (Des Moines, Iowa, 1891), 732-37; *Homestead*, 15 February 1889, 6 March 1891. In 1891 there were 126 mutual insurance companies operating in Iowa, although only 41 had been organized since 1884 and could be plausibly considered Alliance companies; see Iowa Auditor of State, *Annual Report on Insurance, 1891* (Des Moines, Iowa, 1891), 72-77. On elevators, see E. G. Nourse, *Fifty Years of Farmers' Elevators in Iowa*, Iowa Agricultural Experiment Station Bulletin 211 (Ames, Iowa, 1923), 245. It would be mistaken to conclude, as does Lawrence Goodwyn, *Democratic Promise: The Populist Moment in America* (New York, 1976), 260-62, that the Iowa Alliance rejected populism because its leadership was unaware of economic cooperation.

6. *Homestead*, 13 September 1889. For the inequities in state taxation systems in the late nineteenth century, see Morton Keller, *Affairs of State: Public Life in Late Nineteenth Century America* (Cambridge, Mass., 1977), 323-24, and Clifton K. Yearley, *The Money Machines: The Breakdown and Reform of Governmental and Party Finance in the North, 1860-1920* (Albany, N.Y., 1970), 77-95. Jeremiah W. Jenks, "School-Book Legislation," *Political Science Quarterly* (March 1891): 90-125, discusses the "school book trust" and proposals to reduce the cost of textbooks.

7. *Homestead*, 20 July 1888. Voters were allowed to cast votes for three of the six candidates. The results were Spencer Smith (Republican), 225,928; Frank T. Campbell (Republican) 224,808; Peter Dey (Democrat), 201,265; John Mahin (Republican), 200,075; Christian L. Lund (Democrat), 176,327; Herman Wills (Democrat), 175,049. See Iowa Secretary of State, *Official Register of the State of Iowa, 1889* (Des Moines, Iowa, 1889), 192. Party affiliations are not given in the official returns. See *Homestead*, 7 September 1888, for a list of the Democratic nominees.

8. Charles Beardsley to William B. Allison, 7, 20 September, 4 October 1888, Allison Papers; Congressional Quarterly, *Congressional Quarterly's Guide to U.S. Elections*, 2d ed. (Washington, D.C., 1985) 342, 814; W. B. Bonnifield to John F. Lacey, 10 November 1888, J. F. Oliver to John F. Lacey, 10 November 1888, box 247, John F. Lacey Papers, State Historical Society of Iowa, Des Moines.

9. N. M. Hubbard to William B. Allison, 12 January 1889, Allison Papers, and Leland Sage, *William Boyd Allison* (Iowa City, Iowa, 1956), 239.

10. Frank T. Campbell to William B. Allison, 26 January 1889, Allison Papers.

11. *Iowa State Register* (Des Moines), 28 July and 9 July 1889.

12. The *Homestead* had little to say about the GOP gubernatorial nomination, but the defeat of Wheeler at the state convention was clearly a disappointment to the Alliance; see the remarks of August Post in *Homestead*, 13 September 1889. The *Iowa State Register*, 7 July 1889, objected to the characterization of Wheeler as the "farmer candidate" and Hull as the "railroad candidate."

13. J. A. T. Hull to William B. Allison, 19 June 1889; C. B. Hunt to William B. Allison, 1, 12 July 1889; E. C. Lane to William B. Allison, 27 July 1889, Allison Papers.

14. *Iowa State Register*, 15, 16 August 1889.

15. J. S. Clarkson to William B. Allison, 24 August 1889, Allison Papers, and *Iowa State Register*, 18, 25 August 1889.

16. *Des Moines Leader*, 1 September 1889.

17. Ibid., 19 September 1889, and Jean B. Kern, "The Political Career of Horace Boies," *Iowa Journal of History* 47 (July 1949): 216–17.

18. *Des Moines Leader*, 19, 29 September 1889.

19. August Post to Horace Boies, 17 September 1889, quoted in ibid., 15 October 1889; August Post to Joseph G. Hutchison, 9 September 1887, quoted in *Iowa State Register*, 20 September 1889; Horace Boies to August Post, 5 October 1889, quoted in *Des Moines Leader*, 15 October 1889; Joseph G. Hutchison to August Post, 14 September 1889, quoted in *Register*, 20 September 1889.

20. *Des Moines Leader*, 13 October 1889, and *Cedar Rapids Gazette*, quoted in *Leader*, 18 October 1889.

21. *Iowa State Register*, 16 October 1889, and unidentified newspaper clipping, 22 October 1889, scrapbook 3, box 6, Larrabee Papers, State Historical Society of Iowa, Iowa City. There was no truth in the allegation that Ashby had been dismissed from the Alliance; in 1890 he was the lecturer of the National Farmers' Alliance. See Iowa Farmers' Alliance, *Proceedings of the Iowa Farmers' Alliance at Its Annual Meeting, October 29–31, 1890* (Des Moines, Iowa, 1890), 11.

22. *Iowa State Register*, 22, 29 October, 27 October 1889.

23. Boies received 49.9 percent of the vote to Hutchison's 48.1 percent, with the balance going to minor parties; see Congressional Quarterly, *Guide*, 500. The account of the LeMars celebration is in the *Iowa State Register*, 12 November 1889.

24. Assessments of the outcome are in the *Chicago Tribune*, quoted in *Iowa State Register*, 8 November 1889 and 10 November 1889; see also the summary of the range of interpretations for the Republican defeat in *Register*, 23 March 1890. John N. Irwin's discussion of the causes of the debacle, in "Is Iowa a Doubtful State?" *Forum* 13 (April 1892): 257–64, echoes the *Register* in attributing the defeat primarily to prohibition.

25. See Appendix B. Although it is theoretically possible that the Democratic gains among farmers can be attributed to gains among foreign-born antiprohibition farmers since the two categories overlap, the estimates suggest that this was not the case. When the counties are divided into two groups, according to whether they had more or less than 15 percent of the voting-age males of national origin likely to oppose prohibition, the estimates show that the percentage of farmers voting Democratic in the "high" foreign-born counties increased from 31 to 35 percent from 1887 to 1889, and the increase among farmers in the "low" group was greater, rising from 28 percent in 1887 to 34 percent in 1889.

26. Iowa Secretary of State, *Official Register of the State of Iowa, 1890* (Des Moines, Iowa, 1890), 72–76.

27. Rothrock's candidacy was mentioned in N. M. Hubbard to William B. Allison, 9 December 1889, Allison Papers. See also Dan Elbert Clark, *History of Senatorial Elections in Iowa* (Iowa City, Iowa, 1912), 219.

28. C. B. Hunt to William B. Allison, 12 November 1889; Gilbert Pray to William B. Allison, 21 November 1889; J. S. Clarkson to William B. Allison, 20 December 1889, Allison Papers.

29. John A. Evans to William B. Allison, 12 November 1889, Allison Papers.

30. C. A. Schaffter to William B. Allison, 14 November 1889; James Wilson to Wil-

liam B. Allison, 11 December 1889; J. C. Cook to William B. Allison, 9 December 1889; E. S. Ellsworth to William B. Allison, 26 October, 11 November 1889, Allison Papers.

31. D. B. Davidson to William B. Allison, 18 November 1889, and A. F. Meservey to William B. Allison, 22 November 1889, Allison Papers.

32. Frank Jackson to William B. Allison, 5, 7, 11 December 1889, Allison Papers.

33. G. L. Godfrey to William B. Allison, 15 November 1889, and Nathaniel M. Hubbard to William B. Allison, 9 December 1889, Allison Papers. C. A. Schaffter to William B. Allison, 16 December 1889, suggested that Finn desired "the chairmanship of an important committee in the senate." Finn did vote for Allison and was granted the chair of the Committee on Schools, although this was not among the important committees. Iowa Senate, *Journal, 1890* (Des Moines, Iowa, 1890), 77–78.

34. Frank Jackson to William B. Allison, 11, 26 December 1889, Allison Papers, and U.S. Department of the Interior, *Report of the Secretary of the Interior, 1890,* 5 vols. (Washington, D.C., 1890), 3:64.

35. James Wilson to William B. Allison, 11 December, 27 November 1889, Allison Papers. Although Wallace privately urged Larrabee to contest Allison's seat, the *Homestead* did not take a stand on the senate question. See Henry Wallace, *Uncle Henry's Own Story,* 3 vols. (Des Moines, Iowa, 1917–1919), 3:42.

36. *Iowa State Register,* 17, 18 January 1890.

37. By law, balloting for senator commenced the second Tuesday after organization; see ibid., 21 February 1890.

38. Ibid., 24, 28 January, 20 February 1890.

39. Frank Jackson to William B. Allison, 27 January 1890, Allison Papers, and *Iowa State Register,* 7, 12 February 1890.

40. Gilbert Pray to William B. Allison, 14 February 1890, Allison Papers.

41. Gilbert Pray to William B. Allison, 18 February 1890, Allison Papers; *Iowa State Register,* 20 February 1890; Iowa Senate, *Journal, 1890,* 148–49.

42. These quotations are from Stuntz's report at the 1890 Alliance meeting in Iowa Farmers' Alliance, *Proceedings,* 22.

43. A. L. Stuntz to William B. Allison, 6 March 1890, Allison Papers. In a postscript, Stuntz referred Allison to the ubiquitous "Tama Jim," who, one suspects, assisted the Alliance lobbyist in formulating his strategy.

44. *Weekly Bee* (Omaha), 12 March 1890; *Iowa State Register,* 17 April 1890; Iowa Farmers' Alliance, *Proceedings,* 22.

45. Edgar E. Mack to George D. Perkins, 30 September 1890, George D. Perkins Papers, State Historical Society of Iowa, Des Moines.

46. These quotations are from separate addresses given by Post at the annual meetings of 1889 and 1890. *Homestead,* 13 September 1889, and Iowa Farmers' Alliance, *Proceedings,* 27.

47. *Homestead,* 7 December 1888.

48. Ibid., 24 October 1890. The Butterworth antioption bill and the Hatch antioption bill of 1892 both lumped together futures and options, although these were distinct operations. The Chicago Board of Trade was not against eliminating options but opposed these laws as they would effectively bar trading in futures. Neither of the two bills became law, despite intense lobbying by the Alliance and strong support by Alliance-influenced legislators. See Jonathan Lurie, *The Chicago Board of Trade, 1859–1905: The Dynamics of Self-Regulation* (Urbana, Ill., 1979), 107–26.

49. Herman C. Nixon, "The Cleavage within the Farmers' Alliance Movement," *Mississippi Valley Historical Review* 15 (June 1928): 22–33.

50. Bills to restrict compound lard were introduced several times in the early 1890s but were never passed; see Nixon, "Cleavage," 28–31.

51. Wallace, *Uncle Henry's Own Story*, 3:52, and *Homestead*, 31 October 1890.

52. Newton B. Ashby, *The Riddle of the Sphinx* (Des Moines, Iowa, 1890; reprint, Westport, Conn., 1975), 314–15, 326–28, 338–39.

53. *Iowa State Register*, 18 January 1890. These membership figures are estimates from Appendix A.

54. *Weekly Bee*, 4 February 1891.

55. Iowa Commissioner of Labor Statistics, *Biennial Report, 1890–91* (Des Moines, 1891), 60, 67, 71, 77, 79, 82. The vast majority of the respondents said nothing of solutions since the commissioner only requested their views on conditions, but that even two farmers volunteered the land-loan plan as a solution suggests that many others would have if asked.

56. Iowa Farmers' Alliance, *Proceedings*, 32–33.

57. See Appendix B. The Democrats won six of the eleven congressional seats; see Congressional Quarterly, *Guide*, 818.

58. I have found no evidence of women orators or lecturers in the Iowa Alliance. In 1889 the *Homestead* began devoting one page to a women's column, which primarily counseled women about domestic work, including how to mend tablecloths or store onions. The column rarely touched on political economy and then only peripherally, as when one woman expressed hope for a "second Abraham Lincoln" to emancipate farmers from the "shackles" upon the "over-worked, over-charged, and over-taxed farmer"; see *Homestead*, 18 October 1889.

CHAPTER 9. WHY WAS THERE NO POPULISM IN IOWA?

1. John D. Hicks, *The Populist Revolt: A History of the Farmers' Alliance* (Minneapolis, Minn., 1931; reprint, Lincoln, Nebr., 1961), 119–22; Herman C. Nixon, "The Cleavage within the Farmers' Alliance Movement," *Mississippi Valley Historical Review* 15 (June 1928): 22–33; O. Gene Clanton, *Populism: The Humane Preference In America, 1890–1900* (Boston, 1991), 20–23.

2. Homer Clevenger, "The Farmers' Alliance in Missouri," *Missouri Historical Review* 39 (October 1944): 37–39; Hicks, *Populist Revolt*, 226; and Lawrence Goodwyn, *Democratic Promise: The Populist Moment in America* (New York, 1976), 249–53.

3. Peter H. Argersinger, *Populism and Politics: William Alfred Peffer and the People's Party* (Lexington, Ky., 1974), 81; Hicks, *Populist Revolt*, 207–9; and Goodwyn, *Democratic Promise*, 226–29.

4. Nebraska had 42 of 103 delegates; there were 18 delegates from Ohio and 17 from Iowa. *Weekly Bee* (Omaha), 4 February 1891.

5. Richard Harvey Barton, "The Agrarian Revolt in Michigan, 1865–1900," Ph.D. diss., Michigan State University, 1958, 159–62; Ernest D. Stewart, "The Populist Party in Indiana," *Indiana Magazine of History* 14 (December 1918): 342–43; and Roy V. Scott, *The Agrarian Movement in Illinois, 1880–1896* (Urbana, Ill., 1962), 87–102.

6. *Homestead* (Des Moines), 6 June 1890.

7. Ibid., 20 December 1889, 27 June 1890.

8. Iowa Farmers' Alliance, Proceedings . . . at Its Annual Meeting, October 29-31, 1890 (Des Moines, 1890), 20, 29, 11.

9. Ibid., 9-10.

10. Congressional Quarterly, Congressional Quarterly's Guide to U.S. Elections, 2d ed. (Washington, D.C., 1985), 818; Weekly Bee, 4 February 1891; and Fred E. Haynes, Third Party Movements since the Civil War with Special Reference to Iowa (Iowa City, Iowa, 1916), 312.

11. Henry S. Wilcox to L. H. Weller, 4 January 1888, Weller Papers, and Herman C. Nixon, "The Populist Movement in Iowa," Iowa Journal of History and Politics 24 (January 1926): 31.

12. E. O. Davis to L. H. Weller, 16 June 1888, Weller Papers; Haynes, Third Party Movements, 197; and Nixon, "Populist Movement," 31.

13. Des Moines Leader, 5, 11 September 1890.

14. Iowa Tribune, 25 March 1891. L. L. Polk's biographer observes that "it was with the blessing of Weaver that Polk organized the Iowa branch of the NFA & IU." Stuart Noblin, Leonidas Lafayette Polk: Agrarian Crusader (Chapel Hill, N.C., 1949), 260.

15. Iowa Tribune, 29 April, 6 May 1891.

16. J. Shearer to L. H. Weller, 29 April 1891, Weller Papers.

17. Homestead, 10 April, 15 May 1891.

18. Ibid., 10 April, 12 June, 15 May 1891.

19. Ibid., 16 October 1891; Iowa Farmers' Alliance, Proceedings, 18; J. H. Sanders, "President's Letter No. 3," 30 November 1891, and "President's Letter No. 2," 1 December 1891, Weller Papers.

20. Robert Michels, Political Parties: A Sociological Study of the Oligarchical Tendencies of Modern Democracy, trans. Eden and Cedar Paul (New York, 1915).

21. Homestead, 26 June 1891. Secretary Post reported in October 1891 that district Alliances had been organized in ten of Iowa's eleven congressional districts; see ibid., 16 October 1891.

22. Des Moines Leader, 5 September 1891. Westfall was listed as district organizer for the eleventh district in Homestead, 6 March 1891.

23. Will N. Sargent to L. H. Weller, 6, 16 April 1891, Weller Papers.

24. H. L. Loucks to L. H. Weller, 27 April 1891. As evidence of Weller's commitment to work within the old Alliance, he honored Sargent's request to remove the names of the new Alliance leaders from his newspaper. See Will N. Sargent to Weller, 30 April 1891, and the Farmers' Alliance (Independence, Iowa), 17 December 1891, Weller Papers.

25. Homestead, 23 October 1891.

26. Iowa Tribune, 10 June 1891.

27. Iowa State Register, 4 June 1891.

28. Saturday Evening Post (Burlington), 13 June 1891, quoted in Haynes, Third Party Movements, 317.

29. Iowa State Register, 7 June 1891.

30. Ibid., 17 June 1891.

31. Des Moines Leader, 4 June 1891.

32. Jean B. Kern, "The Political Career of Horace Boies," Iowa Journal of History 47 (July 1949): 223-24.

228 NOTES TO PAGES 164-172

33. Ibid., 229–34, 241–43, and *Iowa State Register*, 24, 26 December 1890, 1, 20, 23 January 1891.

34. *Iowa State Register*, 30 July, 16 August 1891.

35. *Des Moines Leader*, 25 June 1891.

36. Richard Jensen, *The Winning of the Midwest: Social and Political Conflict, 1888–1896* (Chicago, 1971), 114.

37. *Iowa State Register*, 25 July, 8 September 1891.

38. Ibid., 12 June 1891.

39. Ibid., 22 July 1891.

40. Ibid., 20 June 1891. For further instances of the *Register's* flattery of the Iowa Alliance see 17, 30 September, 13 October 1891.

41. Quoted in ibid., 7 August 1891,

42. Argersinger, *Populism and Politics*, 80–87, 99–100. A list of campaign meetings in the *Iowa Tribune*, 21 October 1891, shows appointments for Lease in Iowa from 20 October through 2 November. The only other speaking engagements listed were for Iowa candidates.

43. *Alliance* (Lincoln), 13 August 1891, and *Chicago Sentinel*, quoted in ibid., 30 July 1891. The *Alliance*, 18 February, 7 July 1892, endorsed the subtreasury.

44. Congressional Quarterly, *Guide*, 500. The estimated percentage of farmers voting Republican increased from 51 to 53 percent, the estimated percentage voting Democratic from 34 to 37 percent. An estimated 64 percent of antiprohibition voters voted Democratic in 1891, with 36 percent not voting, leaving zero as the estimated percentage voting Republican. See Appendix B.

45. *National Economist* (Washington, D.C.), 13 August 1892.

46. *Iowa Tribune*, 24 August, 5, 26 October 1892. At Raleigh, N.C., 10,000 heard Weaver; in Des Moines, only 1,200. Fred E. Haynes, *James Baird Weaver* (Iowa City, Iowa, 1919), 326; *Iowa Tribune*, 26 October 1892.

47. *Iowa Tribune*, 14 September and 7 September 1892.

48. *Iowa State Register* (weekly edition), 10 June 1892, quoted in Walter Ellsworth Nydegger, "The Election of 1892 in Iowa," *Iowa Journal of History and Politics* 25 (July 1927): 426.

49. Nydegger, "Election of 1892," 381, 424; Jensen, *Winning of the Midwest*, 201; and *Iowa State Register*, 30 October 1892.

50. The Republicans also benefited from an increase in turnout among foreign-born voters who were not antiprohibition (primarily Scandinavians); see Appendix B.

51. Harrison won 49.6 percent, compared to 44.3 percent for Cleveland, 4.7 percent for Weaver, and 1.4 percent for John Bidwell, the Prohibition Party candidate. Congressional Quarterly, *Guide*, 342.

52. *Iowa State Register*, 29 October 1892.

53. Kirk H. Porter and Donald B. Johnson, eds., *National Party Platforms, 1840–1964* (Urbana, Ill., 1966), 89–90.

54. Iowa Farmers' Alliance, *Proceedings*, 22; *Homestead*, 23 October 1891; August Post to L. H. Weller, 19 June 1891, J. H. Sanders to L. H. Weller, 9 December 1891, Weller Papers.

55. *Homestead*, 10 July, 20 November 1891.

56. The 1891 Alliance convention adopted the resolutions of a year before, which called for free coinage of silver and government ownership of railroads. See Iowa

Farmers' Alliance, *Proceedings*, 33, and *Homestead*, 23 October 1891. The 1892 platform also endorsed free silver although it called for the milder government "control" of railroads. *Homestead*, 21 October 1892.

57. Post's lobbying activities can be seen in August Post to L. H. Weller, 14 July 1892, Weller Papers, and August Post to William Toole, 17 March, 14 July 1892, William Toole Papers, State Historical Society of Wisconsin, Madison. On the 1893 Iowa State Revenue Commission, see John E. Brindley, *History of Taxation in Iowa*, 2 vols. (Iowa City, Iowa, 1911), 1: 292.

58. *Homestead*, 14 October 1892, 20 October 1893. There is no mention of an annual meeting in the 1894 issues of the *Homestead*.

59. Henry Wallace, *Uncle Henry's Own Story*, 3 vols. (Des Moines, Iowa, 1917–1919), 3:55, 65, and *Homestead*, 11 January 1895.

60. Biography of A. M. Post, in *Past and Present of Appanoose County, Iowa* (Chicago, 1913), 33–36; Earley Vernon Wilcox, *Tama Jim* (Boston, 1930), 17; H. J. Stevens to Governor Drake, Records of the Governor, "Appointments," file no. GII.338, Iowa Department of History and Archives, Des Moines; Newton B. Ashby, *The Ashbys in Iowa* (Tucson, Ariz., 1925), 45–46.

61. Rumors of Wallace as a Republican gubernatorial candidate in 1891 were reported in the *Des Moines Leader*, 16 April 1891. See Wallace, *Uncle Henry's Own Story*, 3:67, and Russell Lord, *The Wallaces of Iowa* (Boston, 1947), 132.

62. James Bryce, *The American Commonwealth*, 3d ed., 2 vols. (New York, 1904), 2:21.

63. Jensen, *Winning of the Midwest*; Frederick C. Luebke, *Immigrants and Politics: The Germans of Nebraska, 1880–1900* (Lincoln, Nebr., 1965); and Paul Kleppner, *The Cross of Culture: A Social Analysis of Midwestern Politics, 1850–1900* (New York, 1970).

64. Morton Keller, *Affairs of State: Public Life in Late Nineteenth Century America* (Cambridge, Mass., 1977), 552–64; and Richard F. Bensel, *Sectionalism and American Political Development, 1880–1980* (Madison, Wis., 1984), 62.

65. For an evaluation emphasizing the openness of state legislatures to popular pressures, see Ballard Campbell, *Representative Democracy: Public Policy and Midwestern Legislatures in the Late Nineteenth Century* (Cambridge, Mass., 1980).

CHAPTER 10. THE FATE OF POPULISM

1. Frederick Jackson Turner, *The Frontier in American History* (New York, 1920), 32.

2. John D. Hicks, *The Populist Revolt: A History of the Farmers' Alliance* (Minneapolis, Minn., 1931; reprint, Lincoln, Nebr., 1961), 337.

3. McKinley's margin of victory was 22.9 percent in Wisconsin, 15.7 percent in Minnesota, 13.0 percent in Illinois, 12.6 percent in Iowa, and 10.5 percent in Michigan; he won by 4.8 percent in Ohio and 2.8 percent in Indiana. See Congressional Quarterly, *Congressional Quarterly's Guide to U.S. Elections*, 2d ed. (Washington, D.C., 1985) p. 344.

4. J. Thompson to George D. Perkins, 16 July 1896, Perkins Papers.

5. H. G. McMillan to J. S. Clarkson, 5 September 1896, Clarkson Papers. McMillan's letter summarized the situation in mid-August.

6. Leland L. Sage, *William Boyd Allison: A Study in Practical Politics* (Iowa City, Iowa, 1956), 267; Stanley L. Jones, *The Presidential Election of 1896* (Madison, Wis., 1964), 277, 295, 310, 346; Robert Durden, *Climax of Populism: The Election of 1896* (Lexington, Ky.,

1965), 51, 63, 126; and Gilbert Fite, "Republican Strategy and the Farm Vote in the Presidential Campaign of 1896," *American Historical Review* 65 (July 1960): 789.

7. Richard Hofstadter, *The Age of Reform: From Bryan to F.D.R.* (New York, 1955), 100.

8. Jean B. Kern, "The Political Career of Horace Boies," *Iowa Journal of History* 47 (July, 1949): 238–41, and Herman C. Nixon, "The Populist Movement in Iowa," *Iowa Journal of History and Politics* 24 (January 1926): 80, 89–90, 95–98.

9. Leland L. Sage, *A History of Iowa* (Ames, Iowa, 1974), 213–15, and Jones, *Presidential Election of 1896*, 282–83, 301–2.

10. The politics of fusion in Kansas and Nebraska can be followed more closely in Peter H. Argersinger, *Populism and Politics: William Alfred Peffer and the People's Party* (Lexington, Ky., 1974), 123–24, 134–35, 176–82, 201, 230–32, 267–68, and Robert W. Cherny, *Populism, Progressivism, and the Transformation of Nebraska Politics, 1885–1915* (Lincoln, Nebr., 1981), 36, 40–45. There is little evidence supporting Lawrence Goodwyn's contention (*Democratic Promise: The Populist Moment in America* [New York, 1976], 204–10, 316–17, 388–400, 590–92) that populism in Nebraska was merely a "shadow movement" for free silver and that in Kansas it was a pure form that strongly opposed fusion on a free-silver platform. There were no more midroaders in Kansas than in Nebraska, and in both states most Populists eventually determined that fusion offered significant political advantages.

11. Robert C. McMath, Jr., *American Populism: A Social History, 1877–1898* (New York, 1993), 154.

12. The extent to which my findings for Iowa are applicable elsewhere, of course, will await further investigation, but hints of the dynamics of party competition in Missouri are found in Homer Clevenger, "Missouri Becomes a Doubtful State," *Mississippi Valley Historical Review* 29 (March 1943): 541–48; Clevenger, "The Farmers' Alliance in Missouri," *Missouri Historical Review* 39 (October 1944): 35–43; David P. Thelen, *Paths of Resistance: Tradition and Dignity in Industrializing Missouri* (New York, 1986), 211; and, for Indiana, in Ernest D. Stewart, "The Populist Party in Indiana," *Indiana Magazine of History* 14 (December 1918): 332–67, and Russell M. Seeds, *History of the Republican Party of Indiana* (Indianapolis, Ind., 1899), 73. Roy V. Scott, *The Agrarian Movement in Illinois, 1880–1896* (Urbana, Ill., 1962), 91–102, indicates that with the Farmers' Mutual Benefit Association (FMBA) threatening third-party action in Illinois in 1890, Democrats and Republicans responded by nominating FMBA officials and adopting antimonopoly platforms. On the abortive attempt to establish a Labor/Populist alliance in Chicago, see Chester M. Destler, *American Radicalism, 1865–1901* (New London, Conn., 1946; reprint, Chicago, 1966), 175–211.

13. The history of populism in South Dakota has been neglected, but see Herbert S. Schell, *History of South Dakota* (Lincoln, Nebr., 1968), 226–27, who links the Alliance's move toward a third party in 1890 to the Republican-dominated legislature's defeat of Alliance candidates for U.S. senator.

14. On the weakness of parties in the West, see Paul Kleppner, "Voters and Parties in the Western States, 1876–1900," *Western Historical Quarterly* 14 (January 1983): 49–68. James E. Wright, *The Politics of Populism: Dissent in Colorado* (New Haven, Conn., 1974), and Robert W. Larson, *Populism in the Mountain West* (Albuquerque, N.Mex., 1986), demonstrate that Rocky Mountain populism was not simply a free-silver movement.

15. This would be the approach suggested by V. O. Key, Jr., *Southern Politics in State and Nation* (New York, 1949).

16. From the preamble to the Omaha platform; see Kirk H. Porter and Donald B. Johnson, eds., *National Party Platforms, 1840–1964* (Urbana, Ill., 1966), 90.

17. Ibid.

APPENDIX A: FARMERS' ALLIANCE MEMBERSHIP

1. *Nonconformist* (Winfield, Kans.), 10 April 1890; *Alliance* (Lincoln), 11 October, 1890. Scott McNall, *The Road to Rebellion: Class Formation and Kansas Populism, 1856–1900* (Chicago, 1988), 238–44, discusses the problems of taking Alliance membership claims at face value.

2. *Advocate* (Meriden, Kans.), 17 August 1889, and *Nonconformist*, 7 March 1889.

3. McNall, *Road to Rebellion*, 242.

4. *Homestead* (Des Moines), 1887–1890.

5. Membership Journal, 1889, and quarterly reports of suballiances for the quarters ending 30 June and 30 September 1893, Nebraska Farmers' Alliance papers.

6. MaryJo Wagner, "Farms, Families, and Reform" (Ph.D. diss., University of Oregon, 1986), 17, 48–51.

7. *Kansas Farmer* (Topeka), 6 July 1890.

APPENDIX B: REGRESSION-BASED ESTIMATES FOR IOWA ELECTIONS, 1880–1892

1. J. Morgan Kousser, "Ecological Regression and the Analysis of Past Politics," *Journal of Interdisciplinary History* 4 (Autumn 1973): 237–62.

2. Only .07 percent in 1885 of voting-age men were aliens; in 1895 this figure was .04 percent. Iowa Secretary of State, *Census of Iowa for the Year 1895* (Des Moines, 1896), table 20.

3. In intermediate years I estimated the number of farmers per county by subtracting the smaller from the larger figure of the two census-year figures, multiplied the remainder by the number of years after the first census, divided this figure by five (for the number of years between each census), and then added it to the first census-year figure. Thus, if a county had an estimated 2,000 farmers in 1880 and an estimated 2,500 in 1885, the estimated number of farmers in 1883 would have been 2,300. I followed a similar procedure for estimating the number of total voters at each election.

4. Iowa Secretary of State, *Census of Iowa for the Year 1885* (Des Moines, 1885), table 3; and *Census of Iowa, 1895*, tables 32, 46. The results for the prohibition referendum of 1882 are found in Iowa Secretary of State, *Official Register of the State of Iowa, 1889* (Des Moines, Iowa, 1889), 207–8.

Bibliography

PRIMARY SOURCES

Manuscripts

Allison, William Boyd. Papers. State Historical Society of Iowa, Des Moines.
Blumberg, Dorothy R. "Mary Elizabeth Lease: Populist Campaigner." Unpublished manuscript, Kansas State Historical Society, Topeka.
Clarkson, James S. Papers. Library of Congress, Washington, D.C.
Dolliver, John P. Papers. State Historical Society of Iowa, Iowa City.
Hartford Center Farmers' Alliance. Minutes. State Historical Society of Iowa, Iowa City.
Humphrey, Lyman U. Papers. Kansas State Historical Society, Topeka.
Iowa. Governor's Letter Books. Iowa State Archives, Des Moines.
———. Records of the Governor. Appointments. Iowa State Archives, Des Moines.
Kansas Governor's Office. Letter Press Books. Kansas State Historical Society, Topeka.
Lacey, John F. Papers. State Historical Society of Iowa, Des Moines.
Larrabee, William. Papers. State Historical Society of Iowa, Clermont.
———. Papers. State Historical Society of Iowa, Iowa City.
Lone Tree Alliance. Minutes. Kansas State Historical Society, Topeka.
Mack, Edgar E. Papers. State Historical Society of Iowa, Iowa City.
Maxwell, Samuel. Papers. Microfilm edition. Nebraska State Historical Society, Lincoln.
Nebraska Farmers' Alliance. Papers. Microfilm edition. Nebraska State Historical Society, Lincoln.
Perkins, George D. Papers. State Historical Society of Iowa, Des Moines.
Thayer, John Milton. Papers. Nebraska State Historical Society, Lincoln.
Toole, William. Papers. State Historical Society of Wisconsin, Madison.
Weaver, James B. Papers. State Historical Society of Iowa, Des Moines.
Weller, Luman H. Papers. State Historical Society of Wisconsin, Madison.

Newspapers

Cedar Rapids Evening Gazette, 1887.
(Chicago) *Daily Inter-Ocean*, July–November 1887.
(Chicago) *Western Rural and American Stockman*, 4 September, 17 September 1887.

Clarinda [Iowa] *Herald*, July–November 1887.
(Des Moines) *Homestead*, 1885–1895.
(Des Moines) *Iowa State Register*, 1884–1892.
(Des Moines) *Iowa Tribune*, 1884–1892.
Des Moines Leader, 1884–1892.
Lake City [Iowa] *Graphic*, July–November 1887.
(Lincoln) *Alliance*, August 1889–December 1889.
(Lincoln) *Daily Nebraska State Journal*, November 1889–1890.
(Lincoln) *Farmers' Alliance*, 1890–1892.
(Meriden, Kans.) *Advocate*, August 1889–December 1889.
New York Times, 6 January 1890.
(Omaha) *Republican*, 1886–1889.
(Omaha) *Weekly Bee*, 1886–1891.
Onawa [Iowa] *Weekly Democrat*, 16 January 1896.
Sioux City Journal, 1 January 1896.
(Topeka) *Advocate*, 1890–1892.
(Topeka) *Alliance-Tribune*, 1890.
(Topeka) *Capital-Commonwealth*, November 1888–March 1889.
(Topeka) *Daily Capital*, 1886, July 1888–October 1888, July 1889–November 1890.
(Topeka) *Kansas Farmer*, 1888–1890.
(Washington, D.C.) *National Economist*, 1889–1890, July–November 1892.
(Winfield, Kans.) *American Nonconformist and Kansas Industrial Liberator*, October 1886–
    September 1891.
Winterset [Iowa] *Madisonian*, July–November 1887.

Government Documents

Hinman, Eleanor, and J. O. Rankin. *Farm Mortgage History of Eleven Southeastern Ne-
    braska Townships, 1870–1932.* Nebraska Agricultural Experiment Station Research
    Bulletin 67. Lincoln, Nebr., 1933.
Houk, Howard J. *A Century of Indiana Farm Prices, 1841 to 1941.* Purdue University Agri-
    cultural Experiment Station Bulletin 476. Lafayette, Ind., 1943.
Illinois. Bureau of Labor Statistics. *Biennial Report, 1888.* Springfield, 1888.
_____. *Biennial Report, 1890.* Springfield, 1890.
Iowa. Auditor of State. *Annual Report on Insurance, 1891.* Des Moines, 1891.
Iowa. Board of Railroad Commissioners. *Annual Report, 1885.* Des Moines, 1885.
_____. *Annual Report, 1886.* Des Moines, 1886.
_____. *Annual Report, 1887.* Des Moines, 1887.
_____. *Annual Report, 1888.* Des Moines, 1888.
_____. *Annual Report, 1890.* Des Moines, 1890.
_____. *Annual Report, 1891.* Des Moines, 1891.
_____. *Annual Report, 1892.* Des Moines, 1892.
Iowa. Commissioner of Labor Statistics. *Biennial Report, 1890–91.* Des Moines, 1891.
_____. *Biennial Report, 1895–96.* Des Moines, 1897.
Iowa. House. *Journal, 1886.* Des Moines, 1886.
_____. *Journal, 1888.* Des Moines, 1888.
_____. *Journal, 1890.* Des Moines, 1890.

Iowa. Secretary of State. *Census of Iowa for the Year 1885.* Des Moines, 1885.
_____. *Census of Iowa for the Year 1895.* Des Moines, 1896.
_____. *Official Register of the State of Iowa, 1889.* Des Moines, 1889.
_____. *Official Register of the State of Iowa, 1890.* Des Moines, 1890.
_____. *Official Register of the State of Iowa, 1893.* Des Moines, 1893.
Iowa. Senate. *Journal, 1886.* Des Moines, 1886.
_____. *Journal, 1888.* Des Moines, 1888.
_____. *Journal, 1890.* Des Moines, 1890.
Jenks, Jeremiah W. "Industrial Combinations and Prices." In *Preliminary Report on Trusts and Industrial Combinations.* U.S. Industrial Commission. Washington, D.C., 1900
Kansas. Board of Railroad Commissioners. *Annual Report, 1890.* Topeka, 1890.
Kansas. Bureau of Labor and Industrial Statistics. *Annual Report, 1887.* Topeka, 1887.
_____. *Annual Report, 1893.* Topeka, 1893.
Kansas. Legislature. *Proceedings of the Joint Committee of the Legislature . . . to Investigate the Explosion which Occurred at Coffeyville, Kansas, October 18, 1888.* Topeka, 1891.
Kansas. Secretary of State. *Biennial Report, 1888–90.* Topeka, 1890.
Kansas. State Board of Agriculture. *Monthly Report, September 30, 1890.* Topeka, 1890.
Kemmerer, Edwin W. *Seasonal Variations in the Relative Demand for Money and Capital in the United States.* 61st Cong., 2d sess., S. Doc. 588, 1910.
Massachusetts. Commissioner of Foreign Mortgage Corporations, *Annual Report, 1895.* Boston, 1895.
Missouri. State Department. *Official Manual of the State of Missouri, 1893–94.* Jefferson City, 1893.
Murray, William G. *An Economic Analysis of Farm Mortgages in Story County, Iowa, 1854–1931.* Iowa Agricultural Experiment Station Research Bulletin 156. Ames, Iowa, 1933.
Nebraska. Attorney General. *Biennial Report, 1889–90.* Omaha, 1890.
Nebraska. Board of Transportation. *Annual Report, 1890.* Lincoln, 1890.
Nebraska. Bureau of Labor and Industrial Statistics. *Biennial Report, 1889–1890.* Lincoln, 1890.
_____. *Biennial Report, 1891–92.* Lincoln, 1892.
_____. *Biennial Report, 1893–94.* Lincoln, 1894.
_____. *Biennial Report, 1895–96.* Lincoln, 1896.
Nebraska. House. *Journal, 1889.* (Omaha, 1889).
Nebraska. Legislative Reference Council. *Nebraska Blue Book and Historical Register, 1918.* Lincoln, 1918.
Nebraska. Senate. *Journal, 1889.* (Omaha, 1889).
New York. Banking Department. *Annual Report of the Superintendent . . . Relative to Foreign Mortgage Loan, Investment, and Trust Companies, 1891.* Albany, 1891.
Norton, L. J. Norton, and B. B. Wilson. *Prices of Illinois Farm Products from 1866 to 1929.* University of Illinois Agricultural Experiment Station Bulletin 351. Urbana, Ill., 1930.
Nourse. E. G. *Fifty Years of Farmers' Elevators in Iowa.* Iowa Agricultural Experiment Station Bulletin 211. Ames, Iowa, 1923.
Strand, Norman V. *Prices of Farm Products in Iowa, 1851–1940.* Iowa State Agricultural Experiment Station Bulletin 303. Ames, Iowa, 1942.
U.S. Census Office. *Agriculture*, pt. 1, "Farms, Livestock, and Animal Products." Washington, D.C., 1902.

_____. *Report on Farms and Homes: Proprietorship and Indebtedness in the United States at the Eleventh Census: 1890*. Washington, D.C., 1896.

_____. *Report on Real Estate Mortgages in the United States at the Eleventh Census: 1890*. Washington, D.C., 1895.

_____. *Report on the Population of the United States at the Eleventh Census: 1890*. Washington, D.C., 1895–1897.

_____. *Report on the Statistics of Agriculture in the United States at the Eleventh Census: 1890*. Washington, D.C., 1895.

_____. *Statistics of Population of the United States at the Tenth Census*. Washington, D.C., 1883.

U.S. Congress. *Hearings before the Subcommittee of the Joint Committee on Rural Credits*. 64th Cong., 1st sess., 1915.

U.S. Country Life Commission. *Report*. 60th Cong., 2d sess., 1909, S. Doc. 705.

U.S. Department of Agriculture. Bureau of Statistics. *Corn Crops of the United States, 1866–1906*. Bulletin 56. Washington, D.C., 1907.

_____. *Report of the Statistician (1884–1891)*.

U.S. Department of the Interior. *Report of the Secretary of the Interior, 1890*. 5 vols. Washington, D.C., 1890.

U.S. Industrial Commission. *Report*. Vol. 13. Washington, D.C., 1901.

U.S. Interstate Commerce Commission. *Interstate Commerce Reports*. Vol. 3. Rochester, N.Y., 1893.

_____. *Railways in the United States in 1902*, pt. 2, "A Forty Year Review of Changes in Freight Tariffs." Washington, D.C., 1903.

U.S. Senate. *Report of the Senate Select Committee on Interstate Commerce*, 49th Cong., 1st sess., 1886, S. Rept. 46, pt. 2.

_____. *Testimony Taken by the United States Pacific Railway Commission*, vol. 3, 50th Cong., 1st sess., 1888, S. Ex. Doc. 51, pt. 4.

_____. *Wholesale Prices, Wages, and Transportation*, 52d Cong., 2d sess., 1893, S. Rept. 1394, pt. 2.

Valgren, V. N., and Elmer N. Engelbert. *Bank Loans to Farmers on Personal and Collateral Security*. U.S. Department of Agriculture Bulletin 1048. Washington, D.C., 1922.

Books, Articles, and Pamphlets

Ashby, Newton B. *The Ashbys in Iowa*. Tucson, Ariz., 1925.

_____. *The Riddle of the Sphinx*. Des Moines, Iowa, 1890. Reprint, Westport, Conn., 1975.

Barr, Elizabeth N. "The Populist Uprising." In *A Standard History of Kansas and Kansans*, 2 vols. Compiled by William P. Connelley. Chicago, 1919.

Barton County, Kansas, Alliance Exchange Company. *Rules of the Barton County Alliance Exchange Company*. Great Bend, Kans., 1890. Vol. 5, People's Party Pamphlets. Kansas State Historical Society, Topeka.

Berge, George W. *The Free Pass Bribery System*. Lincoln, Nebr., 1905.

Bliss, William D. P. *Encyclopedia of Social Reform*. New York, 1897.

Congressional Quarterly. *Congressional Quarterly's Guide to U.S. Elections*. 2d ed. Washington, D.C. 1985.

Darrow, Edward N. *A Treatise on Mortgage Investments*. Minneapolis, Minn., 1892.

Diggs, Annie L. "The Women in the Alliance Movement." *Arena* 6 (June 1892): 161–79.

Dunn, J. P., Jr. "The Mortgage Evil." *Political Science Quarterly* 5 (March 1890): 65–83.

Emery, Sarah E. V. *Seven Financial Conspiracies Which Have Enslaved the American People*. Lansing, Mich., 1892.

Fairall, Henry S. *Fairall's Manual of Iowa Politics, 1883*. Iowa City, Iowa, 1883.

———. *Fairall's Manual of Iowa Politics, 1884*. Iowa City, Iowa, 1884.

———. *Fairall's Manual of Iowa Politics, 1885*. Iowa City, Iowa, 1886.

Frederiksen, D. M. "Mortgage Banking in America." *Journal of Political Economy* 2 (March 1894): 203–34.

Gleed, James W. "Western Mortgages." *Century* 9 (March 1890): 93–105.

Indianapolis Commission of the Indianapolis Monetary Conference. *Report*. Chicago, 1898.

Iowa Farmers' Alliance. *Proceedings of the Iowa Farmers' Alliance at Its Annual Meeting, October 29–31, 1890*. Des Moines, Iowa, 1890.

Iowa State Improved Stock Breeders' Association. *Proceedings of the Seventeenth Annual Meeting, December 3–5, 1890*. Des Moines, Iowa, 1891.

Irwin, John N. "Is Iowa a Doubtful State?" *Forum* 13 (April 1892): 257–64.

Ise, John. *Sod and Stubble: The Story of a Kansas Homestead*. New York, 1936.

Jenks, Jeremiah W. "School-Book Legislation." *Political Science Quarterly* (March 1891): 90–125.

Larrabee, William. *The Railroad Question: A Historical and Practical Treatise in Railroads, and Remedies for their Abuses*. Chicago, 1893.

McPherson, T. B. "Cattle as Mortgage Security." *Proceedings of the Second Annual Convention of the National Livestock Association, January 24–27, 1899*. Denver, Colo., 1899.

Marshall, William V. *Cumulative Taxation*. Winfield, Kans., 1890.

Past and Present of Appanoose County, Iowa. Chicago, 1913.

Peffer, William A. *The Farmers' Side: His Troubles and Their Remedy*. New York, 1891.

———. *Populism: Its Rise and Fall*. Edited and with an introduction by Peter H. Argersinger. Lawrence, Kans., 1992.

The Plot Unfolded! or a History of the Famous Coffeyville Dynamite Outrage. Winfield, Kans., 1889. People's Party Pamphlets. Kansas State Historical Society, Topeka.

Populist Handbook for Kansas: A Compilation from Official Sources of Some Facts for Use in Succeeding Political Campaigns. Indianapolis, Ind., 1891.

Porter, Kirk H., and Donald B. Johnson, eds. *National Party Platforms, 1840–1964*. Urbana, Ill., 1966.

Quick, Herbert. *The Hawkeye*. Indianapolis, Ind., 1923.

Rightmire, W. F. "The Alliance Movement in Kansas—Origin of the People's Party." *Transactions of the Kansas State Historical Society* 9 (1905–1906): 1–8.

Scott, S. M. *The Champion Organizer of the Northwest, or My First Sixty Days Work as an Organizer*. McPherson, Kans., 1890.

———. *The Sub-Treasury Plan and the Land and Loan System*. Topeka, Kans., 1891.

Seeds, Russell M. *History of the Republican Party of Indiana*. Indianapolis, Ind., 1899.

Shambaugh, Benjamin F., comp. and ed. *The Messages and Proclamations of the Governors of Iowa*. 7 vols. Iowa City, Iowa, 1903–1905.

Stork, Frank S., and Cynthia A. Clingan. *The Iowa General Assembly: Our Legislative Heritage, 1846–1980.* Des Moines, Iowa, 1980.

Thompson, J. M. "The Farmers' Alliance in Nebraska: Something of Its Origin, Growth, and Influence." *Proceedings and Collections of the Nebraska State Historical Society* 10 (1902): 199–206.

Tracy, Harry. "The Sub-treasury Plan." In James H. Davis, *A Political Revelation.* Dallas, 1894.

Vincent, Leopold, comp. *The Alliance and Labor Songster.* Indianapolis, Ind., 1891. Reprint, New York, 1975.

Wallace, Henry. *Uncle Henry's Own Story.* 3 vols. Des Moines, Iowa, 1917–1919.

Warner, A. G. "Railroad Problems in a Western State." *Political Science Quarterly* 6 (March 1891): 66–89.

Warren, George F., and Frank A. Pearson. *Prices.* New York, 1933.

Wells, David A. *Recent Economic Changes and Their Effect on the Production and Distribution of Wealth and Well-Being of Society.* New York, 1893.

White, William Allen. "What's the Matter with Kansas?" *Emporia Gazette,* 25 August 1896. United States History Collection of Pamphlets, vol. 25. New York Public Library.

SECONDARY SOURCES

Theses and Dissertations

Barnhart, John D. "The History of the Farmers' Alliance and of the People's Party in Nebraska." Ph.D. diss., Harvard University, 1930.

Barton, Richard Harvey. "The Agrarian Revolt in Michigan, 1865–1900." Ph.D. diss., Michigan State University, 1958.

Cook, Robert J. "Puritans, Pragmatists, and Progress: The Republican Coalition in Iowa, 1854–1878." Ph.D. diss., Oxford University, 1986.

Fosbury, Eva May. "Biography of John Mellon Thurston." Master's thesis, University of Nebraska, 1920.

Gildner, Judith A. "An Organizational History of the Iowa Farmers' Alliance, 1881–1890." Master's thesis, Drake University, 1972.

Miller, Raymond Curtis. "The Populist Party in Kansas." Ph.D. diss., University of Chicago, 1928.

Petrowsky, Clarence L. "Kansas Agriculture before 1900." Ph.D. diss., University of Oklahoma, 1968.

Rickard, Louise E. "The Impact of Populism on Electoral Patterns in Kansas, 1880–1900: A Quantitative Analysis." Ph.D. diss., University of Kansas, 1974.

Silverman, Max. "A Political and Intellectual History of the Silver Movement in the United States, 1886–1896." Ph.D. diss., New York University, 1986.

Throne, Mildred. "A History of Agriculture in Southern Iowa, 1833–1890." Ph.D. diss., State University of Iowa, 1946.

Trojanowski, Joseph M. "The Stability of Freight Rate Agreements at Minor Railroad Junctions in Iowa and Kansas, 1880–1910." Ph.D. diss., Yale University, 1980.

Wagner, MaryJo. "Farms, Families, and Reform: Women in the Farmers' Alliance and Populist Party." Ph.D. diss., University of Oregon, 1986.

Books and Articles

Adams, Pauline, and Emma S. Thornton. *A Populist Assault: Sarah E. Van De Vort Emery on American Democracy, 1862–1895.* Bowling Green, Ohio, 1982.

Argersinger, Peter H. " 'A Place on the Ballot': Fusion Politics and Antifusion Laws." *American Historical Review* 85 (April 1980): 287–306.

———. *Populism and Politics: William Alfred Peffer and the People's Party.* Lexington, Ky., 1974.

———. "Religion, the Farmers' Alliance, and the Gospel of Populism." *Kansas Quarterly* 1 (Fall 1969): 24–35.

———. "Road to a Republican Waterloo: The Farmers' Alliance and the Election of 1890 in Kansas." *Kansas Historical Quarterly* 33 (Winter 1967): 443–69.

———. "The Value of the Vote: Political Representation in the Gilded Age." *Journal of American History* 76 (June 1989): 59–60.

Argersinger, Peter H., and John W. Jeffries. "American Electoral History: Party Systems and Voting Behavior." In *Research in Micropolitics: Voting Behavior.* Edited by Samuel Long. 2 vols. Greenwich, Conn., 1986.

Arnett, Alex M. *The Populist Movement in Georgia.* New York, 1922.

Bader, Robert Smith. *Prohibition in Kansas: A History.* Lawrence, Kans., 1986.

Bailyn, Bernard. *The Ideological Origins of the American Revolution.* Cambridge, Mass., 1967.

Bancroft, Hubert Howe. *History of the Life of Leland Stanford: A Character Study.* Oakland, Calif., 1952.

Barnes, Donna A. *Farmers in Rebellion: The Rise and Fall of the Southern Farmer's Alliance and People's Party in Texas.* Austin, Tex., 1984.

Barnhart, John D. "Rainfall and the Populist Party in Nebraska." *American Political Science Review* 19 (August 1925): 527–40.

Barton, D. Scott. "Party Switching and Kansas Populism." *Historian* 52 (May 1990): 453–67.

Beer, Samuel H. "The Modernization of American Federalism." *Publius* 3 (Fall 1973): 49–95.

Bensel, Richard Franklin. *Sectionalism and American Political Development, 1880–1980.* Madison, Wis., 1984.

Beth, Loren. *The Development of the American Constitution, 1877–1917.* New York, 1971.

Bloch, Marc. "Toward a Comparative History of European Societies." In *Enterprise and Secular Change.* Edited by Frederic C. Lane and Jelle C. Riemersma. Homewood, Ill., 1953.

Bogue, Allan G. *From Prairie to Corn Belt: Farming on the Illinois and Iowa Prairies in the Nineteenth Century.* Chicago, 1963.

———. *Money at Interest: The Farm Mortgage on the Middle Border.* Ithaca, N.Y., 1955.

———. "The New Political History in the 1970s." In *The Past before Us: Contemporary Historical Writing in the United States.* Edited by Michael Kammen. Ithaca, N.Y., 1980.

Bogue, Margaret B. *Patterns from the Sod: Land Use and Tenure in the Grand Prairie, 1850–1900.* Springfield, Ill., 1959.

Bowman, John D. "An Economic Analysis of Midwestern Farm Land Values and Farm Land Incomes, 1860–1900." *Yale Economic Essays* 5 (Fall 1965): 317–52.

Bowman, John D., and Richard H. Keehn. "Agricultural Terms of Trade in Four Mid-western States, 1870–1900." *Journal of Economic History* 34 (September 1974): 592–609.

Boyle, James Ernest. *The Financial History of Kansas.* Madison, Wis., 1908.

Briggs, John E. *William Peters Hepburn.* Iowa City, Iowa, 1919.

Brindley, John E. *History of Taxation in Iowa.* 2 vols. Iowa City, Iowa, 1911.

Brock, William R. *Investigation and Responsibility: Public Responsibility in the United States.* Cambridge, 1984.

Bryce, James. *The American Commonwealth.* 3d ed. 2 vols. New York, 1904.

Buck, Solon Justus. *The Granger Movement: A Study of Agricultural Organization and Its Political, Economic, and Social Manifestations, 1870–1880.* Cambridge, Mass., 1913.

Buhle, MariJo. *Women and American Socialism, 1870–1920.* Urbana, Ill., 1981.

Campbell, Ballard C. "Did Democracy Work? Prohibition in Late Nineteenth-Century Iowa: A Test Case." *Journal of Interdisciplinary History* 8 (Summer 1977): 87–116.

———. *Representative Democracy: Public Policy and Midwestern Legislatures in the Late Nineteenth Century.* Cambridge, Mass., 1980.

Carleton, William G. "Why Was the Democratic Party in Indiana a Radical Party, 1865–1890?" *Indiana Magazine of History* 42 (September 1946): 207–28.

Cherny, Robert W. "Lawrence Goodwyn and Nebraska Populism: A Review Essay." *Great Plains Quarterly* 1 (Summer 1981): 181–94.

———. *Populism, Progressivism, and the Transformation of Nebraska Politics, 1885–1915.* Lincoln, Nebr., 1981.

Clanton, O. Gene. *Kansas Populism: Ideas and Men.* Lawrence, Kans., 1969.

———. *Populism: The Humane Preference in America, 1890–1900.* Boston, 1991.

Clark, Dan Elbert. "The History of Liquor Legislation in Iowa, 1861–1878." *Iowa Journal of History and Politics* 6 (July 1908): 339–74.

———. "The History of Liquor Legislation in Iowa, 1878–1908." *Iowa Journal of History and Politics* 6 (October 1908): 503–608.

———. *History of Senatorial Elections in Iowa.* Iowa City, Iowa, 1912.

Clark, George T. *Leland Stanford: War Governor of California, Railroad Builder, and Founder of Stanford University.* Stanford, Calif., 1931.

Clark, Thomas D. "The Furnishing and Supply System in Southern Agriculture since 1865." *Journal of Southern History* 12 (February 1946): 24–44.

Clevenger, Homer. "The Farmers' Alliance in Missouri." *Missouri Historical Review* 39 (October 1944): 24–44

———. "Missouri Becomes a Doubtful State." *Mississippi Valley Historical Review* 29 (March 1943): 541–56.

Cogswell, Seddie, Jr. *Tenure, Nativity and Age as Factors in Iowa Agriculture, 1850–1880.* Ames, Iowa, 1975.

Colbert, Thomas Burnell. "Disgruntled 'Chronic Office Seeker' or Man of Political Integrity: James Baird Weaver and the Republican Party in Iowa, 1857–1877." *Annals of Iowa* 49 (Winter/Spring 1988): 187–207.

Cole, Cyrenus. *A History of the People of Iowa.* Cedar Rapids, Iowa, 1921.

Commons, John R. et al. *History of Labour in the United States.* 4 vols. New York, 1918–1919.

Cox, Thomas C. *Blacks in Topeka, Kansas, 1865–1915.* Baton Rouge, La., 1982.

Davis, David Brion. *The Slave Power Conspiracy and the Paranoid Style.* Baton Rouge, La., 1969.

_____, ed. *The Fear of Conspiracy: Images of Un-American Subversion from the Revolution to the Present.* Ithaca, N.Y., 1971.

Davis, Kenneth S. *Kansas: A Bicentennial History.* New York, 1976.

Dawson, Richard E. "Social Development, Party Competition, and Policy." In *The American Party Systems.* Edited by William N. Chambers and Walter Dean Burnham. 2d ed. New York, 1975.

Denison, John D. *Iowa Democracy: A History of the Politics and Personalities of the Democratic Party.* 4 vols. Des Moines, Iowa, 1939.

Destler, Chester McArthur. *American Radicalism, 1865-1901.* New London, Conn., 1946. Reprint, Chicago, 1966.

Dilla, Harriette M. *The Politics of Michigan, 1865-1878.* New York, 1912.

Dixon, Frank H. "Railroad Control in Nebraska." *Political Science Quarterly* 13 (December 1898): 617-47.

_____. *State Railroad Control with a History of Its Development in Iowa.* New York, 1896.

Dunbar, Willis Frederick. *Michigan: A History of the Wolverine State.* 2d ed. Grand Rapids, Mich., 1970.

Durden, Robert. *Climax of Populism: The Election of 1896.* Lexington, Ky., 1965.

Dykstra, Robert. "Iowa: 'Bright Radical Star.'" In *Radical Republicans in the North: State Politics during Reconstruction.* Edited by James C. Mohr. Baltimore, 1976.

Eichengreen, Barry. "Mortgage Interest Rates in the Populist Era." *American Economic Review* 74 (December 1984): 995-1015.

Elazar, Daniel J. *American Federalism: A View From the States.* 2d ed. New York, 1972.

Eliot, Clara. *The Farmers' Campaign for Credit.* New York, 1927.

Faragher, John Mack. *Sugar Creek: Life on the Illinois Prairie.* New Haven, Conn., 1986.

Farmer, Hallie. "The Railroads and Frontier Populism." *Mississippi Valley Historical Review* 13 (December 1926): 387-97.

Fink, Deborah. *Agrarian Women: Wives and Mothers in Rural Nebraska, 1880-1940.* Chapel Hill, N.C., 1992.

_____. *Open Country, Iowa: Rural Women, Tradition, and Change.* Albany, N.Y., 1986.

Fink, Leon. *Workingmen's Democracy: The Knights of Labor and American Politics.* Urbana, Ill., 1983.

Fisher, Irving. *The Theory of Interest.* New York, 1930.

Fite, Gilbert. "Republican Strategy and the Farm Vote in the Presidential Campaign of 1896." *American Historical Review* 65 (July 1960): 787-806.

Flora, Snowden. "Climate of Kansas." In *Report of the Kansas State Board of Agriculture, June 1948.* Topeka, Kans., 1948.

Fogel, Robert William, and Jack L. Rutner. "The Efficiency Effects of Federal Land Policy, 1850-1900: A Report of Some Provisional Findings." In *The Dimensions of Quantitative Research in History.* Edited by William O. Aydelotte, Allan G. Bogue, and Robert William Fogel. Princeton, N.J., 1972.

Foner, Eric. *Free Soil, Free Labor, Free Men: The Ideology of the Republican Party before the Civil War.* New York, 1970.

_____. *Reconstruction: America's Unfinished Revolution, 1863-1877.* New York, 1988.

Gates, Paul W. *Frontier Landlords and Pioneer Tenants.* Ithaca, N.Y., 1945.

Gehring, Lorraine A. "Women Officeholders in Kansas, 1872-1912." *Kansas History* 9 (Summer 1986): 48-57.

Gienapp, William E. *The Origins of the Republican Party, 1852-1856.* New York, 1987.

————. "The Republican Party and the Slave Power." In *New Perspectives on Race and Slavery in America: Essays in Honor of Kenneth M. Stampp.* Edited by Robert H. Abzug and Stephen E. Maizlish. Lexington, Ky., 1986.

Goodwyn, Lawrence. *Democratic Promise: The Populist Moment in America.* New York, 1976.

Grodinsky, Julius. *The Iowa Pool: A Study in Railroad Competition, 1870-1884.* Chicago, 1950.

Hammarberg, Melvyn. *The Indiana Voter: The Historical Dynamics of Party Allegiance during the 1870s.* Chicago, 1977.

Hammond, Matthew B. *The Cotton Industry: An Essay in American Economic History.* New York, 1897.

Harmer, Marie V., and James L. Sellers. "Charles H. Van Wyck—Soldier and Statesman." *Nebraska History* 12 (October–December 1929): 324-35.

Haynes, Fred Emory. *James Baird Weaver.* Iowa City, Iowa, 1919.

————. *Third Party Movements since the Civil War with Special Reference to Iowa.* Iowa City, Iowa, 1916.

Hays, Samuel P. *The Response to Industrialism.* Chicago, 1957.

Hicks, John D. *The Populist Revolt: A History of the Farmers' Alliance.* Minneapolis, Minn., 1931. Reprint, Lincoln, Nebr., 1961.

————. "The Sub-Treasury: A Forgotten Plan for the Relief of Agriculture." *Mississippi Valley Historical Review* 15 (June 1928–March 1929): 355-73.

Higgs, Robert. "Railroad Rates and the Populist Uprising." *Agricultural History* 44 (July 1970): 291-97.

————. *The Transformation of the American Economy, 1865-1914.* New York, 1971.

Hofstadter, Richard. *The Age of Reform: From Bryan to F. D. R.* New York, 1955.

————. *The Paranoid Style in American Politics and Other Essays.* New York, 1965.

Holmes, William F. "Populism: In Search of Context." *Agricultural History* 64 (Fall 1990): 26-58.

Holt, Michael. *The Political Crisis of the 1850s.* New York, 1978.

Hopkins, John R., Jr. *Economic History of the Production of Beef Cattle in Iowa.* Iowa City, Iowa, 1928.

Jacob, Herbert. "State Political Systems." In *Politics in the American States: A Comparative Analysis.* Edited by Herbert Jacob and Kenneth N. Vines. Boston, 1965.

Jeffrey, Julie Roy. "Women in the Southern Farmers' Alliance: A Reconsideration of the Role and Status of Women in the Late Nineteenth-Century South." *Feminist Studies* 3 (Fall 1975): 72-91.

Jenkins, J. Craig. "Resource Mobilization Theory and the Study of Social Movements." *Annual Review of Sociology* 9 (1983): 527-53.

Jensen, Richard. *The Winning of the Midwest: Social and Political Conflict, 1888-1896.* Chicago, 1971.

Johnson, Keach. "Iowa Dairying at the Turn of the Century." *Agricultural History* 45 (April 1971): 95-110.

Jones, Eliot. *The Trust Problem in the United States.* New York, 1921.

Jones, Stanley L. *The Presidential Election of 1896.* Madison, Wis., 1964.

Keller, Morton. *Affairs of State: Public Life in Late Nineteenth Century America.* Cambridge, Mass., 1977.

Kelley, Bruce Gunn. "Ethnocultural Voting Trends in Rural Iowa, 1890–1898." *Annals of Iowa* 44 (Fall 1978): 441–61.

Kerber, Linda K. *Women of the Republic: Intellect and Ideology in Revolutionary America.* Chapel Hill, N.C., 1980.

Kern, Jean B. "The Political Career of Horace Boies." *Iowa Journal of History* 47 (July 1949): 215–46.

Key, V. O., Jr. *Southern Politics in State and Nation.* New York, 1949.

Kleppner, Paul. *The Cross of Culture: A Social Analysis of Midwestern Politics, 1850–1900.* New York, 1970.

———. *The Third Electoral System, 1853–1892: Parties, Voters, and Political Cultures.* Chapel Hill, N.C., 1979.

———. "Voters and Parties in the Western States, 1876–1900." *Western Historical Quarterly* 14 (January 1983): 49–68.

Kousser, J. Morgan. "Ecological Regression and the Analysis of Past Politics." *Journal of Interdisciplinary History* 4 (Autumn 1973): 237–62.

Larson, Robert W. *Populism in the Mountain West.* Albuquerque, N.Mex., 1986.

Laurie, Bruce. *Working People of Philadelphia, 1800–1850.* Philadelphia, 1980.

Lee, Susan P., and Peter Passell. *A New Economic View of American History.* New York, 1979.

Lichtman, Allan J. "Political Realignment and 'Ethnocultural' Voting in Late Nineteenth Century America." *Journal of Social History* 16 (Spring 1983): 55–77.

Lipset, Seymour Martin. *Agrarian Socialism: The Cooperative Commonwealth Federation in Saskatchewan.* New York, 1968.

———. "Radicalism in North America: A Comparative View of the Party Systems in Canada and the United States." *Transactions of the Royal Society of Canada.* Series 4, 14 (1976): 19–55.

Livingston, James. *Origins of the Federal Reserve System: Money, Class, and Corporate Capitalism, 1890–1913.* Ithaca, N.Y., 1986.

Lockard, Duane. "State Party Systems and Policy Outputs." In *Political Research and Political Theory.* Edited by Oliver Garceau. Cambridge, 1968.

Lord, Russell. *The Wallaces of Iowa.* Boston, 1947.

Lowi, Theodore J. "Party, Policy, and Constitution in America." In *The American Party Systems.* Edited by William N. Chambers and Walter Dean Burnham. New York, 1974.

———. "Why Is There No Socialism in the United States? A Federal Analysis." In *Why Is There No Socialism in the United States?* Edited by Jean Heffer and Jeanine Rovet. Paris, 1988.

Luebke, Frederick C. *Immigrants and Politics: The Germans of Nebraska, 1880–1900.* Lincoln, Nebr., 1969.

Lurie, Jonathan. *The Chicago Board of Trade, 1859–1905: The Dynamics of Self-Regulation.* Urbana, Ill., 1979.

McCarthy, John D., and Mayer N. Zald. "Resource Mobilization and Social Movements: A Partial Theory." In *Social Movements in an Organizational Society.* Edited by John D. McCarthy and Mayer N. Zald. New Brunswick, N.J., 1987.

McCormick, Richard L. "Ethno-Cultural Interpretations of Nineteenth-Century American Voting Behavior." *Political Science Quarterly* 89 (June 1974): 351–77.

McFarlane, Larry. "British Investment in Midwestern Farm Mortgages and Land, 1875–

1900: A Comparison of Iowa and Kansas." *Agricultural History* 48 (January 1974): 179–98.

McGuire, Robert A. "Economic Causes of Late-Nineteenth Century Agrarian Unrest: New Evidence." *Journal of Economic History* 41 (December 1981): 835–52.

McMath, Robert C., Jr. *American Populism: A Social History, 1877–1898.* New York, 1993.

————. "Populist Base Communities: The Evangelical Roots of Farm Protest in Texas." *Locus* 1 (Fall 1988): 53–63.

————. *Populist Vanguard: A History of the Southern Farmers' Alliance.* Chapel Hill, N.C., 1975.

————. "Preface to Populism: The Origin and Economic Development of the 'Southern' Farmers' Alliance in Kansas." *Kansas Historical Quarterly* 42 (Spring 1976): 55–65.

McNall, Scott G. *The Road to Rebellion: Class Formation and Kansas Populism, 1865–1900.* Chicago, 1988.

Malin, James C. "The Kinsley Boom of the Late Eighties." *Kansas Historical Quarterly* 4 (February–March 1935): 23–49, 164–87.

————. *Winter Wheat in the Golden Belt of Kansas: A Study in the Adaptation to Subhumid Geographical Environment.* Lawrence, Kans., 1944.

Marcus, Robert D. *Grand Old Party: Political Structure in the Gilded Age, 1880–1896.* New York, 1971.

Mayer, George H. *The Republican Party 1854–1964.* New York, 1964.

Mayhew, Anne. "A Reappraisal of the Causes of Farm Protest in the United States, 1870–1900." *Journal of Economic History* 32 (June 1972): 464–75.

Merrill, Horace Samuel. *Bourbon Democracy of the Middle West, 1865–1896.* Baton Rouge, La., 1953.

Meyers, Marvin. *The Jacksonian Persuasion: Politics and Belief.* New York, 1960.

Michels, Robert. *Political Parties: A Sociological Study of the Oligarchical Tendencies of Modern Democracy.* Translated by Eden and Cedar Paul. New York, 1915.

Miller, George H. *Railroads and the Granger Laws.* Madison, Wis., 1971.

Miller, Worth Robert. *Oklahoma Populism: A History of the People's Party in the Oklahoma Territory.* Norman, Okla., 1987.

Mills, George. "The Fighting Clarksons." *Palimpsest* 30 (September 1949): 283–89.

Miner, Craig. *West of Wichita: Settling the High Plains of Kansas, 1865–1890.* Lawrence, Kans., 1986.

Mitchell, Theodore R. *Political Education in the Southern Farmers' Alliance, 1887–1900.* Madison, Wis., 1987.

Moore, Charles. *History of Michigan.* 4 vols. Chicago, 1915.

Moses, John. *Illinois: Historical and Statistical.* 2 vols. Chicago: 1889–1892.

Murphy, Paul L. "Mary Marsh Todd." In *Notable American Women, 1607–1905.* Vol. 3. Edited by Edward L. James et al. Cambridge, Mass., 1971.

Murray, William G. *Agricultural Finance: Principles and Practice of Farm Credit.* Ames, Iowa, 1941.

Neilson, James W. *Shelby M. Cullom: Prairie State Republican.* Urbana, Ill., 1962.

Nesbit, Robert C. *The History of Wisconsin: Volume 3; Urbanization and Industrialization, 1873–1893.* Madison, Wis., 1985.

Nixon, Herman C. "The Cleavage within the Farmers' Alliance Movement." *Mississippi Valley Historical Review* 15 (June 1928): 22–33.

_____. "The Populist Movement in Iowa." *Iowa Journal of History and Politics* 24 (January 1926): 3–107.

Noblin, Stuart. *Leonidas LaFayette Polk: Agrarian Crusader*. Chapel Hill, N.C., 1949.

North, Douglass C. *Growth and General Welfare in the American Past*. 2d ed. Englewood Cliffs, N.J., 1974.

Nugent, Walter T. K. *Money and American Society, 1865–1880*. New York, 1968.

_____. *The Tolerant Populists: Kansas Populism and Nativism*. Chicago, 1963.

Nydegger, Walter Ellsworth, "The Election of 1892 in Iowa." *Iowa Journal of History and Politics* 25 (July 1927): 359–449.

Obserschall, Anthony. "Theories of Social Conflict." *Annual Review of Sociology* 4 (1978): 291–315

Olson, James C. *History of Nebraska*. Lincoln, Nebr., 1955.

_____. *J. Sterling Morton*. Lincoln, Nebr., 1942.

Painter, Nell Irwin. *Exodusters: Black Migration to Kansas after Reconstruction*. New York, 1977.

Palmer, Bruce. *'Man Over Money': The Southern Populist Critique of American Capitalism*. Chapel Hill, N.C., 1980.

Palmero, Patrick F. "The Rules of the Game: Local Republican Political Culture in the Gilded Age." *Historian* 47 (August 1985): 479–96.

Parsons, Stanley B. *The Populist Context: Rural versus Urban Power on a Great Plains Frontier*. Westport, Conn., 1973.

Parsons, Stanley B. et al. "The Role of Cooperatives in the Development of the Movement Culture of Populism." *Journal of American History* 69 (March 1983): 866–85.

Pease, George S. *Patriarch of the Prairie: The Story of the Equitable of Iowa, 1867–1967*. New York, 1967.

Philips, Clifton J. *Indiana in Transition: The Emergence of an Industrial Commonwealth, 1880–1920*. Indianapolis, Ind., 1968.

Piehler, Harold. "Henry Vincent: Kansas Populist and Radical-Reform Journalist." *Kansas History* 2 (Spring 1979): 14–25.

Pollack, Norman. *The Just Polity: Populism, Law, and Human Welfare*. Urbana, Ill., 1987.

_____. *The Populist Response to Industrial America: Midwestern Populist Thought*. Cambridge, Mass., 1962.

Pope, Jesse E. "Agricultural Credit in the United States." *Quarterly Journal of Economics* 28 (August 1914): 701–46.

Preston, Howard H. *History of Banking in Iowa*. Iowa City, Iowa, 1922.

Ridge, Martin. *Ignatius Donnelly: The Portrait of a Politician*. Chicago, 1962.

Riley, Glenda. *Frontierswomen: The Iowa Experience*. Ames, Iowa, 1981.

Ripley, William Z. *Railroads, Rates and Regulation*. New York, 1912.

Rogin, Michael P. *The Intellectuals and McCarthy: The Radical Specter*. Cambridge, Mass., 1967.

Roseboom, Eugene, and Francis Weisenburger. *A History of Ohio*. New York, 1934.

Ross, Earle D. *Iowa Agriculture: An Historical Survey*. Iowa City, Iowa, 1951.

Ross, Thomas Richard. *Jonathan Prentiss Dolliver: A Study in Political Integrity and Independence*. Iowa City, Iowa, 1958.

Rothman, David J. *Politics and Power: The United States Senate, 1869–1901*. Cambridge, Mass., 1966.

————. "The Structure of State Politics." In *Political Parties in American History*. Edited by Felice A. Bonadio. 3 vols. New York, 1974.

Rozman, David. "Land Credit in the Town of Newton, Manitowoc County, Wisconsin, 1824-1926." *Journal of Land and Public Utility Economics* 3 (November 1927): 371-84.

————. "Land Credit in Walnut Grove Township, Knox County, Illinois." *Journal of Land and Public Utility Economics* 4 (August 1928): 305-12.

Ryan, Mary P. *Women in Public: Between Banners and Ballots, 1825-1880*. Baltimore, 1990.

Sachs, Carolyn. *The Invisible Farmers: Women in Agricultural Production*. Totowa, N.J., 1983.

Sage, Leland L. *A History of Iowa*. Ames, Iowa, 1974.

————. *William Boyd Allison: A Study in Practical Politics*. Iowa City, Iowa, 1956.

Saloutos, Theodore, "Radicalism and the Agrarian Tradition." In *Failure of a Dream? Essays in the History of American Socialism*. Revised edition. Edited by John H. M. Laslett and Seymour Martin Lipset. Berkeley and Los Angeles, 1984.

Scarrow, Howard A. "Duverger's Law, Fusion and the Decline of American 'Third' Parties." *Western Political Quarterly* 39 (December 1986): 634-47.

Scharnau, Ralph. "Workers and Politics: The Knights of Labor in Dubuque, Iowa, 1885-1890." *Annals of Iowa* 48 (Winter/Spring 1987): 353-77.

Schattschneider, E. E. *Party Government*. New York, 1942.

Schell, Herbert S. *History of South Dakota*. Lincoln, Nebr., 1968.

Schwartz, Michael. *Radical Protest and Social Structure: The Southern Farmers' Alliance and Cotton Tenancy, 1880-1890*. New York, 1976.

Schwieder, Dorothy. "Labor and Economic Roles of Iowa Farm Wives, 1840-1880." In *Farmers, Bureaucrats, and Middlemen: Historical Perspectives on American Agriculture*. Edited by Trudy Huskamp Peterson. Washington, D.C., 1980.

Scott, Roy V. *The Agrarian Movement in Illinois, 1880-1896*. Urbana, Ill., 1962.

————. "Milton George and the Farmers' Alliance Movement." *Mississippi Valley Historical Review* 45 (June 1958): 90-109.

————. "The Rise of the Farmers' Mutual Benefit Association in Illinois, 1883-1891." *Agricultural History* 32 (January 1958): 44-55.

Severson, Robert F., Jr., Frank F. Niss, and Richard D. Winkelman. "Mortgage Borrowing as a Frontier Developed: A Study of Farm Mortgages in Champaign County, Illinois, 1836-1895." *Journal of Economic History* 26 (June 1966): 147-68.

Sewell, William H., Jr. "Marc Bloch and the Logic of Comparative History." *History and Theory* 6 (1967): 208-18.

Shannon, Fred A. *The Farmers' Last Frontier: Agriculture, 1860-1897*. New York, 1945.

Shefter, Martin. "Trade Unions and Political Machines: The Organization and Disorganization of the American Working Class in the Late Nineteenth Century." In *Working-Class Formation: Nineteenth-Century Patterns in Western Europe and the United States*. Edited by Ira Katznelson and Aristide R. Zolberg. Princeton, N.J., 1986.

Sheldon, Addison Erwin. *Nebraska: The Land and the People*. 3 vols. Chicago, 1931.

Sheridan, Richard. *Economic Development in South Central Kansas*, part 1A, *An Economic History, 1500-1900*. Lawrence, Kans., 1956.

Skowronek, Stephen. *Building a New American State: The Expansion of National Administrative Capacities, 1877-1920*. Cambridge, 1982.

Smith, Henry Nash. *Virgin Land: The American West as Symbol and Myth*. New York, 1950.

Sombart, Werner. *Why Is There No Socialism in the United States?* White Plains, N.Y., 1976.

Sorauf, Frank J. *Political Parties in the American System.* Boston, 1964.

Stewart, Ernest D. "The Populist Party in Indiana." *Indiana Magazine of History* 14 (December 1918): 332–67.

Stock, James H. "Real Estate Mortgages, Foreclosures, and Midwestern Agrarian Unrest, 1865–1920." *Journal of Economic History* 44 (March 1983): 89–105.

Stromquist, Shelton. *A Generation of Boomers: The Pattern of Railroad Labor Conflict in Nineteenth-Century America.* Urbana, Ill., 1987.

Summers, Lawrence H. "The Nonadjustment of Nominal Interest Rates: A Study of the Fisher Effect." In *Macroeconomics, Prices and Quantities.* Edited by James Tobin. Washington, D.C., 1983.

Swierenga, Robert P. *Acres for Cents: Delinquent Tax Auctions in Frontier Iowa.* Westport, Conn., 1976.

Sylla, Richard Eugene. *The American Capital Market, 1846–1914: A Study of Public Policy on Economic Development.* New York, 1975.

Thelen, David P. *The New Citizenship: Origins of Progressivism in Wisconsin, 1885–1900.* Columbia, Mo., 1972.

———. *Paths of Resistance: Tradition and Dignity in Industrializing Missouri.* New York, 1986.

Thornthwaite, C. Warren. "The Climate of North America According to a New Classification." *Geographical Review* 21 (October 1931): 633–55.

Throne, Mildred. "The Anti-Monopoly Party in Iowa, 1873–1874." *Iowa Journal of History* 52 (October 1954): 289–326.

———. *Cyrus Clay Carpenter and Iowa Politics, 1854–1898.* Iowa City, Iowa, 1974.

———. "The Grange in Iowa, 1868–1875." *Iowa Journal of History* 47 (October 1949): 289–324.

———. "The Repeal of the Iowa Granger Law, 1878." *Iowa Journal of History* 51 (April 1953): 97–130.

Tilly, Charles. *From Mobilization to Revolution.* New York, 1978.

Trask, David S. "Nebraska Populism as a Response to Environmental and Political Problems." In *The Great Plains: Environment and Culture.* Edited by Brian W. Blouet and Frederick C. Luebke. Lincoln, Nebr., 1979.

Truman, David B. "Federalism and the Party System." In *Politics and Social Life: An Introduction to Political Behavior.* Edited by Nelson W. Polsby, Robert A. Dentler, and Paul A. Smith. Boston, 1963.

Turner, Frederick Jackson. *The Frontier in American History.* New York, 1920.

Turner, James. "Understanding the Populists." *Journal of American History* 67 (September 1980): 354–73.

Unger, Irwin. *The Greenback Era: A Social and Political History of American Finance, 1865–1879.* Princeton, N.J., 1964.

Valelly, Richard M. *Radicalism in the States: The Minnesota-Farmer Labor Party and the American Political Economy.* Chicago, 1989.

Webb, Walter Prescott. *The Great Plains.* New York, 1931.

Wellborn, Fred. "The Influence of the Silver Republican Senators, 1889–1891." *Mississippi Valley Historical Review* 14 (March 1928): 462–80.

Whitaker, James W. *Feedlot Empire: Beef Cattle Feeding in Illinois and Iowa, 1840–1900.* Ames, Iowa, 1975.

Wiebe, Robert. *The Search for Order, 1877–1920.* New York, 1967.

Wilcox, Early Vernon. *Tama Jim.* Boston, 1930.

Williams, Burton J. *Senator John James Ingalls: Kansas' Iridescent Republican.* Lawrence, Kans., 1972.

Williams, Jeffrey. "Economics and Politics: Voting Behavior in Kansas during the Populist Decade." *Explorations in Economic History* 18 (July 1981): 233–56.

Winters, Donald L. *Farmers without Farms: Agricultural Tenancy in Nineteenth-Century Iowa.* Westport, Conn., 1978.

Wood, Gordon S. *The Creation of the American Republic: 1776–1787.* New York, 1972.

Woodward, C. Vann. *Origins of the New South, 1877–1913.* Baton Rouge, La., 1951.

Workman, J. Brooke. "Governor Larrabee and Railroad Reform." *Iowa Journal of History* 57 (July 1959): 231–66.

Wright, Ivan. *Bank Credit and Agriculture under the National and Federal Reserve Banking Systems.* New York, 1922.

Wright, James Edward. *The Politics of Populism: Dissent in Colorado.* New Haven, Conn., 1974.

Yearley, Clifton K. *The Money Machines: The Breakdown and Reform of Governmental and Party Finance in the North, 1860–1920.* Albany, N.Y., 1970.

Zornow, William Frank. *Kansas: A History of the Jayhawk State.* Norman, Okla., 1957.

Index

and Nebraska Republican Party, 75, 114–15
proposals to nationalize, 101, 152
Reagan bill (interstate commerce), 49–52
Redemption laws, 84–85, 122
Reese, M. B., 114
Regency. *See under* Republican Party, Iowa
Republicanism, 132
Republican Party, Iowa
 antimonopoly in, 54, 59–60, 62, 68
 bloody shirt tactics of, 46, 49, 63, 163
 decline in dominance, 47, 53, 210n.23
 dominance after Civil War, 37
 dominance after 1893, 176–77
 factionalism in, 37, 54–55, 136, 138
 and free silver, 176
 and the Grange, 38
 and the Greenback Party, 39
 political philosophy of, 150
 and prohibition, 41, 138, 165
 and railroad managers, 41, 54
 and railroad regulation, 68, 138, 140–41
 and the Regency, 37, 38, 40, 60, 62, 63, 136–37
 response to the Farmers' Alliance, 59–60, 166
 response to Populist Party, 162–64, 169–70
 responsiveness of, 132, 168
 and tariff, 164–65
Republican Party, Kansas
 abuses Populist women, 129–30
 antimonopolists in, 74
 bloody shirt tactics of, 72, 126
 and Coffeyville bombing, 83
 dominance in 1889 legislature, 83
 dominance of, 10, 72, 74, 76, 210n.23
 1888 platform of, 82
 and election of 1890, 132
 factionalism in, 74–75
 and interest rate regulation, 84–86
 response to populism, 125–26, 129–30
 unresponsiveness of, 111, 117–18, 120, 132
Republican Party, national
 antimonopolists in, 9
 dominance after Civil War in Midwest, 8
 and Populist Party, 155
 threats to dominance of, 9
Republican Party, Nebraska
 antimonopolists in, 74, 119–20, 123
 bloody shirt tactics of, 72, 126
 controlled by railroads, 114–15
 dominance of, 10, 72, 74, 76, 210n.23
 and election of 1890, 132
 factionalism in, 75–76, 87
 and railroad regulation, 87–89
 response to Populist Party, 125–26
 unresponsiveness of, 111, 120, 123, 132
Resource-mobilization theory, 6, 190n.13
Rice, John H., 155
Richards, Lucius D., 125

Roberts, G. W., 115
Robinson, Charles, 125
Rock Island Railroad, 61
Rosewater, Edward, 73, 75, 87, 119, 123, 125
Rothrock, James H., 142
Russell, Edward, 116

St. John, John P., 74
Sanders, J. H., 160, 172
Sandusky, H. W., 96
Sargent, Will N., 157, 160
Sawyer, Philetus, 8
Schaller, Phil, 60
Scott, F. M., 104
Scott, S. M., 97–99, 110
Scott, Walter, 162
Scully, William, 23
Sectionalism, 154–55, 163
Shearer, Jonathan, 159
Short-term loans, 17, 18–22, 86. *See also* Interest rates
Silver. *See* Free silver
Simpson, Jerry, 126–27, 128
Sioux City and Pacific Railroad, 42
Slavery, 77, 78, 128
Smith, A. W., 82
Social gospel, 107
Sombart, Werner, 2–3
South Dakota, 4, 19, 87, 178
South Dakota Farmers' Alliance, 155, 159
Southern Alliance. *See* National Farmers' Alliance and Industrial Union
Sovereign, James R., 158
Stanford, Leland, 104–5, 121, 218n.61. *See also* Land loan plan
State Party systems
 diversity of, 173
 and Farmers' Alliance, 8
 importance of, 7, 10, 111, 120–21, 122, 159, 177–79
Stay-of-execution and redemption laws, 84–85, 122
Stivers, Henry, 165
Streeter, A. J., 83
Stuntz, A. L., 146–47, 150
Sturdevant, Phelps D., 73
Subtreasury plan
 explanation of, 102–3
 and land-loan plan, 78, 211n.31
 opposition in Iowa to, 151, 152, 157, 160, 164
 opposition in Kansas to, 105
 opposition in Missouri to, 154
 opposition in Nebraska to, 167, 218n.63
Sweeney, J. H., 66

Tariff, 73, 99, 173
 as political issue in Iowa, 44, 47, 49, 139, 140, 152, 164–65, 169